VIDEOCONFERENCE AND REMOTE INTERPRETING IN CRIMINAL PROCEEDINGS

D1743914

VIDEOCONFERENCE AND REMOTE INTERPRETING IN CRIMINAL PROCEEDINGS

Sabine Braun and Judith L. Taylor

Editors

intersentia

Cambridge – Antwerp – Portland

Intersentia Publishing Ltd
Trinity House | Cambridge Business Park | Cowley Road
Cambridge | CB4 0WZ | United Kingdom
Tel.: +44 1223 393 755 | Email: mail@intersentia.co.uk

Videoconference and Remote Interpreting in Criminal Proceedings
Sabine Braun and Judith L. Taylor, editors

AVIDICUS
Assessment of Videoconference Interpreting in Criminal Proceedings
http://www.videoconference-interpreting.net

EU Criminal Justice Programme
Project JLS/2008/JPEN/037, 2008-2011

Contact:
Dr Sabine Braun
Centre for Translation Studies
University of Surrey
Guildford
GU2 7XH
United Kingdom
s.braun@surrey.ac.uk

With financial support from the Criminal Justice Programme
European Commission – Directorate-General Justice
THE VIEWS EXPRESSED IN THIS BOOK ARE THE SOLE
RESPONSIBILITY OF THE AUTHORS AND DO NOT NECESSARILY
REFLECT THE VIEWS OF THE EUROPEAN COMMISSION

© 2012   Intersentia
          Cambridge – Antwerp – Portland
          www.intersentia.com | www.intersentia.co.uk

Cover image © arturbo

ISBN 978-1-78068-097-2
D/2012/7849/85
NUR 820

British Library Cataloguing in Publication Data. A catalogue record for this book is
available from the British Library.

CONTENTS

INTRODUCTION

Sabine Braun and Judith L. Taylor

University of Surrey

In response to increasing mobility and migration in Europe, the new European Directive on strengthening the rights to interpretation and translation in criminal proceedings[1] aims at a more consistent implementation of the rights set out in the European Convention on Human Rights and encourages the development of minimum standards for legal interpreting and translation in Europe. At the same time, the economic situation is putting pressure on public services and translation/interpreting service providers alike, jeopardizing quality standards and fair access to justice for all European citizens. In the area of interpreting, the use of videoconference technology has been promoted by the European e-Justice initiative and is now being widely considered as a potential solution for gaining cost-effective and timely access to qualified legal interpreters and thus for improving access to justice.

These developments give rise to many questions, including: how technological mediation through videoconferencing affects the quality of interpreting; how this is related to the actual videoconference setting and locations of participants and interpreter; and ultimately whether the emerging forms of videoconference and remote interpreting are sufficiently reliable for achieving the specific goals of legal communication such as evidence and information gathering, decision-making and delivering justice.

In other words, much is at stake. Communication in criminal proceedings is a highly sensitive type of communication, combining, for example, emotionally loaded communication, conflicting goals, asymmetry of power relations, varying levels of education and language proficiency and, in the case of other-language speakers, often an additional degree of vulnerability. According to prior research on videoconference communication, none of these characteristics suggests that legal communication would be an easy type of communication to manage via video link.

The question of viability from a communicative perspective is, therefore, a crucial one. It arguably overrides all other considerations, including cost savings. This is particularly so if it turns out that the 'human cost' is too

---

[1] Directive 2010/64/EU of the European Parliament and of the Council on the right to interpretation and translation in criminal proceedings. Available at http://www.europarl.europa.eu/oeil/ file.jsp?id=5840482.

high. At the same time, it may not be affordable to forego the option of video-mediated interpreting where it turns out to be viable.

It is against this backdrop that the AVIDICUS (2008-11) Project, co-funded by the European Directorate-General Justice,[2] set out to research the quality and viability of video-mediated interpreting in criminal proceedings.

To cover the increasing diversification of interpreting situations involving a video link, the project made a broad distinction between *videoconference interpreting* (VCI) and *remote interpreting* (RI). VCI is the form of interpreting that is used when the proceedings take place at two video-linked locations (e.g. court and prison), with the interpreter being situated at either end of the link. RI is the form of interpreting that is used when the proceedings take place at a single location (e.g. a courtroom), with the interpreter working via video link from a remote location (e.g. another courthouse). This distinction will be made throughout this volume.

The findings of the AVIDICUS Project indicate that there is a growing demand for the use of different forms of video-mediated interpreting in a wide variety of settings to cater for specific local situations and demand throughout Europe, i.e. a generic solution will not suffice. This suggests that there is also a great demand for further locale-based research beyond the initial steps made in AVIDICUS.

At the same time there is a considerable lack of knowledge about the different forms of interpreting among both legal practitioners and interpreters. This, in turn, suggests that training and familiarisation, for example through the training modules devised by AVIDICUS, are crucial to a well-informed and broad-based approach to interpreting in technologically mediated situations. In fact, a realistic assessment of the viability of video-mediated interpreting could be said to be predicated on a basic level of training and familiarisation for all stakeholders.

Most importantly, however, the aims and findings of the AVIDICUS Project need to be seen in context and to be complemented by further research, recommendations and legislation. The final AVIDICUS Symposium, which was held in London in February 2011 and on which the present volume is based, was an attempt to contextualise the AVIDICUS findings and to combine them with complementary research, especially in the area of sign-language interpreting. The present book thus provides a cross-section of the AVIIDICUS findings and their wider context, as well as recommenda-

---

[2] This project was carried out with financial support from the Criminal Justice Programme of the European Commission – Directorate-General Justice (JLS/2008/JPEN/037). The views expressed in this book are the sole responsibility of the authors and do not necessarily reflect the views of the European Commission.

tions for judicial services, legal practitioners and police officers, and legal interpreters. The contributions are divided into five sections.

Section one examines the legislative background and technological context of video-mediated interpreting in criminal proceedings. In the opening contribution, *Caroline Morgan* introduces the European Directive on the right to interpreting and translation in criminal proceedings, describing the path leading to the Directive in its current form, adopted on 20th October 2010, before detailing the scope of the application of the Directive and the right to interpreting and translation. Again from a European perspective, *Evert-Jan van der Vlis* highlights the European E-Justice Action Plan and some of its components, in particular videoconferencing, its applicability to judicial cooperation and mutual recognition, problems of videoconferencing and its relationship to the ECHR.

Section two focuses on research into VCI and RI in criminal proceedings: *Sabine Braun* and *Judith L. Taylor* firstly provide an overview of current research and practice in using video-mediated interpreting in criminal proceedings and other areas. They follow this with a chapter presenting the results of two European surveys into video-mediated interpreting. The surveys, targeted at legal practitioners and legal interpreters, were designed to elicit information regarding current and planned uses of videoconference and remote interpreting in criminal proceedings, and attitudes towards these. Following on from the survey findings, the next three chapters in this section outline the results of the AVIDICUS comparative studies. The studies were designed to elicit information on the viability of videoconference and remote interpreting in criminal proceedings, and in particular to determine whether interpreting via video link impacts upon the quality of the interpretation. The AVIDICUS consortium partners who were responsible for the comparative studies investigated different settings: The University of Surrey partners, *Sabine Braun* and *Judith L. Taylor*, investigated remote interpreting in police interviews, using traditional face-to-face interpreting as a 'control'. The partners at Lessius Hogeschool, *Katalin Balogh* and *Erik Hertog*, explored different configurations of videoconference and remote interpreting in a police interview setting, examining the effect of having participants at different locations, again using face-to-face interpreting as a control. Similarly, the Polish partners at TEPIS, *Joanna Miler-Cassino* and *Zofia Rybińska*, also examined different configurations of videoconference and remote interpreting, but in this case a prosecution setting was adopted. The police and prosecution settings were selected, because the initial survey work showed that the greatest need for video-mediated interpreting is in the early stages of criminal proceedings. Furthermore, it was decided that an investigation of small-group communication settings such as initial police interviews, rather than complex settings such as trials, should be the focus of the comparative studies. It was assumed that the problems that occur in these small-group settings will persist, and possibly be magnified, in more complex settings such as the courtroom. The exploration of these small group communications is also felicitous, in that prior research on the use of video-mediated interpreting in legal proceedings has focused on courtroom communication. Following the presentation of the AVIDICUS comparative studies, *Dirk Rombouts* focuses on one setting examined in the AVIDICUS studies, the police interview. He looks at the relationship dynamics between interviewer and interviewee, and provides insight into how the addition of a legal interpreter via video link affects this relationship. Moving to a complementary research perspective, in a paper dealing with sign-language interpreting in Australia, *Jemina Napier* describes a study of video-based sign-language interpreting in courts in New South Wales, examining issues of communication, perceptions of video-based interpreting, and concluding with recommendations made to the Department of Justice and Attorney General (DJAG) on the use of sign-language interpreters via video link.

Section three looks at technological issues surrounding video-mediated interpreting. *Peter van Rotterdam* and *Ronald van den Hoogen* describe the concept of 'true-to-life' videoconferencing and its importance for legal proceedings, and set out the minimum technical standards for the implementation of this concept. *Jose Esteban Causo* discusses conference interpreting using video links, and looks at the technical guidelines and solutions offered by the European Commission's Directorate General for Interpretation.

Section four addresses the issue of training for the various parties involved in video-mediated legal proceedings. Three new training modules are presented, all designed, developed and piloted by the partners of the AVIDICUS Project. The modules are targeted towards interpreting students, practising legal interpreters, and finally legal practitioners. The contribution by *Sabine Braun et al.* contains for each module an introduction, an in-depth outline of the syllabus including teaching materials, a description of the pilot sessions, and an evaluation of the pilot modules by those participating.

Section five of this volume draws conclusions and considers the implications of video-mediated interpreting in criminal proceedings for the future. In the penultimate chapter, *Ann Corsellis* reviews the context and purpose of the AVIDICUS Project, before outlining the project's wider implications as well as future considerations. Finally, in the concluding chapter, *Sabine Braun* presents recommendations for video-mediated interpreting in criminal proceedings and best practice. The recommendations are targeted towards judicial authorities planning to implement video-mediated interpreting, legal practitioners and legal interpreters, and cover, *inter alia*, technological, practical and ethical issues.

Sabine Braun and Judith L. Taylor
Guildford, June 2011

THE NEW EUROPEAN DIRECTIVE ON THE RIGHTS TO INTERPRETATION AND TRANSLATION IN CRIMINAL PROCEEDINGS

Caroline Morgan

European Commission

1   INTRODUCTION

On 20 October 2010, the European Parliament and the Council adopted Directive 2010/64/EU on the right to interpretation and translation in criminal proceedings. The Directive is the first legislative instrument in the field of criminal law to be adopted under the Lisbon Treaty. This is the first step of a programme designed to increase mutual trust between Member States in relation to their criminal justice systems. The Commission is committed to this procedural rights package so as to honour our commitment, via the EU Charter, to protect fundamental rights in the EU and to facilitate the operation of mutual recognition between judicial authorities in the EU.

2   BACKGROUND

In its criminal law legislation, the EU uses a concept called "mutual recognition". It is borrowed from the internal market, where it is an economic concept: if an item is suitable for sale in one Member State, then all the Member States should accept it for sale without further enquiry. That notion has been adapted to judicial decisions. European measures such as the Framework Decision on the European Arrest Warrant[1] (a mutual recognition measure whereby an arrest warrant is recognised as valid and executed rapidly and without the formal procedure of extradition, which has now been almost entirely abolished throughout the EU) have been adopted, and they in turn have generated a demand for the EU to consider fundamental rights, especially the rights of the defence, in a rather more concrete way.

The Commission decided, in 2001, to present a proposal that would set in place basic minimum standards for defence rights throughout the EU. This was important if we are to recognise each others' judicial decisions as

---

[1]   Framework Decision 2002/584/JHA of 13 June 2002 on the European Arrest Warrant and the surrender procedures between Member States, OJ L 190, 18.7.2002, p. 1.

equivalent to domestic judicial decisions and all that entails (e.g. sending one's nationals to another Member State to face trial, sending evidence across borders for use in trials, receiving one's nationals back from another Member State where they have been sentenced to prison in order that they serve their sentence back home).

In the research phase for the proposal, it became quickly clear that there was a problem with the varying standards of legal interpreting and translation available in criminal proceedings throughout the EU. All Member States are signatories to the ECHR (this is a requirement for joining the EU) and the ECHR provides that anyone facing a criminal charge should be provided with the services of an interpreter, free of charge, if s/he doesn't understand the language of the proceedings. However, the information we received suggested that this requirement was not complied with in a satisfactory way in all EU Member States.

The Commission held an experts' meeting held in October 2002. At that meeting, experts from various institutions (the Institute of Linguists, the Committee for Legal Translators and Court Interpreters of the International Federation of Translators (FIT) and Lessius Hogeschool) set out their "vision". The experts suggested that minimum requirements for court translators and interpreters should be a good, broad educational background and a knowledge of as many subjects as possible, including cultural specificities as well as linguistic skills, that linguistic training be as full as possible (for example for interpreters learning not just conference interpreting but also whispered, consecutive and simultaneous interpreting), that there be training in the legal systems of the countries that they use the languages of, with visits to courts, police stations and prisons, leading to a recognised qualification, that Member States introduce a system of accreditation or certification for these translators and interpreters, and that the accrediting body work in collaboration with the Ministry of Justice of the country in question, that accreditation be by way of a scheme of registration that is not "once and for all", but rather subject to review so as to encourage professionals to keep their language skills and knowledge of court procedures up to date. It was also suggested that there be a system of Continuous Professional Development, a Code of Ethics and Guidelines for Good Practice and that Member States undertake to train lawyers and judges to work with translators and interpreters. Member States that didn't have any training system should be made to offer one.

In some Member States, translators and interpreters were found to work under very poor conditions, e.g. even a prisoner's cellmate could be used as an interpreter.

Cost was often mentioned as a reason why Member States do not fulfil their ECHR obligations in this respect. The Commission took the view that Member States should make funds available for this purpose. Court interpreters and translators should be offered competitive rates of pay so as to make this career option more attractive to language graduates. This should not be seen simply as a question of salary. Better rates of pay would attract more people into the profession, but there are other factors too, such as treating language professionals with more respect, consulting them about court procedures and involving them in such a way as to ensure that their specialist skills are acknowledged and valued.

The Commission's own research confirmed that there were problems. During police questioning, a qualified interpreter was not always present, with defendants sometimes being offered the services of lay persons who had some knowledge of the defendant's language. There were limitations on the documents translated for defendants. At trial, interpreters were sometimes provided for the benefit of the judge and/or prosecutor, rather than for the defendant. In some instances, the judge's or prosecutor's statements were not interpreted for defendants and the role of the interpreter was limited to interpreting the judge's direct questions to the defendant and his replies back to the judge, rather than ensuring that the defendant could understand the proceedings.

The Commission also noted that Member States had difficulty in recruiting sufficient legal/court translators and interpreters. In some Member States, the profession of public service interpreter/translator has official status, with training organised at national level, registration, accreditation and continuous professional development. This is not the case in all Member States. The Commission found that the profession suffers from a lack of status, with translators and interpreters sometimes being poorly paid, not having social benefits (such as paid sick leave and pension rights) and complaining that they are not consulted enough by their counterparts in the legal profession.

This Commission wanted Member States to be required to ensure that the arrangements they offer to legal translators and interpreters were such as to make this an attractive career choice. It is essential that there are enough translators and interpreters in each Member State to cover the needs of foreign defendants.

The Commission followed up this experts' meeting with a Green Paper in 2003 and then, in 2004, a proposal for European legislation covering a number of rights, including the right to interpretation and translation, in criminal proceedings. The proposal did not take up all the suggestions of the linguistic experts but it represented a start.

The proposal was discussed for nearly 3 years in a working group made up of the Commission, the Council and representatives of all the Member States. Prior to the Lisbon Treaty entering into force, when dealing with criminal law matters, there was a requirement of unanimity. Despite our best efforts, unanimous agreement could not be reached, and the proposal was finally shelved in June 2007.

Under the 2009 Swedish Presidency, it was decided to try again to put forward legislation on rights, but this time, not to put forward a proposal covering all rights, but rather a number of separate proposals covering a number of different rights. The agreement to do this is known as the "Roadmap for strengthening procedural rights of suspected or accused persons in criminal proceedings".

The first measure in the roadmap is on translation and interpretation.[2] The Commission put forward a proposal for a Framework Decision, the old pre-Lisbon Treaty instrument, in July 2009. The Lisbon Treaty entered into force on 1 December 2009. In the immediate aftermath, Member States put forward a proposal for a Directive, using the text that had been agreed as a result of the negotiation on the Commission's July 2009 text. That Member State proposal is what formed the basis for the text finally adopted in October 2010.

In July 2009, when the Commission presented its proposal for a Framework Decision, the Swedish Presidency presented an accompanying draft Resolution on "best practice". This Resolution fell within the scope of the Roadmap, according to which action to strengthen the rights of suspected and accused persons could comprise legislation "*as well as other measures*". The proposed Resolution encouraged Member States to promote measures on the involvement of bodies representing interpreters and translators, qualification of interpreters and translators, training, registration of qualified interpreters and translators, remote access to interpretation, and codes of conduct and guidelines on best practice. In October 2009, unanimous agreement was reached on the text. The Resolution was not formally adopted, however, since it was linked to the draft Framework Decision, which had to be "abandoned" after the entry into force of the Lisbon Treaty.

During the negotiations for the adoption of the Directive, particular attention was paid to the European Convention on Human Rights (ECHR) and the case law of the European Court of Human Rights in Strasbourg (ECtHR). The Directive had to be "Strasbourg-proof", meaning that the text should, as a minimum, meet the standards of the ECHR, as interpreted in the case law of the ECtHR.

3   DETAILS OF THE DIRECTIVE

3.1   Scope (Art. 1)

Art. 1 of the Directive deals with the scope of application of the instrument, both from the objective point of view (types of proceedings covered) and from the temporal point of view (moment in time from which the rights apply).

---

2   Resolution of the Council of 30 November 2009, OJ C 295,4.12.2009, p. 1

According to Art. 1(1), the Directive applies to criminal proceedings as well as to proceedings for the execution of a European Arrest Warrant (EAW).

The Directive does not give a definition of "criminal proceedings": this legal concept should be interpreted in the light of the case-law of the ECtHR with respect to the field of application of Art. 6 ECHR. The specific reference to EAW proceedings was necessary in view of the fact that extradition procedures do not fall within the scope of application of this ECHR provision. It was decided that the Directive should not lay down cumbersome obligations where the offences were minor, e.g. traffic offences following roadside checks, where sanctions/fines are imposed "on the spot" by police. It would not be reasonable to require that interpreters be available for such roadside checks. In order to address this concern, Art. 1(3) of the Directive provides that "where the law of a Member State provides for the imposition of a sanction regarding minor offences by an authority other than a court having jurisdiction in criminal matters, and the imposition of such a sanction may be appealed to such a court, this Directive shall apply only to the proceedings before that court following such an appeal".

3.2 Right to Interpretation (Art. 2)

The right of the suspected or accused person to benefit from the services of an interpreter is set out in Art. 6(3)(e) ECHR. There is a divergence in Member States about their legal and practical implementation of this principle. The greatest divergence relates to client-lawyer communication. Whereas in some Member States, interpretation of communication between the accused and his lawyer is provided almost without limit, in others, such communication is not interpreted at all or only with substantial restrictions.[3]

Under this provision, interpretation of client-lawyer communication is to be provided (free of charge) "where necessary for the purpose of safeguarding the fairness of the proceedings". In order to prevent possible abuses of this right, the communication should be "in direct connection with any questioning or hearing during the proceedings or with the lodging of an appeal or other procedural application". Article 2(2) provides that interpretation is to be provided during any appeal or "other procedural application". This term has been left vague; recital 20 refers to the example of an "application for bail".

---

[3] The restrictions are justified in various ways: the most important is costs, but the restrictions may also serve to prevent the defence from using a request for interpretation to slow down proceedings. In some Member States, interpreters are at the service of the court and not the suspected or accused person, so that the only communication to be interpreted is that between the court and the suspected person.

Art. 2(6) provides for the possibility of "remote interpretation". In order to allow for the prompt assistance of an interpreter in situations where there is no interpreter at hand at short notice, interpretation can be facilitated via videoconference, telephone, or Internet. This is already apparently successfully employed in several Member States (e.g. in cases of rare languages if an interpreter cannot – for reasons of time or distance – attend the location of the proceedings). However this option can only be used if the physical presence of the interpreter is not required "to safeguard the fairness of the proceedings".

3.3   Right to Translation (Art. 3)

Art. 3 provides for the right to translation of *essential documents*. This right is not expressly included in Art. 6 ECHR. It can be implied from the ECtHR case-law since other ECHR rights (Art. 6(1) and (3) ECHR) can only be effective if the suspected or accused person who does not speak or understand the language of the proceedings, is able to understand the content of the trial.[4]

Art. 3(1) states that suspected or accused persons who do not understand the language of the criminal proceedings shall be provided with a written translation of "all" documents that are "essential" to ensure that they are able to exercise their right of defence and to safeguard the fairness of the proceedings.

Art. 3 (2) specifies three types of essential document that must always be translated: "any decision depriving a person of his liberty, any charge or indictment, and any judgment".[5]

Art. 3(7) allows "an oral translation or oral summary" of essential documents. The case-law of the ECtHR[6] allows an oral translation or oral summary to be provided instead of a written translation.

The "competent authorities" of the Member States will be responsible for applying these provisions. Under Art 3(3), it is for them to decide which documents are to be considered essential – apart from those listed in Art 3(2) – and which documents may be translated in part (Art 3(4)) or orally (Art 3(7)).

---

[4]   See Kamasinki v. Austria, 19 December 1989, in particular par. 74.

[5]   But NB Art. 3(4) excludes from the scope of the right to translation "passages of essential documents which are not relevant for the purposes of enabling suspected or accused persons to have knowledge of the case against them".

[6]   Hermi v. Italy, 18 October 2006, par. 70, "This suggests that oral linguistic assistance may satisfy the requirements of the Convention [...]. The fact remains, however, that the interpretation assistance provided should be such as to enable the defendant to have knowledge of the case against him and to defend himself".

Art. 3(7) provides that a suspected or accused person may waive the right to translation, if they "have received prior legal advice or have otherwise obtained full knowledge of the consequences of such a waiver, and that the waiver was unequivocal and given voluntarily".

3.4 Other Provisions

The need to ensure quality of the translation or interpretation provided to the suspected or accused person is the object of specific provisions in Arts. 2(8) and 3(9), which require a "quality sufficient" to ensure "that suspected or accused persons have knowledge of the case against them and are able to exercise their right of defence". Furthermore, the quality of the service provided may be the object of a specific review procedure according to Arts. 2(5) and 3(5).

The Directive also addresses the question of practical availability of qualified legal interpreters and translators. Art. 5(2) invites Member States to set up "a register of independent translators and interpreters who are appropriately qualified", which, where appropriate, should be made available to legal counsel and relevant authorities.[7]

Recital 32 provides that the level of protection of the Directive should never fall below the standards stipulated by the ECHR and by the Charter. Indeed, the Directive is supposed to be "Strasbourg- and Charter-proof" and should be interpreted and applied in such a way.

Recital 33 provides that the provisions of this Directive that correspond to rights guaranteed by the ECHR or the Charter should be interpreted and implemented consistently with those rights.

Art. 8 contains an important non-regression clause: nothing in this Directive shall be construed as limiting or derogating from any of the rights and procedural safeguards that are ensured under the ECHR, the Charter, other relevant provisions of international law, or the law of any Member State that provides a higher level of protection.

Member States have to transpose the Directive by 27 October 2013.

---

[7] See recital 31, which encourages Member States to provide wider access to the registers by way of the e-Justice portal.

VIDEOCONFERENCING IN CRIMINAL PROCEEDINGS

Evert-Jan van der Vlis

Ministry of Security and Justice, The Hague

1 INTRODUCTION

Information and communication technology (IT) is going through a spectacular development. In less than 10 years, it has become possible to effect all information processing and communication anywhere and at all times in a safe, reliable and affordable manner. Virtual communication is developing at breakneck speed. Internet, email, smart phones, netbooks and iPads enable us to consult information and to communicate at any time. Working, together or alone, has become independent of time and place. It is impossible to imagine life today without the mobile phone, and 'free' communication tools such as Skype and Windows Live Messenger are becoming more and more popular. Video meetings and conferencing are used increasingly often. The difference between physical and virtual meeting is become smaller. This rapid development of information and communication technology does not pass the judiciary by unnoticed. The procedure before the courts used to be dominated by paper files, written exchange of documents and hearing persons in court, but these matters are changing fast. IT applications are increasingly applied when bringing cases before the court, preparing court sessions, hearing cases in court and when drawing up and publishing court decisions. Within the European Union (EU), many Member States are busy improving digital access to the administration of justice. Striving for digital access is one of the key objectives for EU judicial policy for the coming years. Videoconferencing is the central focus of this contribution.

2 EUROPEAN E-JUSTICE ACTION PLAN 2009-2013

The Ministers of Justice of the Member States of the European Union have decided to assign a high priority to E-Justice. The European E-Justice action plan 2009-2013 is intended to improve European and national procedures by making use of the possibilities offered by modern technology.[1] It is important in this connection that a great deal of legislation and regulations date

---

[1] (2009/C75/01) http://eur-lex.europa.eu/LexUriServ.do?uri=OJ:C:2009:075:0001:0012:EN: PDF.

from before the digital era. The possibilities offered by IT were not taken into account when said legislation and regulations were drawn up. Where the law, for example, requires identification of persons, signatures and sending documents or a personal appearance, it is not always clear whether this can also include digital identification, signatures or despatch and whether persons are allowed to appear by means of a video link. All of the above is often experienced as an obstruction to the progress of digitisation. It has to be clear whether the law allows the use of modern technology, and, if it does, the conditions under which this should happen. The E-Justice action plan intends to make a contribution to the above. In doing so, the focus is on four areas:

- setting up a European E-Justice portal;
- deploying IT for communication between judicial authorities (cross-border videoconferencing has been designated a priority in that connection);
- using IT for specific procedures, for example the European order for payment procedure.[2]
- cross-border access to national registers, such as trade and insolvency registers, the land registry, Central Register of Wills, criminal registers and linking registers of legal interpreters and translators.

3   E-JUSTICE PORTAL

The E-Justice portal was launched in 2010. It forms a one-stop system. It focuses on citizens, companies, lawyers and judges with cross-border legal questions and promotes knowledge of the various legal systems. The portal contains more than 12,000 pages in 22 languages.[3] The portal site contains, for example, information on legal assistance, personal injury, training legal staff and videoconferencing, and links to judicial databanks and online insolvency registers and land registries. For example, a Dutch tourist can read in Dutch what his rights are as a traffic victim in Italy, and a Pole can read in Polish how to obtain legal assistance in Belgium. The portal will be further expanded to include interactive user options. It is the intention that as a result cross-border procedures can be conducted in a secure manner and in one's own language and that persons can also consult foreign registers in their own language.

---

[2]   http://eur-lex.europa.eu/Result.do?arg0=payment+procedure&arg1=&arg2=&titre=titre&chlang= en&RechType=RECH_mot&Submit=Search&ihmlang=en.

[3]   https://e-justice.europa.eu/home.do.

4   VIDEOCONFERENCING

The simplification and encouragement of the use of videoconferencing when hearing experts and witnesses is another component of the action plan. Hearing persons by means of videoconferencing refers to the situation in which a direct live image and sound connection is created between, for example, the judge hearing the case and the party being heard (for example a witness) with direct communication options for both sides. They are not present in the same room, but they can see and hear each other. The hearing party can ask questions and receive a direct answer as if the witness or expert were present in the same room. Hearing witnesses and experts by means of videoconferencing should be distinguished from recording a hearing on video with the aim of playing it back at a later stage, for example during the hearing in court. Characteristic of videoconferencing is that the hearing takes place directly, albeit by means of closed circuit video. This does not detract from the fact that hearings can be recorded on tape or disk.[4]

4.1   Examples

The need for videoconferencing in criminal cases arose in first instance in countries with a large territory. The development of modern communication techniques in combination with the need to save time and money has led to the introduction of the possibility of hearing suspects, witnesses and experts by means of videoconferencing. Other reasons for introduction include:

- the wish to protect minor and other vulnerable witness from confrontation with the suspect;
- the reduced risk of escapes and problems that could arise from an escape, such as personal injury and mass police deployment;
- increasing the quality of the process: witnesses who otherwise would not be able, or in a less direct form, to contribute to establishing the truth, are now available to the parties and the judge;
- reducing delays because the suspect cannot be present in court on time as a result of traffic jams or for other reasons.

In Australia, a statutory regulation has for some time provided conditions for the use of videoconferencing when hearing the suspect. There is a separate regulation for hearing witnesses who reside abroad in cases concerning sex tourism involving children.[5] Canada has legislation in place for hearing

---

[4]   https://e-justice.europa.eu/content/Presentation.do?idTaxonomy=69&plang=en&init=true%vmac=iUbSi_fISE9lBi_tE6pwdPNeSKJOPos8A-VH6IkSGm9Ll3SV0i28d7NU51 mU2BsibN5W5RnohdpLCCcBsz9XAAAEngAAAAH.

[5]   Federal Magistrates Act 1999, s.69 and Crimes Act s 50EA.

witnesses by means of videoconferencing and recording statements that can serve as evidence.[6] Hearing witnesses by means of videoconferencing is applied on a large scale in the United States,[7] especially during the initial appearance, i.e. the first time the suspect is brought before the court (generally within 24 hours after arrest), and with respect to hearing a suspect who fails to pay a fine or compensation.[8] The suspect is usually located in a detention centre or a police station from which communication with the judge, who has to decide on the decision to detain the person involved, can take place by means of a closed circuit television system. The suspect's lawyer is also present at the place of detention. The Public Prosecutor is in the same location as the judge.[9]

In Italy, the security of trials against mafia suspects provided a reason to introduce videoconferencing in criminal proceedings in 1992. This regulation was expanded significantly in 1998. The regulation is linked to the special detention status of the person to be heard. In addition to remote videoconferencing, hearing persons in another courtroom via videoconferencing has also been regulated. The same applies to splitting up the video image to observe several suspects remotely at the same time. Large numbers of suspects are mainly found in trials against members of the mafia.[10]

Germany applies a regulation for hearing witnesses using video links whose wellbeing could be jeopardised. A similar regulation exists for hearing children and vulnerable witnesses. A regulation that provides for hearing witnesses, experts and suspects during the preliminary investigation using videoconferencing has been in place in Belgium since 2002.[11]

At the International Criminal Tribunal for the former Yugoslavia (ICTY), the judge can take measures to protect victims and witnesses pursuant to the Rules of Procedures and Evidence.[12] The International Criminal Court applies a similar regulation.[13]

---

[6] Federal Court Rules 1998. http://www.canlii.org/ca/laws/regu/si-98-78/si-98-78.html.

[7] It was decided in the case Edwards vs. Logan, 38 F. Supp. 2d 463, 465-68, that a prisoner who has initiated compensation proceedings against a guard guilty of using excessive force does not have the right to appear in person. The costs of transferring Edwards from New Mexico to Virginia would amount to $8652. http://www.wsba.org/info/bog/sept09tab16.pdf.

[8] Mols, G.P.M.F. Het telehoren van verdachten en getuigen, Metro, 1995. Federal Rules of Criminal Procedure, Rule 5(f).

[9] Law decree 356/1992.

[10] Le procès à distance au moyen de la vidéoconférence: l'experience Italienne (A/Conf. 187/Italy/2).

[11] Criminal Code § VII, article 112/317.

[12] Rules of Procedures and Evidence (Testimony by Video link) 71bis. http://www.icty.org/.

[13] http://www.icc-cpi.int/Menus/ICC/Legal+Texts+Tools/Official+Journal/Rules+of+Procedures+and+Evidence.htm.

This general overview makes it clear that videoconferencing is applied for various reasons.[14] Bridging large distances, which involves significant cost, and the efficiency gains to be made in that connection, particularly play a role in countries with an extensive territory and in international cooperation. The verification of provisional deprivation of liberty (initial appearance) concerns both shorter distances and the need imposed by law to perform the hearing within a relatively short period of time. Videoconferencing mostly prevents a large number of short-distance movements and in doing so can contribute to efficiency and cost savings. An entirely different reason is the application of videoconferencing with a view to the physical or psychological protection of witnesses (minors, victims of sexual abuse or protected witnesses). Hearing by videoconferencing can contribute to the protection of these witnesses against reprisal by the suspect and his/her accomplices. Improving the quality of the administration is also important. Witnesses who otherwise could not contribute, or not contribute as directly, to establishing the truth, can be heard using videoconferencing.

4.2   EU convention on mutual assistance

The use of videoconferencing is increasing all the time within the EU as a result of the EU convention on mutual legal assistance (Mutual Assistance in Criminal Matters between Member States). It has been laid down in this convention that Member States can make use of videoconferencing when performing cross-border witness hearings.[15, 16]

Article 10

If a person is in one Member State's territory and has to be heard as a witness or expert by the judicial authorities of another Member State, the latter may, where it is not desirable or possible for the person to be heard to appear in its territory in person, request that the hearing take place by videoconference, as provided for in paragraphs 2 to 8.

The requested Member State shall agree to the hearing by videoconference provided that the use of the videoconference is not contrary to fundamental principles of its law and on condition that it has the technical means to carry out

---

[14] The E-Justice website contains information per Member State on the use of videoconferencing. https://e-justice.europa.eu/contentPresentation.do?idTaxonomy=151&plang=en&vmac=6PfEnQngpnf80JIWvBoLEl_T5MPbj5jBudB5G8N03mrxYOaqDzX9OZZ0fpZ3OsNoV4e-RttOsACOHMBYRObgAAG4sAAAAV.

[15] 2000/c97/01. http://europa.eu/legislation_summaries/justice_freedom_security/. judicial_cooperation_in_criminal_matters/l33108_en.htm.

[16] A treaty with a similar provision was signed between the EU and Japan. http://eur-lex.europa.eu/Notice.do?mode=dbl&lang=en&ihmlang=en&lng1=en,nl&lng2=bg,cs,da,de, el,en,es,et,fi,fr,hu,it,lt,lv,mt,nl,pl,pt,ro,sk,sl,sv,&val=508413:cs&page=.

> the hearing. If the requested Member State has no access to the technical means for videoconferencing, such means may be made available to it by the requesting Member State by mutual agreement.

The above provision enables one Member State to request another Member State to hear a witness or expert using videoconferencing. In this case, the hearing is performed under the supervision of the requesting foreign authority, for example in Belgium, while the witness or expert is located in France. The laws of both Member States apply to the video hearing and the same rules apply that would apply to a hearing in which the witness is physically present. The consent of the person to be heard is required. In addition to hearing witnesses and experts, hearings using videoconferencing are also possible with respect to suspects, provided that the Member States involved consider this to be necessary, their judicial authorities agree thereto and the suspect consents as well (article 10, paragraph 9).[17]

5   JUDICIAL COOPERATION

The argument for including the possibility of using videoconferencing in the EU convention is that the technology and quality of videoconferencing links have developed to such an extent that it is responsible to make use of it within the context of judicial cooperation. Judicial cooperation is high on the EU agenda. It has become simpler for persons to move from one Member State to another as a result of the disappearance of internal borders.[18] Millions of people now travel abroad, partly as a result of the emergence of low budget airlines. An ever larger group of persons move to a different Member State of the EU to settle there temporarily, to work or with the intention of settling there permanently. Increasing mobility is not limited to holidays and (labour) migration. Those involved in drug trafficking, human trafficking and financial fraud also benefit from the open borders. Criminal organisations easily move from one country to the next. Judicial cooperation and exchange of information is essential if the aim is to prevent offenders from moving from one Member State to another without being punished. This is why it was agreed during a session of the European Council in Tampere (1999) that mutual recognition of court decisions and judgments have to become the cornerstone of judicial cooperation within the EU.[19]

---

[17] As regards civil law, the provision has been included in the EU Evidence Regulation that a court can request another Member State that use is made of videoconferencing. http://eur-lex.europa.eu/LexUriServ/LexUirServ.do?uri=OJ:C:2000:314:0001:0020:EN:PDF.

[18] http://europa.eu/legislation_summaries/justice_freedom_security/free_movement_of_persons_asylum_immigration_/l33020_en.htm.

[19] The Presidency conclusions at the Tampere European Council, Oct 15-16, 1999 §33-37.

5.1   Mutual recognition

The starting point is that Member States recognise and implement each other's court decisions without a great deal of red tape. Said starting point is based on the notion that there is mutual confidence among the Member States as regards the constitutionality, legitimacy and honesty of each Member State's legal system. The underlying thought in this connection is that all Member States are bound by the European Convention on Human Rights and Fundamental Freedoms (ECHR). There are two sides to confidence. One the one hand, the implementing state whose cooperation is requested has to be confident that the procedure in the requesting Member State on which the request is based occurs in accordance with the law and the guarantees of the ECHR. The requesting state, on the other hand, has to be confident that the procedure in the implementing state also occurs in accordance with the law. Mutual recognition renders harmonisation of criminal justice systems – something that is considered a bridge too far in Europe[20] - unnecessary. Mutual recognition should thus facilitate judicial cooperation and prevent a thorough review of each other's criminal justice system.[21]

The first instrument that was based on mutual recognition is the European Arrest Warrant (EAW) that has replaced the various extradition procedures within the EU. This regulation makes it much simpler, for example, to extradite a British citizen who is alleged to have committed an offence during a holiday in Portugal to said country.[22] The number of requests for extradition between Member States has increased significantly as a result of this regulation.[23] There are furthermore (draft) framework decisions on the taking of evidence in criminal proceedings and the harmonisation of the criminalisation of, for example, human trafficking, money laundering, drug trafficking, terrorism and victim care, mutual recognition of default judgments and the implementation of criminal justice sanctions.

---

[20] National criminal law of all Member States was developed over centuries, it symbolizes a national identity and culture. Each Member State treasures its own characteristics.

[21] Mutual confidence is also the essence of the ruling in the Güzütuk and Brügge Case 187/C and Case-385/01. According to the Court, it is necessary 'that Member States have mutual confidence in their respective criminal justice systems and that each Member State accepts the application of the criminal justice system in place in the other Member States, also if its own criminal justice system would lead to a different outcome'.

[22] Several examples can be found on the Fair Trials International website. See: http://www.fairtrials.net/cases/spotlight/garry_mann/.

[23] http://ec.europa.eu/justice/policies/criminal/extradition/docs/com_2011_175_en.pdf.

5.2 Roadmap Stockholm Programme

A problematic aspect of mutual recognition is that it mainly focuses on the repressive side of criminal law. It often fails to consider that in each Member State evidence is formed in a context of legal guarantees. That context makes the evidence legal and reliable, or illegal and unreliable. The relevant rules differ from country to country and the guarantees are shaped in different phases. For example, in Belgium the caution need not be given prior to a hearing, in Poland it is permitted to monitor communication between a lawyer and a detainee during the first fourteen days and in Finland nearly half of all criminal cases are settled without the presence of the accused or in writing.[24]

The context factors are removed if evidence is transferred to a different country without that country being allowed to consider its formation. If in France a lawyer is not allowed to be present during every phase of the hearing of the witness, this is compensated in a later phase of the criminal proceedings. Mutual recognition compels the Member State to refrain from examining a specific aspect (the foreign evidence) concerning its compatibility with the right to a fair trial as laid down in Article 6 of the ECHR. As a result, mutual recognition can be on strained terms with Article 6 of the ECHR.

Practical application of the EAW raises questions regarding whether the same standards are applied throughout Europe, despite the fact that the law and criminal procedures in all Member States are subject to the standards of the ECHR. A person can apply to the European Court of Human Rights (ECtHR) to enforce his rights, but this is only possible if there is an alleged violation and all national remedies have been exhausted. It has become clear that this is not an effective means of guaranteeing that Member States comply with the standards of the ECHR.

This situation has prompted the European Commission to draft a roadmap to strengthen the procedural rights of suspects and accused persons in criminal procedures. This Roadmap comprises a phased plan that was included in the Stockholm Programme, which was adopted by the European Council in December 2009.[25] The first step is formed by the right established in October 2010 to interpretation and translation.[26] The next steps include a directive

---

[24] Ed Cape, Zaza Namoradze, Roger Smith and Taru Spronken, Effective Criminal Defence in Europe, Intersentia 2010.

[25] http://europa.eu/legislation_summaries/human_rights/fundamental_rights_within_european union/jl0036_en.htm and http://ec.europa.eu/.../planned.../22_jls_stockholm_programme_ en.pdf.

[26] See the contribution of Caroline Morgan – The New European directive on the rights to interpretation and translation in criminal proceedings.

relating to the information on the rights of suspects, the 'Letter of Rights'[27] and a directive on the right to legal assistance. Directives concerning vulnerable suspects and the right to communication of detained persons with family, their employer and the appropriate consulate are also anticipated.

6   VIDEOCONFERENCING IS NOT WITHOUT PROBLEMS

Hearing suspects, witnesses and experts by means of videoconferencing is not without problems. In the United States research has been carried out among users for some time.[28] Judges were generally enthusiastic about hearing using videoconferencing. They indicated that the handling of cases progressed more smoothly than in traditional arraignments. Handling progressed more quickly (fewer delays caused by bringing in the suspect), while, in their opinion, the use of videoconferencing did not have a negative influence on control of the trial, the behaviour of the suspect or communication with him/her. Terry and Surette (1985) note in their video-based study that:

> They [judges] all felt the video either increases or has little effect upon the speed of the arraignments, the effectiveness of the defendant's legal representation, or the humanization of the arraignment. Finally they felt that the use of video did not increase the likelihood of defendant's pleading guilty.[29]

Public Prosecutors were also enthusiastic, but less so than the judges. They considered that videoconferencing led to reduced quality of communication between the defendant and the other trial participants. The defence lawyers proved much more critical. In their view, the judge is less able to control the proceedings, communication is complicated and as a result the quality and effectiveness of legal assistance to the defendant is negatively influenced. Opinions differed among the defendants that were interviewed. The opinions of the defendants that were interviewed are set out in the table in Table 1.[30]

American literature also highlights the risk that the wish to save costs will become dominant and that – despite criticism from defendants and lawyers – the application of videoconferencing will be expanded ever further. This may jeopardise the right to confrontation,[31] the right to due process, a public trial and the right to effective legal assistance. It is pointed out in this connection

---

[27]   http://ec.europa.eu/prelex/detail_dossier_real.cfm?CL=en&DisId=199549.

[28]   Ray Surrete – W.C. Terry – Media Technology and the courts: the case of closed circuit video arraignments in Miami, Florida, 1990.

[29]   Terry, W.C. and Surette, R. (1985), 'Video in the Misdemeanor Court: The South Florida Experience'. IN *Judicature* 69 (10), 18.

[30]   Terry and Surette (1985: 19).

[31]   The United States recognises the defendant's constitutional right to directly confront those who accuse him of a criminal act. This right has been laid down in the Sixth Amendment.

that pronouncing a judgment forms such a central element of criminal proceedings that it would be undesirable in principle to sentence persons via a television screen. This in fact also applies to adopting a position with regard to the question of whether the defendant is guilty of the matters s/he is charged with.

Survey item	(N)	Yes %	No %	Unsure %
I think that using video limited my ability to argue my case	345	31.6	64.3	4.1
There were questions I wanted to ask but didn't because I was on TV	338	20.1	78.4	1.5
I acted or spoke differently because I was on TV	339	18.9	78.4	2.1
The use of TV made me nervous	342	29.2	70.2	0.6
I feel that the use of TV violated my legal rights	342	15.2	79.5	5.3
If I wasn't on TV I would have pled differently	338	10.7	85.5	3.8
I think that using TV for court appearance is a good idea	348	72.1	20.4	7.5
I was happy with my televised court appearance	344	78.5	19.5	2.0
I feel that the use of video made my case go faster	340	84.4	12.1	3.5

Table 1: Defendants' attitudes towards video links (source: Terry and Surette 1985).

Hoogstraten points out the risk that the parties involved will *stare* at the image instead of having actual eye contact (monitor capture or TV watching). If a defendant addresses the court and the judge is (unconsciously) staring at the TV screen (displaying the defendant) this can be very confrontational for the defendant.[32]

Orie, a judge on the International Criminal Tribunal for the Former Yugoslavia, emphasises the importance of the procedural context in which videoconferencing is applied.[33] He emphasises the fact that the technical quality of

---

[32] Hoogstraten, J. – Verdachten en verhoren, Amsterdam 1995.
[33] Orie, A.M.M. – De verdachte in beeld?, Deventer 2004.

videoconferencing is mainly a matter of money. A good connection is no longer a problem using current technology. However, the reason for using videoconferencing is often decisive for the procedural context. At a short distance, a lawyer will have a choice of being in court or with the defendant. That choice will often not exist if large distances have to be bridged. Who monitors the hearing and the room in which it takes place? Conversely, if the lawyer is not physically present with the defendant, this will not benefit the communication. A separate telephone line will not always prevent the defendant from feeling abandoned and alone. If the lawyer is present in the detention centre, he will miss direct contact with the judge and the impression that more is required to convince him will easily arise. Who bears responsibility for the hearing and according to what law (the right to refuse to give evidence, taking the oath and witness protection)? The answer to these questions is relevant to the decision to make use of videoconferencing.

7   VIDEOCONFERENCING IN RELATION TO THE ECHR

This paragraph deals with the question of how hearing via videoconference link corresponds to the demands it makes of the law of criminal procedure. Articles 5 and 6 of the ECHR are relevant in this context. Article 5 ECHR protects the personal freedom of citizens. If someone is deprived of his/her liberty such must occur in accordance with a procedure described in law. This provision grants a suspect who has been arrested the right to be brought before the competent court. Article 6 contains the principles for the proper administration of justice. For example, in the determination of his/her civil rights and obligations or when determining the lawfulness of a prosecution brought against him/her, everyone has the right to a fair and public handling of his/her case, within a reasonable term by an independent and impartial court. This concerns the principle of a fair trial.

Art. 5. Right to liberty and security

1.   Everyone has the right to liberty and security of person.
No one shall be deprived of his liberty save in the following cases and in accordance with a procedure prescribed by law:
(a) the lawful detention of a person after conviction by a competent court;
(b) the lawful arrest or detention of a person for non-compliance with the lawful order of a court or in order to secure the fulfilment of any obligation prescribed by law;
(c) the lawful arrest or detention of a person effected for the purpose of bringing him before the competent legal authority on reasonable suspicion of having committed an offence or when it is reasonably considered necessary to prevent his committing an offence or fleeing after having done so;
(d) the detention of a minor by lawful order for the purpose of educational supervision or his lawful detention for the purpose of bringing him before the competent legal authority;

(e) the lawful detention of persons for the prevention of the spreading of infectious diseases, of persons of unsound mind, alcoholics or drug addicts or vagrants;

(f) the lawful arrest or detention of a person to prevent his effecting an unauthorised entry into the country or of a person against whom action is being taken with a view to deportation or extradition.

2. Everyone who is arrested shall be informed promptly, in a language which he understands, of the reasons for his arrest and of any charge against him.

3. Everyone arrested or detained in accordance with the provisions of paragraph 1 (c) of this Article shall be brought promptly before a judge or other officer authorised by law to exercise judicial power and shall be entitled to trial within a reasonable time or to release pending trial. Release may be conditioned by guarantees to appear for trial.

4. Everyone who is deprived of his liberty by arrest or detention shall be entitled to take proceedings by which the lawfulness of his detention shall be decided speedily by a court and his release ordered if the detention is not lawful.

5. Everyone who has been the victim of arrest or detention in contravention of the provisions of this Article shall have an enforceable right to compensation.

Art. 6. Right to a fair trial

1. In the determination of his civil rights and obligations or of any criminal charge against him, everyone is entitled to a fair and public hearing within a reasonable time by an independent and impartial tribunal established by law. Judgment shall be pronounced publicly but the press and public may be excluded from all or part in the trial of the interests of morals, public order or national security in a democratic society, where the interests of juveniles or the protection of the private life of the parties so require, or to the extent strictly necessary in the opinion of the court in special circumstances where publicity would prejudice the interests of justice.

2. Everyone charged with a criminal offence shall be presumed innocent until proved guilty according to law.

3. Everyone charged with a criminal offence has the following minimum rights:

(a) to be informed promptly, in a language which he understands and in detail, of the nature and cause of the accusation against him;

(b) to have adequate time and facilities for the preparation of his defence;

(c) to defend himself in person or through legal assistance of his own choosing or, if he has not sufficient means to pay for legal assistance, to be given it free when the interests of justice so require;

(d) to examine or have examined witnesses against him and to obtain the attendance and examination of witnesses on his behalf under the same conditions as witnesses against him;

(e) to have the free assistance of an interpreter if he cannot understand or speak the language used in court.

Article 5, third paragraph, provides, briefly, that anyone who has been arrested or detained must be brought promptly before a judge. This provision serves to limit the actual possibility of arbitrariness and to prevent abuse of detainees. As far as is known, the ECHR never made any provision on the manner in which the arraignment before a judicial agency should be structured.

It is clear that when the ECHR as drafted in 1950, the physical arraignment of the defendant before the judge was assumed. The same applies to the hearing of witnesses and experts. On the other hand, the ECHR is a dynamic instrument that does not remain untouched by modern technologies. It is established ECtHR case law that the ECHR is "a living instrument which must be interpreted in light of present-day conditions".[34] The objective of the arraignment is important when answering the question whether, according to current standards, a different manner of arraigning defendants or hearing witnesses can withstand review against the ECHR. The ECtHR rendered an opinion in this context in the Schiesser case.[35] According to the ECtHR, that objective lies in offering persons who have been deprived of their liberty a court procedure, by way of special guarantee, in order to prevent arbitrary deprivation of liberty and to ensure that the deprivation of liberty will be as short as possible. Article 5, third paragraph, ECHR contains, according to the ECtHR, a procedural and substantive requirement: the relevant authority will, on the one hand, have to hear the opinion of the defendant brought before it and, on the other hand, assess whether there are reasons for continuing the detention. In its assessment, it will also want to take into consideration whether the person is physically able to undergo detention and has not been subjected to disproportionate violence during arrest. In this light, physical arraignment is the starting point, but a different manner of arraignment using modern techniques need not be excluded in advance, provided the video and audio connection satisfies the relevant quality requirements.

7.1 The right to be present

According to the ECtHR, Article 6 of the ECHR provides for the right to be present at the hearing. Not until the defendant, or his lawyer, is present at the hearing, will he be able to exercise his rights such as examining witnesses. The term hearing will have a different meaning if videoconferencing is applied. The hearing will take place in the courtroom, but the judge and the others present in the courtroom will receive part of the proceedings via a video connection, which is different to the classic manner. The defendant is also present in court during the videoconference session, albeit not physically. The quality requirements set by law in respect of the audio and video connection can moreover ensure that the right to follow the court hearing is sufficiently implemented.[36]

---

[34] ECtHR 25 April 1978, Tyrer v. United Kingdom, Series A no. 26, at § 31.
[35] ECtHR 4 December 1979, Series A 34, at § 30-31.
[36] ECtHR 23 February 1994, Series A, vol. 282-A.

The defendant has the right to participate actively in the court hearing. The defendant is in principle able to follow the proceedings, can ask questions and consult his lawyer via videoconference link.

It is furthermore important whether hearing by videoconference constitutes a sufficiently public handling of the case. The public nature of the hearings where this applies need not be impaired by a hearing using videoconferencing, provided the setup of the TV screens or other screens is such that persons other than the judge can also see the images. The requirement of a public handling of the case has been satisfied if any member of the public can have a seat in the courtroom in the customary manner and has a good view of the screens.

7.2 Hearing witnesses

Hearing an incriminating witness is partly intended to check his or her testimony for reliability and credibility. A direct confrontation can simplify this check because the judge of the defence is better able to respond to the body language of the witness. It is furthermore plausible that a witness is less inclined to lie during a direct confrontation. The ECtHR has decided, however, that it is not necessary that incriminating witnesses are heard in all cases, provided the defendant has had an adequate and proper opportunity to examine the witnesses or have them examined.[37] All of the above does not detract from the fact that, according to case law of the ECtHR the right to examine witnesses can also be satisfied if the lawyer of the defendant has had the opportunity to ask questions. It will therefore depend on the specific case whether the absence of the defendant was so serious the right to examine witnesses was violated.[38]

In the case of Marcello Viola versus Italy[39] – a criminal case against a person suspected of several homicides and membership of the mafia – Viola, who was detained, had the opportunity during the appeal proceedings of attending his trial via videoconference link. He was also able to communicate confidentially with his lawyers. Before the ECtHR, Viola invoked violation of Article 6, paragraphs 1 and 3, of the ECHR. The ECtHR commenced with an explanation of the right of a defendant to personally appear at the criminal proceedings. The interests of victims and witnesses should not be disregarded in this connection, even if their interests are not included in Article 6 ECHR. Article 6 guarantees the defendant's right to actually participate in his trial. But the personal appearance of the defendant during appeal

---

[37] ECtHR Saïdi v. France Publication: A 261 C.
[38] ECtHR King/UK, 26 January 2010, no. 9742/07.
[39] ECtHR 5 October 2006, no. 45106/04 (Viola).

proceedings is not of the same importance as during the first instance, not even if the court of appeal is fully competent, both factually and with respect to the questions of law. The court of appeal in the Viola case was fully competent, both with respect to establishing the facts and the law. It had to assess the guilt or innocence of the defendant, which is why the defendant's participation in the trial was necessary. However, this can also occur via videoconference link. Italian law provides for this option. The ECtHR also pointed out several international law instruments that provide for participation in the trial using videoconferencing. Such a manner of participation is, in itself, not contrary to Article 6 ECHR. In the Viola case, the security risks inherent in transport had to be taken into account. Viola was accused of very serious, mafia-related crimes and the risk of collusion or escape was taken seriously. On the other hand, other considerations, such as the right to adjudication within a reasonable term, may be taken into account within the context of the decision whether the public debate after the first instance provided for a need. Using videoconferencing in this case served to protect public order, to prevent crime, to guarantee the rights of witnesses and victims, and to facilitate the handling of the case within a reasonable term. In order to answer the question of whether the manner in which the defendant was enabled to participate in his trial satisfied the requirements of Article 6 ECHR, the Court considered it important that the defendant could hear and see from detention the persons who played a role in the courtroom and that he could be heard and seen by the judges and witnesses. The defence lawyers were able to communicate with him in a confidential manner, both from the courtroom and in the place of detention. This manner of participation in the trial did not essentially prejudice the position of the defence when compared with the position of the other parties to the trial. The defendant had the opportunity to exercise the rights guaranteed by the requirements of due process and Article 6 ECHR was therefore not violated.

No violation of Article 6 §§ 1 and 3

Marcello Viola v. Italy (no. 45106/04)

The applicant complained that his participation in the hearing by videoconference had amounted to a violation of Article 6 (right to a fair trial). Relying on Article 4 of Protocol No. 7 (right not to be tried or punished twice), he further complained that he had been tried twice for the same offence.

In the Court's opinion, it was undeniable that the transfer of a prisoner such as the applicant entailed particularly stringent security measures and a risk of absconding or attacks. It could also provide an occasion to renew contact with the criminal associations to which the applicant was suspected of belonging.

In the present case, the applicant was accused of serious crimes related to the mafia's activities. The fight against that scourge could, in certain cases, require the adoption of measures intended to protect, in particular, public safety and order and to prevent other criminal offences. With its rigid hierarchical structure and very strict rules and its substantial power of intimidation based on the rule of silence and the difficulty in identifying its followers, the Mafia represented a sort of criminal opposition force capable of influencing public life directly or indirectly and of infiltrating the institutions. It was not therefore unreasonable to consider that its members could, even by their mere presence in the courtroom, exercise undue pressure on other parties in the proceedings, especially the victims and witnesses who had turned state evidence.

In those circumstances, the Court considered that the applicant's participation at the appeal hearings by videoconference pursued legitimate aims, namely the protection of public order, the prevention of crime, protection of the right to life, freedom and security of witnesses and victims of offences, and compliance with the "reasonable time" requirement in judicial proceedings. In addition, the Court found that the arrangements for the conduct of the proceedings had respected the rights of the defence. It therefore concluded, unanimously, that there had been no violation of Article 6 §§ 1 and 3.

The case of Zagaria versus Italy is also interesting.[40] In this case, the European Court did consider that Article 6, paragraph 3, at c, had been violated. In this case, a violation of Article 6, paragraph 3, at c, ECHR in combination with Article 6, paragraph 1, ECHR was assumed, because no confidential communication with the lawyer had been possible during the court hearing, because the telephone connection used for communication between the lawyer and the defendant had been tapped. This case also concerned crimes related to the mafia. Zagaria was located in prison and was connected to the courtroom by means of videoconference link. He communicated confidentially with his lawyer using the telephone. In the file, however, his lawyer found a written report drawn up by a police officer of a conversation with his client concerning a fax and a man called RG. It is essential to a fair trial that a defendant can give his lawyer instructions in a confidential manner when his case is discussed and the evidence is produced. A violation of Article 6(3) occurred, despite the fact that the lawyer did not find out that the conversation had been listened in on until after the trial. At that time, the proceedings against RG were still pending and several other procedures were pending as well. In view of the weak response of the government with respect to the police officer who had violated the confidentiality - said person was neither prosecuted nor subjected to disciplinary measures - there is no guarantee that the incident will not occur again. Zagaria had a justified fear that conversations were listened in on, which could be reason for him to hesitate to put forward issues that could be relevant to the case brought against him.

---

[40] ECtHR 27 November 2007, no. 58295/00.

7.3   Position of the interpreter

There is no case law yet concerning the position of the interpreter during videoconferencing in criminal cases. In this connection, the general rule applies that the responsibility of the government is not limited to appointing an interpreter, but that it should also ensure that the interpreter and his/her interpretation are of sufficient quality. This is to guarantee that the right to the assistance of an interpreter free of charge is 'practical' and 'effective'. Sufficient quality is a logical consequence, as the right to the assistance of an interpreter would otherwise hardly be a safeguard. In the case of Cuscani versus England, the ECtHR further tightened this line.[41] Cuscani, the manager of an Italian restaurant, whose command of English was poor, was prosecuted for tax evasion. The judge had been informed, shortly before the hearing, of Cuscani's poor command of English and his inability to follow the trial without the assistance of an interpreter. The judge then decided that an interpreter had to be present during the court hearing. No interpreter was present during court hearing, however, and the judge was persuaded by Cuscani's lawyer to let communication progress via his brother. It was later established that the brother did not translate everything during the court hearing.

The ECtHR established that the judge was under the obligation to ascertain – following consultation with Cuscani himself – that Cuscani was able to fully participate in a trial that could potentially have serious consequences for him. The Court concludes that the judge failed to comply with this obligation: the judge did not consult with Cuscani himself and relied on Cuscani's brother without testing his language skills. According to the Court, it is correct that the actions of the defence are primarily a matter for the defendant and his lawyer. However, the ultimate guardian of the fairness of the trial is the presiding judge who was aware of the difficulties that could have arisen for the defendant in view of the absence of an interpreter. The ECtHR establishes in this connection that the national courts have argued themselves that the judges have to look after the interests of the defendant with scrupulous care:

> However, the ultimate guardian of the fairness of the proceedings was the trial judge who had been clearly apprised of the real difficulties which the absence of interpretation might create for the applicant. It further observes that the domestic courts have already taken the view that in circumstances such as those in the instant case, judges are required to treat an accused's interest with 'scrupulous care'.[42]

---

[41]   ECtHR 24 September 2002, application no. 00032771/96 (Cuscani vs. United Kingdom)

[42]   ECtHR, Cuscani vs. United Kingdom, (2003) 36 EHRR 1, §39.

If the services of an interpreter are used during videoconferencing, the judge, under whose responsibility the hearing takes place, will have to assess explicitly whether the assistance rendered by the interpreter can be considered to be of sufficient quality. In this respect, the judge cannot hide behind an excessively careless attitude on the part of the lawyer.[43] However, practice does contain many examples of situations in which the judge is not sufficiently critical where the quality of interpreters is concerned. Judges are, however, faced with a difficult task. They are expected, on the one hand, to monitor the reliability of the interpretation, while, on the other hand, they are usually unable to assess the quality of the interpretation. The interpreter is responsible for her/his work, the judge for the entire case, including the interpretation that is at the basis of his/her ultimate decision. After all, it is the duty of the judge to establish the truth. Effective communication creates an important condition for complying with this responsibility and to guarantee the quality of the examination in court. This is only possible if communication with the assistance of an interpreter progresses without problem. The findings of tests conducted within the context of AVIDICUS make it clear that interpreting in criminal cases in which videoconferencing is used requires additional skills. It is generally accepted that that these skills can only be obtained in sound interaction with the legal practice. Deploying judges, police detectives, Public Prosecutors and lawyers as teachers in the training of interpreters is therefore essential. It is also important that judges, police detectives, Public Prosecutors and lawyers are aware of the (im)possibilities when working with an interpreter during videoconferencing. They should develop the skill to approach the activities of interpreters with a sufficiently critical attitude.

8   SOME CONCLUSIONS

The introduction of videoconferencing in criminal proceedings clearly has advantages. As regards witnesses, think for example of the protection of vulnerable witnesses or witnesses who, due to the large distance or otherwise, cannot be heard or only with great difficulty. There are also advantages in terms of costs savings and efficiency benefits with respect to the administration of justice, mainly as a result of decreasing movement of defendants and hearing defendants residing abroad. The technical possibilities seem limitless, but caution is required. Attending a trial remotely using videocon-

---

[43] Also in the case of Hermi versus Italy, the ECtHR concludes that the judge is obliged to guarantee the effectiveness of the defence for the defendant, even if the defendant has not informed the competent authorities or contacted his counsel himself. ECtHR 18 October 2006, application: 18114/02.

ferencing is in itself not contrary to the ECHR, provided its application serves a legitimate purpose and the manner of implementation is compatible with the rights of the defence. Alienation or mechanisation of the administration of criminal justice can easily occur if videoconferencing is applied en masse. If society gets the impression that handling court cases using videoconferencing impairs the quality of the administration of justice, the danger arises that videoconferencing ultimately impairs the legitimacy of the administration of justice. This is all the more pertinent for defendants who doubt the quality of the proceedings and consequently the correctness of the outcome of their criminal proceedings. In view of the increasing use of videoconferencing, it is very important that, when training judges, Public Prosecutors and lawyers, there is also attention to the use of videoconferencing in legal practice. This also applies to being able to assess critically the quality of the assistance offered by an interpreter.

VIDEO-MEDIATED INTERPRETING: AN OVERVIEW OF CURRENT PRACTICE AND RESEARCH

Sabine Braun and Judith L. Taylor

University of Surrey

1 INTRODUCTION

This chapter reports on one of the outcomes of the AVIDICUS Project. Against the backdrop of recent developments in Europe, especially the promotion of the use of videoconferencing in criminal proceedings, for example in the European E-Justice Action plan,[1] the AVIDICUS Project set out to evaluate the quality of video-mediated interpreting in criminal proceedings and its viability from an interpreting point of view. To achieve this overarching aim, the project had three specific objectives:

(1) To identify situations in the criminal justice sphere where video-mediated interpreting would be most useful and specify a set of relevant situations;

(2) To assess the reliability of video-mediated interpreting in these situations from an interpreting perspective through a series of comparative case studies and formulate a set of recommendations for EU criminal justice services on the use of video-mediated interpreting in criminal proceedings;

(3) To devise and pilot three training modules on video-mediated interpreting based on the findings from (2): one for legal practitioners, including the police; one for interpreters working in the legal services; and one for interpreting students.

The first of these objectives included a review of current practice of video-mediated interpreting, especially in legal proceedings, which will be discussed in this chapter, and two European surveys, one among legal practitioners, and the other among legal interpreters, which will be presented in the following chapter.

Current practice was assessed through an analysis of the small body of research and reports on existing projects and studies. The aim of this was to

---

[1] European E-Justice Action Plan of the European Council (OJ No. C 75/01, 31-03-2009). Available at http://eur-lex.europa.eu/LexUriServ/LexUriServ.do?uri=OJ:C:2009:075:0001:0012:EN:PDF. See also van der Vlis (in this volume).

sketch out as broad an initial picture of video-mediated interpreting use as possible, to draw together practical and academic views and to identify possible benefits and real or potential problem areas.

This was complemented by an expert meeting in the initial phase of the project, which included representatives of European and national institutions who had gathered experience in video-mediated interpreting, videoconferencing experts, representatives from the legal professions and the police, interpreters, interpreting researchers and interpreter trainers.

Furthermore, all members of the AVIDICUS consortium engaged in field observation of current practice, i.e. observation of use of live video links, both with and without interpreting, in judicial settings, e.g. in the court rooms of their respective countries. They also held numerous informal consultations with legal interpreters, legal practitioners and police personnel.

The aggregate findings from the above tasks helped shape the AVIDICUS comparative studies, which are discussed later in this volume. The review of current practice ensured that these studies were conducted in relevant settings and would lead to relevant and valid recommendations.

The review confirms that what is described here as 'video-mediated interpreting' is in fact a blanket term for a variety of forms of interpreting. A broad distinction will be made in this chapter and throughout this volume between *videoconference interpreting* (VCI) and *remote interpreting* (RI). Videoconference interpreting is the form of interpreting that is used when the proceedings take place at two video-linked locations (e.g. court and prison), with the interpreter being situated at either end of the link. Remote interpreting (RI) is the form of interpreting that is used when the proceedings take place at a single location (e.g. a courtroom), with the interpreter working via video link from a remote location (e.g. another courthouse).

Section 2 of this chapter will outline the context in which the discussion of VCI and RI in criminal proceedings is embedded and will also give more comprehensive definitions for both forms. Section 3 will give an overview of current practice and research. This is based on the review of reports on other projects and initiatives, the outcomes of the expert meeting, informal consultations and field work. Section 4 draws conclusions with regard to the current and projected pictures of VCI and RI use in criminal proceedings.

2 BACKGROUND

A survey conducted by the European Council Working Party on Legal Data Processing (Working Party on e-Law) in 2008 shows that the use of video-conferencing (VC) is increasing in both **national and cross-border criminal proceedings** to speed up judicial co-operation, to reduce costs or to increase security.[2] The survey also asked whether the respondents had experience in using videoconferencing for translation or interpretation.

Austria, Bulgaria, the Czech Republic, France, Ireland, Italy, Latvia, Luxembourg and Malta replied that they had no such experience. Denmark reported that remote interpreting (RI) had been used in a trial. Hungary, Romania and Sweden stated that they had limited experience in using VC equipment and interpreting. Estonia, Germany, Slovenia and Spain reported occasional or frequent use of simultaneous interpreting in video links in court. Poland reported carrying out moot court trials involving interpreters to test RI via phone and video link. The Netherlands replied that interpreters participate frequently in video links between courts and prisons and that they are located either in court or in the prison. Finland responded that interpreters were involved in video links between Finnish district courts and Swedish prisons, with one interpreter in the prison and another interpreter in court. The UK reported that England and Wales used video links between police custody suites and courts, and interpreters, when involved, were located in court. In Scotland, however, interpreters involved in videoconferences would generally be seated next to the witness.

These responses point to a wide range of different forms of video-mediated interpreting, with primary interlocutors and interpreters being positioned in different locations. This chapter focuses on the details of the various situations in which videoconferencing and interpreting coincide.

2.1 Context

The European Union has promoted the use of videoconference technology in legal proceedings[3] for a number of reasons. VC technology is seen as being capable of:

- supporting judicial co-operation,
- speeding up legal proceedings,
- saving costs in legal proceedings, especially cross-border proceedings,
- helping to resolve security concerns and avoiding the transport of detained persons,
- giving access to interpreting services.

---

[2] European Council Working Party on Legal Data Processing (2008), *Questionnaire on videoconferencing – Compilation of responses*, 6709/08 JURINFO 19. Brussels: European Commission.

[3] Especially through the European e-Justice initiative launched by the DG Justice and the ensuing Multi-Annual European e-Justice Action Plan 2008-13 (Council of the European Union (2008), *European e-Justice Action Plan*, 15315/08 JURINFO 71. Brussels: European Union.)

Because greater migration and mobility rates have entailed an increase in the number of bi- and multilingual proceedings both at national level and in cross-border cases, gaining access to legal interpreters has become a critical issue in Europe. Timely access to qualified legal interpreters for a wide range of languages, including 'rare' languages, is therefore crucial, and video-conference technology is seen by judicial services and the European e-Justice initiative as having the potential to ensure this timely access is achieved.

As the use of videoconferencing in legal proceedings (administrative, criminal and immigration) has become more frequent, it has also become the subject of academic debate. Current academic thinking posits that videocon-ference technology should be used with utmost care and that further research on its effects is required before it can be used more widely (e.g. Poulin 2004, Federman 2006, Haas 2006, Wiggins 2006, Sossin & Yetnikoff 2007, Havard Law School 2009).

Referring to criminal justice, Poulin has argued, for example, "that courts should not extend their reliance on videoconferencing further and instead must undertake studies to explore the impact of the technology in criminal proceedings" (2003: 1089). With regard to VC use in immigration proceed-ings and based on extensive reference to experimental research on the differ-ences between face-to-face and videoconference communication, the Harvard Law Review has recently warned that VC use in this setting may result in a system "in which individuals gain speedier entrance [to an immi-gration court] but fewer receive the opportunity to be heard in a meaningful manner" (2009: 1193). At the same time, the Harvard Law Review does acknowledge the practical requirements of, and pressures on, immigration courts. It concedes that "improving the technology used, limiting use to preliminary hearings, and requiring the respondent's consent could help balance the efficiency videoconferencing purportedly provides with the substantive requirements of the immigration court system" (2009: 1192).

Some projects report positive results, although empirical evidence for the positive conclusions is not always provided. However, recent projects which have aimed or are aiming to gather empirical evidence for their conclusions range from the 'Gateways to Justice' project in Australia[4] project (2007-10), to prison-court video links in Canada,[5] which are embedded in the Criminal justice reform/bail reform in British Columbia launched in 2007, or a video-conferencing project in the London Probation services in 2006.[6]

---

[4] http://www.justiceenvironments.edu.au/attachments/progress-report-2-nov-v3.pdf
[5] http://www.criminaljusticereform.gov.bc.ca/en/justice_reform_projects/bail_reform/index.html.
[6] Unpublished report.

One issue that the Harvard Law Review does not address is the growing number of European initiatives that focus on such aspects as improving technology and the audiovisual environment in which videoconferencing takes place. The work on legal videoconferencing undertaken by the Dutch Ministry of Justice,[7] for example, has been concerned with the conditions under which videoconference technology may be used both in immigration and criminal justice. This work has taken into account the specifics of legal communication in court and a wide range of other factors, and can serve as a starting point for the consideration of videoconference (and remote) interpreting:

> A courtroom is an area where communication between different parties in proceedings is of primary importance and where certain legal, traditional and ceremonial aspects also play an important role. Like a courtroom, the chambers of an examining magistrate, a witness room and the interrogation room in a penitentiary institution are no ordinary workplaces. The special feature of such rooms is that each of the participants has a fixed role, as a result of which they may or may not sit (or stand) opposite or next to one another, often in a specific place in the room. Considerable importance is moreover attached to ensuring that each participant can see and hear all the other participants clearly and observe both verbal and non-verbal reactions. The use of videoconferencing in alien and criminal law proceedings as a means of hearing aliens, suspects, witnesses and experts at a distance therefore imposes such stringent requirements on equipment components and the composition, positioning and adjustment thereof that the audiovisual solution may generally be regarded as a tailor-made solution.[8]

The work conducted in the Netherlands in this area has resulted in a set of recommendations for the use of videoconferencing in legal proceedings and a publically available handbook on videoconferencing,[9] which in turn has become a basis for the handbook on videoconferencing developed by the European Council Working Party on Legal Data Processing, available through the e-Justice portal.[10] What is noteworthy is the 'holistic' approach, which goes far beyond emphasising the importance of the quality of the videoconferencing equipment (see also van Rotterdam and van den Hoogen in this volume).

Criticism at a deeper level in relation to legal videoconferencing and video-mediated interpreting in criminal proceedings has been voiced by the Law Societies in Europe. The main argument is that irrespective of the quality the technology, the use of VC links as a replacement for the physical

---

[7] http://www.rijksoverheid.nl/onderwerpen/videoconferentie.

[8] SN 1759/08, February 2008, p.2.

[9] http://www.justitie.nl/onderwerpen/recht_en_rechtsbijstand/videoconferentie/.

[10] https://e-justice.europa.eu/attachments/vc_booklet_en.pdf; http://bit.ly/1QY6MA.

presence of a defendant in court, for example, is inconsistent with human rights.[11] The criticism is, however, targeted at the use of videoconferencing as such and does not arise from concerns over the quality of video-mediated interpreting, which has been the focus of the AVIDICUS project. The debate as to whether or not the use of videoconferencing in criminal proceedings is appropriate from a legal point of view is outside the scope of AVIDICUS.

In reality, the growing use of videoconferencing in legal proceedings has also increased the demand for interpreting in videoconference situations. The above examples from bail hearings, probation and court settings could easily be imagined with the involvement of an interpreter.

Furthermore, the increasing mobility and migration in Europe and the new legal framework (especially the new EU Directive on strengthening the rights to interpretation and translation in criminal proceedings)[12] are likely to lead to a higher demand for legal interpreting. This also demands a cost-effective solution for the provision of interpreting, especially at a time when the economic climate puts pressure on public services and interpreting service providers alike, jeopardizing quality standards and fair access to justice for all European citizens.

---

[11] In a declaration published by the Law Societies Joint Brussels Office in June 2009, the office states the following with reference to the AVIDICUS expert meeting in June 2009 and the issue of legal videoconferencing and video-mediated interpreting:

> On 4 June 2009 the Law Societies Joint Brussels Office participated in an experts meeting on an EU sponsored study on the Assessment of Video-conference Interpreting in the Criminal Justice Services. We emphasised the importance of the right to a fair trial and the right to be brought promptly before a judge. We drew attention to the Council of Europe European Committee for the Prevention of Torture and Inhuman or Degrading Treatment or Punishment (CPT) report to the UK Government published on 1 October 2008.
>
> In relation to extensions of pre-charge detention by video-link it emphasises that the physical presence of a detainee should be seen as an obligation, not as an option open to the judicial authority. We emphasised that a person charged with a criminal offence should, as a general principle based on the notion of a fair trial, be entitled to be present at his hearing. We would also emphasise that videoconferencing must not be used as a means to water down the right to interpretation.
>
> We are very concerned that virtual courts piloted in the UK are being billed as good practice. [...]. This fails to consider or even acknowledge the disadvantages including in terms of inconsistency with human rights. (The Law Societies Joint Brussels Office 2009: 36-37)

[12] Directive 2010/64/EU of the European Parliament and of the Council on the right to interpretation and translation in criminal proceedings. Available at http://www.europarl.europa.eu/oeil/ file.jsp?id=5840482.

It does not come as a surprise, therefore, that public service providers and interpreting agencies look towards videoconferencing technology as a potential solution for gaining cost-effective and timely access to qualified legal interpreters and thus for improving access to justice.

However, some of the many issues arising include how the technological mediation through videoconference link affects the quality of interpreting; how this is related to the actual videoconference setting and the locations of participants and interpreter; and ultimately whether the emerging forms of videoconference and remote interpreting are sufficiently reliable for achieving the specific goals of legal communication such as evidence and information gathering, decision-making and delivering justice.

Much like videoconference communication *per se*, the viability of video-mediated interpreting has thus become the subject of much debate. While some see these forms of interpreting as ways of speeding up communication processes and providing timely access to qualified interpreters, others are concerned that they will have adverse affects on the interpreters' working conditions and the quality of interpreting.

Given the strongly opposing views in this area and the scarcity of systematic research, it was considered vital in the AVIDICUS project that a better overview of the situation be obtained before attempting to answer questions regarding the viability and quality of video-mediated interpreting. This chapter thus summarises the current extent of video-mediated interpreting. Whilst the focus is on criminal justice, reference will also be made to other areas of relevance that provide insight into the method of video-mediated interpreting.

One point that has become clear is that the notion of videoconferencing and interpreting covers a range of configurations. The next section will provide definitions of the prototypical configurations.

2.2   Videoconferencing and interpreting: definitions

What has been termed 'video-mediated interpreting' thus far is in fact a host of different settings in which interpreting is delivered via video link or in a videoconference. The AVIDICUS project from the outset made a distinction between two basic forms of video-mediated interpreting in criminal proceedings: videoconference interpreting and remote interpreting. In practice, these have variations, outlined as follows:

1. Videoconference interpreting

Videoconference interpreting (VCI) is the form of interpreting that arises when the proceedings take place at two different locations that are video-linked and an interpreter is required to facilitate the communication. This includes, for example, links between a courtroom in one country and a remote witness in another country, links between courts and police custody suites (e.g. for first hearings) or links between courts and prisons (e.g. for remand extension hearings).

When the proceedings are bilingual, requiring the services of an interpreter, there are two ways of integrating an interpreter in the videoconference situation, leading to two variants of videoconference interpreting, as shown below. On the one hand, the interpreter can be with the participants in the main room, e.g. the court room (videoconference interpreting A). On the other hand, the interpreter can be co-located with the other-language speaker in a custody suite, prison or in another court house (videoconference interpreting B).[13]

Figure 1: VCI (A) – interpreter present in the main room

Figure 2: VCI (B) – interpreter located with the other language-speaker

Current national legislation varies in terms of what is permissible, and the location of the interpreter varies. Examples of this are given in the following chapter of this volume.

2. Remote interpreting

Remote interpreting (RI) is the form of interpreting used when the proceedings take place at a single location (e.g. a courtroom), with the interpreter

---

[13] In a cross-border setting, the co-presence of the interpreter with a witness, suspect or prisoner in another country raises a number of logistical questions, e.g. who is responsible for sourcing, booking, vetting, briefing and paying the interpreter.

working via video link from a remote location (e.g. another courthouse or a central interpreting hub).

Figure 3: Remote interpreting – interpreter in a different location

The major difference between 'remote interpreting' and 'videoconference interpreting' in legal proceedings is that the former uses videoconference technology for the sole purpose of linking a legal interpreter to the proceedings, whilst 'videoconference interpreting' uses a video link to enable legal proceedings to take place across a distance, i.e. to connect primary participants who are not at the same location.

VCI and RI have different motivations. RI has become attractive to the judicial services to gain timely access to qualified legal interpreters but also to save interpreter travel costs and cut down on waiting times for interpreters, whilst VCI is simply a consequence of having bilingual proceedings take place via videoconference link.

3. Videoconference interpreting + Remote interpreting

The two settings can, of course, be combined. This happens when the proceedings take place at two different locations and the interpreter is stationed at a further location.

Figure 4: Videoconference and remote interpreting combined

This setting may look complex at first sight, but it may help to overcome some of the drawbacks of videoconference interpreting with the interpreter being located at one of the two sites. However, at present, this setting does not seem to play a significant role in video-mediated criminal proceedings.

3   CURRENT PRACTICE

This section will focus on the analysis of ongoing and recently completed projects that use videoconference technology to facilitate or enable interpreting services. The focus is on projects in legal contexts. However, brief reference will be made to other contexts (e.g. supranational organisations, healthcare) where such initiatives help to create a broader picture (section 3.1). Section 3.2 will cover VCI and RI in legal proceedings, including immigration and criminal justice settings. In accordance with the focus of the AVIDICUS project, the overview takes account of spoken-language interpreting only. There are also projects under way in video-mediated sign-language interpreting. For an overview, see e.g. Napier (in this volume).

3.1   Videoconference-mediated interpreting outside the judicial system

Most of the insights into video-mediated interpreting outside the judicial system come from conference interpreting. Experiments with remote interpreting began as early as the 1970s and triggered a body of experimental research that has, over time, generated an interesting pattern, namely a discrepancy between 'objective' measures for the performance of the interpreters in RI and their 'subjective' perceptions of their performance, well-being and satisfaction with this method of interpreting. Another area in which remote interpreting has been applied for a number of years is healthcare, but very little reliable information and empirical research is available in this area. One experimental study has been conducted in relation to VCI and RI in business settings.

3.1.1   Conference interpreting in supra-national institutions

Supra-national organisations have experimented with the use of remote (simultaneous) conference interpreting via video link since the 1970s (see overviews in Andres & Falk 2009, Böcker & Anderson 1993, Mouzourakis 1996, 2003, 2006, Moser-Mercer 2003, Roziner & Shlesinger 2010). From the 1990s onwards, one of the driving forces behind these efforts was the linguistic and logistical challenge entailed by the expansion of the European Union, and in particular the anticipated shortfall of interpreting booths in the European institutions after the EU expansion (Mouzourakis 2003). The aim was to set up interpreters in other rooms – i.e. in a centralised interpreter hub – with video screens providing them with the audio and video images from the actual meeting room.

Early experiments incurred extremely negative reactions from conference interpreters (Mouzourakis 2003). A variety of factors may have contributed to this, ranging from shortcomings of early (ISDN-based) videoconference technology, with limitations especially in sound quality, to resistance to change. However, when the experiments were repeated under different technical conditions and in different institutions, the picture did not change much. Mouzourakis notes:

> It has become clear that interpreter complaints were not only due to the inferior technological conditions, but also the result of a number of physiological (sore eyes, back and neck pain, headaches, nausea) and psychological complaints (loss of concentration and motivation, feeling of alienation) stemming from the remote interpreting conditions. These complaints resurfaced in subsequent experiments, conducted in a variety of technical conditions and by a number of multilingual organisations; it would thus be difficult to attribute them solely to a particular technical setup or even to the working conditions provided by a particular organisation. (Mouzourakis 2006: 52)

Two experimental studies deserve particular attention. A study conducted for the ITU in 1999 (Moser-Mercer 2003) included 12 conference interpreters. Six of them worked from English into French. Their performance was sampled over several days of traditional and remote interpreting. The subsequent analysis focused on errors. One of the recent studies conducted for the Interpreting Service of the European Parliament in 2004 (Mertes-Hoffman 2005,[14] Roziner & Shlesinger 2010) included 36 interpreters working in several language combinations. Their performance in traditional and remote interpreting was sampled over a period of two weeks.

As well as investigating the interpreters' performance, the two studies also surveyed subjective factors, such as the interpreters' emotional responses to RI, and measured 'objective indices' ranging from stress indicators (such as blood pressure, heart rate and cortisol levels of the interpreters) to aspects of the working environment (temperature, lighting etc). The main results can be summarised as follows:

Stress

According to the ITU study, "repeated psychological self-assessment by interpreters during the experiment indicated that they found working under remote conditions more stressful, although these results did not reach statistical significance" (Moser-Mercer 2003: 11). Similarly, stress hormone values in the interpreters who participated in the ITU experiment were found to be higher for RI compared to traditional on-site interpreting, but this difference did not reach statistical significance (Moser-Mercer 2003:12). The European Parliament (EP) study comes to a partially different conclusion, conceding that "the RI condition was perceived as significantly more stressful than on-

---

[14] Mertens-Hoffman Management Consultants Ltd. (2005). Final report on the December 2004 remote interpreting test at the European Parliament. Unpublished. Executive summary: http://www.euractiv.com/31/images/EPremoteinterpretingreportexecutive_summery_tcm31-151942.pdf

site. The experience of high workload and high tension remained nearly unchanged during the various activities in the RI workday. [...]. These subjective ratings of stress are in sharp dissonance with objective measures of stress [...] where no such differences were found" (Roziner & Shlesinger 2010: 235).

Sense of discomfort and self-ratings of performance

Despite the lack of statistical significance in the self-ratings, the ITU study – like previous studies – discerned a sense of discomfort among the interpreters. Roziner and Shlesinger confirm this view: "In most of the studies based on subjective measures of performance, interpreters rated their own performance during RI as inferior to that of on-site interpreting" (2010: 238). They concede, however, that "the interpreters' low self-ratings could have stemmed from their initial objection to RI" (2010: 238).

Aspects of the working environment

Most aspects were found to be similar between RI and traditional interpreting, leading Roziner and Shlesinger to the conclusion that "the slight variations that did occur could not, in themselves, account for the interpreters' sense of discomfort" (2010: 242).

Performance rating (error analysis)

In the relatively small ITU study, the interpreters' RI performance declined faster than their on-site performance, and this was explained by an earlier onset of fatigue in RI: "Interpreters tire significantly more quickly, as evidenced by a faster decline in quality of performance over a 30-minute turn" (Moser-Mercer 2003: 1). In the larger-scale EP study, a direct comparison of the interpreters' performance in the two conditions resulted in slightly lower rates for RI but the difference failed to reach statistical significance. A more refined analysis, using multiple linear regression analysis, still yielded similar results but the difference became statistically significant. However, Roziner and Shlesinger believe that the difference "may be regarded as rather minor in practical terms" (2010: 241).

The most striking result of these studies, then, seems to be the discrepancy between objective findings and subjective perception. Roziner and Shlesinger conclude for the EP study that "[w]hereas the interpreters themselves were significantly less satisfied with their own performance in RI, the objective judgments of a panel of judges (two for each excerpt), based on 1,059 different judgments, point to almost no decline in quality, with a possible acceleration in the rate of decline, compared with the rate in on-site interpreting" (2010: 242).

A different, more technically oriented approach was taken by the Interpreting Service of the European Commission (SCIC) in 2010. The aim of a study conducted by the Fraunhofer Institute for the SCIC was to define the minimum quality of digital video and audio sources required to provide on-site and remote simultaneous interpretation. A total of 36 conference interpreters underwent a series of tests in which they rated, for example, different audio and video qualities, albeit without performing any actual interpreting task. The so-called 'human factors', which were found to be important in other studies (see above) were not included in this study. The findings resulted in a comprehensive list of technological recommendations for video and audio transmission (see Esteban Causo in this volume). Whether the use of the equipment recommended in this study will improve the interpreters' subjective perception of RI during their interpreting task remains to be seen.

3.1.2   Healthcare settings

In healthcare settings, remote interpreting seems to have increased over the past decade, but empirical studies of interpreter performance, accuracy etc. are largely absent.

Settings of remote interpreting in healthcare include both RI via video link and RI via audio link.[15] Relevant video-mediated settings include solutions for doctor-patient conversations at GP surgeries, communication in hospitals,[16] pharmacies[17] and other settings.

Research conducted before 2005 mostly relies on survey data, i.e. participant perceptions, and is summarised in Azarmina & Wallace (2005). As Azarmina and Wallace note, "[t]he findings of the selected studies suggest that remote interpretation is at least as acceptable as physically present interpretation to patients, doctors and (to a lesser extent) interpreters themselves" (2005: 44). In spite of the conspicuous absence of any rating of interpreter performance,[18] the authors conclude: "Remote interpretation

---

[15]   The latter is sometimes referred to as telephone interpreting. However, in line with the terminology used here for video-mediated interpreting, a difference should be made between 'telephone interpreting', which involves a telephone conversation between two parties with the help of an interpreter, and 'remote interpreting via audio link', which is the audio-based counterpart of remote interpreting via video link.

[16]   E.g. http://www.post-gazette.com/pg/11067/1130381-28.stm, http://www.fortmorgantimes.com/ci_17065663.

[17]   E.g. http://www.prnewswire.co.uk/cgi/news/release?id=173514.

[18]   There is no performance rating in any of the studies on RI by video link. However, Azarmina & Wallace also included studies on RI by audio link, in particular a study conducted by Hornberger et al. (1996) in which the performance of remote simultaneous interpreting in doctor-patient conversations was compared to traditional on-site consecutive interpreting in such situations and was interestingly found to be more accurate. In addition, doctors and patients preferred the remote simultaneous mode to on-site consecutive interpretation, whilst interpreters felt the opposite.

appears to be associated with levels of accuracy at least as good as those found in physically present interpretation (2005: 44).[19]

A more recent study on RI in healthcare using internet-based videoconferencing technology conducted by the Belgian Ministry of Health is ongoing. In contrast to earlier studies, which mostly focused on potential or real cost savings through the use of RI, this pilot takes account of the features of interpreted interaction and intercultural mediation, and makes recommendations for the behaviour in such video links (Verrept 2011).

Based on initial results from the pilot, which was conducted in four Belgian hospitals, the study has recently concluded that the healthcare interpreters involved in the study "needed supplementary training to make adequate use of the equipment" and that RI in this setting "is more complex than face-to-face interpreting: important aspects are procedures to check sound and image quality at the beginning of the intervention, the moderate use of gestures, note taking and the management of turn taking". However, as the study also concedes, "the main issue seems to be to make health care providers familiar with the system and to make them rely on it when they encounter a linguistic or socio-cultural barrier that makes the intervention of the mediator necessary" (Verrept 2011).[20]

The review of mainly remote interpreting in healthcare settings suggests strongly that research and practice in this area have some way to go before it will be possible to ascertain where remote interpreting can be a means of support and how it would have to be done.

3.1.3 Business settings

Braun (2004, 2006, 2007) analysed the performance of interpreters in a combination of videoconference and remote interpreting. The data for this study were gathered in a collaborative videoconferencing project (ViKiS – Videoconferencing with Integrated Simultaneous Interpretation) funded by the German government in the 1990s. At that time, the advent of ISDN- and desktop-based VC solutions had brought the cost of videoconferencing down considerably and had made VC technology an attractive communication solution for smaller companies, allowing them to communicate globally.

Recognising the language barriers that smaller companies in particular face in the global marketplace, the point of departure of the ViKiS project was that the appeal of VC technology for smaller companies could be further improved if it were possible to integrate an interpreter into the VC situation. The project created a prototype of a VC-based interpreter workstation which

---

[19] See also Braun (2006).
[20] http://tisp2011.tucongreso.es/ti2011/files/book-abstracts.pdf.

could connect to two VC sites. According to the definitions given in section 2.2, the setting falls into the fourth category, videoconference interpreting combined with remote interpreting. The illustration of this setting is repeated below. However, in contrast to an ordinary three-point videoconference, which would only allow consecutive interpretation, the ViKiS interpreter workstation manipulated the sound channels to enable bi-directional simultaneous interpretation between the two sites.

Figure 5: Videoconference and remote interpreting combined

The empirical work in ViKiS focused on the viability of interpreting using the ViKiS station. In contrast to the settings of remote conference interpreting described in section 3.1.1, the focus was on small-group business communication with a maximum of two to three participants at each of the two sites connected through the interpreter workstation. Whilst it might have been hypothesised that the small-group setting would make the interpreter's work easier than in remote conference interpreting, ViKiS started from the assumption that each interpreting situation comes with its own difficulties and that the combined complexity of interpreting and videoconferencing would make interpreting a difficult task in any setting. The aim of the study was to investigate the extent to which the interpreters would be able to adapt to the novel situation.

The study was based on 11 simultaneously interpreted bilingual VC sessions (English<>German and French<>German), involving four interpreters, in which job interviews and information-gathering conversations about job opportunities were simulated. The primary interlocutors acted in roles that were similar to their real-life jobs (e.g. human resources managers). The interpreters were trained (conference) interpreters who – with one exception – had many years of experience. The sessions were recorded and played back to the informants, who were asked to verbalise everything they could remember from their interpretation (retrospective 'thinking aloud'). Both the VC sessions and the think-aloud protocols were transcribed and analysed with regard to interpreting problems and adaptation strategies.

As in other studies, the data revealed a number of problems. Firstly, in spite of the dyadic and interactive nature of the communication in small groups, both the primary interlocutors and the interpreters reported that the communication via VC was more fatiguing than traditional face-to-face communication and that it was more difficult to establish a rapport with the other participants. Secondly, due to the low sound quality of the ISDN connections, the sound quality was problematic for the interpreters. The interpreters' task was further complicated by the fact that the lack of rapport frequently led the primary interlocutors to produce long-winded, repetitive and incoherent utterances which were difficult to comprehend. Finally, because of the interlocutors' inability to solve interaction problems in the VC situation, the interpreters were required to adopt the role of a moderator, which posed a number of ethical and other problems.

In spite of these problems, however, the interpreters believed that interpreting in this setting was feasible in principle, especially if the sound quality could be improved. This impression is corroborated by the interpreters' ability to adapt to the VC setting. Three stages of adaptation were observed, both within one VC and across several VCs (see especially Braun 2006). The initial stage was one of problem discovery and awareness raising. At this stage, an initial *reduction of the interpreters' performance* and the use of *ad hoc and local problem-solving strategies* dominated. The second stage was characterised by an intense reflection on how to deal with the problems encountered (manifest in the retrospective think-aloud protocols) and by experimenting with 'new' strategies (manifest in the VC sessions themselves). As a result, more *global problem-solving strategies* were used. However, these still mainly served to *repair* problems which had already occurred. A third stage began with the use of *global avoidance and preventive strategies* to prevent problems that are difficult to repair from occurring altogether.

Whilst the quality of the interpretation was not the focus of the study, the data reveal a number of problems in this respect. Not all of the numerous listening comprehension problems could be resolved by activating additional mental resources and background knowledge to bridge the comprehension gap, which resulted in omissions, generalisations and inaccuracies. Moreover, the interpreters' focus on source text comprehension led to problems with their output, which was often uneven and full of hesitations and pauses. The adaptation was more successful in the area of interaction. The interpreters were able to develop appropriate strategies for communication management to avoid overlapping speech and other turn-taking problems.

What remains to be investigated is whether improved sound quality and the use of the consecutive mode of interpreting, which enables the interpreter to intervene for clarification, will help overcome problems and make a combination of VCI and RI possible without compromising the accuracy and completeness of the interpretation.

3.2 Video-mediated interpreting in legal proceedings

As a consequence of increased VC use in legal settings, the use of video-mediated interpreting in legal proceedings is also increasing. It is now frequent in many different types of legal proceeding throughout Europe and beyond (see also section 2 and Braun & Taylor's report about the AVIDICUS surveys in this volume), with VCI (settings A and B) being most common. Meanwhile, reports on practice are scarce and only refer to selected immigration and criminal justice settings. For the most part, the available material (mainly reports of pilot studies) indicates that there are still many unknowns when videoconferencing technology and interpreting are combined to provide access to justice.

3.2.1 Immigration settings

With regard to the application of videoconferencing and interpreting in immigration settings, reports are available in relation to asylum interviews, immigration hearings before an immigration court/tribunal and immigration bail hearings. The first of these reports, addressing asylum interviews, also shows that the practical solutions are at times less straightforward than the four configurations described in section 2.2 imply.

Videoconference and remote interpreting in asylum interviews

An initiative concerned with the use of VC technology to provide interpreters in asylum interviews is the GDISC project. [21] This initiative, which is partly funded by the European Commission and led by the immigration services in the Netherlands, aims to provide a solution for asylum interviews for which no qualified interpreter is available in a particular country (and language combination). Participating immigration services have access to the interpreter services used by the immigration services of other participating Member States by means of a videoconference link. The method of interpretation used is 'relay interpretation', which entails the use of two interpreters who use a pivot language, in combination with a video link. The mode of interpreting is consecutive. The interpreter who speaks the immigration case worker's language is co-located at the main site, together with the case worker and the applicant. The second interpreter, who speaks the language of the applicant, is located at a remote site, in another country that participates in the pool project. According to GDISC, mainly African and Oriental languages, e.g. Tamil, Punjabi, Bengali, Somali and Efefe, have been requested to date.

---

[21] http://www.gdisc.org/index.php?id=548.

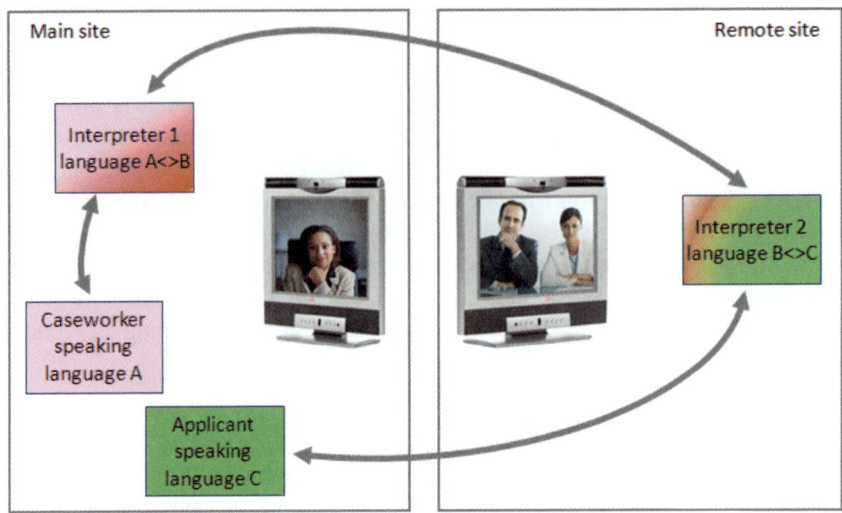

Figure 6: GDISC project (Source: Adapted from Dutch Ministry of Justice)

The project has produced some operational guidelines as well as detailed specifications for the videoconference equipment, which are largely in line with the appeal made by researchers and practitioners that the best possible equipment should be used.[22] Furthermore, the initiative has been described by GDISC as being "very successful" and the evaluation has been "very positive".[23] However, this is an administrative assessment that is not underpinned by empirical research on e.g. the quality of the interpretation and other crucial aspects of the communication taking place in this setting.[24]

In 2008 Bulgaria, one of the beneficiary countries in the GDISC project, requested feedback on the project. Responses were obtained from 18 countries, revealing opposing views:[25]

> Czech Republic: 'we have no practical experience with it so far. We were able to find a proper interpreter in our country in all cases we have dealt with. […] There is no legal regulation of remote interpretation, so we might imagine two problems in the court. First, the asylum seeker could challenge reliability of dual interpretation per se as this way a shift in content can happen. Second, with remote inter-

---

[22] GDISC Interpreters' Pool Project (2007).

[23] http://www.gdisc.org/index.php?id=548.

[24] "Successful" appears to mean simply having access to an interpreter in the first place (personal communication with the project managers).

[25] http://irm.gov.hu/i/irm.gov.hu/files//downloads/Fooldal/Europai_Unios_palyazatok/ Europai_Migracios_Halozat/EMH_eredmenyek/summary_of_gdisc_interpreters_pool-recognition_of_interviews.doc.

pretation, the original signature of the interpreter, which is required, could not be provided.

Netherlands: 'The experiences within this project with video conferencing are very encouraging. Experience shows that the project is an adequate solution to combat the shortage of interpreters in the new as well as the candidate member states of the EU. The project also fits very well into the goals of GDISC, which is to stimulate and where possible facilitate practical cooperation among immigration services.'

Videoconference interpreting in immigration hearings

In 2004, the Canadian Immigration and Refugee Board (IRB) commissioned a feasibility study on the use of videoconference links in refugee hearings. The study related to hearings which involved an interpreter (Ellis 2004).[26] The study notes that of approximately 23,000 refugee hearings completed in Canada between September 2003 and August 2004, approximately 1,000 were held via video link between offices of the Canadian Refugee Protection Division (RPD) in Toronto and RPD offices in other Canadian cities. The immigration judge, the refugee protection officer and the interpreter were together in the Toronto office, whilst the refugee and his/her lawyer were in one of the other cities. The method of interpreting was thus what was defined in section 2.2 as videoconference interpreting setting (A). The mode was consecutive.

To assess the viability of such videoconferences, the study conducted interviews with 14 immigration lawyers, and obtained questionnaire responses from 25 immigration judges, 16 refugee protection officers and 17 interpreters, all with comparable experience of immigration hearings including hearings via VC. In addition, three academics (a media expert, a social psychologist and a sociologist, but no interpreting researcher) were asked to provide background information.

The broad conclusion of the study is that the immigration lawyers were mostly sceptical about the suitability of VC, whilst the other three groups were generally more positive. There are, however, some critical voices too. For example, the report notes that when the informants were asked for suggestions on how to improve VC-based hearings, "[t]here was a general reluctance to buy into this question because the respondents generally were not comfortable with the premise" and that one of the interpreters "declined to offer any suggestion because he (or she) didn't like to even think of video-conferencing as a long-term proposition" (Ellis 2004: online).

One of the major problems reported was that the interpreter was not located with the refugee, and a number of different dimensions of this prob-

---

[26] Ellis (2004) http://www.irb-cisr.gc.ca/eng/disdiv/proeva/revs/video/Pages/index.aspx.

lem were identified. Firstly, the personal rapport between the interpreter and the refugee was found to be weak, although the comment that there was "no opportunity, while waiting for the hearing to commence or during breaks, for the claimant and interpreter to talk together" (*ibid*) raises some questions with regard to interpreter ethics, given that current codes of conduct would not endorse such practice. The report emphasises, however, that in the view of the respondent interpreters such conversations with the refugee "have traditionally contributed importantly to a claimant's comfort both with the interpreter and with the hearing environment generally" (*ibid*).

Secondly, the co-ordination of the communication was found to be more difficult. According to the study, "[w]ith the interpreter sitting beside the claimant - or other witnesses - in an in-person hearing, a touch on the arm will quietly signal the need for the claimant to pause and wait for the translation. When the interpreter is located in the member's room, similar non-intrusive control is not possible" (*ibid*). Thirdly, the translation of documents presented by the refugee was a problem due to the interpreter's location at the other site. Finally, some judges highlighted that the interpreter's physical separation from the refugee made it impossible to use whispered interpreting. They felt that consecutive interpreting was disruptive especially when they delivered their final submissions.

The VC-based hearings tended to be longer and were considered to be more fatiguing than comparable face-to-face hearings. One judge furthermore wondered whether the physical separation of the refugee would "impact on the way they give their evidence" and whether the refugees "feel justice is being done" (*ibid*). The lawyers had similar concerns. One of the interpreters claimed, however, "that people sometimes may feel intimidated by having their hearing through video-conference but in my opinion you can make someone feel comfortable and relaxed to testify through a camera as well as in person" (*ibid*).

The interpreters were concerned that body language and emotions were not transmitted as efficiently in the VC as they were face-to-face and that this might undermine the refugee's credibility. The interpreters also felt that the VC communication involved more repetition and overlapping speech, which was difficult to resolve and impeded accurate interpretation. This coincides with the findings of Braun (2004, 2007) in her study on video-mediated interpreting in business settings (see section 3.1.3). In spite of the concerns and problems, some of the interpreters also highlighted positive aspects of the VC situation. One of them found, for example, "that video conferencing is good. You are clearly able to see the expressions on the claimant's face and it is possible to hold the hearing in a fair, expeditious manner if everybody is in agreement with the process" (Ellis 2004: online).

Some of the informants requested training and one interpreter suggested that the equipment should briefly be explained to the refugee at the beginning of the hearing.

In contrast to some of the positive views expressed by those who participated in the immigration hearings, one of the academics who commented on the study claimed that "the mediation effects created through videoconferencing introduces the significant possibility of inconsistency, inaccuracy, and altered judgement" (*ibid*). The second researcher came to the conclusion that "the current literature does not speak in favor of interpersonal interactions through videoconferencing versus face-to-face interactions" (*ibid*). The third researcher also referred to the findings of prior research on the psychological impact of VC communication and claimed on the basis of these studies that "where sensitive and highly emotional information has to be transmitted, we can conclude that videoconferencing might not be the most efficient and comfortable way to communicate for the refugee / asylum seekers" (*ibid*).

However, the report emphasises that the researchers did not want "to rule out the use of videoconferencing without first attempting such a study" and that in one researcher's view it would not be "impossible that a well thought out use of videoconferencing in a refugee hearing context might present advantages" (*ibid*). One of the main conclusions of the researchers was that a final decision on the appropriateness of using VC technology in refugee hearings should not be made "without further and more sophisticated trials and investigation" and that after the study it would be too early to say whether the problems "could not be solved with some felicitous adjustments in the protocol, procedures and technical facilities, at least perhaps for a significant proportion of cases" (*ibid*).

The investigator who conducted the study made several recommendations. Most importantly, he recommended that "cases involving allegations of physical or sexual abuse or torture should be removed from the videoconferencing regime immediately" (*ibid*). Furthermore he highlighted the importance of ensuring that the refugee understands the VC conditions and of finding a solution for the spontaneous interpretation of documents presented at the refugee's location. With regard to technical problems (which seem to have occurred), the report points out that it would be "unseemly to leave these Board responsibilities on the shoulders of counsel or interpreters" (*ibid*).

The investigator also recommended that a substantial pilot study should be undertaken. This should be a comparative study of VC-based and face-to-face hearings during which the VC should be set up in the best possible way. He recommended that such a comparative study "ought to be done by academics" with appropriate qualifications. Federman (2006: 450) states that the IRB rejected Ellis' recommendation for a pilot study.

Whilst the study did not attempt to measure any 'objective' factors, such as the interpreters' performance or the refugees' and the judges' reception of the communication, it made some highly interesting observations about the setting, the location of the interpreter and the perceptions of those involved in the hearings. It is arguably one of the most comprehensive studies on legal videoconferencing with interpreting conducted prior to the AVIDICUS project. Some of the perceptions reported in this study corroborate the findings of the studies conducted in remote conference interpreting (see section 3.1.1) and video-mediated business interpreting (see section 3.1.3).

Videoconference interpreting in immigration bail hearings

In 2008, two British charities – Bail for Immigration Detainees (BID) and the British Refugee Council – conducted a study on immigration bail hearings via video link (BID 2008),[27] which aimed at gauging the views of bail applicants. Of the 16 hearings analysed, 11 required an interpreter. In these hearings, videoconference interpreting (A) setting was used, i.e. the interpreter was located in the courtroom together with the immigration judge, legal representative, sureties and Home Office representative, while the bail applicant was in a detention centre. Of the 11 applicants who had an interpreter, 3 stated (in the questionnaire used for the study) that they had difficulty following what happened in the courtroom and that only the questions directed towards them and their answers were interpreted; 5,stated that everything said in the courtroom was interpreted; and 3 applicants did not give details about this. Three applicants also had technological difficulties: they had problems seeing and hearing what was happening in the courtroom. The study comes to the conclusion that:

> Whilst video link bail hearings may well work for some detainees (particularly those who have previously been let down by escort failures), BID and the Refugee Council believe video hearings must only be used where detainees are consulted about their impact, informed about the process and given a meaningful choice between a video link and an in-court hearing. This monitoring exercise presents evidence, albeit based on a limited sample size, of how bail applicants are being affected by video link bail hearings and recommends action from the AIT [Asylum and Immigration Tribunal], the Home Office and the Legal Services Commission.[28]

BID and the British Refugee Council make recommendations to various groups involved in the running of the bail hearings process. To the Asylum and Immigration Tribunal, it was recommended, inter alia, that the roll-out of video hearings should be closely monitored to evaluate the impact on bail applicants, and until this is done, the roll-out should be suspended. The fact that bail applicants can request an in-court hearing, and how this should be carried out, should be clearly explained to them. In addition, video hearings

---

[27] http://www.refugeecouncil.org.uk/policy/position/2008/bail_hearings.
[28] 'Immigration bail hearings by video link: a monitoring exercise by Bail for Immigration Detainees and the Refugee Council,' March 2008, p.5.

in prisons 'must not arbitrarily end after 45 minutes because of the commercial requirements of a private contractor.'[29] It was also stated that, where an interpreter is used, judges should ensure that everything said in court is interpreted for the bail applicant.

As was the case in the study commissioned by the Canadian immigration services,[30] the BID study highlights some of the tensions and pressures immigration services face. It demonstrates that if video-mediated communication is to be used in such sensitive settings, the initiatives mentioned at the beginning of section 3.2.1, which aim to specify minimum quality standards for legal videoconferencing, are as urgently needed as informed guidance for the use (and non-use) of video-based interpreting (see Braun in this volume).

3.2.2   Criminal proceedings – outside the European Union

Anecdotal evidence suggests that VCI and RI are used in many countries around the world. Videoconferencing per se has been used in legal criminal proceedings in many English-speaking countries – e.g. Australia, Canada, New Zealand, South Africa and the US – since the late 1990s, mainly for bail and remand hearings but also for first hearings and hearings of a remote witness, with the effect that VC equipment was installed some in court houses, prisons and also police stations.[31] The implementation was normally preceded by feasibility studies, which in some cases engaged with the advantages and disadvantages of VC technology. A study conducted in South Africa in 2003, for example, considered the advantages of VC in terms of time and cost savings and security, but also the psychological effects and the possible scope of VC use in criminal proceedings.[32] In contrast to the conclusions drawn by academics who conducted research into VC communication, the conclusion in the feasibility studies was normally that VC can be used in criminal proceedings under certain circumstances, especially in pre-trial hearings, that pilots should be conducted, and *grosso modo*, the 2000s saw a worldwide spread of VC technology in criminal proceedings. Other non-EU countries using VC include, for example, Norway,[33] Israel,[34] and Kenya.[35]

---

[29]   Immigration Bail Hearings by video link: monitoring exercise report, p.3.

[30]   The observations made in the BID report suggest that the authors were not aware of the findings from the study commissioned by the Canadian immigration services in 2004.

[31]   See overview in http://www.justice.ie/en/JELR/VIDEOen.pdf/Files/VIDEOen.pdf.

[32]   http://www.justice.gov.za/salrc/reports/r_prj113_2003jul.pdf.

[33]   http://www.ccbe.org/fileadmin/user_upload/document/E-Justice_Portal/17-18_02_2009/ Abstracts/23_abstract_Videoconferencing_Norway.pdf; http://www.ccbe.org/fileadmin/user_upload/document/E-Justice_Portal/17-18_02_2009/ Presentations/23_Videoconferencing_in_Norwegian_courts.pdf.

[34]   http://www.haaretz.co.il/hasite/spages/808333.html.

[35]   http://www.lantech.co.ke/index.php?option=com_content&view=article&id=57& Itemid=74.

Videoconference interpreting

Given the multicultural nature of all of the countries named above, the use of VC in criminal proceedings is likely to involve various forms of 'videoconference interpreting' (VCI) as well. However, references to interpreters in VC-based proceedings are scarce. Some practical references to the integration of interpreters can be found in the VC guidelines issued by some courts. The guidelines of the Supreme Court of Tasmania for court-prison video links state, for example, that if an interpreter is required, s/he can be located either in court or in prison (a provision that has, however, been disputed in immigration settings, see section 3.2.1). The procedure that should be followed when the interpreter is in prison is described:

> Where, for any reason, a third party (i.e. prison officer, technical assistant, interpreter at a remote point) is present in the room from where the video conference is being transmitted then that person should, at the start of the proceedings, be introduced (by prosecutor or counsel as appropriate) and their purpose for being present explained to the Court. [36]

Whilst it is good to see that the interpreter is mentioned in these guidelines (albeit only twice), it seems that everything which happens after the introductions is considered to be 'business as usual' for an interpreter working in a VC. Such assumptions are in contrast with the findings of studies in immigration settings (see section 3.2.1) and also contradict the personal perceptions of many interpreters (see Braun & Taylor's report about the AVIDICUS surveys in this volume).

The only other point in these guidelines that indirectly concerns the interpreter is the guidance for the beginning of VC-based proceedings, which make a clear statement regarding the responsibilities for the technology:

> Commencement of proceedings: At the commencement of a video conference the judicial officer/court clerk/video co-ordinator will check that the link has been established. The presiding judicial officer should confirm that the witness/person at the remote point can be seen and heard clearly and similarly that the witness at the remote point can clearly see and hear the judicial officer. [37]

Other than this example, available reports on video-mediated interpreting in criminal proceedings focus on 'remote interpreting' (RI) and are mostly from the United States. Therefore, the remainder of this section is based on information available from the US, where both VCI and RI are widely used.

---

[36] http://www.supremecourt.tas.gov.au/about_us/courtroom_technology/ video_conferencing_guidelines.

[37] http://www.supremecourt.tas.gov.au/about_us/courtroom_technology/ video_conferencing_guidelines.

Video-based interpreting in US courts

A general assessment of video-based interpreting in US criminal courts was given in 2009 by the United States' National Center for State Courts:

> States that have integrated videoconferencing into the courtroom report the advantage of expediency in providing language services when no interpreter is available on-site, and when they use credentialed in-state interpreters, there is no question about the quality of the service. In addition, most of the systems available are portable, mobile, wireless, and fairly simple to incorporate into the existing courtroom network. This method is already being successfully used by courts for arraignments and jail interviews, and the possibilities of additional areas of use are limitless. (Green & Romberger 2009: 2)[38]

The authors imply a potentially wide range of settings of both videoconference and remote interpreting but do not give a description of the details, e.g. the effect of having the interpreter at different locations, nor is it clear from whose point of view this method of interpreting is "successful".

As previously shown, such statements are not unknown in relation to video-based interpreting (see GDISC project in section 3.2.1), but they clash with some of the research findings in relation to legal videoconferencing, VCI in legal proceedings and remote conference interpreting. Yet, as in immigration, the appeals by researchers (and some legal professionals) for caution have not stopped the use of VC in legal proceedings (with or without an interpreter) nor the use of VC technology for remote interpreting. The examples below show that RI is common practice in US court rooms. In many cases, the interpretation is delivered in simultaneous mode.

Remote interpreting in the Circuit Courts in Florida, USA

A prominent example of the use of remote interpreting is the Ninth Circuit Court in Florida, which introduced a central interpreter hub in 2007 to address the challenge of having to interpreters for over 25,000 court hearings each year with only eight employed interpreters and a reduced budget for hiring freelance interpreters. The situation was exacerbated by the fact that the Ninth Judicial Circuit covers sixty-seven courtrooms spread over more than 2,000 square miles, entailing high travel costs for interpreters.[39] In other words, the introduction of this hub was mainly a cost-cutting exercise.

The interpreter hub serves all judicial locations that fall under the jurisdiction of the Ninth Judicial Circuit from a single point (one of the court

---

[38] http://contentdm.ncsconline.org/cdm4/item_viewer.php?CISOROOT=/accessfair&
CISOPTR= 184&CISOBOX=1&REC=1.

[39] http://www.ninthcircuit.org/programs-services/court-interpreter/downloads/
CentralizedInterpretingPresentation.pdf.

houses). The interpreters' workstations are configured to provide remote *simultaneous* interpreting.[40] A demo video is available at the court website.[41]

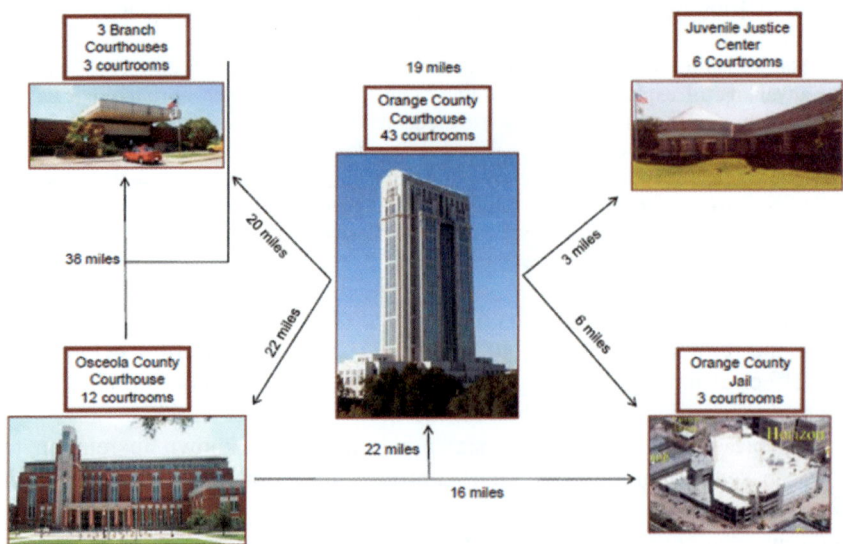

Figure 7: RI in the US (Source: Ninth Judicial Circuit Court, Florida, USA)

A study of the interpreters' workload appears to have taken place, but it is not clear how the figures were gathered (for example, with regard to the savings made by using remote interpreting). In any case, the results of the study are mainly couched in financial terms. For the most part, the need for freelance interpreters (as opposed to the staff interpreters, who are directly employed), has diminished, due in part to the fact that a single staff inter-preter now provides remote services to several locations. Travel time for staff interpreters has also been reduced. Since January 2008, there has reportedly been a 16% reduction in spending on staff interpreter services.[42]

In the meantime, other circuit courts followed, and a report published by the Commission on Trial Court Performance & Accountability of the Supreme Court of Florida in 2010 states that "13 circuits report using some

---

[40] The interpreters' workstations are equipped with Pentium Dual Core computers, audio and visual network connectivity, dual 17"-19" monitors, and analogue touch-tone telephones. The courtroom is fitted out with an audio-mixer-biamp flex (12 microphone units, telephone interface card with two inputs), a video camera (security camera on network), and headphones (3 per courtroom). – http://www.ninthcircuit.org/programs-services/court-interpreter/downloads/CentralizedInterpretingPresentation.pdf.

[41] http://www.ninthcircuit.org/programs-services/court-interpreter/centralized-interpreting/.

[42] http://www.ninthcircuit.org/programs-services/court-interpreter/downloads/CentralizedInterpretingPresentation.pdf.

remote audio or audio/video technology to provide court interpreting services".[43] The report provides some guidelines for the use of RI via video link, similar to the guidelines developed by other courts in the US (see Wisconsin example below), and also highlights some of the shortcomings of remote interpreting via telephone, which have entailed that some courts "choose not to use the services".[44]

Remote interpreting in Arizona Municipal Court, Mesa

The Arizona Municipal Court in Mesa (US) introduced new videoconference equipment in 2009, mainly to cater for video links between courts and prisons (Webster 2009).[45] The feasibility was evaluated by the National Centre for State Courts. The evaluation report touches on the issue of the interpretation:

> [A] critical issue is the role of the interpreter. The interpreter may be needed during conversations with the financial officer, public defender, prosecutor, and clerk. The interpreter also is needed during the court hearing. Finally, an interpreter may be required by the victim or witnesses. Careful choreography is required to ensure that the interpreter is available at the right time in each of these areas. The use of interpreters adds a layer of complexity to the design of a video-conferencing solution. (Webster 2009: 5)

No comment is offered on other potential issues with the interpretation. However, the report makes some interesting technical observations:

> Control over the audio-video environment is essential. At present, the court has a panel of button presets for various arrangements of speakers, interpreters, etc. In the new videoconferencing environment, this control must include the video feed, as well. (2009: 13)
>
> Full duplex audio is required. Since two videoconferencing signals are recommended, the audio signal for one link can work in one direction, and the audio signal for the second link can function in the other direction. Without full duplex audio, interpreters must change their approach to translation from simultaneous to sequential, which will slow the proceedings. (2009: 14)

This suggests that as in the Florida circuit courts, the interpretation is routinely delivered in the *simultaneous* mode, a situation that is partially

---

[43] Recommendations for the Provision of Court Interpreting Services in Florida's Trial Courts; http://www.remoteinterpreting.com/media/PDFs/TCP&A_Full_Recommend.pdf, p. 51.

[44] Recommendations for the Provision of Court Interpreting Services in Florida's Trial Courts; http://www.remoteinterpreting.com/media/PDFs/TCP&A_Full_Recommend.pdf, p. 55.

[45] http://contentdm.ncsconline.org/cdm4/item_viewer.php?CISOROOT=/tech&CISOPTR=708&REC=5.

different from the situation in most European countries (see Braun & Taylor on the AVIDICUS surveys this volume).

Remote interpreting in the Wisconsin Court Interpreters' Program, US

The Wisconsin Court Interpreter Program is another example of a coordinated effort to use remote interpreting in order to keep costs down and to gain timely access to an interpreter (Wisconsin Court Interpreter Program 2010). The programme has used remote interpreting in *consecutive* mode via both video link and telephone for a number of years and has developed guidelines for the use of remote interpreting in a courtroom setting. These include recommendations for when RI can be used and when it should not be used.

The recommended uses include interpretation involving rare languages, situations when timely access to an interpreter is required or a certified interpreter is not available locally and when the cost of getting an interpreter on site is "high relative to the length or importance of the court session".[46] However, there is no specification of what "high" means and how the "importance" of a court session is measured. According to the recommendations, RI should not be used in trials, in proceedings longer than 15 minutes[47] or for situations involving many people, intensive cross-examination or 'emotionally charged situations'. The guidelines furthermore point out that "the interpreter should be allowed to establish communication before the hearing" and that "all participants should speak clearly, slowly, and one at a time." In terms of technical requirements, the guidelines highlight that the use of high-quality equipment is crucial and that time for testing should be taken (see also Braun in this volume).

It seems that communication among the Wisconsin judiciary and court interpreters is limited. In 2009, an 'experiment' was carried out between an interpreter in Madison city and a court in Door county [both in Wisconsin], taking a surprisingly amateurish view on how RI could be implemented and how cost savings could be achieved.[48] Revealing the plan of using wireless technology and "free trial software from Polycom" for RI, a court administrator commented in the News Magazine of the Wisconsin judiciary that "this was just a test, but had it been the real thing, the state and Door County would have saved hundreds of dollars and the availability of a certified court interpreter for almost any language would have been assured". No reference was made to Wisconsin's ambitious Court Interpreter Program, whose rather

---

[46] http://www.wicourts.gov/services/interpreter/docs/telephoneinterpet.pdf.

[47] It is interesting to note that the 2006 version of the guidelines recommended 30 minutes as the maximum, whilst the (current) 2010 version reduced this to 15 minutes.

[48] http://www.wicourts.gov/news/thirdbranch/docs/spring09.pdf.

elaborate guidelines for RI suggest that thought has been given to the challenges of this method of interpreting.

3.2.3　Criminal proceedings – in the European Union

In the EU, Article 9 of the Second Additional Protocol to the European Convention on Mutual Assistance in Criminal Matters[49] allows for the hearing of evidence via VC, and the increasing number of cross-border proceedings suggests a growing demand for this technology in European courts. This is supported by the E-Justice Action Plan of the European Council,[50] which focuses on the application of VC and other electronic tools in criminal justice. This development also shapes the demand for, and practice of, video-mediated *interpreting* in criminal proceedings the EU, which at present focuses more on 'videoconference interpreting' (VCI) than on 'remote interpreting'. However, there are indicators that the demand for RI is expanding in the EU (see also Braun & Taylor on the AVIDICUS reports in this volume). The new European Directive on strengthening an accused person's rights to interpreting and translation in criminal proceedings[51] includes the possibility of remote access to interpretation by videoconference link (and telephone).

Whilst 'remote interpreting' is still a rather novel development in criminal proceedings in the EU, the use of video links is well established in the criminal justice systems of some EU member states, and accordingly, there is a considerable amount of experience with the various forms of 'videoconference interpreting', especially in relation to first hearings and remand extension hearings (see also Braun & Taylor on the AVIDICUS reports in this volume).

Videoconference interpreting in remand extension hearings

Although logically not the first stage of criminal proceedings, the area of remand hearings is reported first here, because it seems to be an area of criminal justice in which videoconference technology has been used for more than a decade in some European countries. In the UK, VC technology is used for 'court-prison video links'.[52] Owing to the age of these video links, the

---

[49]　http://conventions.coe.int/Treaty/en/Treaties/Html/182.htm.

[50]　http://eur-lex.europa.eu/LexUriServ/LexUriServ.do?uri=OJ:C:2009:075:0001:0012:EN: PDF.

[51]　See FN 12.

[52]　See http://www.justice.gov.uk/publications/corporate-reports/hmps for England and Wales, http://news.bbc.co.uk/1/hi/scotland/3183662.stm for Scotland, and http://www.justice.ie/en/JELR/VIDEOen.pdf/Files/VIDEOen.pdf, pp. 9-11, for England, Wales, Scotland and Northern Ireland.

technology is often obsolete, especially in the lower courts (Magistrates Courts). Given that these courts deal with approximately 95% of all criminal cases, the equipment is known to most interpreters and has left a bitter taste about videoconference interpreting (see also Braun & Taylor on the AVIDICUS reports in this volume). Using narrowband ISDN connections and small, low quality screens, this video equipment often makes it difficult to hear properly and to recognise anyone at the remote site.[53] Some of the problems arising from this for an interpreter are outlined by Fowler (2007). However, there is some justified hope that this technology will soon be confined to history.

The 2009/10 Annual Report of the Courts Services for England and Wales (Her Majesty's Court Services Annual Report), for example, notes that the Court Services had "completed a further series of upgrades and replacement of video link equipment in the Crown Court and magistrates' courts" during the reporting period.[54] The British Home Office Resource Accounts Report 2009-10 notes for the same period: "During the past year we renewed our focus on ensuring maximum efficiency and effectiveness in the CJS [Criminal Justice System], particularly in dealing with serious crime through better information technology, use of video links and more efficient processes."[55] Initiatives such as the bail reform project in Canada (see section 2) also sound more promising in terms of technology.

In other countries, similar practices of using video links for remand hearings are reported to be becoming increasingly frequent. The development in France is particularly interesting. In 2006, eight years after VC use in French courts had been authorised for various purposes, including court-prison links,[56] an evaluation report identified several technical and logistical problems and concluded that the introduction of VC technology had failed to produce the intended uptake.[57] However, in 2009, the number of remand hearings by video link saw a sharp rise. Up to 5,000 VCs appear to have taken place in the first half of 2009, representing a 400% increase from

---

[53] Webster describes what appears to be similar technology in courts in Mesa, Arizona (US): "A small number of initial appearances are conducted via a videoconferencing link with the county jail, but the technology that is used is antiquated and not very effective, and the time allotted by the county to conduct these hearings is inadequate" (2009: 4).

[54] http://www.hmcourts-service.gov.uk/cms/files/HMCS_Annual_Report2009-2010_web. pdf, p. 25.

[55] http://www.homeoffice.gov.uk/publications/about-us/corporate-publications/resource-accounts/resource-accounts-09-10?view=Binary/, p. 6.

[56] http://www.unjf.fr/c2i/B5/Module-B5-html/genWebUNJF/co/B5_Uc67.html.

[57] http://www.justice.gouv.fr/actualite-du-ministere-10030/lutilisation-de-la-visioconference-dans-les-services-judiciaires-12065.html; full report: http://www.audits.performance-publique.gouv.fr/ bib_res/v3_200606_rapport_rapport-v3-justice-visioconference.pdf.

2008.[58] There is no information about the use of interpreters, but it is likely that some of the video links will have involved interpretation.

The Irish Ministry of Justice commissioned a feasibility study for the use of VC to conduct bail and remand hearings in 2003. In contrast to some similar studies, this study examined the situation in Europe and worldwide, making reference, for example, to the feasibility study conducted in South Africa (see 3.2.2), which included a more thorough discussion of potential benefits and problems of VC use than other such studies. As a result, the Irish study recommended "the introduction of a modern videoconferencing system"[59] and a pilot involving four court rooms and five prisons. In addition to bail and remand hearings, the study suggested that other pre-trial applications be considered during the pilot, including applications to the court, adjournment and appellate proceedings, and consultations between lawyers and prisoners. For this purpose, the installation of soundproof VC booths in prisons and the locations of the lawyers (e.g. the Law Society and solicitor's offices) was recommended.[60] As is so often the case, however, no reference was made to the integration of interpreters.

First hearings in Virtual Courts

The other type of pre-trial hearings that the criminal justice services in the EU have focused on are first hearings of defendants, victims and witnesses. As in prison-court links, different practices of interpreting have begun to emerge in such hearings.

In the Netherlands, for example, where videoconferencing has been used in pre-trial hearings since 2007, the prosecutor is normally at one police station and communicates with the defendant in custody at another police station, whilst the interpreter can choose the location, but is normally at the location of the defendant (i.e. 'videoconference interpreting' B).[61] This practice seems to be in line with the observations about the interpreter's location made in immigration settings, especially in the Canadian study (see section 3.2.1). This configuration enables the interpreter to continue using the interpreting modes which are most common in European courts: consecutive interpreting when rendering the non-native speaker's utterances into Dutch, and whispered interpreting when interpreting from Dutch into the language of the non-native speaker.

---

[58] http://archives.lesechos.fr/archives/2009/LesEchos/20578-11-ECH.htm.

[59] http://www.justice.ie/en/JELR/VIDEOen.pdf/Files/VIDEOen.pdf, p. 49. Parallel technological consultancy projects were under way to identify appropriate technology.

[60] Curiously, the report notes that the implementation of these booths had begun in 2004, i.e. before the final report of the feasibility study had been submitted (in 2005).

[61] http://www.justitie.nl/onderwerpen/recht_en_rechtsbijstand/videoconferentie/.

In England, 2007 saw the introduction of the 'Virtual Courts' for first hearings, i.e. video links between Magistrates Courts and defendants in police custody. According to the British Office for Criminal Justice Reform (OCJR), the intention was to speed up proceedings. A factsheet published by the OCJR notes that the Virtual Court "reduces the time from charge to first hearing from days to just a few hours in most instances, which improves the service to victims by disposing of first hearings within hours of charge". [62] The OCJR also draws attention to the fact that the virtual courts are intended to combine VC technology with "an on-line 'virtual' collaboration space – allowing case files to be shared electronically".[63]

The 2007 pilot phase linked Camberwell Green magistrates' court to four local police stations.[64] The second pilot phase in 2009/10 ran in two magistrates' courts in London and North Kent, linking to 15 police stations in London and one in north Kent.[65] Whilst the initial pilot excluded hearings that require an interpreter,[66] the second pilot phase, which ran in 2009/10,[67] included cases in which interpreters were required. Anecdotal evidence suggests that the interpreter is normally – but not always – in court.

Both pilot phases were evaluated in terms of the efficiency of the virtual court concept. The final report of the first pilot phase claimed that as a concept it was "a clear success, enabling both custody and bail first hearings to take place in a single day, indeed in an average time of just three-and-a-half hours".[68] The final report of the second pilot phase, published in December 2010, produced more mixed findings.[69] With regard to cases involving an interpreter, the report makes few but insightful observations:

> Time delays in the audio link were reported by practitioners as being common, and were witnessed during courtroom observations. While the delays themselves

---

[62] Virtual Court Factsheet, OCJR 2008, http://frontline.cjsonline.gov.uk/_includes/downloads/guidance/better-use-of-technology/20081107_Virtual_Court_Factsheet_V5.pdf, p.1.

[63] Virtual Court Factsheet, OCJR 2008, http://frontline.cjsonline.gov.uk/_includes/downloads/guidance/better-use-of-technology/20081107_Virtual_Court_Factsheet_V5.pdf, p. 1.

[64] London ICV Newsletter, Metropolitan Police Authority, July 2007, http://www.mpa.gov.uk/downloads/partnerships/icv/newsletter/2007-07.pdf, p.1.

[65] http://www.justice.gov.uk/downloads/publications/research-and-analysis/moj-research/virtual-courts.pdf, p. iii.

[66] "The virtual court can be used, with the defendant's consent, in all first hearings except those involving multiple defendants, appropriate adults, interpreters, youths or in complex and sensitive cases." London ICV Newsletter, Metropolitan Police Authority, July 2007, p.1, http://www.mpa.gov.uk/downloads/partnerships/icv/newsletter/2007-07.pdf.

[67] http://www.mpa.gov.uk/downloads/partnerships/icv/newsletter/2010-02.pdf, p. 2.

[68] Virtual Court Factsheet, OCJR 2008, http://frontline.cjsonline.gov.uk/_includes/downloads/guidance/better-use-of-technology/20081107_Virtual_Court_Factsheet_V5.pdf, p.2.

[69] http://www.justice.gov.uk/downloads/publications/research-and-analysis/moj-research/virtual-courts.pdf.

were quite short (a second or less), it was sufficient to cause individuals to repeat themselves on several occasions, and people on opposite ends of the link spoke over one another (similar to some long distance telephone calls). This did not appear to be a problem in the majority of cases, in that it did not result in confusion or delays to the hearing process. However, it did cause some communication problems where a defendant had language difficulties, or where an interpreter was being used.[70]

Some magistrates and District Judges felt that some cases were not suitable to be handled in Virtual Courts due to their complexity and the time that was required to hear them. While opinions varied, this included cases requiring interpreters and cases involving complex bail applications, both of which were more likely than most to need more time or flexibility than was available. Courtroom observations confirm that these cases tended to take longer to be heard than the 15 minutes allowed in the pilot, which caused knock-on delays for other cases heard during the same session.[71]

These results are less than surprising. Delays in video-mediated communication have long been documented as a source of disruption (e.g. the various papers in Finn *et al.* 1997), and it is also well-known (and perhaps obvious) that interpreter-mediated communication tends to take longer than monolingual communication. The request that there must be more flexibility in the duration of the video link is one of the points that had also been made in the study on immigration bail hearings conducted by BID in 2008 (see 3.2.1).

4 CONCLUSIONS

Videoconference and remote interpreting have become common practice in many areas of criminal justice and in other settings. There are indications that the practice is growing, partially owing to the expansion of videoconferencing per se in criminal proceedings, and partially owing to the criminal justice services' search for solutions to rising costs of interpreting, timely access to an interpreter and other aspects. It may, however, be that some of the recent results, e.g. regarding virtual courts, have dampened the original expectations.

The main outcomes of the review presented here can be summarised as follows.

Research on legal videoconferencing has identified a number of communication problems in VC communication and has expressed scepticism concerning the adequacy of videoconferencing in legal proceedings.

---

[70] http://www.justice.gov.uk/downloads/publications/research-and-analysis/moj-research/virtual-courts.pdf, p. 7.

[71] http://www.justice.gov.uk/downloads/publications/research-and-analysis/moj-research/virtual-courts.pdf, p. 22.

At the same time, some important initiatives, promoted and partially funded by the European Commission, are under way to improve videoconferencing technology in court rooms and other criminal justice settings. These initiatives have begun to specify minimum standards for videoconferencing technology to be used in criminal proceedings and in connection with remote conference interpreting. The specifications also extend to the audio-visual environment including lighting, seating arrangements, duration of VC use and other aspects.

Judicial institutions or those who conduct pilot and evaluation studies on their behalf are often unaware of prior research, evaluation exercises and pilot studies. In the UK, for example, court-prison video links (used mainly for remand hearings), virtual courts (used for first hearings) and developments in remote interpreting in the police seem to exist in parallel universes without much cross-fertilisation and seemingly without learning lessons from pilot projects in closely related areas (e.g. immigration) in the UK or elsewhere.

Research on video-mediated *interpreting* is scarce, except in the area of remote conference interpreting, and has produced mixed results.

A recurring result from the studies on remote conference interpreting is a discrepancy between 'objective' measures (e.g. of the interpreters' performance, stress levels and other factors) and the interpreters' individual perceptions, i.e. the 'human factor'. This is corroborated by some studies in other areas, e.g. in immigration.

Very little is known, however, about the adaptability of interpreters in video-mediated interpreting. A small-scale study in business settings suggests that interpreters are able to adapt within limits, but that the technological environment, and possibly other factors, play a crucial role in pushing the boundaries of adaptation. Longitudinal studies in this area are absent.

Most importantly, there is very little academic research on VCI/RI in legal proceedings and, to the best of our knowledge, no published research on VCI/RI in criminal proceedings. Available (practice-based) reports on video-mediated interpreting in legal proceedings focus either on immigration settings or – in criminal justice – on courts, court-prison links and court-custody links, whilst other elements of criminal proceedings, including police interviews, prosecution and consultation with a lawyer, have been neglected.

No study has systematically investigated the quality of the interpreters' performance in video-mediated interpreting in criminal proceedings, nor has there been a systematic survey of the parties involved in video-mediated and interpreted events in criminal proceedings.

Against this backdrop, the two surveys conducted in the AVIDICUS project, addressing legal interpreters and legal practitioners to find out about current experience with, and planned uses of, video-mediated interpreting in legal settings, constituted an important step towards a systematic analysis of these forms of interpreting. Another crucial step was the series of empirical studies conducted in AVIDICUS, in which the quality of various forms of video-based interpreting was compared with the quality of traditional interpreting in legal settings. The outcomes of the surveys and the comparative studies will be reported in the following chapters of this volume.

5 REFERENCES

Andres, D. and Falk, S. (2009), 'Remote and Telephone Interpreting'. In: Andres, D. and Pöllabauer, S. (eds.), Spürst Du wie der Bauch rauf runter? Fachdolmetschen im Gesundheitsbereich/Is everything all topsy turvy in your tummy? Health Care Interpreting. München: Martin Meidenbauer, 9-27.

Azarmina, P. and Wallace, P. (2005), 'Remote interpretation in medical encounters: a systematic review', *Journal of Telemedicine and Telecare*, 11, 140-145.

Böcker, M. and Anderson, B. (1993), 'Remote conference interpreting using ISDN videotelephony: a requirements analysis and feasibility study'. In: *Proceedings of the Human Factors and Ergonomics Society, 37th annual meeting*, 235-239.

Braun, S. (2004), Kommunikation unter widrigen Umständen? Fallstudien zu einsprachigen und gedolmetschten Videokonferenzen. Tübingen: Narr.

Braun, S. (2006), 'Multimedia communication technologies and their impact on interpreting'. In: Carroll, M., Gerzymisch-Arbogast, H. and Nauert S. (eds.), *Audiovisual Translation Scenarios. Proceedings of the Marie Curie Euroconferences MuTra: Audiovisual Translation Scenarios Copenhagen, May 2006*. Available at http://www.euroconferences.info/proceedings/2006_Proceedings/2006_Braun_Sabine.pdf.

Braun, S. (2007), 'Interpreting in small-group bilingual videoconferences: challenges and adaptation processes', *Interpreting*, 9 (1), 21-46.

Council of the European Union (2008), *European E-Justice Action Plan*, 15315/08 JURINFO 71. Brussels: European Union.

Ellis, S.R. (2004), *Videoconferencing in Refugee Hearings. Ellis Report to the Immigration and Refugee Board*. Ottawa: Immigration and Refugee Board of Canada Audit and Evaluation Committee. Available at http://www.irbcisr.gc.ca/eng/disdiv/proeva/revs/video/ Pages/index.aspx.

European Council Working Party on Legal Data Processing (2008), *Questionnaire on videoconferencing – Compilation of responses*, 6709/08 JURINFO 19. Brussels: European Union.

Federman, M. (2006), 'On the Media effects of immigration and refugee board hearings via videoconference', *Journal of Refugee Studies*, 19 (4), 433-452.

Finn, K., Sellen, A. and Wilbur, S. (eds.) (1997), *Video-mediated communication*. Mahwah, NJ: Erlbaum.

Fowler, Y. (2007), 'Interpreting into the ether: interpreting for prison/court video link hearings', *Proceedings of the Critical Link 5 conference, Sydney, 11-15/04/2007*. Available at http://www.criticallink.org/files/CL5Fowler.pdf.

GDISC Interpreters' Pool Project (2007), *Project Operational Guidelines*. Unpublished report.

Green, C.E. and Romberger, W. (2009), 'Leveraging Technology to Meet the Need for Interpreters', Future Trends in State Courts 2009, 36-39. Available at http://contentdm.ncsconline.org/cdm4/itemviewer.php?CISOROOT=/accessfair &CISOPTR=184&CISOBOX=1&REC=1.

Haas, A. (2006), 'Videoconferencing in Immigration Proceedings', *Pierce Law Review*, 5 (1), 59-90.

Harvard Law School (2009), 'Access to Courts and Videoconferencing in Immigration Court Proceedings', *Harvard Law Review*, 122 (1151), 1181-1193.

Hornberger, J., Gibson, C., Wood, W., Dequeldre, C., Corso, I., Palla, B. and Bloch, D. (1996), 'Eliminating language barriers for non-English-speaking patients', *Medical Care*, 34 (8), 845-856.

Johnson, M. and Wiggins, E. (2006), 'Videoconferencing in criminal proceedings: Legal and empirical issues and directions for research', *Law and Policy*, 28 (2), 211-227.

Lee, J. (2007), 'Telephone interpreting: Seen from the interpreters' perspective', *Interpreting*, 9 (2), 231-252.

Lee, J. (2009), 'Interpreting inexplicit language during courtroom examination', *Applied Linguistics*, 30 (1), 93-14.

Moser-Mercer, B. (2003), 'Remote interpreting: assessment of human factors and performance parameters'. *Communicate!* Summer 2003. Available at http://www.aiic.net/ViewPage. cfm/article879.htm.

Mouzourakis, P. (1996), 'Videoconferencing: techniques and challenges', Interpreting, 1 (1), 21-38.

Mouzourakis, P. (2003), 'That feeling of being there: vision and presence in remote interpreting'. *Communicate!* Summer 2003. Available at http://www.aiic.net/ViewPage.cfm/article911.htm.

Mouzourakis, P. (2006), 'Remote interpreting: a technical perspective on recent experiments', *Interpreting*, 8 (1), 45-66.

Poulin, A.B. (2004), 'Criminal justice and videoconferencing technology: the remote defendant', *Tulane Law Review*, 78 (1089), 1089-1167.

Roziner, I. and Shlesinger, M. (2010), 'Much ado about something remote: Stress and performance in remote interpreting', *Interpreting*, 12 (2), 214–247.

Sossin, L. and Yetnikoff, Z. (2007), 'I can see clearly now: Videoconference hearings and the legal limit on how tribunals allocate resources', *Windsor Yearbook of Access to Justice*, 25 (2), 247-272.

The Law Societies Joint Brussels Office (2009), *Criminal Law Reform Update*. June 2009. Available at http://international.lawsociety.org.uk/files/EUCriminalLaw ReformUpdateJune2009.pdf.

Verrept, H., (2011), 'Intercultural mediation through the Internet in Belgian hospitals', *4th International Conference on Public Service Interpreting and Translation, 13th-15th April 2011*. Abstract available at http://tisp2011.tucongreso.es/ti2011/files/book-abstracts.pdf.

Webster, L.P. (2009), *Evaluation of Videoconferencing Technology: Mesa Arizona Municipal Court Final Report*. Denver: National Centre for State Courts. Available at http://contentdm. ncsconline.org/cdm4/item_viewer.php? CISOROOT=/tech&CISOPTR=708&REC=5.

Wisconsin Court Interpreters Program (2010), 'Best Practices: Remote Interpreting in Court. *Telephone, Videoconferencing and VRI (Video Remote Interpreting)'*. Available at http://www.wicourts.gov/services/interpreter/docs/telephone inter pret.pdf.

Wisconsin Judiciary (2009), 'Technology links Madison court interpreter to courts in Door, Trempealeau', *The Third Branch,* 17 (2), 2. Available at http://www. wicourts.gov/ news/thirdbranch/docs/spring09.pdf.

VIDEO-MEDIATED INTERPRETING IN CRIMINAL PROCEEDINGS: TWO EUROPEAN SURVEYS

Sabine Braun and Judith L. Taylor

University of Surrey

1   INTRODUCTION

As part of gaining an overview of how video-mediated interpreting is used the criminal justice system, the AVIDICUS Project conducted two surveys in European Union member states: the first aimed at judicial services and legal practitioners; the second at legal interpreters. Each survey had its own distinct objective.

- The aim of the survey among legal practitioners and judicial institutions was to gauge the extent to which different forms of video-mediated interpreting are currently employed in Europe and to elicit information regarding planned uses, as well as the underlying motivations for use on the part of the judicial services.
- The survey among legal interpreters was intended to capture the informants' views, attitudes and current experience with different forms of video-mediated interpreting and to obtain a self-assessment of interpreting performance under videoconference conditions, the perceived difficulties and requirements for training.

As with the overview of current practice (reported in the previous chapter), the results of the two European surveys helped shape the AVIDICUS comparative studies (see Balogh & Hertog, Braun & Taylor, and Miler-Cassino & Rybińska in this volume) ensuring that the settings tested were relevant and would lead to valid, appropriate recommendations on the use of videoconference interpreting (VCI) and remote interpreting (RI) in legal proceedings (for definitions, see the review of current practice by Braun & Taylor in this volume).

Although a number of surveys have been conducted among public service interpreters to investigate their self-perception and/or to contrast the views of public services interpreters and service provides (e.g. Angelleli 2003; Lee 2009; Martin & Abril Martí 2008; Martin & Ortega-Herráez 2009; Ortega Herráez & Foulquié Rubio 2008), none of them has focused on video-mediated interpreting to date.

Section 2 outlines the methodological basis for conducting the two surveys. Section 3 presents the results. This includes responses on the frequency of VCI and RI use, the main settings in which they are employed, the legal, social and political contexts of VCI and RI use, the technological context, attitudes to video-mediated interpreting, and views on the need for specialised training. Section 4 draws conclusions from these responses, and ties together the two points-of-view represented by the surveys.

2   METHODOLOGY

2.1   The surveys

The legal practitioners' survey targeted judicial institutions in Europe, and more specifically those employing individuals with knowledge of current and planned uses of videoconference and remote interpreting in criminal proceedings. In order to gain as full a picture of the situation as possible, legal and judicial *institutions* were contacted with a questionnaire and invited to identify appropriate persons in their respective countries who would be able to provide information. The questionnaire was circulated in paper-based form, and participation was sought on the understanding that the information provided would be released in anonymised form and that, where relevant, reports would refer to a country's institutions in general (e.g. "the district courts of country X" or "the police force in country Y") but would not identify any specific institution by name nor location. The European Council Working Party on Legal Data Processing helped to disseminate the questionnaire and a number of national judicial institutions supported the dissemination of the questionnaire at national level.

The interpreters' survey was aimed at legal interpreters who have experience with VCI and/or RI in criminal proceedings in particular, and more especially those who have worked in such settings more than once in the last five years. The survey was conducted online on the understanding that participation would be anonymous and that the responses would not be attributable to any participating individual. The link to the survey was sent to, and distributed by, professional interpreter associations and institutions throughout Europe for circulation to members and associates.

The two questionnaires were phrased differently, given the different purposes and respondent groups, but they covered the same and/or complementary information on the following aspects:

- The frequency with which VCI and RI are employed in different areas
- The main settings in which these forms of interpreting are employed
- The (perceived) reasons and motivations for their use
- The technology used and perceptions of its appropriateness
- The procedures for the use of VCI and RI
- Reactions to VCI and RI
- Perceptions regarding co-operation between judicial services and interpreters

The legal practitioners were also asked whether there is a legal basis, policy and guidance for VCI and RI. The interpreters were invited to give a self-assessment of various aspects of their performance in VCI/RI and to give their views on training for this method of interpreting. The surveys were intended to constitute a 'snapshot' of existing and planned uses of VCI and RI and attitudes towards them, and as such were not intended to be exhaustive.

2.2 The respondents

In total, the legal practitioners' questionnaire received 35 responses from institutions in 17 European Union Member States. These included responses from all parts of the criminal justice system, including, though not limited to, probation services, national ministries of justice, prosecution bodies, courts, and the police. In addition, one immigration service responded. While this does not constitute a criminal justice institution, the responses are insightful and informative, and are thus included here in the interests of completeness.

It should be noted that some of the institutions already use VCI and/or RI in some way, while others do not; therefore, not all the questionnaires were completed in their entirety.

The interpreters' survey garnered 201 responses from 31 countries. 166 of these were completed and subsequently analysed. Of these 166 interpreters, 150 had interpreted in a VC situation (VCI or RI) at least once. In other words, 16 interpreters who completed the survey had never done VCI or RI. Given the nature of many questions, their views nevertheless provided valuable insights.

Most European countries were represented in the interpreters' questionnaire. Responses were received from EU member states (152) and from European countries outside the EU (2). The highest number of respondents (84) was from the UK. There were also individual responses from outside Europe (12) including Australia, Brazil, Cambodia, Canada, Mexico, Morocco, Turkey and the United States.

Of the 166 respondents to the interpreters' questionnaire who completed the questionnaire, 121 were female (i.e. 73%), and 45 male (i.e. 27%).

As figure 1 shows, the largest group of respondents were aged between 40-49 (33.7%). Only 1.8% were aged between 20-29; 18.1% were between 30-39; 27.1% were between the ages of 50 and 59; and 19% were over 60 years old.

Amongst the interpreters, 48 languages were said to be spoken natively, with the largest groups speaking English (26 respondents), Spanish (22), German (17), Portuguese (15), Dutch (14), Polish (13), Finnish (8), French (8), Chinese (7) and Turkish (5). Interpreters were then asked to state the non-native language(s) in which they work. 99.5% of respondents gave one working language, 78.7% also gave a second working language, and 36.1% a third language.

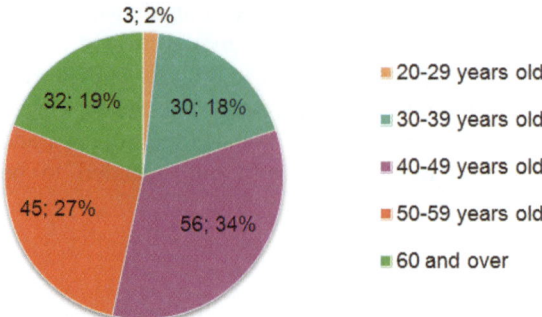

Figure 1: Distribution of age groups among the interpreters

Interpreting experience ranged from very experienced (66.7% had done more than 2000 hours of general interpreting; 41.5% had carried out more than 2000 hours of interpreting in criminal justice proceedings) to far less experienced (9.3% had done less than 400 hours of general interpreting; in terms of criminal justice interpreting, 18.9% had done less than 400 hours of work). The work experience in terms of working hours generally correlated with the interpreters' age. The two categories were therefore analysed together.

When asked in which areas of criminal justice they work, all areas were represented in the interpreters' answers. The survey specifically asked whether respondents had interpreted for the police, investigating judges, courts or prisons, but the interpreters also added that they had worked for, inter alia, probation services, defence counsel, customs, and forensic departments. Most interpreters stated that they also work in other areas, including other legal fields (immigration, civil law) as well as healthcare, business, conference, media and educational contexts (one respondent stated s/he was a staff interpreter for a university), charity and ecclesiastical areas, and the military.

3   RESULTS OF THE EUROPEAN SURVEYS

3.1   Frequency of use

One of the questions in each of the surveys attempted to elicit information about the extent of VCI and RI. The legal practitioners were asked to rate the estimated overall frequency of use in their respective countries and to comment on the areas in which uses of VCI and RI are planned. According to the responses, in some countries, VCI and RI are used very frequently; in others, it is rarely or never employed. However, its use is planned at all levels of criminal justice in Europe. The following table shows the situation in 2009, based on the self-assessment by the judicial institutions responding to the survey:

Used regularly	Used occasionally	Used rarely	Used but frequency unknown	Not (yet) used
Estonia Netherlands United Kingdom	Germany Poland Sweden	Czech Rep. Denmark Malta Slovakia	Austria Belgium France	Lithuania

Table 1: Use of video-mediated interpreting by country

To give an example of the extent of available videoconferencing facilities – as an indirect indicator for the possible use of video-mediated interpreting – in February 2010, the British Ministry of Justice reported the following to the House of Commons:[1]

Each UK jurisdiction has a wide range of video-conferencing facilities as detailed below. Most of these can be used in cross-border situations in accordance with relevant national and EU legislation. The use of video-conferencing between the UK and other Member States has to date been fairly limited; however, as capacity increases it is anticipated that so will its use.

England and Wales:

— Over 40% of Crown and Magistrates' Courts have videoconferencing facilities.

— 389 Crown Court rooms have videoconferencing facilities in 85 sites.

— 468 Magistrates' Court rooms have videoconferencing facilities in 274 sites.

— There are video-conferencing links in 58 of 218 County Court sites.

— 28 prisons have a total of 38 video links which could be used in cross-border situations—this is in addition to the Prison Court Video Link network which connects 151 Magistrates' and 30 Crown Courts with 66 prisons and young offender institutions (where the facilities are for domestic use only).

— It is expected that equipment will be deployed to all 139 prison establishments in future.

— 160 National Probation Service sites have a total of 172 video links.

— 42 prisons and 38 probation sites will have 99 IP video links by the end of March 2010.

While the early roll out of video-conferencing facilities focused on connecting prisons and courts, in England and Wales we encourage the use of available facilities and are in the process of increasing the capacity of available equipment and modernising the underlying technology.

---

[1]   http://www.publications.parliament.uk/pa/cm200910/cmselect/cmjust/162/162we13.htm.

Figures are also reported for the other jurisdictions of the UK, i.e. Scotland and Ireland.

Another example is Poland, which replied that VCI and RI are used "occasionally". However, during 2004 and 2005, Poland experienced a sharp increase in the number of video-mediated court hearings, from 22 in 2004 to 126 in 2005. By 2007, the number had increased to 431, of which 22 were cross-border cases. 2008 saw 774 video-mediated court cases, including 35 cross-border cases. During the period 2006-2008, 90 courtrooms in 45 regional Polish courts were equipped with VC terminals. 2009 saw district courts begin to be fitted with VC facilities, as well as 21 prisons and detention centres. 11 public prosecutors' offices were furnished with VC equipment in 2007.

The interpreters were asked about the extent of their personal experience with VCI and RI. The responses (Figure 2) suggest that VCI is currently more common than RI both in judicial proceedings and other situations, as the following diagram shows. Given that most respondents are from Europe (154 of 166), this can be taken as an indicator for the situation in Europe. As was pointed out in Braun & Taylor's chapter in this volume on current practice, the distribution of VCI and RI outside Europe appears to be different.

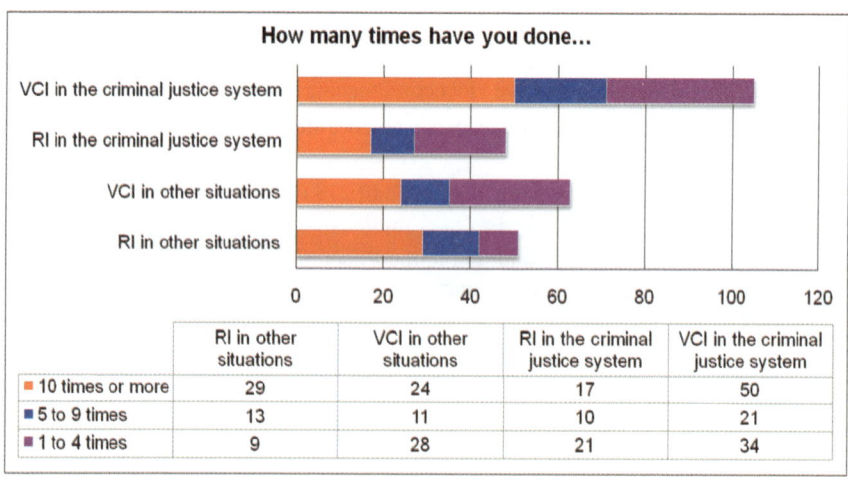

Figure 2: Interpreter experience with videoconference and remote interpreting

The chart is based on the responses of the 150 interpreters (out of 166 who completed the survey) who had done VCI or RI at least once. The total number of responses is higher than 150 because multiple replies were possible here.

3.2   Main settings

Another question in both surveys was aimed at ascertaining the settings in which video-mediated interpreting is used in criminal proceedings. The legal practitioners were asked to describe the settings and stages of the proceedings in which their respective countries or institutions have a need for video-based interpreting. According to the responses garnered in this practitioners' survey, VCI and RI are used, in principle, for all types of crime, and at all stages of criminal proceedings, albeit with varying frequency and restrictions.

Apart from differences in legislation and views on the permissible uses of VCI/RI, it seems to be the geography, politics and judicial structures of different countries that result in different needs. For example, Denmark reported using RI for court interpreting, owing to the fact that it has many small islands which constitute a challenge for the timely access to an interpreter. Thus, in the Danish scenario, RI is often 'more practical and flexible' than face-to-face interpreting. Interestingly, the mode of interpreting is simultaneous if possible.

All other countries that replied use VCI at the court stage of proceedings. The Scottish court services, for example, were of the opinion that 'courts are more likely to use VCI than RI [...]. Regarding RI, it is likely that using this would need to be raised with the judiciary in any given case as it is not a familiar concept'.

VCI settings include pre-trial hearings, and especially first hearings and bail and remand hearings. According to the responses from judicial authorities, the settings vary with regard to the location of the interpreter. In the Netherlands, for example, the interpreter is generally co-located with the non-native speaker, but can in fact choose his/her location. In Belgium, the interpreter is generally co-located with the legal practitioner, e.g. the prosecutor. In Poland, the location of interpreter is not regulated in law. In the UK, the location of the interpreter is not regulated, but in practice the interpreter is more frequently situated with the legal practitioner (in court) than with the non-native speaker (in prison or police custody).

In all of these cases, the mode of interpreting in VCI was reported to be consecutive. Only in some cases, when the interpreter is co-located with the non-native speaker, is whispered interpreting used.

The emphasis on VCI in court settings does not mean that there is no demand for RI in criminal proceedings in Europe. RI is a setting which is being considered by a number of European police forces. It is currently being introduced by the Metropolitan Police Service in London. The intention is to place interpreters in centralised hubs, similar to those in the Florida circuit courts (see Braun & Taylor's chapter on current practice in this volume), although the mode of interpreting will be consecutive. The Metropolitan Police Newsletter of October 2009 explained the plans as follows:

In order to speed up access to linguistic support, a new video conferencing platform will be created. Video equipment will be installed in each custody suite involved in the trial [meaning: a pilot phase], and in selected interview rooms for dealing with witnesses and victims. This network will be supported by the creation of 8 'interpreter hubs', strategically placed around London, to take account of demand and interpreter availability.[2]

In the counterpart survey, the interpreters were questioned once again about their experiences of the settings in which VCI and RI had been used. As shown in the legal practitioners' responses, the interpreters' responses also indicate that VCI and RI are used at all stages of criminal proceedings, from initial police interview to charge, pre-trial (bail, remand), trial and post-sentence, as well as for lawyer-defendant communication. The following chart shows the distribution of interpreter experience with VCI and RI at different stages of criminal proceedings (multiple replies were possible):

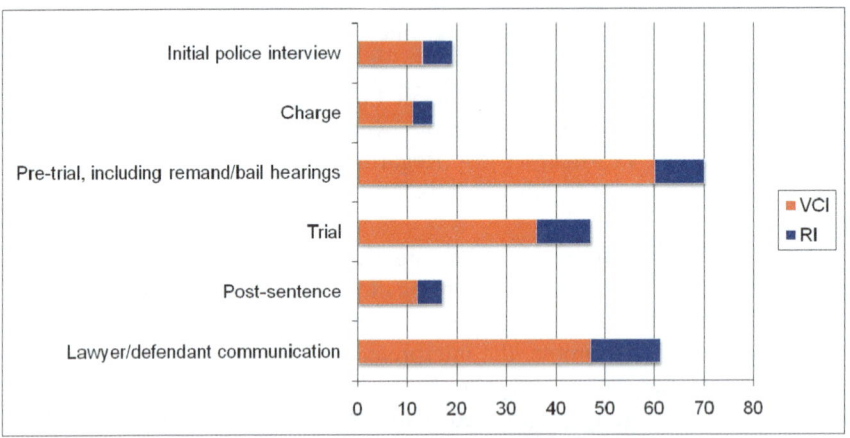

Figure 3: Interpreter experience with VCI/RI in criminal justice

As above, the chart is based on the responses of the 150 interpreters (out of 166 who completed the survey) who had done VCI or RI at least once. The total number of responses is higher than 150 because multiple replies were possible here.

The distribution of experience among the interpreters seems to confirm that VCI is currently much more common than RI in Europe at all stages of the proceedings. The distribution of VCI is to a certain extent a reflection of the use of videoconferencing in criminal proceedings. Many of the reports cited in Braun & Taylor's review of current practice (in this volume)

---

[2]   http://www.mpa.gov.uk/downloads/partnerships/icv/newsletter/2009-10.pdf, p. 3.

indicated that videoconferencing is most commonly used at the pre-trial stage, i.e. for first hearings and bail/remand hearings. What is clearly under-represented in the reports however, is lawyer-defendant communication.

The average duration of the communication also varied. Most of those who had interpreted for pre-trial and for lawyer-defendant consultations stated that the link lasted less than 30 minutes. Trials, however, generally lasted for more than an hour. Other uses for VCI and RI included witness interviews, pre-sentence reports and probation assessment.

Interpreters were invited to describe a typical experience of VCI or RI use. A male, UK-based Polish-English interpreter, for example, described his experiences working in magistrates' courts, interpreting via video link for lawyer-defendant communications and for pre-trial hearings lasting around 10 – 15 minutes. He reported that he is normally in court and sits next to the legal practitioner, using a mixture or consecutive and whispered interpreting, depending on the layout of the court and the quality of the equipment used for the hearing. He reported only being able to see the outline of the person for whom he was interpreting on the video screen, and stated that the image and sound quality are generally far from sufficient to allow him to do his job satisfactorily. More specifically, the problems he has encountered include connection failures, time lags, interference, and ignorance on the part of the court staff as to how the VC equipment works.

This interpreter's experience of VC rather contradicts the view expressed by some of the legal practitioner respondents (and some other interpreters) that there are no problems associated with using a video link to interpret. However, several respondents to the legal practitioners' questionnaire did report serious technological problems.

The above interpreter also mentioned that he had never seen VCI used in trials or for 'complex issues'. However, another UK-based interpreter describes an instance of VCI use during a Crown Court trial involving a domestic violence case. The VC link was necessary during the cross-examination of a witness. The interpreter was located with the witness at the remote site (in this case, another room within the court building). The mode of interpreting was consecutive. The respondent stated that, on the video screen, they were only able to see whoever was addressing the witness at that particular moment, but that the image quality and sound quality were excellent, and no problems occurred.

These two examples illustrate the difference in quality between the video links used in different types of court even within a single country, which is a source of different experiences and potentially varying attitudes of interpreters towards VCI and RI.

3.3   Reasons for use, legal basis, policy and guidance

Both groups were asked about the reasons they see for using VCI or RI in legal proceedings. The responses revealed strongly opposing views between the judicial authorities/legal practitioners and the interpreters. The interpreters' perception of the reasons for the implementation of VCI and RI is generally negative. Many interpreters believe that these forms of interpreting are implemented for the sole purpose of cutting interpreting costs. The interpreters' responses suggest that some interpreters feel threatened by this development, as they fear a drop in earnings.

The judicial authorities gave a wide range of reasons, including the following:

'More efficient use of resources'

'Reduces travel and waiting times'

'More practical and flexible'

'Better for environment'

'Safer'

'Not used to save money – rather it gives access to qualified legal interpreters for rare languages for which there is no qualified interpreter nearby. As long as a qualified interpreter is available locally, this is the preferred option'

'Means of providing access to justice for non-English speakers'

Indirectly, some of these responses confirm that cost cutting is an important element in the introduction of VCI and RI. The argument that VCI and RI are better for the environment may generally be interpreted as a post-hoc justification of cost cutting. What is noteworthy in some of the responses, however, is a level of dissatisfaction in the judicial services with the way interpreting is currently delivered. The points about timing and flexibility of VCI/RI indicate that the current arrangements are seen as being unsatisfactory, and VCI/RI are perceived as being a means of dealing with this.

At the same time, the legal practitioners' survey shows that when it comes to applying VCI or RI, the judicial services sometimes find themselves in a state of legal limbo. In response to the question of whether there is a legal basis for the use of VCI and RI, only some respondent countries referred to a concrete piece of legislation (see table 2). Others referred to general regulations regarding the use of VC in criminal proceedings but stated that no specific regulations on the use of interpreters in video links exist. Not all countries replied to this question.

It is interesting to note that some respondent countries cited different pieces of legislation that in their opinion allowed or prohibited the use of VCI/RI. This suggests that there is some uncertainty as to which VCI and RI uses are actually covered by current legislation. Reference is also made to changing legislation with regard to the usage of VCI and RI.

Does the national law of your country make any provisions regarding the use of VCI/RI in criminal proceedings? If yes, please give details.	
UK, Police	'32 1 (a) Criminal Justice Act 1988 -- essentially the discretion of the court.' 'PACE (Police and Criminal Evidence Act)' 'No plans to use in custody at present, because of the requirement for change in law. ... We would be very willing to consider it if it was legal.'
Scotland, Courts	'The Crown considers each case on its merits and if VC/RI were to facilitate court proceedings, it would be implemented.'
England/ Wales, Courts	'A bill has been laid before Parliament that will legitimise, if passed, the use of VCI in court proceedings.' 'The law in England and Wales makes provision for a 'Live Link.' [...] Whilst a defendant's court attendance can be achieve under law by live link from a prison or other custodial environment, there are restrictions. Such a link is permissible for preliminary proceedings but not for trials. Sentencing is permissible in certain circumstances. Evidence by witnesses via a live link is permissible in restricted circumstances. The location of an interpreter who is appointed to assist a defendant, a witness or a court is subject to judicial direction which is most likely but not exclusively to be in favour of having the interpreter sitting with the person or persons he is required to assist. Accordingly, an interpreter may be required to assist from somewhere away from the courtroom. The precise location of an interpreter is not dictated by statute.'
Northern Ireland	'Criminal Justice (NI) Order 2008 (earlier legislation repealed and all consolidated in this Order) and the Criminal Appeal (NI) Act 1980'
Denmark	'Art 149, section 7, of the Danish Administration of Justice Act regards interpretation via VC in both civil and criminal proceedings. The provision will come into force on 1st October 2009. So far VC has only been in use on a voluntary basis from all parties, including the interpreter. According to art 149, section 7, an interpreter can participate in the proceeding via VC if it would imply disproportionate difficulties if the interpreter participated in the proceedings at the same place as the party (includes the suspect/defendant in criminal proceedings), witness or expert. It is a condition that interpretation via VC can be performed in an adequate/reassuring way. According to the article, the interpreter can participate via VC if s/he has to travel far. This could be the case if only a few interpreters know a particular language. Furthermore, it follows from article 149, section 7, that when the interpreter interprets for a party, witness, or expert who participates in the proceedings via VC, the interpreter should as far as possible

	participate in the proceedings from the same place as the party, witness or expert. However, the interpreter may, in exceptional cases, participate from another place to the party, witness or expert.'
Germany	'The EU Legal Assistance Agreement of 29 May 2009, which regulates witness hearings via VC. Also art 1 of the European Legal Assistance Agreement of 1959.'
France	'The final paragraph of art 706-71 of the Code of Criminal Procedure permits the use of RI via VC in the course of a hearing, questioning or confrontation of parties by the juge d'instruction. It is used, where absolutely necessary, if the interpreter cannot be present with other participants. Art 694-5 of the same Code makes art 706-71 applicable for the carrying out, by French authorities, of a request for mutual assistance.'
Poland	'Criminal Procedure Code, art 117, item 1 - this article allows the use of VC in criminal procedures. Hearing/interrogation shall be done in the presence of a sworn interpreter.'
Netherlands	'www.justitie.nl/onderwerpen/recht_en_rechtsbijstand/Videoconfer entie/Wetten (in Dutch). Does not make any specific provision regarding RI.'
Estonia	'No, it does not'
Czech Republic	'Provision of the Czech Code of Criminal Procedure relating to VC are located in Provision 444 (hearing by videophone and telephone) and Provision 445 (Provision 444 - foreign state requests the carrying out of a hearing via video/telephone in the Czech Rep; provision 445 - Czech Rep requests hearing via video/telephone of a foreign state)'
Slovakia	'The Slovak national law does not contain any special provisions regulating VC in criminal proceedings. However, the provisions of the Slovak Code of Criminal Procedure regulate the hearing of witnesses and these provisions contain special situations, where the witness shall be heard by the use of technical equipment dedicated to the transmission of sound and picture.'
Malta	No provisions
Belgium	'There is a law dated 1 May 2005 (Belgian State Gazette 66/02/2005), which implements art 34 of the treaty of 29 May 2000 and the protocol dated 16 Oct 2001. Assistance of an interpreter is a safeguarded by the European Convention on Human Rights.'

Table 2: Legal basis for the use of video-mediated interpreting in criminal justice

The situation is similar with regard to policies and guidance on the use of VCI and RI. Whilst some countries referred to general guidelines for videoconferencing, there appear to be no specific guidelines for VCI and RI in criminal proceedings as yet in the respondent countries. Responses such as the following are symptomatic of the situation:

'The judge decides in each individual case.' (Denmark)

'There is no specific policy on the use of VCI/RI.' (Netherlands)

'No instructions or guidelines. There is only a reference in an internal bylaw "for prosecutor and courts concerning MLA saying that they can use VC". It is up to a prosecutor or a court to ask for a hearing to be conducted via VC'. (Czech Republic)

3.4   Technological basis

Legal practitioners reported a mixture of VC systems and connection types in use across Europe and, indeed, within individual institutions. The different types of hardware also varied in age. Accordingly, differences in the quality of 'basic' technology – for example, viewing screens – were reported. Furthermore, differing communication protocols and network capacities seem to cause problems in connectivity.

The following table exemplifies the type of connection and hardware employed in different countries and institutions:

Country	What type of VC connection does your institution use?	What type of hardware is used?
Czech Rep.	4xISDN. No possibility of running VC on IP network	IPOWER 9000
Denmark	Fibre	Sony and Creator or Tandberg
Estonia	Mainly ITU H323 standard IP. In international hearings, ISDN based on ITU H320 standard.	Mainly Tandberg; in courtrooms Bosch DCN. Prosecutors, attorneys, and experts also use PC-based VC software Polycom PVX to attend remotely.
France	ISDN, H320, two BRI bandwidth 256KB/s	Tandberg T1000, T990, T6000
Germany	BIAMP Audia VoIP-2	Beyerdynamic SIS
Malta		Polycom USX 8000, Full VC system and recording of session

Netherlands	Both ISDN and IP	Tandberg
Poland	During national sessions: broadband connection (above 2MB). During international sessions: ISDN connection.	Sony
Slovakia	ISDN	Tandberg 550 (TTC7-05)
UK	Various types of connections and hardware were reported, e.g.	
England/Wales	Martin Dawes Link UK, Courts Direct ISDN Link, ISDN telephone connectivity 384KB	Polycom VSX 7000
England/Wales	IP for Prison Link network. Witness links use ISDN or PBX. For ISDN links, 3 or 4 lines recommended. Internal witness links use CAT 5 cabling. Old AEL witness links in Crown Court connect internally using Coax cabling.	Mostly Polycom VSX7000s or VSX7000e. Prison Link network uses Sony PCS 1 or Sony 1600. Witness links use 2x42" plasma screens (courtroom); 32" LCD or TFT monitor in witness room. Prison links: dual 42" plasma screens (Crown Court); dual 28" CRT screens (Magistrates Court) with 28-32" CRT screen in witness room.
Northern Ireland	At time of survey– ISDN connectivity, but due to move to IP in prisons. ISDN retained in county courts at present. Investigating IP to IP connectivity for Belfast courts.	Tandberg equipment (linkages to Court Service equipment may involve other manufacturers). T6000 units used mostly in courts, T85 Edge mostly in prisons with T1700 to be installed for office/consultation use.

Table 3: Technological basis for the use of video-mediated interpreting in criminal justice

Among the problems that were highlighted by many interpreters and some legal practitioners were problems with the sound and image quality of the videoconferences. On the other hand, several institutions reported no problems with the technology. Interpreter respondents frequently reported never being able to move the camera, adjust the volume, or see relevant documents.

3.5 Reactions

As a general rule, both legal practitioners and interpreters felt that face-to-face interpreting is always preferable to any form of video-mediated interpreting. Some legal institutions reported, however, that there were no problems with VCI and RI and no difference in quality. Interpreter opinion ranged from seeing absolutely no value in VCI and RI to 'everything is good'. The following table outlines the common ground and points of contention between institutions and interpreters:

Legal Practitioners	Interpreters
'There is no comparison: a one-to-one is the ideal scenario.'	'Everything is good.' 'Avoidance of contact with violent or dangerous detainees.' 'Useful in international cases'. 'Avoids unnecessary travelling'. 'Useful in an emergency.'
'The respondent's view is that face-to-face interpreting is preferable to VC interpreting. However, she thinks that VC interpreting is better than telephone interpretation and in an instant world has its place as a valid means of communication.'	'Quick, operative. I fully support VCI'. 'I think you quickly get used to it.' 'You can never be absolutely sure that you have been understood.'
'Face-to-face usually preferable (depends on technical quality of VC device).'	'RI is vital for traumatised witnesses.' 'Should only be used when protecting the young and vulnerable. Not to be generalised.'
'The respondent is not aware of any reports of difference in quality.' 'No difference, either in sound or picture/presence.' 'No particular problems.' '[They are] of the same quality.' 'VCI is usually of an inferior quality.' 'The quality [...] has not been discussed or investigated.'	'From the interpreting point of view, I am afraid to say it doesn't have any good points; unless a high-tech system is developed and used, such as 3-dimensional megascreens with perfect sound.' 'I cannot find any good points of VCI from the point of view of the interpreter.' 'I cannot see any advantages, it is just an experiment which is 'flavour of the month' at the moment.' 'Not adequate for legal settings'. 'Sound quality needs drastic improvement.' 'Picture quality needs drastic improvement.'

	'Technology is still rudimentary.' 'Insufficient awareness of the difficulties caused by sound problems or lack of documents.' 'Good points are sound quality and picture clarity.'
'Feedback has been positive.'	'Lack of rapport between interpreter and other participants.' 'Unreal feeling, isolation.' 'More tiring' 'Very few, if any, good points.' 'It is more difficult than FtF due to background noise, slower reaction time.'

Table 4: Legal practitioner and interpreter reactions to VCI and RI

3.6 Co-operation

Interpreters were asked about their involvement in the decision to use a VC link in a criminal justice setting (see figure 4). When asked whether it had ever been explained to the interpreter why a particular interpreting assignment needs to involve either VCI or RI, of the total 149 respondents to this question, 39.6% (59) replied 'Yes, always'; 26.2% (39) responded 'sometimes'; and 34.2% (51) answered 'never'. The question of whether the interpreter had ever been informed beforehand that a video link will be involved was answered by 143 interpreters. Of them, 48.3% (69) stated that they were 'always' informed beforehand; 25.2% (36) said they were informed 'sometimes'; 26.6% (38) reported that they were 'never' informed. Finally, the interpreters were asked whether they had ever been consulted regarding the appropriateness of using VCI or RI. 14.2% (21) replied 'yes' and 85.8% (127) said 'no'.

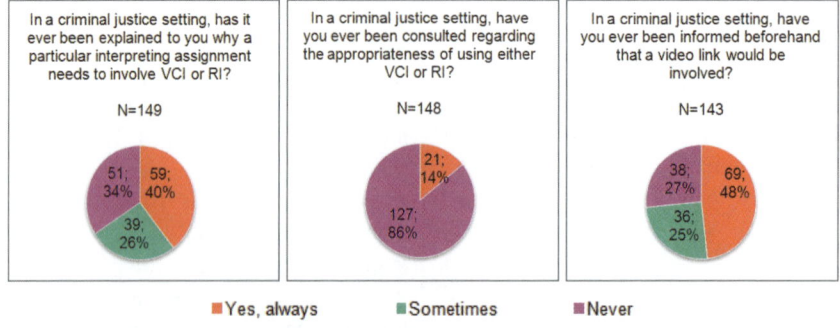

Figure 4: Interpreter consultation on the use of VCI/RI

Comments appended to the responses to these questions were varied and enlightening. One interpreter stated that 'there has been discussion between interpreters and a certain criminal justice authority on the appropriateness of using VCI and RI.' Apart from that, opinion was divided. Several other interpreters took the view that explaining the situation to them or consulting them was not necessary. Others thought the opposite or felt that their views were not seen as important. The following examples are representative of the comments made:

'Interpreters are usually never consulted on the use of VCI/RI. It appears we do not count'.

'The service user or the establishment never consider interpreters' comment important or useful.'

'Decision to use VCI/RI usually taken before an interpreter is consulted.'

'They just say, "get on with it"'.

'We need to be part of the process and not just leave it to the "techies"'.

'Closer cooperation between interpreter and person conducting investigation is required'

'You can ask the court official for some guidance'.

'I usually find out the reasons through asking'.

'The purpose of VCI in court with the defendant in custody is quite straightforward and self-explanatory.'

'An explanation isn't necessary'

Despite the variety of responses, many of them suggest that an increase in dialogue is required to avoid misapprehensions and prevent the perception among interpreters that they are a marginalised group whose opinion is inconsequential. At present the feeling that "we do not count" seems to be prevalent among interpreters. This perception may have influenced the interpreters' self-assessment of their performance in VCI and RI situations, which will be reported in the next section.

3.7   Interpreter Self-Assessment

The interpreters who had experienced VCI/RI were invited to assess their performance and satisfaction levels when carrying out VCI and RI, basing their comparison on their general face-to-face interpreting experience.

Firstly, respondents were asked to rate their VCI performance, specifically in criminal proceedings (Figure 5). The majority of respondents judged their performance to be of a lesser standard than they would expect in a face-to-face scenario, irrespective of their level of experience. However, in each of the three parameters represented in the table, a considerable number felt that their performance was the same as in the face-to-face mode (for those who had five or more experiences: comprehension of source text – 21.5%; production of target text – 37.6%; rapport with others – 18.7%).

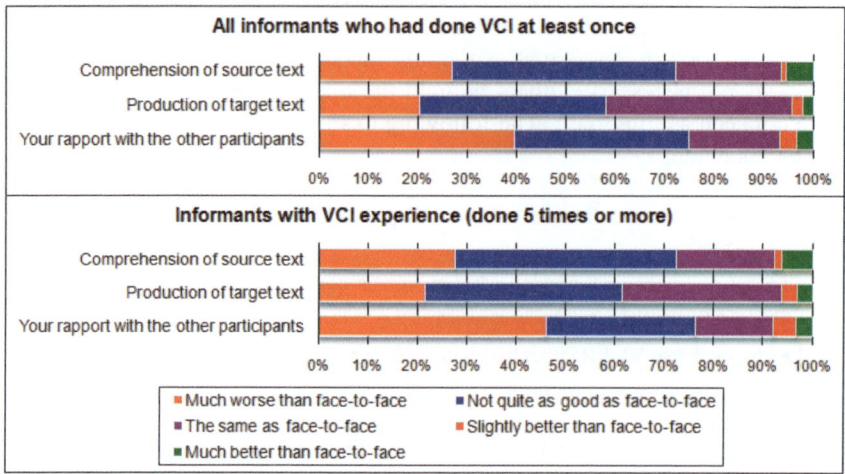

Figure 5: Interpreters' rating of VCI performance

A similar picture emerges in relation to RI. As figure 6 shows, those with more experience of RI gave slightly lower ratings compared to the ratings for VCI in the same group. Yet the general proportions are similar to those for VCI.

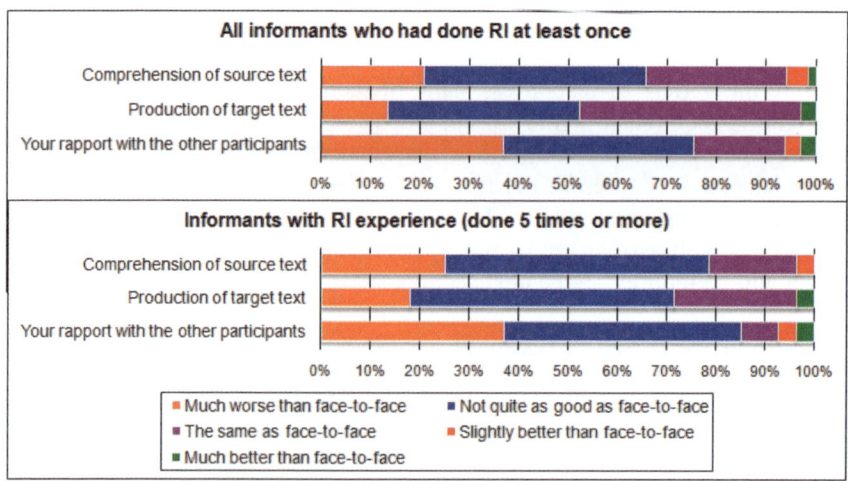

Figure 6: Interpreters' rating of RI performance

The most notable point is that the ratings for target text production are generally higher than the ratings for source text comprehension and rapport with the interlocutors. In other words, some of the interpreters felt that in spite of their problems with source text comprehension and rapport, they would still be able to perform at least as well as in face-to-face interpreting. This does not say anything about the actual interpreting quality in video-mediated interpreting, which does not seem to confirm the self-assessment (see Balogh & Hertog, Braun & Taylor and Miler-Cassino & Rybińska in this volume; see also Moser-Mercer 2003, Roziner & Shlesinger 2010). The perception is, however, interesting as it suggests that approximately 40% of the interpreters who had some experience with VCI and 30% of those who had experience with RI either felt at ease with their own performance or at least chose to say they did.

The interpreters were then asked to gauge their satisfaction levels for the two forms of video-mediated interpreting:

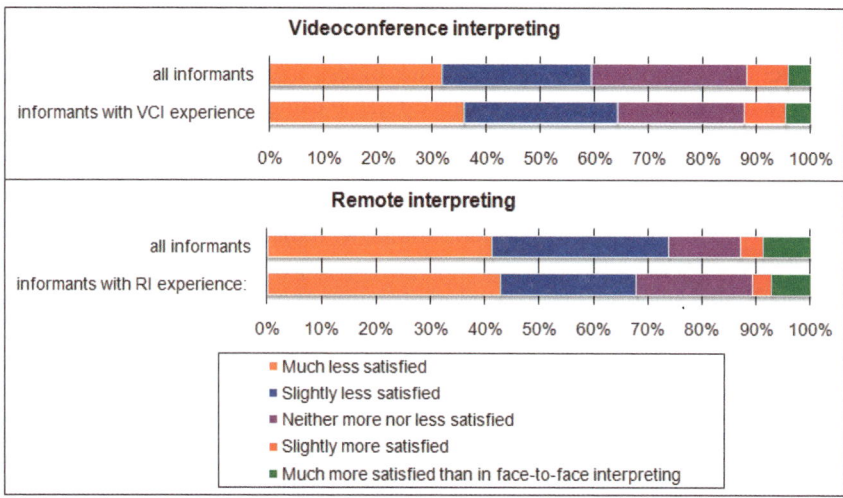

Figure 7: Interpreters' rating of satisfaction levels

Here again, RI was rated slightly lower than VCI; however, the differences are not great and the proportions are again similar. The majority of the interpreters find video-mediated interpreting less satisfactory than traditional face-to-face interpreting.

An interesting difference emerges, however, if the results – performance ratings and satisfaction levels – are broken down into age ranges. The distribution of age ranges, which was reported in section 2 (figure 1), is repeated as here figure 8 for ease of reference:

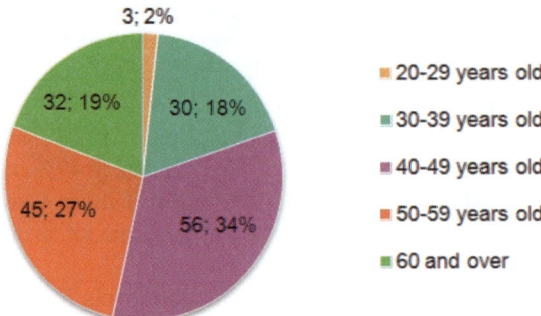

Figure 8: Distribution of age groups among the interpreters

Figures 9, 10 and 11 show the relative distribution of performance and satisfaction ratings by age group. The oldest age group gave the most positive ratings in all three performance-related categories (figures 9 and 10). Moreover, in this age group the discrepancy between the ratings for target text production and the other two categories was lower than in the other groups, who generally rated their target text production higher than their source text comprehension and their rapport with the interlocutors. Given the correlation between age range and interpreting experience in our sample (see section 2), this suggests that general interpreting experience may have a more important role to play in the perception of video-mediated interpreting than specific experience with video-mediated interpreting itself.

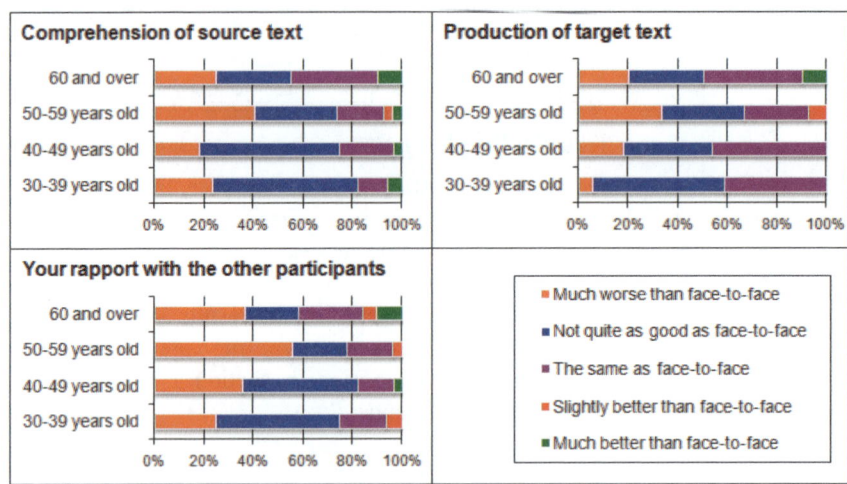

Figure 9: Rating of VCI Performance – by age range

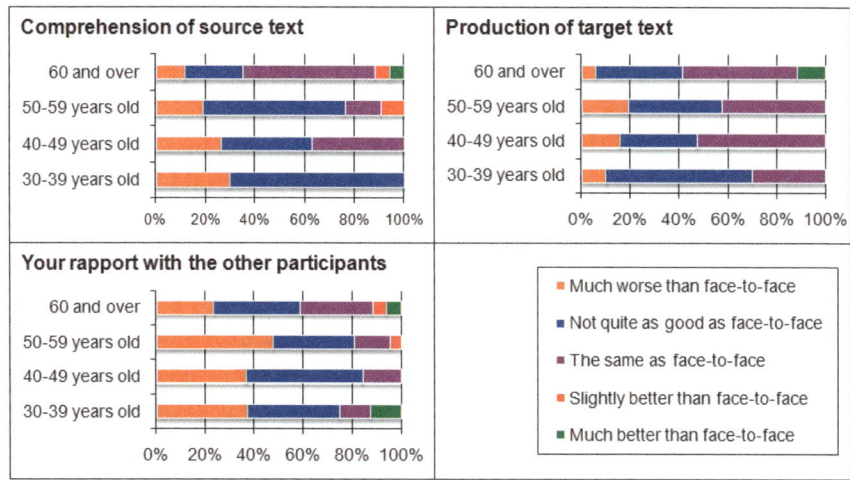

Figure 10: Rating of RI Performance – by age range

Figure 11 shows that, again, the ratings in terms of satisfaction levels were highest in the 60 years and over age group, with more than 50% being at least as satisfied with both RI and VCI as with face-to-face interpreting. It is also noteworthy that 15% in this age group had a slight or strong preference for VCI and 25% for RI compared to face-to-face interpreting.

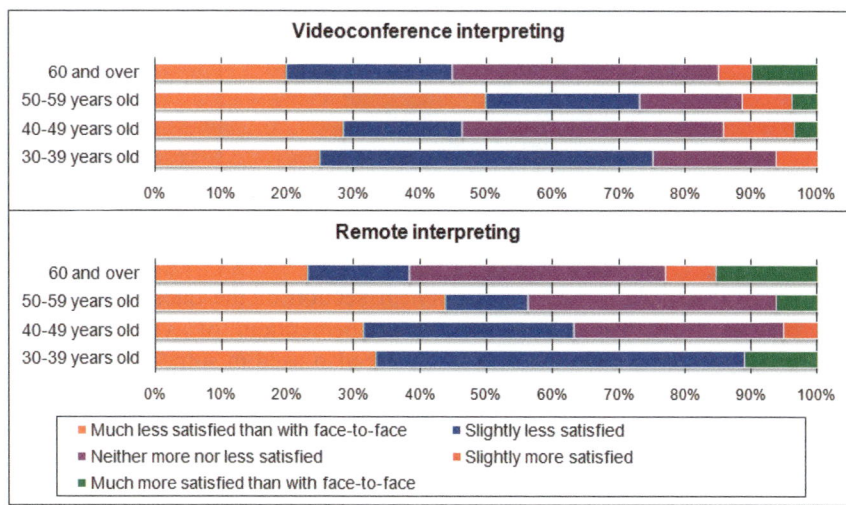

Figure 11: Satisfaction Levels for VCI and RI – by age range

The youngest of the four age groups analysed was the least positive group in terms of satisfaction levels. In this group, 76% and 89% were either slightly or much less satisfied with VCI and RI respectively when compared their level of satisfaction with face-to-face interpreting.

The largest group of respondents to the survey were based in the UK (84 out of the 166 interpreters who completed the questionnaire). As the next chart (figure 12) shows, satisfaction levels among UK-based interpreters are lower in relation to both VCI and RI than among interpreters in other countries. Apart from being generally more positive, the interpreters in other countries also made a greater distinction between VCI and RI, with the latter seen as less satisfactory than the former.

It is possible that the generally negative attitude of UK interpreters has led to their making little distinction between VCI and RI. Another consideration is that video links in many Magistrates courts in England/Wales are based on outdated technology (see also Braun & Taylor's chapter on current practice in this volume), but since they have existed for a long time, they constitute one of the best known types of VC facility among legal interpreters in the UK. The quality of this equipment may be partially responsible for the low satisfaction ratings given by UK interpreters for VCI.

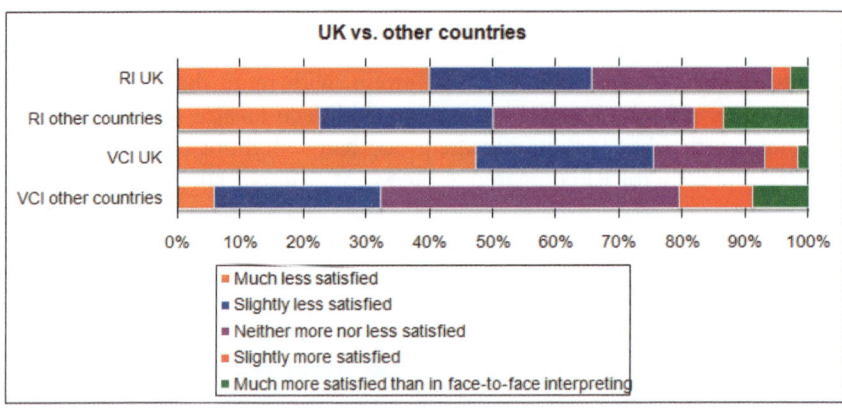

Figure 12: Satisfaction level of interpreters in the UK (N=84) vs. other countries (N=82)

As a final question in the self-assessment section of the questionnaire, the interpreters were asked to rate their perception of video-mediated interpreting in terms of categories that were also used in some of the studies on remote conference interpreting (see Braun & Taylor's chapter on current practice in this volume). The categories included the interpreters' motivation, the perceived level of isolation, stress and fatigue compared to face-to-face interpreting (see figures 13 and 14).

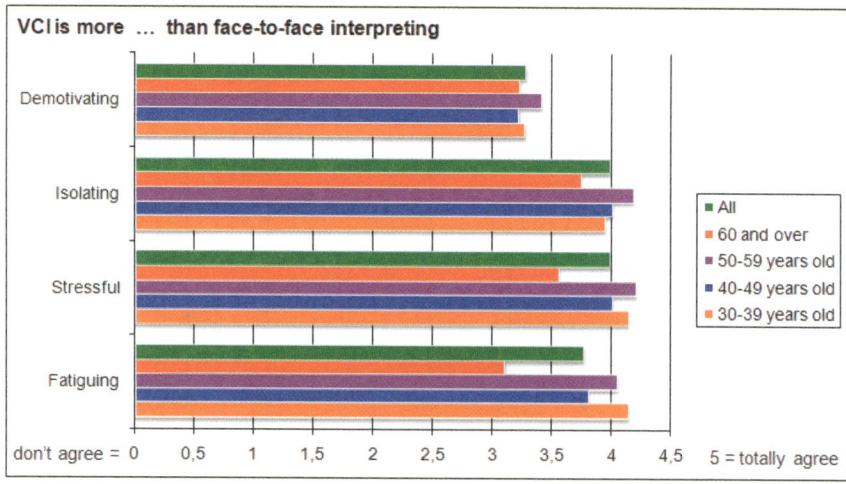

Figure 13: Emotional/physiological responses to VCI

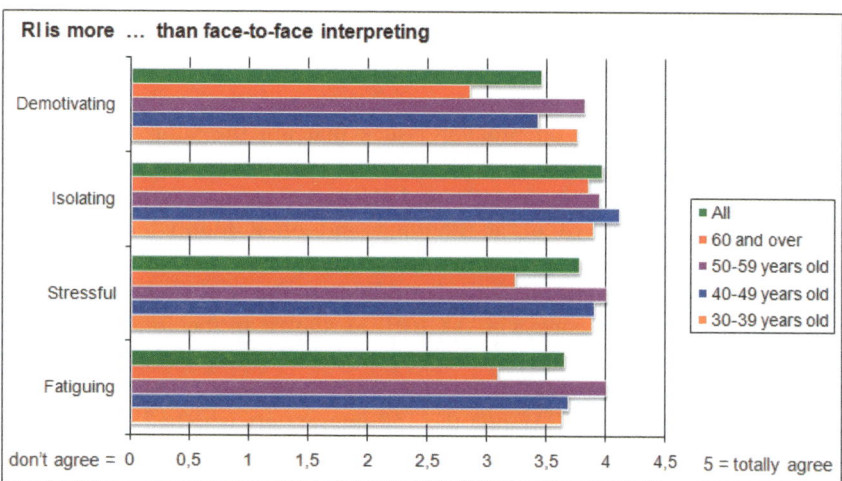

Figure 14: Emotional/physiological responses to RI

As expected, the interpreters rated both VCI and RI as being less motivating, more isolating, stressful and fatiguing than face-to-face interpreting. What is once again noteworthy, however, is that the oldest age group gave more positive ratings in all categories than the other three age groups analysed.

3.8 Training: views and expectations

In another section of the questionnaire, the interpreters were also asked about their views on training in VCI and RI. When asked whether there should be training for VCI/RI, the interpreters responded as shown in figure 15.

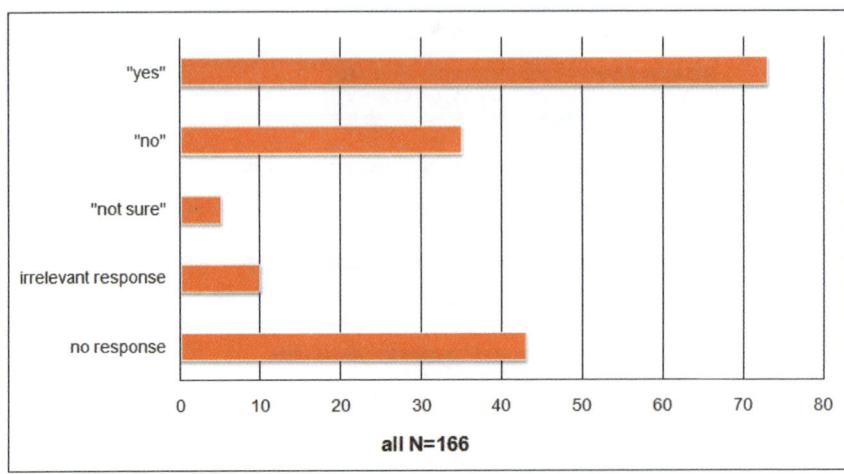

Figure 15: Interpreter views on VCI/RI training

What is remarkable is the relatively large number of "irrelevant responses". As in other sections of the questionnaire, the interpreter respondents often used free comment boxes to describe their own (anecdotal) experience with VCI/RI, to express their general dissatisfaction with the implementation of VCI/RI or to comment on broader issues that are the subject of current debate within the interpreting profession, i.e. comments that do not relate specifically to training or to VCI and RI and their uses. Many of these comments are indicative of an ongoing and often highly emotionalised debate within the interpreter community.

What is equally insightful is the distribution of the responses in relation to the interpreters' experience with VCI/RI, as shown in the following graph (figure 16). Among the 16 interpreters who had never done VCI/RI, 10 (62.5%) felt that training would be necessary and only 1 (6.25%) thought that this was not the case. Among the 150 interpreters who had done VCI or RI at least once, only 63 (42%) agreed that training needs to be provided, whilst 34 (22.7%) deemed it unnecessary. In other words, the number of those who thought there should be training for VCI/RI seems to decrease relative to the experience.

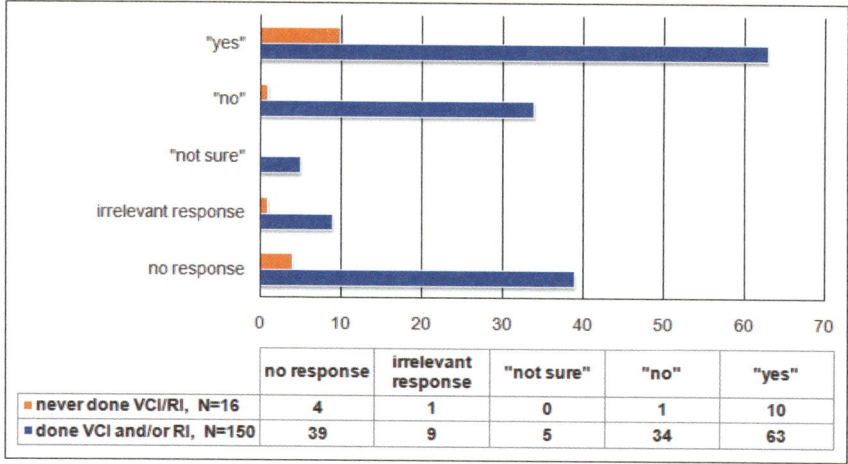

	no response	irrelevant response	"not sure"	"no"	"yes"
▪ never done VCI/RI, N=16	4	1	0	1	10
▪ done VCI and/or RI, N=150	39	9	5	34	63

Figure 16: Interpreter views on VCI/RI training, according to experience

Some of the free comments relating to this question confirm this trend:

'You learn on the job, with mistakes and all.'

'Learned on my own with practice.'

'Court technicians instructed me on how to use the equipment.'

'Not training as such; more supervised hands-on experience.'

'It is quite straightforward and user friendly.'

'I do not think this requires special training.'

A number of other comments reveal that some interpreters thought training needs to be provided to the other participants:

'Not necessarily for the interpreters. However most defendants may have big problems coping with VCI and RI.'

'To date, I feel my experience has been sufficient. However, the parties engaging the interpreter should be trained in the way they use us.'

'I do think that interpreters and all court parties should be adequately trained before considering this modality.'

'Yes, training is necessary. First of all for the technicians, for a good set-up of the cameras (choice of position, sound) is key. Secondly for the users, because the interpreter cannot intervene in the case of wrong use of buttons etc. Thirdly for the interpreter, although there are less changes for him/her.'

Furthermore, the interpreters commented on the kind of training that they would find useful:

'A course to get used to the new technology (sound/image) and the set-up would be useful.'

'Simple explanations of what can be expected and some audio-visual transmission coping techniques would have been welcome.'

'Practice would be helpful.'

'Training in communication and interpersonal skills.'

'Methodology of interpreting.'

An interesting discrepancy emerges when the responses concerning training are compared to the interpreters' self-assessment of their performance and the rating of their satisfaction levels with VCI/RI. Whilst self-assessment and satisfaction are impervious to the level of experience with VCI or RI, which would suggest that not much adaptation takes place, the perceived need for training drops with increasing experience, suggesting that an increased amount of experience may, after all, induce a subtle degree of comfort with the VC condition.

Apart from that, two conclusions emerge from scrutiny of the comments on training. Firstly, if training is necessary, then the other groups involved in the process – for instance, legal practitioners, police officers and court technicians – also require training, in addition to the interpreters. Secondly, there is a wide range of aspects – from practical to 'theoretical' – that interpreters would like to see included in training. Both the necessity for the training of legal practitioners as well as interpreters and the variety of points to be included in training are highlighted in Braun *et al.* in this volume.

4   CONCLUSIONS

This chapter has reported the findings from two surveys carried out in the AVIDICUS project, one among judicial institutions/legal practitioners and one among legal interpreters in Europe. Most of the 35 judicial institutions in Europe who responded to the survey reported that they use or plan to use video-based interpreting in criminal proceedings, either in their institution or at least in their countries, and they gave a variety of reasons for this. The interpreters' survey gathered 166 interpreters, mostly located in Europe, who had at least some experience with these forms of interpreting in criminal proceedings. Both surveys show that VCI is more common in Europe than RI but that both forms of interpreting are currently used at all stages of criminal proceedings.

The interpreters report many different experiences with regard to the settings in which they have encountered VCI or RI and the technological conditions under which they have worked. Accordingly, their views on video-based interpreting are extremely disparate, ranging from 'it doesn't have any good points' to 'everything is good'. The majority of the interpreters, however, have various doubts and anxieties in relation to video-mediated interpreting, which are not always known to, or acknowledged by, the judicial authorities.

Fragmentation of knowledge seems to be one of the biggest problems. A lack of knowledge on both sides can be identified with regard to the judicial institutions' reasons for the use of VCI and RI and the difficulties of video-based interpreting. Judicial institutions may have a range of reasons for using VCI and RI, but the interpreters' perception is that they are mainly of a financial nature. Thus, interpreters feel threatened by the anticipated cost cuts. In terms of difficulties, judicial institutions were inclined to report 'no problems' without making it clear what the basis for this assessment was.

The legal practitioners' survey also shows that there is little by way of specific guidance for VCI and RI and that the technological basis (equipment and type of connection) varies widely. The latter may be partially responsible for the extremely mixed reactions to VCI and RI from both sides, which range from 'sound/picture quality needs drastic improvement' and 'technology is still rudimentary' to 'good points are sound quality and picture clarity'.

Furthermore, many interpreters feel excluded from the process of implementing VCI and RI that is under way in judicial institutions. This may have helped to shape the self-assessment of their performance and satisfaction with VCI and RI. The self-assessment is generally on the negative side, with the exception of the oldest age group. A noteworthy point is, however, that the majority of interpreters rated their own target text production more positively than their ability to understand the source text and to build a rapport with the other interlocutors. On the whole, VCI and RI are perceived as less motivating, more stressful, fatiguing and isolating than face-to-face interpreting.

Because the uses of VCI and RI vary significantly from country to country and, indeed, within individual countries and institutions, it is difficult to put together a clear and accurate picture of video-mediated interpreting in the criminal justice services, and to identify correlations between conditions of use and performance. However, the following major conclusions can be drawn with regard to the current and emerging uses of VCI and RI in criminal proceedings:

- There exists a wide variety of legal communication settings to which both interpreters and legal practitioners need to adapt if the implementation of videoconferencing facilities proceeds.
- This is complemented by a wide variety of technical standards among and within countries, which is likely to make this adaptation process unnecessarily difficult.
- In addition, the continued use of low-quality equipment and connections jeopardises both the quality of legal interpreting in video-based settings and the acceptance of video-mediated interpreting among interpreters and possibly also legal practitioners.
- There are a number of discrepancies between the views of legal practitioners/judicial services and interpreters. For example, whilst

judicial institutions cite a number of reasons for the implementation of VC-based interpreting solutions, interpreters mostly see these as a way to cut interpreting costs[3] and thus feel threatened.

- Although generally speaking the respondents from the judicial services accept that video-mediated interpreting is unlikely ever to be as good as face-to-face interpreting, the judicial services are, as expected, more willing to embrace video-mediated interpreting than the interpreters. This is obviously linked to demand but the lack of knowledge about interpreting and its challenges, which is apparent in the legal practitioners' survey, carries a danger that the difficulties of video-mediated interpreting are underestimated.

- The analysis of the interpreters' responses reveals a marked tension between objective (and obvious) difficulties of video-mediated interpreting and resistance to change on the part of some interpreters. Interpreters feel excluded from discussions about the implementation of VC facilities in judicial institutions. They perceive the use of video-based interpreting as a cost cutting exercise and fear pay losses. Some interpreters also fear a dogged dependence on the technology.

- There is a conspicuous absence of clear rules and procedures, guidelines or policies on the use of VCI and RI.

- This is coupled with a lack of knowledge, cross-fertilisation, dialogue and co-operation among the stakeholders and complemented by a lack of training in, and research into, video-based interpreting, especially in the area of legal interpreting.

Whilst judicial institutions have a vested interest in the use of videoconferencing technology to resolve current problems with the provision of legal interpreting, many interpreters are suspicious of this development. Their anxieties (fear of the unknown in the changing landscape of interpreting, fear of pay loss, increased dependency on technology), the feeling of exclusion from the decision-making and implementation process, and the prevalence of outdated, inadequate equipment in some institutions are only some of the most prominent factors that are likely to shape the interpreters' attitudes towards video-based interpreting.

Equally importantly, the interpreters' perception that video-mediated interpreting is part of an exercise to cut down on interpreting costs is in stark contrast with their experience that video-based interpreting is more demanding, stressful and fatiguing than face-to-face interpreting and that it

---

[3] Discrepancies between the views and attitudes of legal practitioners and interpreters with regard to interpreting are not unknown (Lee 2007 for telephone interpreting; Foley 2006 and Lee 2009 for traditional court interpreting; see also Pöchhacker 2000 for Public Service Interpreting in general).

would therefore, in some interpreters' view, command higher fees. Some interpreters thus see themselves as being caught in a vicious cycle, which may increase the negative attitudes.

Some caveats are in order. The two surveys presented can only provide snapshots of the current situation. This can be illustrated by the observation that the interpreters' responses often focus on a particular setting. There is a striking reluctance on the part of some interpreters to accept that some of the problems they encountered may have been due to the idiosyncrasies of a particular setting or piece of equipment.

Given the generally low level of experience with video-mediated interpreting, it is highly likely that some adaptation and familiarisation is yet to take place and that initial reports on problems are as 'exaggerated' as the oversimplified claim made by some legal practitioners, court clerks or other administrators that there are no problems at all. At the same time, the survey results suggest that adaptation cannot be expected to take place on a fast track. The initial VCI/RI experience that some interpreters in our sample had gained did not lead to a more positive perception of the VC situations. Only an increase in the general interpreting experience seemed to be able to achieve this.

The wealth of information derived from the two surveys has provided invaluable input for the development of the AVIDICUS recommendations (see Braun in this volume). However, the question of whether and to what extent video-mediated interpreting can be used in criminal proceedings cannot be answered – and the recommendations would be incomplete – without a thorough analysis of the actual interpreting quality and an assessment of its appropriateness in a legal context.

In other words, a crucial task for research is to disentangle the subjective perceptions and their sources from the actual performance and interpreting quality that can be achieved in video-based interpreting in criminal proceedings. The findings of the AVIDICUS comparative studies in this respect, which have also shaped the recommendations, are covered in several contributions in this volume.

What is urgently required at a political level is an informed dialogue between all parties involved. The narrow focus of some interpreters on their limited experience also goes to show that – in addition to research and dialogue – the current situation also requires much more awareness-raising, education and training to overcome misperceptions, close the knowledge gap and support long-term adaptation processes, if video-mediated interpreting is, in the final analysis, deemed to be adequate in a legal context. Suggestions for the training of the main stakeholder groups are made by Braun *et al.* in this volume.

5 REFERENCES

Angelelli, C. (2003). The interpersonal role of the interpreter in cross-cultural communication: a survey of conference, court and medical interpreters in the US, Canada and Mexico In Brunette, L. et al. (Eds) (2003). *The Critical Link 3. Interpreters in the Community*. Amsterdam: Benjamins, 15-26.

Foley, T. (2006). Lawyers and legal interpreters: Different clients, different culture. *Interpreting* 8:1, 97-104.

Lee, J. (2007). Telephone interpreting: seen from the interpreters' perspective. *Interpreting*, 9 (2), 231-252.

Lee, J. (2009). Conflicting views on court interpreting examined through surveys of legal professionals and court interpreters. *Interpreting* 11 (1), 35-56.

Martin, A. & Abril Martí, I. (2008). Community interpreter self-perception. A Spanish case study. In C. Valero-Garcés, C. & . Martin (Eds) (2008). *Crossing borders in community interpreting. Definitions and dilemmas*. Amsterdam: Benjamins, 203-230.

Martin, A. & Ortega Herráez J.M. (2009). Court interpreters' self perception. In R. de Pedro Ricoy, I.A. Perez & C.W.L. Wilson (Eds), *Interpreting and translating in public service settings: policy, practice, pedagogy*. Manchester: St. Jerome Publishings, pp.141-155.

Moser-Mercer, B. (2003). Remote interpreting: assessment of human factors and performance parameters. *Communicate!* Summer 2003. Available at http://www.aiic.net/ ViewPage. cfm/article879.htm.

Ortega Herráez, J.M. & Foulquié Rubio, A.I. (2008). Interpreting in police settings in Spain: Service providers' and interpreters' perspectives. In C. Valero-Garcés & A. Martin (Eds), *Crossing borders in community interpreting. Definitions and dilemmas*. Amsterdam: Benjamins, 123-146.

Pöchhacker, F. (2000). The Community Interpreter's task: self-perception and provider views. In: R. Roberts, S. Carr, D. Abraham and A. Dufour (Eds), *The Critical Link 2*: Amsterdam: Benjamins, 49-65.

Roziner, I. and Shlesinger, M. (2010). Much ado about something remote: Stress and performance in remote interpreting. *Interpreting*, 12 (2), 214–247.

AVIDICUS COMPARATIVE STUDIES – PART I: TRADITIONAL INTERPRETING AND REMOTE INTERPRETING IN POLICE INTERVIEWS

Sabine Braun and Judith L. Taylor

University of Surrey

1 INTRODUCTION

One of the major aims of the AVIDICUS project was to assess the viability and reliability of video-mediated interpreting in criminal proceedings from an interpreting perspective. There are already many instances of video-mediated interpreting in criminal proceedings (and other legal proceedings), and given the new European Directive on the rights to interpretation and translation in criminal proceedings,[1] which allows the use of video-conferencing to gain access to qualified legal interpreters, the extent of video-mediated interpreting in this area of justice is likely to rise. However, there is a dearth of systematic research in this area. To the best of our knowledge, no study has systematically investigated the quality of the interpreters' performance in video-mediated interpreting in criminal proceedings. In addition, research on video-mediated interpreting conducted in other areas has generated mixed findings, depending on the setting investigated and the research methods used (see Braun & Taylor's contribution on current practice in this volume for an overview).

Videoconferencing technology is often introduced in the judicial system to save costs. Sossin & Yetnikoff (2007: 248) argue (albeit with reference to immigration) that "questions of financial resources and structures" cannot be separated "from the question of fairness and reasonableness" of judicial decision-making. Procedural fairness is closely linked to the quality of the communication, and in national and transnational cases involving more than one language the quality of the interpretation is a crucial element.

A sufficient quality of interpreting performance must therefore be regarded as a *conditio sine qua non* for the use of video-mediated interpreting in criminal proceedings. The question of the viability of video-

---

[1] Directive 2010/64/EU of the European Parliament and of the Council on the right to interpretation and translation in criminal proceedings. Available at http://www.europarl.europa.eu/oeil/ file.jsp?id=5840482. See also Morgan (in this volume).

mediated interpreting must override all considerations of potential financial savings, especially if it turns out that the use of video-mediated interpreting changes the proceedings beyond what is acceptable to ensure procedural fairness.

At the same time, the potential benefits of videoconferencing, when appropriately used, must not be cursorily dismissed, especially at a time when the European effort to strengthen the rights of European citizens to translation and interpreting in criminal proceedings and the ensuing likely growth of demand for legal interpreting in Europe coincide – and sometimes compete – with financial constraints imposed on Public Service institutions.

It was with a view to the absence of research-based guidance and in anticipation of the increasing use of video-mediated interpreting in criminal proceedings that the AVIDICUS project set out to investigate the quality of interpreting in such circumstances. After reviewing current and planned uses of video-mediated interpreting in a number of European countries and identifying those settings in the justice sphere in which the use of videoconferencing in connection with interpreting is most likely (see Braun & Taylor's contribution on the AVIDICUS surveys in this volume), the project consortium designed a series of experiments to compare the quality of traditional interpreting in such settings with different forms of video-mediated interpreting.

The present chapter focuses on part I of this comparative study, the part conducted by the University of Surrey. However, section 2 will first of all give an overview of the study as a whole, including its rationale, aim and the overall approach. Section 3 will outline the specific aims and the theoretical framework of the study conducted by the University of Surrey, section 4 will describe the methodology used for this part of the study, section 5 will present the major findings, and section 6 will conclude this chapter.

2   THE AVIDICUS COMPARATIVE STUDIES

As was pointed out in Section 1, the rationale behind the comparative studies was that interpreting quality is the key to any conclusion regarding the usability of video-based interpreting in criminal justice. The studies were conducted at three test sites (Surrey – Great Britain; Antwerp/Utrecht – Belgium/Netherlands and Warsaw – Poland).

The AVIDICUS comparative studies have distinguished two forms of video-mediated interpreting: Videoconference interpreting (VCI) is the form of interpreting that is used when the proceedings take place at two different locations (e.g. court and prison) that are video-linked, with the interpreter being situated either at the main site (variant A) or at the site of the other-language speaker (variant B). Remote interpreting (RI) is the form of interpreting that is used when the proceedings take place at a single location

(e.g. a courtroom), with the interpreter working via video link from a remote
location (e.g. another courthouse).

The aim of the studies was to provide a quantitative and qualitative
assessment of the interpreting performance in criminal proceedings that
involve a video link (either to link two judicial locations or to link a judicial
location and an interpreter). The focus was on the identification of critical
instances in the interpretations.

Given the lack of an agreed research method for this novel area of
research, it was decided to adopt an eclectic approach to the collection and
analysis of the data, albeit with a common core, which consisted of the
following elements:

1. All studies should be comparative in nature, comparing one or more
   forms of video-mediated interpreting with traditional face-to-face
   interpreting in the same setting.
2. All studies would be based on simulations, using legal practitioners,
   legal interpreters and role players as suspects or witnesses.
3. The focus should be on the early stages of proceedings, because it had
   been found that the small body of research on video-mediated
   interpreting in a legal context had focused on court proceedings (see
   Braun & Taylor's overview of current practice in this volume).
4. A further reason for focussing on the early stages of proceedings was
   that these stages were anticipated to require increased attention in the
   near future because of the reinforced right to translation and
   interpreting in criminal proceedings, as reflected in the new EU
   Directive.[2]
5. The focus should be on small-group communication as a first step
   before testing more complex settings such as court proceedings.

In line with these premises, the following research designs were used:

- The **Surrey site** conducted an in-depth comparison of traditional face-
  to-face interpreting and remote interpreting, using a police interview
  setting and comparing eight instances of each type of interpreting,
  resulting in a total of 16 interpreting sessions (see sections 3-5 below).
- The **Antwerp/Utrecht site** expanded the comparison to include face-
  to-face interpreting, remote interpreting and videoconference inter-

---

[2]   In addition to the directive on the right to translation and interpreting in criminal
proceedings, the European 'Roadmap for strengthening procedural rights of suspected or
accused persons in criminal proceedings' (see Morgan in this volume) also foresees further
rights, such as the right to legal aid and the right to information, whose implementation
may have an impact on the extent of interpreting services needed especially in the early
stages of criminal proceedings.

preting variants A and B. The setting was also a police interview, and four instances of each were compared, resulting in a total of 16 interpreting sessions (see Balogh & Hertog in this volume).

- The **Warsaw** site compared traditional face-to-face interpreting and the two forms of videoconference interpreting (variant A and B) in a prosecution setting, comparing 3 instances of each, i.e. a total of nine instances (see Miler-Cassino and Rybińska in this volume).

Thus, each of the three relevant forms of video-mediated interpreting was covered at two sites, with a combination of different small-group communication settings (police and prosecution). A total of 41 interpreting sessions was conducted, of which 12 included remote interpreting, 14 used the two variants of videoconference interpreting and 15 involved face-to-face interpreting. All sessions were video-recorded, transcribed, and then analysed quantitatively and qualitatively, using the transcripts and video recordings. The analysis was based on a set of analysis criteria drawn from research into interpreting quality, verbal, non-verbal and visual communication. In addition, semi-structured interviews with the participants were conducted to elicit further qualitative data.

Distinctions were made with regard to the focus of comparison. Since remote interpreting (RI) is perceived by many interpreters to be the most difficult form of video-based interpreting (see Braun & Taylor's contributions on current practice and on the AVIDICUS surveys in this volume), it was decided to conduct one in-depth study on this form of interpreting (Surrey). Moreover, the study of RI is important because it may be the form that is in highest demand, especially in the initial stages of criminal proceedings (interviews with suspects, witnesses), but also in other settings (e.g. healthcare). At the same time, a comparison of all forms of video-mediated interpreting was envisaged, hence the studies in Antwerp and Warsaw. These studies took into account the need for cross-border videoconferencing with distributed participants, and focused on different settings (police and prosecution interviews [at pre-trial stage], see Balogh & Hertog and Miler-Casino & Rybińska in this volume respectively).

3   THE SURREY STUDY: AIM AND THEORETICAL FRAMEWORK

The specific aim of this part of the comparative study was an in-depth analysis of the interpreting quality in police interviews with suspects involving remote interpreting compared to the interpreting quality in interviews using traditional interpreting, in order to assess the viability of remote interpreting in the context of criminal justice.

The study drew on a variety of complementary theoretical frameworks relating to communication, interpreting and videoconferencing. Using a genre-based approach to communication, the police interview with a suspect is conceptualised here as a purpose-driven communicative event with specific goals and hence specific moves and 'rules' (see e.g. Berk-Seligson 2009 and Rombouts in this volume). This implies that whilst there are different types of interview, core elements such as eliciting a suspect's version of events and asking in-depth questions constitute common 'moves' in most suspect interviews. Furthermore, police interviews are understood here as instances of dyadic, i.e. two-way communication, following basic rules of communication management, especially rules of turn-taking and alignment of the participants (Sacks *et al.* 1974; Goffmann 1981, Gumperz 1982; Schiffrin 1994), which contribute to the meaning and the dynamics of the communication.

The use of an interpreter in a police interview inevitably changes the dynamics of the interview to a certain extent, for two reasons. The first and perhaps most obvious of these is that the type of interpreting normally required in police interviews, i.e. two-way consecutive interpreting, is a type of interpreting that gives the interpreter relatively high 'visibility' (compared to e.g. simultaneous conference interpreting, where the interpreter works in a booth). Two-way consecutive interpreting is therefore normally perceived as a 'triadic' situation with specific patterns of communication management, and the interpreter has been shown to play an important part in the alignment of the participants and the coordination of the talk in such situations (Wadensjö 1998; Mason 1999, 2001).

The other reason for the change in the dynamics of the communication is that interpreting is a highly strategic cognitive-linguistic process of discourse comprehension and production (Alexieva 1998; Gile 1991, 1993; Kohn & Kalina 1996; Kalina 1998; Mead 2002; Braun 2004; Riccardi 2005) in which the interpreter forms his/her (own) understanding of the source text and produces his/her version of this in the target language. In other words, each interpreter will produce a different version. Due to the cognitive complexity of interpreting, involving multitasking (Gile 1991, 1993) and rapid decision-making (Alexieva 1998), interpreters often work at the limit of their mental capacity and have to act highly strategically to balance different requirements such as the accuracy and completeness of the message, the appropriateness of expression and register, and the fluency and timeliness of delivery. At the same time, the specific requirements of legal interpreting (see e.g. Berk-Seligson 1990, 2009; Hale 2007, Hertog 2001, 2003; Kadric 2001; Mikkelson 2000; see also Braun in this volume), for example, in terms of accuracy and completeness, impose constraints on the use of some common interpreting strategies, especially coping strategies such as generalisations or omissions of parts of the message. Legal interpreting commands special emphasis on achieving accuracy, completeness and avoidance of misunderstandings, e.g. through asking for clarification of meaning. It also requires the accurate reproduction of different registers and of features of the source text delivery, since the choice of register (e.g. colloquial language) may be as meaningful in a legal context as a stutter or hesitant delivery. Any potential change in the dynamics or meaning of the communication needs to be minimised.

Prior research suggests, however, that in video-mediated communication and video-mediated interpreting it may be even more difficult than in traditional interpreting situations to grasp and relay meaning reliably and that the technological mediation may change the dynamics of the communication even further, depending, for example, on the distribution of the interlocutors and the interpreter (see Braun & Taylor's overview of current practice in this volume for an overview of prior research on video-mediated communication and interpreting).

What was unknown prior to commencing this study was to what extent traditional and video-mediated legal interpreting would differ in terms of quality, and whether video-mediated legal interpreting would be reliable enough especially for evidential purposes (see also Corsellis 2006). These were the major research questions of the study reported here.

The challenge was to develop a methodology that would enable the researchers to isolate those problems of video-mediated interpreting that are specifically caused by the technological mediation rather than by the challenges of legal interpreting or interpreting as such. To this end, a comparative study was designed, and existing approaches to assessing interpreting quality (Kalina 2002, 2005; Kurz, 2001, Pöchhacker 1994, Shlesinger 1997) were adapted to suit the needs of assessing the quality of interpreter performance in video-meditated interpreting in a legal context. One aspect that was given particular attention was prior work on non-verbal and visual communication in the context of interpreting (Bühler 1985; Poyatos 1997; see also Knapp & Hall 2009[5]). The role of this prior work and the category system derived from it will be explained in the following section, which outlines the research methodology used in the Surrey study.

4 METHOD

4.1 Informants and design of the study

The study was based on a simulation of police interviews. It involved

- eight experienced legal interpreters working between French and English,3 all with a minimum of five years experience interpreting in police interviews,
- three English police officers with experience in working with interpreters,
- two French native speakers in the role of a 'detainee'

---

[3] All but one of the interpreters were native speakers of French.

Two interview scripts were used, one based on a case of physical assault, another based on fraud and obtaining money by deception. The scripts were based on anonymised records of real police interviews from two police constabularies in England.

The interpretation was delivered sequentially in short-consecutive mode. Each interpreter worked with one interview in the face-to-face session and another one in the videoconference session. The two interviews were used as shown in the test matrix in Table 1.

Interpreter	1	2	3	4	5	6	7	8
Traditional interpreting interview script:	A	B	A	B	A	B	A	B
Remote interpreting interview script:	B	A	B	A	B	A	B	A

Table 1: Test matrix

In the traditional setting, the police officer and the detainee faced each other, and the interpreter sat next to the detainee, as is common practice in police interviews in England (see Figure 1).

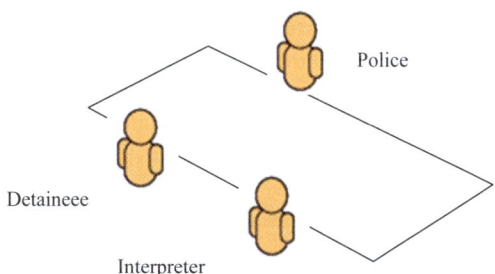

Figure 1: Seating order in the face-to-face sessions

In the interviews that involved a video link between the interview room and the interpreter, an Access Grid videoconference system, based on H.264 standard, with high-quality sound, boom microphones and four cameras was used. In the interview room, the images were projected onto a wall. In the interpreter's room, a 19" screen flat screen, one camera and a table microphone were used. Although the interpretation was consecutive, the interpreters wore a headset to ensure good sound quality and to avoid disturbances.

The police officer and the detainee, who were in the 'interview room', faced each other, as in the face-to-face interviews. The wall onto which the video images were projected was perpendicular to them. All participants saw the following (see Figure 2): an overview of the interview room with police officer and detainee, a close-up of the police officer and the detainee, and a close-up of the interpreter. However, the interpreters were able to choose whether or not they wanted to see their own image. Some interpreters chose not to see it, which led to problems during the session (see below).

Police officer 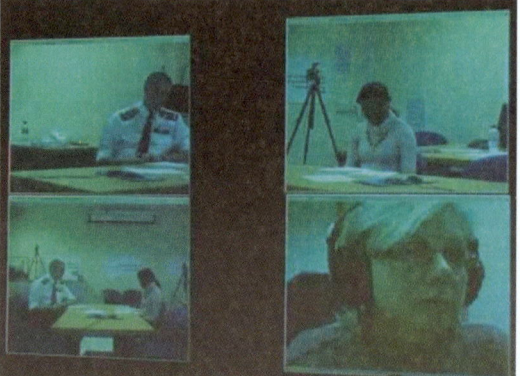 Detainee

Overview of
Police officer
and detainee

Interpreter

Figure 2: View on the videoconference screen

4.2   Data collection and analysis

Video recordings of interviews were made in the 'interview room', using two camcorders. A total of eight hours of interpreting were recorded and subsequently transcribed, amounting to a data corpus of 67,000 words. In addition, the participating interpreters and police officers completed a pre-session questionnaire and were interviewed after their sessions to elicit their views on how the sessions went.

Based on Kalina's (2002) criteria for the assessment of interpreting performances, a comprehensive category system which mainly refers to conference interpreting, a set of analysis categories was developed which included categories that were adapted to two-way consecutive interpreting in a legal context. Moreover, categories for the analysis of non-verbal and visual communication were added. The following steps were carried out in the analysis:

1.   The two police interviews were divided into genre 'moves', i.e. small, meaningful units of interaction, including:

    1.   Introduction
    2.   Caution
    3.   Preliminary Enquiries
    4.   Suspect's version
    5.   Police Officer's in-depth questions
    6.   Conclusion of the interview

2. As stated above, a category for the analysis of communication problems and interpreting quality was devised, including:

   - Language-based categories, e.g., omissions, additions, inaccuracies, lexical/terminological problems, turn-taking problems
   - Non-verbal and visual categories, e.g. problems with gaze, being out of shot

3. Using these categories, the interviews were coded by three raters. A final agreement was achieved in discussions between them.
4. A quantitative analysis was carried out, i.e. a comparison between data from face-to-face and remote interpreting.
5. An additional qualitative analysis was conducted to assess the scale of the emerging problem areas and identify critical instances.
6. The data were triangulated with the survey results and post-test comments made by the interpreters and police officers.

The following section reports the main results of the study.

5   MAIN RESULTS

5.1   Overview: quantification of problems

The quantitative analysis of the 16 interviews (8 in face-to-face mode and 8 in remote mode; 67000 words in total) in terms of the major categories of problems resulted in the breakdown shown in Table 2.

	Face-to-face interpreting (FTF)	Remote interpreting (RI)	RI / FTF FTF=100%
Inaccuracies	89 (11.1)	110 (13.8)	124%
Omissions	68 (8.5)	108 (13.5)	159%
Additions	10 (1.3)	29 (3.6)	290%
Linguistic problems: lexis/terminology, idiomaticity, grammar, style/ register, coherence, language mixing	204 (25.5)	260 (32.5)	127%
Paralinguistic problems 1: articulation, hesitation, repetition	316 (39.5)	417 (52.1)	132%
Paralinguistic problems 2: false start, self-repair	261 (32.6)	287 (34.9)	110%
Synchronisation problems (turn-taking)	34 (4.3)	110 (13.8)	324%

Table 2: Distribution of problems (in brackets: average per interview)

The focus of the analysis categories was in line with the priorities of the specific requirements of legal interpreting as outlined in Section 3. Among the major categories were, therefore, for example, omissions, additions and inaccuracies. The expectation was that the number of problems would be higher in remote interpreting in all of these categories, and this expectation was confirmed by the analysis, albeit to varying degrees. In the category of inaccuracies, for example, the difference between the two forms of interpreting seems to be small, with 89 inaccuracies in traditional interpreting and 110 in remote interpreting. However, an in-depth analysis of the instances in this category revealed a number of important differences, as shown in Table 3.

	FTF	RI	RI / FTF FTF=100%
Distortions	19 (2.4)	38 (4.8)	200%
Minor shifts	15 (1.9)	15 (1.9)	100%
Minor other inaccuracies	43 (5.4)	40 (5.0)	93%
Inaccurate names and numbers	12 (1.5)	17 (2.1)	142%
Total	89 (11.1)	110 (13.8)	124%

Table 3: Distribution of different types of inaccuracies (in brackets: average per interview)

Distortions, the most problematic of all of the 'inaccuracy' categories, were twice as frequent in remote interpreting. On average, each interview that used remote interpreting contained five major distortions. They were mainly caused by one more of the following:[4]

- Conceptual misunderstandings of what was said:

  PO: I want you to confirm what happened.
  INTP: Je voudrais vous en parler.
         I would like to talk to you about this.

- Mishearings:

  DET: Elle m'accusait devant tout le monde.
         She was accusing me in front of everybody.
  INTP: And she was abusing me in front of everybody.

---

[4]   PO = police officer; INTP = interpreter; DET = detainee; in italics: English gloss.

- Misrenderings, i.e. apparently correct understanding but wrong rendition:

  PO: This is the rule that was <u>seized</u> today.
  INTP: C'est donc la règle qui a été <u>utilisée</u> aujourd'hui.
  This is the rule that was <u>used</u> today.

- Misrepresentation of the speaker's intentions:

  PO: Is there anything else you want to know before we start?
  INTP: Est-ce que vous voulez, euh, est-ce que vous me comprenez bien? Est-ce que vous m'entendez bien?
  Would you like, uh, can you understand me well? Can you hear me well?

- Summary renditions:

  PO: Then I said, 'The people at the cab office said you did [hit Ms Jones]'.
  INTP: Ensuite-, ensuite, euh, j'ai dit, euh, ce que les employés à la station de taxi ont dit.
  Then, then, uh, I said, uh, what the employees at the taxi stand said.

The in-depth analysis of other categories such as omissions and additions shows a similar picture. Given the specific requirements of legal interpreting, the problems identified in this study seem to put constraints on the use of video-mediated interpreting in criminal proceedings. At least, it would seem reasonable to restrict its use to the simplest cases of low impact crime until further knowledge has been gained, for example, about how the design of videoconference systems and the training of interpreters and legal practitioners may help to reduce the problems currently arising (see also van Rotterdam & van den Hoogen and Esteban Causo in this volume on system design, and Braun in this volume on recommendations for the use of video-mediated interpreting in criminal proceedings).

5.2   Correlations between categories

Some types of problem had a tendency to co-occur with other types of problems. In particular, there was a strong correlation between turn-taking problems and omissions, and this correlation was stronger in RI. Thus, as shown in Table 4, only 3 of the 34 turn-taking problems identified in FTF (i.e. 9%) entailed an omission in the target text, whilst as a conservative estimate at least 16 of the 110 turn-taking problems identified in RI (i.e. 15%) caused an omission in the target text. In most of these cases, the omission went unnoticed and therefore led to a loss of information.

	FTF	RI
Omissions	68	108
Turn-taking problems	34	110
Turn-taking problems with omission	3	16
Proportion of all omissions	4%	15%
Proportion of all turn-taking problems	9%	15%

Table 4: Correlation between turn-taking problems and omissions

The most common type of turn-taking problem, and the source of all related omissions as shown above, was overlapping speech between the interpreter and one of the primary interlocutors, as in the following example (the square brackets indicate overlapping speech):

> DET: Et je travaillais à H et M l'année passée, à [mi-temps.]
> *And I worked part-time for H and M last year.*
> INTP: [Last year], I, I worked with H and M.

The interpreter uses a common interpreting strategy here. She begins to interpret while a primary interlocutor (here the detainee) is still talking but about to complete his/her utterance. In traditional police interpreting, this technique saves time in the communication and is also an efficient way for the interpreter to gain the floor, i.e. to indicate directly that she wants the detainee to stop. In the interviews that were interpreted via video link this did not work so effectively, because overlapping speech normally caused disruption and uncertainty.

Similar problems with overlapping speech in dialogue interpreting via video link were also found by Braun (2004, 2007) and in the 2010 Virtual Court pilot in England (Ministry of Justice 2010). The recurrence of overlapping speech in different settings[5] and its potentially serious consequences suggest that the avoidance of overlapping speech is a particularly important aspect for guidelines and training.

---

[5] Unlike the present study, interpreting in the Virtual Court pilot is an instance of 'videoconference interpreting' with two participant locations and the interpreter being at one of these. However, the mode of interpreting used in the Virtual Courts is consecutive, as in the present study. By contrast, Braun's (2004/2007) setting involved three locations: The primary interlocutors were at two different locations, and the interpreter was at a third location, and the mode used was simultaneous interpreting. In spite of the simultaneous mode, overlapping speech occurred in this setting, for example, when the interlocutors talked over the interpreter, believing that s/he had completed rendering the previous speaker's turn, whilst the interpreter just paused.

5.3 Distribution of problems on a timeline

Another part of the analysis focused on the distribution of interpreting problems on a timeline. For this purpose, the interpreting problems in each genre move were counted separately, as shown in Figure 3 below.

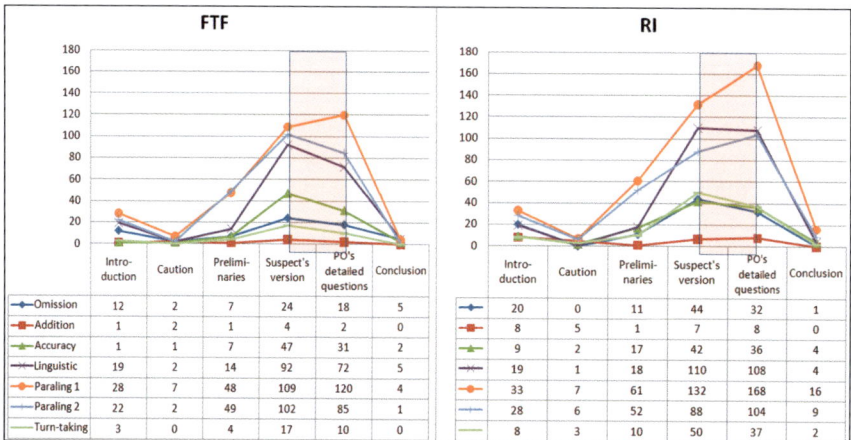

FTF	Intro-duction	Caution	Prelimi-naries	Suspect's version	PO's detailed questions	Conclusion
Omission	12	2	7	24	18	5
Addition	1	2	1	4	2	0
Accuracy	1	1	7	47	31	2
Linguistic	19	2	14	92	72	5
Paraling 1	28	7	48	109	120	4
Paraling 2	22	2	49	102	85	1
Turn-taking	3	0	4	17	10	0

RI	Intro-duction	Caution	Prelimi-naries	Suspect's version	PO's detailed questions	Conclusion
Omission	20	0	11	44	32	1
Addition	8	5	1	7	8	0
Accuracy	9	2	17	42	36	4
Linguistic	19	1	18	110	108	4
Paraling 1	33	7	61	132	168	16
Paraling 2	28	6	52	88	104	9
Turn-taking	8	3	10	50	37	2

Figure 3: Interpreting problems on a timeline in traditional face-to-face interpreting (FTF) and remote interpreting (RI) in the simulated police interviews

What can be seen at first glance is an increase in interpreting problems towards the middle of interviews. However, since the genre moves at the beginning and end (introduction, caution and conclusion) were much shorter than the moves in the middle, this is not surprising. The interesting point is the second observation: At the transition from the genre move entitled 'Suspect's version' to the move entitled 'PO's detailed questions' (highlighted in Figure 3), the number of problems in face-to-face interpreting drops in most categories or at least stops rising steeply (paralinguistic problems 1). By contrast, in the interviews using remote interpreting, the problems in some of the categories (paralinguistic problems 1, omissions and additions) continued to rise, and in the case of the paralinguistic problems, the increase is steep. In other words, the patterns in the two sets of data begin to diverge in the second half of the interview. In the sessions using remote interpreting, the number of problems does not drop as much as in the sessions using traditional interpreting.

Gile (2009) and Mead (2002) have pointed out that paralinguistic problems are often indicative of other, underlying problems with the interpreter' processing capacity. Given the feedback from the interpreters in the comment sessions and also the responses of interpreters to the AVIDICUS survey among legal interpreters (see Braun & Taylor in this volume), the likeliest reason for the steeper increase of problems in remote interpreting in the second half of the interviews is the onset of fatigue half way through the interview.

Given that the simulated sessions were on average 30 minutes long, the findings suggest that problems may arise with the interpreting performance in a real-life situation unless the communication is of very short duration. This result becomes even more critical in view of the differences in length between face-to-face and video-based sessions, which will be reported in the following section.

5.4   Length of interviews and word count

On average, the interviews conducted using remote interpreting were 19% longer than the interviews using traditional face-to-face interpreting. By contrast, the word count of the two sets of interviews was not significantly different, with the result that the average speech rate in the interviews conducted using remote interpreting is lower than the speech rate in the face-to-face sessions.

Word count	FTF	RI	RI / FTF FTF=100%
Total number of words	32681	33931	104%
Police officer	6783	7106	105%
Detainee	8325	8397	101%
Interpreter	17573	18428	105%
Length of interviews in minutes	193	230	119%
Average speech rate (words per minute)	170	147	87%

Table 5: Basic statistics of the interviews

The lower speech rate in the video-based sessions, i.e. the fact that the participants spoke more slowly and/or made more frequent pauses, may have been caused in part by frequent instances of speaking louder than in the face-to-face sessions. Judging by the number of problems in the video-based sessions, however, neither the lower speech rate nor the interlocutors' tendency to speak louder seems to have helped the interpreters with their interpreting task. Conversely, the rise in the number of problems in the second half of the video-based sessions, suggests that the lower speech rate in connection with a raised voice may even have been more tiring for the interpreters to listen to than the more naturally flowing speech in the face-to-face sessions.

Furthermore, whilst the lower speech rate goes some way to explain the longer duration of the video-based sessions, it may not have been the only reason. A more detailed qualitative analysis of the data shows that the video-based sessions also required what Olson, Olson & Meader (1997: 170) called a greater "process overhead", for example to coordinate the communication or to resolve comprehension problems. This would explain why all groups of participants used a slightly higher number of words in the video-mediated sessions. Braun (2004, 2007) also found that videoconference participants (in interpreted videoconferences) were repetitive, their speech marked by redundant expressions. This finding was not replicated by the present study, but it may be argued that the tendency to use redundant expressions was constrained by the fact that the police officers and detainees followed a script. Further research will be required to show whether different conditions will produce more redundant speech in video-mediated criminal proceedings, or whether the communication genres that are relevant in criminal proceedings will counteract this tendency.

In any case, the clear differences in length suggest that the video-based sessions were on the whole less efficient than the face-to-face sessions. This is corroborated by a number of other observations which are more difficult to quantify. Some of these will be discussed in following section.

5.5   Dynamics of the communication

One problem area that is much more difficult to quantify in a meaningful way is the dynamics of the communication. This includes the ways in which turn-taking is co-ordinated, but it is not confined to this. Another important dimension of the dynamics of the communication is the 'rapport' or communicative bond between interlocutors. As Gumperz (1982) has shown, the creation of rapport relies, for example, on the use of a variety of verbal and non-verbal signals (e.g. a quick glance at an important point in the conversation to check whether the message has been understood), and on the addressee's well-timed reactions to such signals (e.g. meeting someone else's quick glance as a way of confirming understanding). When successful, such signals may promote cooperation, agreement and common understanding. By implication, a lack of rapport can contribute to misunderstandings or at least make communication more difficult.

In a videoconference, some of the rapport-creating signals seem to be more difficult to employ effectively, and timely reactions to each other seem to be more difficult to achieve. In particular, gaze and eye contact are very difficult to control even with the best possible positioning of cameras and screens. In one of the interviews conducted using remote interpreting, for example, the interpreter hesitated when rendering the charge. She appears to be searching for the correct expression. The police officer noticed the pause and looked at the screed towards the interpreter, but seemed unable to detect that the interpreter had a problem. After a short while, he continued his utterance without giving the interpreter enough time to complete her interpretation.

To return to turn-taking, Wadensjö (1998) has argued that the way in which the interpreter controls the floor can be seen as more or less cooperative and hence can either strengthen or weaken the communicative bonds. If the interpreter succeeds, for example, in starting to speak while the detainee is completing his or her sentence, and in using this to indicate very 'gently' to the detainee that s/he should stop talking, this is a good communicative achievement, as it avoids disruption and 'fighting' for the floor. However, as was noted in Section 5.2, there were problems with this strategy because of the general problems with overlapping speech in videoconferences. At the same time, another common strategy used by interpreters to gain the floor, raising their hand, also failed at times, because the interpreter's hand was out of shot (one interpreter in particular had chosen not to see her own image and therefore had no control over whether or not her hand was captured by the camera). The only solution for the interpreter to stop a speaker was, therefore, often to intervene verbally. This caused considerable disruption in places, because the interpreter had to raise his/her voice in order to be noticed, with the likely result that the interpreter was perceived as uncooperative or even incompetent.

Furthermore, the problem mentioned in Section 5.4, that the interlocutors, especially the police officers, often raised their voices, is also likely to have an impact on the overall dynamics of the communicative situation, as is the fact that because of the room layout used in this study (officer and detainee facing each other, screen perpendicular to them),[6] the officer and the detainee often looked towards the screen (i.e. towards the interpreter) rather than at each other. The possible impact of these problems on the dynamics and the outcome of the communication as well as the extent to which the interlocutors are able to adapt their behaviour have to be investigated further.[7] In the meantime, it will be important to make reference to such problems in guidelines and training.

6 CONCLUSIONS

Broadly speaking, remote interpreting was found to magnify known problems of (legal) interpreting to a certain extent. This includes linguistic and cultural problems (terminological issues, culture-bound references) as well as problems associated with an overload of the interpreter's cognitive processing capacity (e.g. paralinguistic problems such as hesitations and repairs). As a consequence, the number of serious interpreting problems (e.g. omissions, additions, distortions, lexical/terminological problems, para-

---

[6] This layout was chosen, because it is currently being implemented at the interpreter hubs of the Metropolitan Police Service in London, and will therefore be used in real-life situations soon.

[7] These aspects are currently being investigated in AVIDICUS II (EU DG Justice grant, JUST/2010/ JPEN/AG/1558, 2011-2013).

linguistic problems, turn-taking problems) was higher in remote interpreting compared to face-to-face interpreting. Furthermore, a range of additional problems for the interpreter were observed including, for example, problems with gaze and eye contact, sound and listening comprehension, communication management and the co-ordination of the talk, and rapport with the remote interlocutors.

In line with prior research on remote conference interpreting by Moser-Mercer (2003), the number of problems was found to increase faster during the videoconference sessions than in the face-to-face sessions, suggesting an earlier onset of fatigue of the interpreter.

One of the dilemmas was that familiar interpreting strategies (e.g. the use of visual signs to control the floor), did not always work well in the videoconference situation, whilst their replacement by other strategies (e.g. verbal intervention) seemed to be disruptive or to cause uncertainty.

To interpret these findings, the limitations of the studies have to be borne in mind. Firstly, the study is based on simulations, because real-life data were not available at the time of conducting this research. However, there are also a number of advantages associated with the use of simulations, e.g. the control of variables, which was an advantage at the present stage of the research. Another possible limitation was the use of scripts in the simulations, which meant that interpreting problems did not always have real consequences because the participants tended to return to the given storyline even if it had been distorted by an inaccurate or incomplete interpretation. However, the initial problems could still be analysed, making it possible to extrapolate the scale of problems in real-life situations.

The small size of the sample makes it difficult to assess (and calculate) the significance of the differences found between the two forms of interpreting and puts a limitation on the validity of the findings, although the general trend is that remote interpreting is more difficult and creates more problems than traditional face-to-face interpreting. One further limitation is that only one language pair was involved. However, the other partners in the AVIDICUS Project carrying out comparative studies used different language pairs and came to similar conclusions (see Balogh & Hertog and Miler-Cassino & Rybińska in this volume).

Moreover, this study has focused on one particular setting, a police interview, which is normally highly regulated and formulaic. It remains to be seen what kind of (additional or different) problems other, less regulated settings such as lawyer consultations would generate.

Finally, the analysis in this study has focused on interpreting quality as such. This is only one step on the way to a more comprehensive assessment of the viability of video-mediated criminal proceedings that involve an interpreter. What needs to be analysed in future are further possible changes in the dynamics of the communication beyond the changes described in

Section 5.5, and the potential impact of such changes on the specific goals of the communication in criminal proceedings.

REFERENCES

AIIC (2000). Guidelines for the use of new technologies in conference interpreting. *Communicate!* March-April 2000. Available at http://www.aiic.net/ViewPage.cfm?page_id=120.

Alexieva, B. (1998). Consecutive interpreting as a decision process. In A. Beylard-Ozeroff, J. Králová & B. Moser-Mercer (Eds.), *Translators' strategies and creativity*. Amsterdam: Benjamins, 181-188.

Berk-Seligson, S. (1990). *The bilingual courtroom: court interpreters in the judicial process*. Chicago: University of Chicago Press.

Berk-Seligson, S. (2009). *Coerced Confessions: the discourse of bilingual police interrogations*. New York: Mouton de Gruyter.

Braun, S. (2004). *Kommunikation unter widrigen Umständen? Fallstudien zu einsprachigen und gedolmetschten Videokonferenzen*. Tübingen: Narr.

Braun, S. (2007). Interpreting in small-group bilingual videoconferences: challenges and adaptation processes. *Interpreting* 9 (1), 21-46.

Bühler, H., (1985). Conference interpreting: a multichannel communication phenomenon. *Meta* 30 (1), 49-54.

Corsellis, A. (2006). Making sense of reality. *Linguistica Antverpiensia* 5/2006, 341-350.

Finn, K, Sellen, A. & Wilbur, S. (Eds.) (1997). *Video-mediated communication.* Mahwah, NJ: Erlbaum.

Gile, D. (1991). The processing capacity issue in conference interpretation. *Babel 37* (1), 15-27.

Gile, D. (1993). *Translation/interpretation and knowledge*. In Y. Gambier, &J. Tommola (Eds.), 67-86.

Gile, D. (2009). *Basic Concepts and Models for Interpreter and Translator Training*. Amsterdam: Benjamins.

Goffman, E. (1981). *Forms of Talk*. Pennsylvania: University of Pennsylvania Press.

Gumperz, J. (1982). *Discourse strategies*. Cambridge: CUP.

Hale, S. (2007). *Community Interpreting*. Basingstoke and New York: Palgrave Macmillan.

Hertog, E., (Ed.) (2001). *Aequitas Access to Justice across Language and Culture in the EU*. Antwerp: Lessius University College. Available at http://www.agisproject.com.

Hertog, E., (Ed.) (2003). *Aequalitas Equal Access to Justice across Language and Culture in the EU*. Antwerp: Lessius University College. Available at http://www.agisproject.com.

Kadric, M. (2001). *Dolmetschen bei Gericht: Erwartungen, Anforderungen, Kompetenzen*. Vienna: WUV, Universitätsverlag.

Kalina, S. (1998), *Strategische Prozesse beim Dolmetschen. Theoretische Grundlagen, empirische Untersuchungen, didaktische Konsequenzen,* Language in Performance 18. Tübingen, Gunter Narr.

Kalina, S. (2002). Quality in interpreting and its prerequisites. In C. Garzone & M. Viezzi (Eds.), *Interpreting in the 21st Century: challenges and opportunities*. Amsterdam: Benjamins, 121-130.

Kalina, S. (2005). Quality Assurance for Interpreting Processes. *Meta* 50 (2), 768-784.

Knapp, M. & Hall, J. (2009). *Nonverbal Communication in Human Interaction. (5th ed.)* Wadsworth: Thomas Learning.

Kohn, K. & S. Kalina (1996). The strategic dimension of interpreting. *Meta* 42 (1), 118-138.

Kurz, I. (2001). Conference Interpreting: quality in the ears of the user. *Meta* 47 (2), 394-409.

Mason, I. (Ed.) (1999). *The Translator* 5 (2) (Special issue on dialogue interpreting).

Mason, I. (Ed.) (2001). *Triadic exchanges: studies in dialogue interpreting*. Manchester: St. Jerome.

Mead, P. (2002). Exploring hesitation in consecutive interpreting – an empirical study. In C. Gazone & M. Viezzi (Eds.), *Interpreting in the 21st century*. Amsteram: Benjamins, 73-82.

Mikkelson, H. (2000). *Introduction to court interpreting*. Manchester: St. Jerome.

Ministy of Justice (2010). *Virtual Court pilot Outcome evaluation*. Ministry of Justice Research Series 21/10. Available at http://www.justice.gov.uk/downloads/publications/research-and-analysis/moj-research/virtual-courts.pdf.

Moser-Mercer, B. (2003). Remote interpreting: assessment of human factors and performance parameters. *Communicate!* Summer 2003. Available at http://www.aiic.net/ViewPage. cfm/article879.htm.

Moser-Mercer, B. (2005). Remote interpreting: issues of multi-sensory integration in a multilingual task. *Meta* 50 (2), 727-738.

Mouzourakis, P. (2006). Remote interpreting: a technical perspective on recent experiments. *Interpreting* 8 (1), 45-66.

Olson, J., Olson, G. & Maeder, D. (1997). Face-to-face group work compared to remote group work. In K. Finn, A. Sellen & S. Wilbur (Eds.), *Video-mediated communication*. Mahwah, NJ: Erlbaum, 157–172.

Pöchhacker, F. (1994). *Simultandolmetschen als komplexes Handeln*. Tübingen: Narr.

Poyatos, F., (ed.) (1997). *Nonverbal Communication and Translation: New perspectives and challenges in literature, interpretation and the media*. Amsterdam: Benjamins.

Riccardi, A. (2005). On the evolution of interpreting strategies in simultaneous interpreting. *Meta* 50 (2), 753-767.

Sacks, H., Schegloff, E. & Jefferson, G. (1974). A simplest systematics for the organization of turn taking in conversation. *Language* 50 (4), 696-735.

Schiffrin, D. (1994). *Approaches to discourse*. Oxford & Cambridge, Mass.: Blackwell.

Shlesinger, M. (1997): Quality in simultaneous interpreting. In Y. Gambier, D. Gile & C. Taylor (Eds.), *Conference interpreting: current trends in research*. Amsterdam: Benjamins, 123-131.

Sossin, L. & Yetnikoff, Z. (2007). 'I can see clearly now': videoconference hearings and the legal limit on how tribunals allocate resources. *Windsor Yearbook of Access to Justice* 25 (2), 247-272.

Wadensjö, C. (1998). *Interpreting as interaction*. London: Longman.

AVIDICUS COMPARATIVE STUDIES – PART II: TRADITIONAL, VIDEOCONFERENCE AND REMOTE INTERPRETING IN POLICE INTERVIEWS

Katalin Balogh and Erik Hertog

Lessius University College

1   INTRODUCTION

The Belgian partners in the AVIDICUS project- Lessius University College, Antwerp, and the Antwerp Local Police – set up a number of contrastive experimental tests to observe and analyse the differences in performance and perception between Face to Face (FF), Videoconferencing (VCI) and Remote Interpreting (RI) in criminal proceedings.

There were three full testing days which will be reported on here. Two test days were hosted by the audio-visual centre of the University of Leuven, Belgium, on 1st (when 7 role plays carried out) and 25th February 2010 (when 5 recordings were made). The third test day (7th May 2010, 4 role plays recorded) was organized between Utrecht Court and Zeist Asylum Centre in the Netherlands. The four Belgian partners were present during the tests and were assisted by the on-site technical staff of the host institutions.

The test corpus consists of sixteen role plays of about 25 to 30 minutes each, between Dutch-speaking officials (in this case police officers) and Hungarian-speaking suspects or witnesses. Four role plays were interpreted using traditional face-to-face interpreting (FF), four were of the videoconference interpreting A type (VCI A, i.e. the interpreter sits with the police, the suspect/defendant is in another location); four were videoconference interpreting type B role plays (VCI B, i.e. the interpreter is in the same location as the other language speaker while the police officer is in a different location) and four were remote interpreting settings (RI; i.e. the interpreter is on his or her own, in a different location from the other participants, both the police officer and the suspect or witness).

The topics of the role plays were taken from real-life police interviews and dealt with four situations: police questioning of someone suspected of credit-card fraud; interview of a suspect of human trafficking; interview of a witness to a hold-up in a hotel, and finally, questioning of a suspect of criminal conspiracy. The role plays were not scripted - there was no fixed script to follow – but the participants were briefed on the topic and on the general drift the interrogation or interview should pursue. Occasionally, specific instructions were given to one of the role players on positioning, behaviour, body language, coherence and register to try and gauge the effect of these parameters on the overall interpreting performance. The detailed analysis of the role plays below will highlight a number of these effects.

The role plays were conducted in Dutch and Hungarian, the latter being a language completely unknown to the police officers, which forced them to rely exclusively on the interpreting and prevent them from hazarding any guesses or from being able to check the validity of the interpreting on the basis of their proficiency in a more 'common' language. The participants in the role plays were, first of all, four Dutch-Hungarian interpreters, who had between five to fifteen years of interpreting experience each, including experience in legal interpreting, though not in VCI or RI. The 'actors' playing the role of suspect or witness were all native speakers of Hungarian, with little or no Dutch at all, most of them postgraduate or postdoctoral students at the University of Leuven. The two police officers, one Chief Inspector and one Inspector, one male and one female have long-standing experience of conducting interviews with legal interpreters though, again, not in VCI or RI. In the course of the four test days, every interpreter did one face-to-face (FF) interview, one videoconference interpreting A (VCI A) interview, one videoconference interpreting B (VCI B) session and one RI interview (RI) in random order. All role plays were video-recorded for later analysis.

2   PRODUCT AND PROCESS ANALYSIS

The sixteen recordings were analysed according to two main categories: interpreting categories and audio-visual categories; in other words, analysis took place at the product level and the process level.

The product level itself focuses on overall accuracy in transferring the message (misunderstanding, *contresens*, etc.), and in particular on omissions and additions. Furthermore, at this level the linguistic, paralinguistic, contextual, synchronization and interaction issues of the interpreting performance are also considered. At the process or 'technical' level the primary consideration was whether there was any connection between the interpreting performance and resulting problems on the one hand, and the technical circumstances of the videoconference or remote setting on the other, as compared to the 'default' form of FF interpreting.

The main research question was whether the process influences the product. In particular, consideration was given to whether there are significant differences in interpreting quality and interpreting performance between FF and the other forms, whether the quality of the image or sound – the technical level – affects the quality of the interpreting, and whether, all parameters being equal, a higher technical quality leads to better interpreting quality.

2.1   Product analysis: Interpreting categories

Omissions, additions, inaccuracies

The four interpreters totalled the following number of omissions:

Form of interpreting	Number of omissions
FF	11 (25%)
VCI A	8 (19%)
VCI B	8 (19%)
RI	16 (37%)

As the table shows, the percentage of omissions is much higher in RI than in the other three forms. The lowest number of omissions occurs in VCI A and VCI B. However, it has to be noted that one of the interpreters alone was responsible for 17 omissions or almost 40% (39.5%) of all omissions.

Addition

It was envisaged that the results in the table below would give a general impression of the inclusion of additions in the interpreters' strategies, but once more a discrepancy can be noted:

Form of interpreting	Number of additions
FF	8 (40%)
VCI A	2 (10%)
VCI B	9 (45%)
RI	1 (5%)

Again, these figures should be treated with caution, since one interpreter was responsible for 11 (55%) of the additions, whereas one interpreter had no additions at all.

Accuracy

As far as accuracy is concerned, the figures show a more even distribution of the number of 'misinterpretations'.

Form of interpreting	Number of inaccuracies
FF	16 (24.6%)
VCI A	16 (24.6%)
VCI B	17 (26.2%)
RI	16 (24.6%)

The overall result for inaccuracies across the different forms of interpreting is evenly distributed but if the interpreters are again examined individually it can be seen that one interpreter was responsible for 37 (58%) cases of (in-)accuracy.

2.2 Product analysis: Linguistic issues

This subcategory within the product level looks at the following interpreting issues: Lexical/terminological problems; problems with idiomaticity; grammatical problems; problems with cohesion, coherence and style; and problems of register. The results are as follows:

Form of interpreting	Number of linguistic problems
FF	48 (27%)
VCI A	41 (23%)
VCI B	48 (27%)
RI	42 (23%)

It is again an evenly distributed result. These results suggest that the different forms of interpreting do not have a major impact of the various linguistic problems. A similar picture arose for paralinguistic issues including unnecessary repetition; hesitation; articulation problems; false starts; and voice quality problems. Regarding the performance of the individual interpreters, it could be suggested that every interpreter encountered linguistic problems in the different forms of interpreting more or less equally and that as far as this issue was concerned, it was not an individual phenomenon for one or two of them.

2.3 Product analysis: Paralinguistic issues

The paralinguistic issues that were analysed consist of unnecessary repetition; hesitation; articulation problems; false starts; and voice quality problems.

Form of interpreting	Number of paralinguistic issues
FF	200 (29%)
VCI A	164 (24%)
VCI B	152 (22%)
RI	170 (25%)

This is, again, a reasonably evenly divided result, which seems to suggest that paralinguistic issues do not depend on the form of interpreting. Two of the four interpreters had the most problems with repetition and hesitation.

They were responsible for 30.6% and 36.2% respectively of all the para-linguistic problems in all forms of interpreting.

Synchronisation/Interaction issues

Synchronisation and interaction include the following issues: turn-taking problems; overlap; and artificial pauses. In this subcategory there is a very pronounced shift between the four forms. The overall results are as follows:

Form of interpreting	Number of synchronisation and interaction issues
FF	31 (11%)
VCI A	83 (30%)
VCI B	90 (32%)
RI	77 (27%)

A fuller understanding of these figures necessitates a closer examination of individual issues.

Turn-taking problems

Form of interpreting	Number of turn-taking problems
FF	24 (15%)
VCI A	42 (27%)
VCI B	45 (29%)
RI	45 (29%)

Overlapping speech

Form of interpreting	Number of overlaps
FF	7 (7%)
VCI A	27 (29%)
VCI B	39 (41%)
RI	22 (23%)

Artificial pauses

Form of interpreting	Number of pauses
FF	0 (0%)
VCI A	2 (40%)
VCI B	3 (60%)
RI	0 (0%)

In all of these categories a shift can be observed. All the interpreters had problems with turn-taking and overlap. In the other categories above it can be seen that there were always one or two interpreters who had problems with a specific issue. However, in the case of turn-taking and overlapping, all four interpreters encountered similar problems. At the same time, they made few, if any, artificial pauses. It can be tentatively suggested that the reason for this shift in the area of synchronisation/interaction will be found on the other level, i.e. on the technical process level. Before testing this assumption, however, the other subcategories within the product level should be explored.

Contextual issues

In this subcategory the problems of lack of awareness of the local or cultural context were considered. The results are as follows:

Form of interpreting	Number of contextual issues
FF	2 (15.0%)
VCI A	5 (38.5%)
VCI B	5 (38.5%)
RI	1 (8.0%)

Once again, a shift between the different forms can be discerned, but it should also be noted that these results are based on a very small number of occurrences.

Recall problems

Recall problems such as complete blackouts or disconnection from the event do not occur often enough to draw substantial conclusions from it.

Form of interpreting	Number of recall problems
FF	3 (19%)
VCI A	7 (44%)
VCI B	6 (37%)
RI	0 (0%)

Language mixing

Concerning use of the wrong language and code switching there is again differences between the different forms of interpreting, but in this case too it should be pointed out that these results are based on a very small data sample.

Form of interpreting	Number of instances of language mixing
FF	2 (11%)
VCI A	4 (22%)
VCI B	8 (45%)
RI	4 (22%)

2.4   Product analysis: All categories

The aggregate result of all the interpreting, linguistic and paralinguistic
issues shows a reasonably evenly distributed picture:

Form of interpreting	Number of issues
FF	321 (25%)
VCI A	319 (25%)
VCI B	340 (26%)
RI	317 (24%)

There is no marked discrepancy in the overall results of all the interpreting
categories. The results are equally distributed, which leads to the tentative
conclusion that the difference in the forms of interpreting may not
significantly affect the overall quality of interpreting. There may be specific
problems or issues requiring attention and thus training, but on the whole, the
different forms of interpreting seem to produce similar quality.

2.5   Processs analysis

On the process level audio-visual and technical issues are considered.

Gaze

Whenever there is a screen in a room, people seem to become mesmerised by
it. Even when other people are present, a screen grabs the attention, at the
expense and to the detriment of personal rapport. This is the reason why the
issue of gaze and rapport needs careful consideration and analysis, given the
importance of positioning and rapport in interpreted criminal proceedings
including police interviews.

In general, in the VCI A setting (interpreter with police officer), it was
observed that both police officer and interpreter looked at the screen and
almost never looked at each other. They focused on the suspect/witness in
the remote location and did not realize that they were not looking at each
other when speaking. However, when questioned about this, it became
apparent that they did not see this as a disturbing element.

In the experiment involving a VCI B setting – a case of the criminal
conspiracy – the interpreter was together with the suspect while the police

officer was alone in a remote location. The interpreter was sitting behind the suspect so that the suspect could not see the interpreter. The suspect was clearly disturbed by this set up and always turned towards the interpreter when speaking. Finally the suspect said:

S: Nemlehet, hogyeztígy... nemlátommagátrendesen.
Is it possible, that I ... (the suspect turns her chair towards the interpreter) I don't see you well.

I: Mag ik mijn stoel verzetten? Ik zie de tolk niet.
Can I move my chair? I don't see the interpreter.

PO: U hoeft de tolk niet te zien. De tolk zal gewoon vertalen en wij kijken naar mekaar.
You don't have to see the interpreter. The interpreter will translate and we look at each other.

I: Önneknemkell a tolmácsotlátnia, ööö mi nézzükegymást.
You don't have to see the interpreter, hm we look at each other.

S: Deháténszeretémlátni, hogymitmond. Könnyebbígy.
But I would like to see what he is saying. It is easier for me.

I: Maar ik zou graag willen zien wat de tolk zie... zegt. Zo is het gemakkelijker.
But I would like to see, what the interpreter see... # says. This is easier.

PO: Helpt u dat?
Does it help you?

I: Segítez most?
Does it help you now?

PO: Helpt u dat?
Does it help you?

I: Segítezönnek?
Does it help you?

S: Háttermészetesen, szeretnémlátniazarcátamíg...
Of course, I would like to see his face when ...

I: Euh, natuurlijk ik wil het gezicht van de tolk zien.
Hm # of course, I would like to see the face of the interpreter.

PO: OK? Dat is goed, geen probleem. Als de tolk er geen problemen mee heeft.
OK? It is fine. No problem. If the interpreter doesn't have any problems with it.

I: De tolk heeft daar geen probleem mee.
The interpreter doesn't have any problems with it.

PO: OK, dat is goed.
OK. That's fine.

I: Rendben. Rendben.
Alright. Alright.

Following this exchange, the suspect moved her chair and then seemed to be sitting very comfortably. She was pleased because she could now see the

interpreter. Although she still did not gaze at the interpreter, it seemed to be
necessary for her to see the person who was speaking.

Other non-verbal issues: Posture, gesture, facial expression, actions

It is often said that to some extent interpreters also need to be actors. They
have to pay attention to their posture, gesture, facial expression, tone of
voice, and general behaviour. For the most part, all of the interpreters
involved in this study were very professional. They were generally not
disturbed by the presence of the camera. However, an exception to this
occurred in a VCI B setting, a police interview involving a case of credit-
card fraud.

The interpreter in this case studied law in Hungary but has been living in
Belgium for twenty years. She speaks Dutch fluently and appears to be a
very responsible and reliable legal interpreter. This particular situation,
however, seemed unusual and difficult for her. She became very defensive in
the course of the interview and unconsciously began to act as the suspect's
'advocate'. Consequently, she established a relationship with the suspect and
whispered to her. In her feedback interview she explained that she had
indeed formed a bond with the suspect because of the common language they
shared and because of the situation that found themselves in: sitting in a
darkened room, looking together at the screen with the police officer
speaking to them. She said she felt as if they were in a movie theatre. The
interpreter and her 'friend' the suspect were together in the cinema watching
the screen where the police officer - the 'bad guy' - was playing his role. The
police officer also felt the distance. He felt he was never really part of the
conversation and felt powerless. It seemed as if he could only look at the
screen and could not 'get through' to the suspect. At one point during the
interview there was a strange artificial pause of eight seconds: a significant
time period in this context. The frustrated police officer appeared very much
alone during this pause, looking helplessly at the two people at the other end
of the video link. Thus, the use of the video link in this particular instance
appears to have impacted significantly upon the relationship dynamics of the
police interview. This could potentially harm the quality of the evidence
achieved.

Technical issues

(Not) being in shot

During the role plays, various experimental situations were introduced. In
videoconference or remote interpreting the quality of sound and image is
paramount and should convey as reliable and true-to-life a picture as
possible. The colour of the skin, the size of the person, gestures, movements
and tone of voice should all be conveyed. However, the police officers
indicated that they wanted to see more, or at least have access to more

detailed observations such as the movements of the suspect's hands or his/her eyes. Using the so called fish-eye shot, they wanted to focus on the suspect's body language. With a close-up of the suspect they wanted to get a 'better' picture of the reliability of the information they were receiving. This was tried out in a VCI B situation. The suspect did not notice anything, as the only person using the fish-eye shot was the police officer. However, this raises the question of who 'calls the shots' and who monitors the images.

Sound-cutting out and inaudible segments

The second experiment was in a VCI A situation where the interpreter was together with the police officer, while the suspect was located at a second site. At one stage, the role player was asked to act very anxiously, to behave very nervously and to start moving about in his chair. This movement resulted in poorer sound quality and in an inaudible fragment for the interpreter and for the police officer. As a result, the police officer asked the suspect to sit still. A nervous person can thus be the cause of technical sound and image problems and such situations need consideration.

Visuals

During the VCI B hearing of a witness to a hold-up in a hotel, a document reader was introduced. The police officer asked the witness to draw the location where the hold-up had taken place. She had to place her drawing on the document reader, but the police officer could not see the picture clearly. The witness had used an ordinary biro, but the picture could not be clearly seen at the other end of the video link. The interpreter had a thicker pen with her, and offered it to the witness so she could make a new drawing. Meanwhile the police officer gave instructions to the interpreter on how to turn and adjust the light of the document reader. The experiment shows that training and experience are necessary for both the interpreters and the police officers when it comes to using devices such as document readers.

2.6   Interim conclusion

By way of interim conclusion, it can be suggested that, although there does not seem to be a significant difference in the overall interpreting quality among the four forms of interpreting, videoconference or remote interpreting can be a cause of specific problems on the product level. The first part of this analysis revealed some issues of concern such as increased difficulties with turn-taking and overlap in VCI and RI.

Turn-taking problems in FF only represented **15%** of the total number of turn-taking problems, whereas in VCI A the number rose to **27%**, and in VCI B and RI to **29% each.** On the basis of these results it can be suggested that turn-taking problems occur more frequently when the communication is mediated by technology, which could add a factor of distraction and potential stress. Moreover, in contrast with the other issues highlighted in the study, turn-taking problems were experienced by all four interpreters, irrespective of their linguistic and interpreting skills. This can be illustrated by the following examples:

In VCI A:

W: ... ésígylátszott, hogyittki van gombolva...
[onderbreking/interruption]
... and you could see, that his shirt was

I: Egypillanatra, hogyhamegállna
A moment please, if you could stop.

W: azinge.
open

I: akkorezt is lefordítanám.
I would like to translate what you were saying.

W: Igen.
Yes.

I: [...] dus die droeg een zwarte hemd,
So, he was wearing a black shirt,

W: Ésbelülilyenzsebeivoltak a bőrkabátnakés ...
And inside the leather coat there were some pockets and ...

I: Egypillanatra, egypillanatralegyenszíves!
Legyenszívesegypillanatramegállni, mégnemfordítottam le. Euh, euh
dus een zwarte hemd,
*One moment, one moment please! Stop for a moment please, I didn't
translate yet what you were saying. Hm, hm so a black shirt, ...*

In VCI B:

PO: [...] Ik wil u nogmaals bedanken voor uw bereidwilligheid, en voor
uw opmerkzaamheid bij de feiten.
*I would like to thank you again for your willingness and for your
attentiveness.*

I: St
St (sic)

PO: Als wij nog vragen hebben... Ja zeg maar, zeg maar...
If we have some more questions... Yes, say it, say it ...

I: Ja. Akkorazthiszem, hogymegfelelőmennyiségűfelvilágosítástkaptunk.
Köszönjükazegyüttműködéstés a
részvételtésamennyibenkérdésünklesz... Jazegt u maar voort, hoor!
*Yes. I think we have got enough information. Thank you for your
cooperation and your participation and if we have some more
questions...(in Dutch to the police officer) You can continue!*

PO: Als we nog vragen zouden hebben, kunnen wij u nog contacteren?
So if we have some more questions could we contact you?

I: Tehátamennyiben, mégkérdéseklennénekfelvennékönnel a kapcsolatot.
So if there were any more questions, they would contact you.

In RI:

PO: Dan zou ik willen vragen, dat u zich voorstelt als beëdigde tolk aan mevrouw. Kan u dat even doen?
So I would like to ask you to introduce yourself to the lady as the sworn interpreter. Could you do this?

I: ÖööJónapotkívánok! Üdvözlömkedveshölgyem! A mai nap alkalmávalénleszekazönöööhivatalostolmácsa.
Hm. Good afternoon! Welcome. Today I will be your hm official interpreter.

S: Jó.
That's fine.

I: Ja, ik heb het gedaan.
I did so. (in Dutch to the police officer)

A similar picture can be discerned in the case of overlaps. In FF, overlaps amounted to **7%,** in VCI A to **29%** , in VCI B to **41%**, and in RI to **23%**. Again, these problems are not specifically related to one particular interpreter's performance. All four interpreters had difficulties with overlap in VCI and in RI, as illustrated by the following example:

S: Igen, természetesen. HorváthFerencnekhívnak,
Yes, of course. My name is FerencHorváth,

I: Janatu
Yes, of cou...

S: Ik kom van Honga
I am from Hung...

I: Mijnnaam is FerencHorváth.
My name is FerencHorváth

S: 1986 júniushuszonharmadikán.
On the 23rd of June in 1986.

I: Ik woon in Hongarije ik ben geboren op 23 juni 1980
I live in Hungary and I was born on the 23rd of June in 1986.

S: Egybudapestiutazásiirodánakdolgozom.
I'm working for a travel agency in Budapest.

I: En ik werk voor een reisbureau in Boedapest.
And I'm working for a travel agency in Budapest.

2.7   The role of technology

Because of the importance of the process level, it seems legitimate to ask whether there is a direct relation between technology (process) and product (interpreting). This is the reason why the tests were conducted in two different test sites, one in Belgium (Leuven) and one in The Netherlands (Utrecht/Zeist). In Leuven, in the audio-visual centre of the University of Leuven, the equipment was good but not specific. Similarly, the technician in attendance was not experienced in the legal field. In Utrecht/Zeist, on the other hand, the technology was specifically for court interpreting and was monitored by someone with expertise in this field.

The video-mediated tests were distributed as follows:

Leuven 1:	2 VCI B; 1 VCI A; 1 RI
Leuven 2:	3 VCI A; 1 VCI B
Utrecht/Zeist:	3 RI; 1 VCI B

When the test results are analysed according to location (and implicitly the technology used), the following picture of interpreting problems at each site emerges:

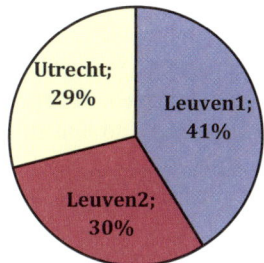

There is a slight improvement in the interpreting quality categories in the last (Utrecht/Zeist) location, i.e. under the better technical circumstances. Most of the problems in the product (interpreting) category occurred on the first day in Leuven. On the second day in Leuven, when both the interpreters and the police officers had gained some experience, an apparent improvement can be observed. In the third location, working with better technology, a further slight improvement can be discerned. Looking at some crucial issues the results revealed in VCI and RI – synchronisation/interaction issues (turn-taking; overlap; artificial pauses) – the following results can be observed:

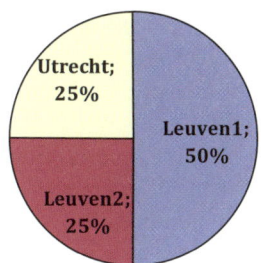

Most of the problems with turn-taking and overlap appear to occur on the first day in Leuven. At that point, the interpreters did not have any experience with videoconference or remote interpreting or with the technical equipment involved. On the second day in Leuven, under the same technical circumstances, the results were better, which seems to point to the importance of experience rather than to an overriding importance of the quality of technology.

In order to answer the question of whether or to what extent better technical circumstances lead to better interpreting quality it would be necessary to carry out more experiments on the relationship between technology and the interpreting product. However, as the participant feedback suggests, the quality of sound and image is paramount for delivering good quality interpreting and, additionally, that training of both the interpreters and police officers on how to conduct video-mediated interpreting sessions is essential.

3 FEEDBACK

In addition to the statistical analysis of both the interpreting product and process, it was considered important to receive personal feedback from all participants involved in the role plays regarding the advantages, disadvantages, points of concern of the various forms of interpreting. To this end the partners organised both written and oral feedback sessions, the salient points of which are summarised below.

3.1 Summary of *written* feedback of the police officers

- In VCI A the police officers experienced a feeling of greater 'distance' than in FF and they found it more difficult to gauge the emotions of the suspect/witness and establish confidence. VCI A made it more difficult for them to follow body language, hence their suggestion to be able to see a close up as well as a whole body image. However, their impression was that the interpreters seemed to be quite at ease in VCI A.
- In VCI B they felt even less 'rapport' with the suspect/witness. They tended to focus on the screen with the result that non-verbal information in particular was lost or not sufficiently picked up. Their main concern was a feeling of 'rapport' between interpreter and suspect/witness in the other location, even to the extent that the suspect appeared to be 'supported' by the interpreter.
- RI, the police officers felt, was characterised by more interruptions and overlaps which made the role plays less fluent. The impression was that this seemed the most difficult form for the interpreter.

3.2 Summary of *written* feedback of the interpreters

- VCI A: Three of the four interpreters claimed they felt there was no significant difference in quality of interpreting. However, they did point out that turn-taking, 'fluency' and contact with the police officer require attention and training. This was because of the interpreters' focus on the screen, watching the suspect/witness, which led to the interpreters' distraction and inattentiveness to the police officer.
- In VCI B the physically closer 'contact' between the interpreter and the suspect/witness (and the decreased contact with the police officer) was considered to be the most significant issue. Three out of four interpreters felt that this form of interpreting was more fatiguing and required more concentration (paying attention to the police officer on the screen), though this was not considered to be the case during the role plays in The Netherlands because of the "excellent" quality of sound and image.
- RI: for three interpreters the turn-taking and interaction were more difficult to handle than in the other forms of interpreting, and the general feeling was that proceedings were "slower". The fact that two participants who do not speak a common language were together in a different location made it more tiring for three of the four interpreters. There was a greater need for note-taking – which could be distracting – and it was generally felt that overall quality and performance satisfaction levels decreased in RI. However, there was one interpreter who had conference ('booth') interpreting experience and who felt quite at ease in RI and, indeed, considered it to be the most efficient setting.
- Generally speaking, the interpreters felt that the quality of interpreting was not fundamentally influenced by VCI or RI provided the quality of image and sound was "excellent". They were, on the whole, satisfied with their performance.

3.3 Summary of individual feedback interviews with the interpreters

The following points were stressed during the individual interviews with the four interpreters:

- There remained a preference for FF on the grounds of their own previous experience in police interviews, the feeling of being more "involved" in the situation, and the greater awareness of non-verbal information and body language.
- However, in the end, they saw no fundamental differences among the four forms of interpreting with regard to guaranteeing interpreting quality and performance.

- As mentioned above, VCI A most resembled interpreters' previous experiences and thus was seen as the easiest new form of interpreting to accommodate. VCI B strengthened the relationship between the interpreter and the suspect/witness at the expense of the police officer, simply because of the physical proximity of two people speaking the same language finding themselves in the same location. VCI B was therefore felt to be more "uncomfortable". RI (at least for 3 out of the 4 interpreters) was the most difficult and "controversial" because of the feeling of distance, the relation to the other participants, the need for greater concentration, an increased need to take notes, difficulties with turn-taking, and the "dominance" of the screen at the expense of live contact.
- Nevertheless, all four interpreters were satisfied with their own performances and felt that VCI or RI were feasible forms of interpreting in criminal proceedings. However, they should only be used on condition that sound and image quality were excellent, training was provided to allow interpreters and legal professionals to become familiar with the specific requirements of VCI A, VCI B and RI and that training take the form of role plays and experiments that should be as realistic as possible.

3.4 Summary of final feedback (round table)

The final feedback session consisted of a round table with the two police officers, three of the four interpreters and the four Belgian project partners. Most of the issues that had already been raised in the responses to the questionnaires or in the interviews were touched upon again. However, the following important points need to be emphasised once more:

- Not surprisingly, there was a general preference for FF because of the immediate interaction it allowed, the better rapport between the interlocutors, the importance of body language cues for the interviewer, the rapport that was felt, the more easily manageable turn-taking and, most importantly, because it allowed the police full use of interviewing strategies (including deliberate use of silence).
- Generally speaking, the video-mediated forms of interpreting were seen to highlight the issues of quality and interpreting competences. For example, source language comprehension, note-taking while watching a screen, turn-taking management, and target language production demanded more assured interpreting skills than in FF. Thus, the suggestion was put forward that a pre-briefing before the assignment should be organised (though, according to the police officers, this should not be too detailed in order to avoid "coloured" interpreting). Both VCI A and VCI B were seen as more distracting for the police because of gaze and turn-taking confusion, screen focus,

and because it was felt that these forms of interpreting encouraged speakers to ramble and hence cause overlaps. VCI B in particular carried the danger of too close a rapport between interpreter and suspect/witness, which made the police officer feel excluded, resulting in problems such as the marked switches to the 3rd person and the loss of non-verbal information for the police. It was suggested that perhaps a different positioning in VCI B might be advisable, i.e. with the interpreter sitting behind the suspect/witness instead of next to him/her, thus allowing a fuller view of the suspect/witness. It was suggested by the police officers that a split screen (two images of the suspect/witness: one close up, one full body) might remedy some of the information loss. They questioned the need to see the interpreter in VCI B and RI, since the interpreter's image, according to the police officers, distracted rather than aided in the interview. As said above, in RI two of the three interpreters present experienced less involvement, though the interpreter with conference experience saw in it a greater opportunity for concentration and the use of resources.

- The suitability of VCI or RI in criminal proceedings was raised as an issue of principle. These forms were seen as feasible for witness interviews, for standard procedures (e.g. a remand hearing), for information exchange procedures, and in cases of serious security risk, but not for serious or difficult in-depth interrogations, evidence assessment or trials. In other words, guidelines should be drawn up as to when these forms can be used and are in line with legal and human rights procedures.

- Finally, two conditions for successful VCI or RI in criminal proceedings were stressed. First, the need for training, both for the police and the interpreters (becoming familiar with camera and screen; coping with a different experience of rapport and feeling of remoteness; gaze and turn-taking management; interpreting skills in a potentially more stressful environment; and interviewing strategies in these forms of interpreting). A considerable part of that training should be directed towards both the police and the interpreters and should involve realistic settings. Secondly, a *conditio sine qua non* is the quality of sound and image (including, among other things, lighting, positioning and synchronicity) without which it is impossible to conduct an efficient and reliable VCI or RI interview.

4   CONCLUSIONS

Summarising all feedback information, the following seem to be the salient points:

- Those involved in the Belgian/Dutch study agreed that FF is the most 'comfortable' and efficient forms of interpreting in police interviews.
- However, there is also consensus among the participants that videoconference and remote interpreting will play an increasingly important role in legal interpreting.
- VCI A, with the interpreter being in the same location as the police officer, seems acceptable to all participants as a form of interpreting.
- RI is also deemed by the police to be acceptable as a form of interpreting, since the police officers feel that they do not really have to see the interpreter. In this case, the more important consideration for them is to be in same location with the crucial participant, i.e. the suspect or witness. The fact that the interpreter is in a different location is not of concern to them. The interpreters, on the other hand, experience RI as a challenging form of interpreting, which they are confident can be mastered with training and experience. This appears to be borne out by the assessment – and quality – produced by the one interpreter who had simultaneous booth experience.
- For all participants VCI B – the suspect and interpreter in the same location, the police officer on his or her own in a different place – turned out to be the most problematic form. The police officer felt distanced, disconnected and powerless to monitor the situation. The interpreters too felt uncomfortable at being 'on their own' with the suspect or defendant. The general feeling was that VCI B should only be used in certain circumstances such as a witness interview. VCI B was the least favourable form of videoconference interpreting.
- Finally, all participants stressed the need for good sound and image quality, for guidelines on how to conduct VCI and RI, and for training.

AVIDICUS COMPARATIVE STUDIES – PART III: TRADITIONAL INTERPRETING AND VIDEOCONFERENCE INTERPRETING IN PROSECUTION INTERVIEWS

Joanna Miler-Cassino and Zofia Rybińska

TEPIS, the Polish Society of Sworn and Specialised Translators

1 INTRODUCTION

Whereas the UK and Belgian partners in the AVIDICUS project focused on various configurations of video-mediated interpreting of police interviews, TEPIS, the Polish partner in the consortium, examined the use of videoconference interpreting to facilitate a prosecutor's questioning of a witness in a criminal case. As in the other partners' test scenarios, the decision was taken to replicate real-life procedure as closely as possible. This was achieved by acting within the constraints of Polish law (at the time of writing, only witnesses and experts may be interviewed via VC link), by using the VC facilities already in place in law enforcement agencies in Poland, and by involving real prosecutors. Authentic scenarios, drafted by prosecutors, were employed, and covered the entire span of a witness interview and included all relevant procedural elements. The scenarios used for the tests involved the pre-trial hearing of a witness:

- in a drug trafficking case (the witness was a tourist who shared a room with a suspected drug trafficker),
- in a car accident case,
- in a credit card fraud case (the witness had used an ATM).

The three test scenarios took the form of a comparative study in three different interpreting configurations:

- Face-to-face;
- VCI A (the interpreter was at the same location as the prosecutor; the foreign language speaking witness was at another location);
- VCI B (the interpreter was at the same location as the foreign language speaking witness; the prosecutor was at another location).[1]

---

[1] For definitions, see the introduction in this volume.

The three scenarios were tested first in the face-to-face setting, followed by VCI (A) and VCI (B). The following persons participated in the tests:

- 3 court interpreters
- 3 prosecutors
- 1 witness
- IT staff: 2 IT experts/technicians
- 2 TEPIS representatives, observing

The three interpreters are Poles around 30 years old. They are certified court translators and interpreters (referred to as "sworn translators" in Poland), which means they hold at least the *magister* (MA) degree, have passed the State examination, and obtained the right to practice the profession and to provide services for the police, public prosecutors' offices and courts. The interpreters had 7, 3 and 2 years of interpreting experience respectively. Each interpreter interpreted a given scenario only once in order to avoid the false effect of 'improvement' in overall interpreting quality as a result of famili-arity with the subject, the content of the prosecutor's questions, and problems arising. All three prosecutors are active at the National Public Prosecutor's Office (now re-named the Office of the Prosecutor General). The tests were carried out in the then National Public Prosecutor's Office in Warsaw, Poland, for three consecutive days from January 12 to 14, 2010.

Day 1	Day 2	Day 3
SCENARIO 1 DRUG TRAFFICKING	SCENARIO 2 CAR ACCIDENT	SCENARIO 3 CREDIT CARD FRAUD
Face-to-face [Interpreter 1]	Face-to-face [Interpreter 3]	Face-to-face [Interpreter 2]
VCI A (the Interpreter with the Prosecutor, the Witness at a remote location) [Interpreter 2]	VCI A (the Interpreter with the Prosecutor, the Witness at a remote location) [Interpreter 1]	VCI A (the Interpreter with the Prosecutor, the Witness at a remote location) [Interpreter 3]
VCI B (the Interpreter with the Witness, the Prosecutor at a remote location) [Interpreter 3]	VCI B (the Interpreter with the Witness, the Prosecutor at a remote location) [Interpreter 2]	VCI B (the Interpreter with the Witness, the Prosecutor at a remote location) [Interpreter 1]

Test Schedule

To ensure the highest degree of authenticity, the videoconference room layout and seating arrangement of the witness, prosecutor and interpreter were as they would be in a real situation.

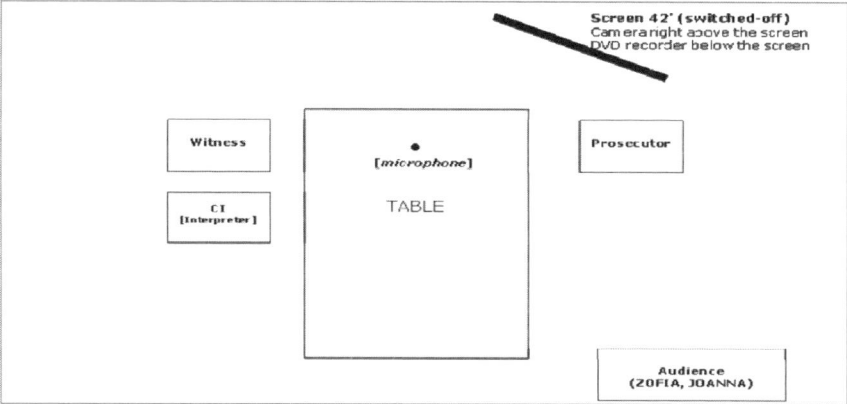

Room arrangement – face-to-face setting

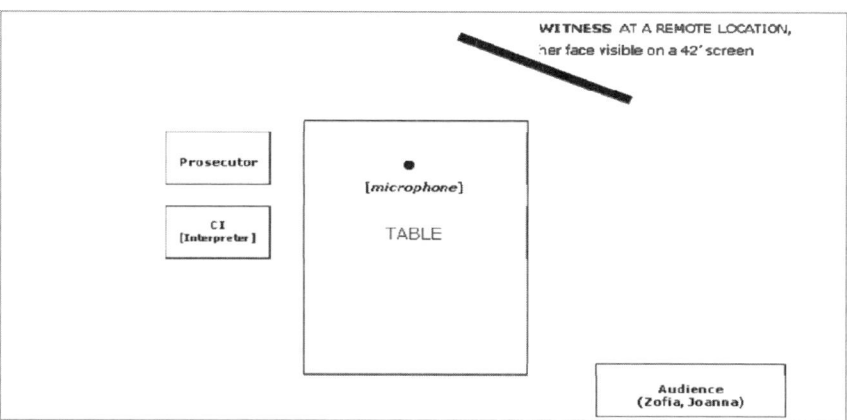

Room arrangement – VCI A setting (interpreter with prosecutor)

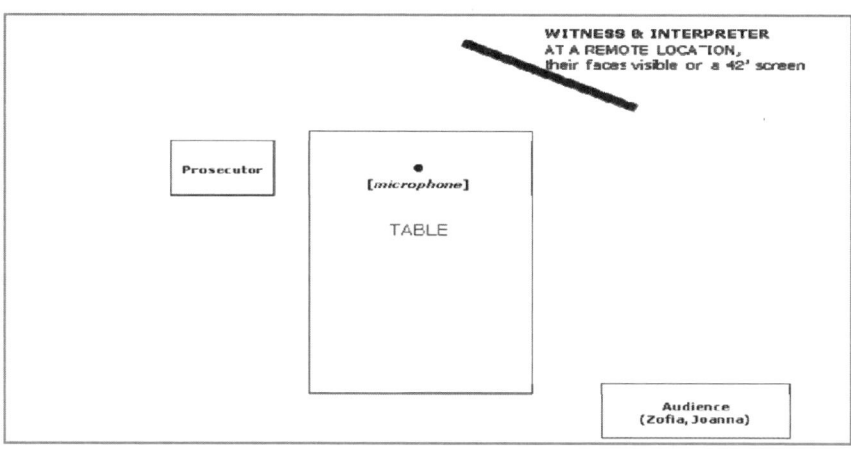

Room arrangement – VCI B setting (interpreter with witness)

2 VIDEOCONFERENCE EQUIPMENT FOR THE TESTS

The tests used the National Public Prosecutor's Office's professional videoconference equipment, namely:

- SONY PCS A –CG 70P Video terminal (encrypting mode – 128b key encryption)
- Recording device: DVD Sony recorder
- Screens: 42' Sony Bravia screen, 17' desktop screen
- Document camera.

The connection used during the tests was of a high quality (2Mbs).

3 TEST ASSESSMENT

3.1 Assessment objectives and criteria

The Polish partner in the AVIDICUS project set out to assess the quality of interpreters' performance in the above three settings and to observe the communicative behaviour of the primary participants, in addition to identifying difficulties arising from the video link. Considering our professional background as interpreters, the main focus during assessment by TEPIS was on interpreting quality and all the factors that affected or might have affected the quality of interpreter's performance in VCI A and VCI B settings, while face-to-face setting served as the 'control'.

In assessing the interpreters' performance, the criteria provided in the 2005 Regulations of the Ministry of Justice, which lay down detailed procedures for the examination of candidates for the profession of sworn translator (legal translators/court interpreters), were adopted. They are used by the State Examination Board in Poland for candidates taking the court interpreting examination and have been compiled specifically for the purpose of evaluating the quality of court interpreting under Poland's legal framework. The applied criteria were as follows:

1. Interpreting equivalence (accuracy in terms of substantive content): 0-10 points
2. Interpreting correctness in terms of specialist terminology and phraseology: 0-15 points
3. Interpreting correctness in terms of grammar and (non-legal) lexis: 0-10 points
4. Proper language register (functional style): 0-10 points
5. Correct pronunciation and intonation, articulation, fluency, pace of speech: 0-5 points

The above system basically corresponds to the AVIDICUS categories applied for analysis in the other test sites.

The assessment was carried out using video recordings of the tests and transcripts of the hearings.

The assessment was aided by opinions of two experts: expert 1, who is a licensed court translator and interpreter with 17 years of interpreting experience and 7 years as a court interpreter and expert 2, a highly skilled and experienced translator and interpreter of the English language.

Interpreting quality analysis was focused on linguistic and para-linguistic categories of the interpreters' performance, such as:

- comprehension of the SL,
- delivery of TL (i.e., accuracy, completeness, appropriateness for the situation, fluency, intonation, etc.),
- interpreter's rapport with the other participants.

In addition to the primary assessment objective, the subsidiary goals involved assessing whether:

- the primary participants changed anything in their communicative behaviour because of the video link (speaking slower, louder, were more repetitive, whether they took notes, changed their posture, etc. and whether there was any 'meta talk' about the video link),
- the remote participant could see/hear/understand everything during the hearing.

The assessors also noted any difficulties or irregularities arising from the video link, including:

- technical problems such as insufficient sound quality or lags in transmission,
- problems with seating order and seeing participants in the context of interpreting comfort,
- problems with communication management (e.g. who manages the floor, turn-taking, overlaps).

3.2   Interpreting quality assessment – day 1

The first day of tests was in fact a "warm-up day" for interpreters, during which the interpreters were not exposed to any specific linguistic difficulties that might have posed problems in interpreting. It was assumed that getting used to interpreting in front of the camera and in the presence of an evaluative audience is in itself an intimidating factor for them.

There were, however, normal and predictable differences in language use between the witness (highly redundant, everyday speech, at a slow pace, occasionally colloquial expressions or words typical of a local variety of English) and the prosecutor (very formal register, long sentences, many dates and numbers of articles from legislative texts, questions often prepared in advance and read out rather quickly or phrases that are used at the beginning of each questioning). In addition, there were also differences in the way the two prosecutors expressed themselves, one of them being easier to interpret, slightly less formal and more cooperative (e.g. willing to cut a long sentences short). Also, the topic of the questioning was quite general, thus reducing the risk of major interpreting errors.

The interpreters did not have any major problems understanding the SL delivery, which is also attributable to the quality of the video link being very good. It seems that any requests they made for a clarification or repetition resulted from their own imperfections or shortcomings rather than from the fact that they interpreted via a video link. In that context, the advantage of the interpreter sitting next to the foreign language speaking witness became noticeable when the interpreter was able to clarify an expression unknown to him with the witness with greater ease than during video-mediated communication.

However, the quality of the interpreters' output was by no means the same. Based on the video-recorded material it was observed that an interpreter with an excellent accent and a very good command of English made the best impression, followed by a second interpreter whose delivery seemed very good, with the interpreter ranked third in terms of perceived interpreting quality being at the bottom of the ranking. However, the sequence reversed after an analysis of the interpreters' output based on transcriptions of their interpretations. In terms of correspondence between the SL and TL deliveries, the person who made the lowest number of substantial departures from the original, omissions or additions was the interpreter who was actually last in the "naked-eye" ranking, followed by the interpreter who made the best impression, while the lowest quality grade based on transcript analysis was assigned to the interpreter who was ranked second based on the video-recorded material.

3.2.1   Face-to-face setting [court interpreter 1]

Comprehension of source text

The interpreter's output demonstrated an absence of major problems with source text comprehension, the only exceptions being the mistake made in the witness's address (SL: 17 Baker street, TL: 70 Baker street). The interpreter did not have to ask for any clarifications, nor did she request any of the speakers to repeat what they said.

Production of target text

In terms of source-target correspondence, in quite a number of instances the interpreter's output was inaccurate (SL: *"... detained for drugs in her luggage"*, TL: *"... detained with her luggage"*; SL: *"She introduced me to him"*, TL: *"She introduced him to me"*) and incomplete (substantial number of omissions and additions). However, departures of the interpretation from the original did not distort the communication process.

The quality of the interpreter's TL production was analyzed with reference to grammatical, syntactical and lexical errors. The interpreter made quite a few grammatical mistakes in the English language (*"Did I said...."*, *'In what language [Eh] Joanna Zys speak..."; "Now [Eh] the [Eh] [Eh] minutes would be [Eh] printed ...."; "... the protocol that have been read out ..."*); had problems with word order in the English language [*"In this activity there would participate as a recording clerk Mr.XXX"*]. A couple of sentences the interpreter produced in her native language, Polish, were also grammatically unacceptable. As regards lexical correctness, the interpreter tended to provide TL words and expressions that were more or less close in meaning to the SL original rather than equivalents. The interpreter in some instances did not know or confused legal terms.

As regards the criterion of fluency, the interpreter paused frequently [*eh, uhm*] which reduced her articulation speed. The pronunciation and intonation were correct, but she spoke with a strong Polish accent.

The interpreter, who was sitting next to the English-speaking witness and in front of the prosecutor, turned her head towards the witness whenever she started speaking, as if the interpreter wanted to see her face (or perhaps the movement of her lips) to better understand what the witness was saying.

The interpreter remained calm and self-assured throughout the interpreting process, did not show any major signs of nervousness, except for some hand gestures and slightly quickened pace of speech when she had problems formulating the TL text. She also tried to look at the person who spoke (prosecutor or witness), which probably helped her better understand the text. The interpreter took notes during her work.

3.2.2   VCI A setting [court interpreter 2]

In this setting, the interpreter was in the prosecutor's office, and the witness was at a remote location.

Comprehension of source text

The interpreter had no problems with understanding the source-language text. No requests for clarifications or repetition were presented.

Production of target text

In terms of source-target correspondence, the interpreter's performance was marked by quite a high level of inaccuracy [SL: *"... a sworn translator, XXX is taking part in this examination proceeding"*, TL"*... you will be interrogated by the sworn translator of the English language, Mrs. XXX"*, SL: *"... the equipment is going to be operated by ...."*: TL: *"... IT specialist is responsible for the equipment"*, SL: *"I, I went with my friends in December*

2008 to the travel agent Neckermann in London where we purchased the holiday in Bangkok.", TL: *"Already met in the travel agency Neckermann where we bought our holiday in Thailand."*; SL: *"Her English was fluent and she seemed friendly, so I assumed there would be no problems [Eh] actually sharing the room with her"*, TL: *"Her English was very fluent. She was a very friendly person. There were no problems"*] and incompleteness – the interpreter omitted several phrases and made some additions that seem to be based on what was said earlier during the proceeding.

The interpreter made a few grammatical and syntactical mistakes in English [*"Please tell me where do you live?"*] but her interpreting output in the Polish language was very good in terms of grammar and collocations.

As regards lexical correctness, the interpreter made a few errors [SL: *"twin bedroom"* TL: *"double bed bedrooms"*,] and in some cases did not provide correct equivalents of legal terms but was able to provide correct English equivalents of such legal terms as *"witness examination record"*.

The interpreter's pronunciation and intonation in English were remarkable. However, she paused quite often while speaking.

3.2.3   VCI B setting [court interpreter 3]

In this setting, the prosecutor was in his office and the interpreter was at a remote location together with the witness.

Comprehension of source text

The interpreter had some problems with understanding the source-language text. He did not know some of the expressions that the witness used ["hunky-dory", "strawberry blond hair"] and asked the witness to explain the meaning of such terms or omitted them in his delivery ["tank-top", "bubble wrap"].

Production of target text

This interpreter's output suffered from substantial level of inaccuracy and a very large number of additions and omissions. The interpreter did not take notes when interpreting. Consequently, he did not interpret whole phrases of considerable significance like names of persons and institutions, hours and dates [SL: *"it is 13.30" "My name is XXX"*, SL: *"Article 233 section 1"* TL: *"Article 233"*], omitted long sentences [e.g. *"...is XXX against whom there is issued an international warrant of arrest as he is accused of being a member of an organized crime group that deals in drug trafficking"*] or had to ask the witness/prosecutor to repeat [date of birth of the witness, her address]. Moreover, the interpreter quite frequently departed from the original, with his TL delivery being only similar in meaning to the original rather than equivalent to it [SL: *"he was in his thirties"* TL: *"He was about thirty years old"*].

The interpreter made some grammatical mistakes in English [*"Did I showed you?", Did XXX offered…?"* but his overall command of the English language was generally good. In terms of lexis, the interpreter had major problems with legal terminology, failing to provide correct English equivalents of even basic terms [SL *"examination of a witness"* TL *"investigation"*; SL: *"recording clerk"* TL *"clerk"*; SL *"examination record"* TL *"protocol"*; SL *"photographic evidence"* TL: *"chart"*], or did not use correct phraseology]SL*"... examined in relation to her acquaintance with..."* TL: *"questioned with regard to the circumstance of her acquaintance with..."*].

The interpreter's pronunciation and intonation in English were good. His rate of articulation was quite fast and, in several cases, he tended to make auto-corrections when he realized he may have inaccurate in his interpreting [SL: *"Parents' first names"* TL *"Your parent, your parents' first names"*; SL *"Does the witness speak Polish at any level?"* TL: *"[Eh] Do you speak Polish? Do you... What is your command of Polish? Do you speak Polish at to... [Eh] at all?"*]

With regard to all three interpreters' communicative behaviour on the first day of tests, one of the experts remarked that it was difficult to assess whether the interpreters changed anything in their communication because of the video link, since the video link was of a high standard. The quality of sound and image was very good. The expert further noted that: *"all the three interpreters seemed to feel comfortable and at ease in the interpreting environment, whether it was "face-to-face" or VC-assisted. They also seemed to be happy with the seating order. In the case of two interpreters, there were no problems with communication management, they waited for the speaker to finish their statement and then proceeded with their deliveries. However, one interpreter tended to interrupt the prosecutor/witness when he wanted to start interpreting."*

There were some organisational flaws which impacted the interpreting process. As one of the experts observed, in the VCI A setting *"neither the prosecutor nor the interpreter could show the witness where to sign, so the technician did it. Yet, at the moment of signing the interpreter sometimes was not allowed to finish the interpretation because too much was going on in both locations. "* The expert also pointed out a drawback of the VCI B setting that *"became apparent when the prosecutor started speaking while the interpreter was signing the record, which seemed to have caused considerable stress to the interpreter (he remained distracted until the end of the interrogation and his performance deteriorated noticeably)."*

Both these situations show the importance of proper management of the communicative situation to avoid overlapping and turn-taking problems.

3.3 Interpreting quality assessment – day 2

Witness questioning on the second day was the most difficult of the three test days. The witness spoke with a Scottish accent and used quite a number of colloquial expressions and Scottish words. Moreover, the manner she spoke was difficult to understand at times: once in a while she "mumbled under her breath" or covered her face with hands, which rendered her speech far more difficult to comprehend than on the preceding day. Also, the witness's testimony embraced a description of a traffic accident, including a precise account of vehicles' locations in relation to the road and passengers' positions in the car, further complicated by the differences in the Polish and British traffic systems (left-hand side and right-hand side).

The interpreters behaved in more or less the same way as on the preceding day. Despite a much higher level of text difficulty than on the preceding day, two interpreters (working in the face-to-face and VCI B settings) provided good, although not impeccable TL output; their pace of speech was quite fast and contributed to a successful examination of the witness. In the overwhelming majority of cases, requests for repetition or clarification resulted from the fact that the interpreters did not know specific terms/colloquialisms.

However, one interpreter's overall performance (in the VCI A setting, when the interpreter was next to the prosecutor, the foreign language speaking witness at a remote location) was far less satisfactory. The interpreter's comprehension problems and repetitive requests for clarification of phrases or single terms turned the examination into an excessively lengthy, chaotic and incoherent experience.

It is not possible to determine the reasons for such a drop in quality of performance based on a single instance. Faced with the same type of difficulties during face-to-face interpreting and VCI A setting (when the interpreter sat next to the witness), the other two interpreters managed well despite similar difficulties. The experts did not comment on this. In the feedback, the interpreter later reported "*a technical problem*" and "*insufficient quality of sound and image*", where in fact, it was the witness who was incoherent, while the sound was the same as in other hearings and insufficient audibility was above all attributable to the witness' mumbling rather than equipment deficiencies.

It seems, therefore, that the interpreter was affected by a combination of unfavourable working conditions (as it was the first time this interpreter worked via video link) coupled with several other factors, such as:

- the interpreter being separated from the witness,
- the witness' speech being inarticulate (the witness spoke very unclearly, too softly, dropped in some colloquial or slang words, muttered under her nose, mumbled, etc.),
- the lack of fluency on the interpreter's part (despite experience)

This clearly demonstrates the need for training interpreters in videoconference interpreting despite their ample experience in face-to-face court interpreting.

3.3.1 Face-to-face setting [court interpreter 3]

Comprehension of source text

The interpreter had no major problems with understanding the source-language text, except for the Scottish *"hoose"* (which he asked the witness to repeat but, apparently, did not know the word and omitted it in his TL delivery; *"just after 3ish"* (which he first took for *"fish"* but after hearing the witness say it again understood and interpreted it as *"about 3 o'clock"*), or *"dreich"* (which he omitted).

Production of target text

The interpreter did not take notes when interpreting. As a result, his delivery suffered, just like his interpreting output in the drug trafficking case (day 1), resulting in a high level of inaccuracy [SL: *"I was taken to downtown"* TL: *"I went to the center"*; SL: *"I don't have anyone in Poland"* TL:" *She does not have a correspondence address in Poland"*; SL: *"I think"* TL: *"As far as I remember"*]. Moreover, his interpreting output contained and a very large number of additions and omissions. In his delivery, he omitted names of persons [*"My name is XXX"* – phrase omitted], made mistakes in first names [SL: *"Marek Sowisło"* TL: *"Piotr Sowisło"*], omitted whole phrases [*"I just remember actually"*, *"I am such an eejit"*, *"I am just a daftie"*,], some of which were of major significance [*"traffic accident which took place on 22 February 2009"* omitted], substituted place names [SL: *"Poznań"* TL: *"Szczecin"*], and provided incomplete references to the Criminal Code [SL: *"Article 233 section 1"* TL: *"Article two three three"*; *"pursuant to Article 147"* – omitted]. Because he took no notes, quite frequently the interpreter had to ask for repetitions and clarifications (case number, date of birth, address *"number 9 Dyce lane, it's flat 2/2)*. Moreover, quite unjustifiably, the interpreter switched to the third person singular instead of using the first person singular "SL: *"I am a doctor"* TL: *"She is a doctor"*].

The interpreter made quite a number of grammatical mistakes in English [SL: *"No, only if you were their relative, then there would be other legal proceeding rights in place for you"* TL: *"No, however, should you be related to those persons, you will be entitled to a different legal rights"*; *"Tell us what do you know..."* '*Please describe how did the accident occur"*, *"How long do you have you're your driving license?"*]. Nevertheless, these mistakes did not affect the witness's understanding of the interpretation.

The interpreter had considerable problems with lexis. The witness's delivery contained quite a number of colloquial or Scottish words that the interpreted either omitted altogether [*"wee"*, *"drookit"* – both omitted], or asked for a clarification [*"jammy sandwich"*]. Similarly, the interpreter failed to provide correct TL equivalents of traffic terms [SL: *"motor vehicles* TL: *"mechanical vehicles"*; SL: *"front nearside door"* TL: *"front door"* or *"front door the closest to me"*; SL: *"crossroad"* TL: *"roundabout"*], some every-day terms [SL: *"occupation"* TL: *"profession"*; SL: *"jacket"* TL: *"coat"*], and legal terms [SL: *"witness examination record"* TL: *"statement"* or "protocol"; SL: *"punishable up to three years of imprisonment"* TL: *"liable to prosecution which is up to 3 years of incarceration"*; SL: *"family name"* TL *"Your maid... your ancestors' name"*].

The interpreter's pronunciation and intonation in English were good, his speech rate of articulation was quite fast, and his delivery was not interrupted by long pauses.

3.3.2   VCI A setting [court interpreter 1]

Comprehension of source text

The interpreter experienced major problems with understanding the English text, especially when the witness used colloquial or Scottish terms, when she provided her account of the car accident or was giving her particulars [SL: *"Taylor"* TL *"Hiller"*; SL: *"At number 9 Dyce Lane"* TL: *"Number 9 Dyce Lee"*]. The interpreter's requests for repetition and clarification were extremely frequent.

Production of target text

The interpreter's output was inaccurate [SL: *"We summoned you ... in order to examine you as a witness using technical devices, while using a remote video terminal..."* TL: *"We summoned you ... and decided to record this interrogation"*] and incomplete (a number of omissions) [SL: *"IT specialist from the Appellate Prosecutor's Office in Poznań and from the Appellate Prosecutor's Office in Szczecin"* TL: *"IT specialists from Poznań and Szczecin"* SL: *"... this proceeding will be recorded by means of audio-visual equipment"* TL: *"... this activity will be recorded."* SL: *"he hit his head"* TL: *"he hit his face"*]. Some of the interpreter's utterances were grammatically incorrect [*"... if was any blood relation between you and these persons"*].

Undoubtedly, the interpreter's biggest problem was with lexis, as she had difficulties providing equivalents of every-day words and phrases [SL: *"As I understand, you have a higher education?"* TL: *"Your profession I assume is higher?* SL: *"one of those... senior citizen things that happen..."* TL: *"one of those serious incidents"* SL: *"Date and place of your birth"* TL: *"Date and place of your birthday"*], colloquialisms and Scottish words used by the witness [*"dreich"*, *"clammy"*, *"hoose"*, *"about 3ish"*], words related to road traffic [SL: *"wee car did a somersault"* TL: *"the car turned"*] and legal terms [SL: *"Code of Criminal Procedure"* TL: *"Criminal Procedure"* SL: *"Article 233 section 1"* TL: *"provision 235 paragraph 1"* SL: *"prosecuted for giving false testimony"* TL: *"punished for giving false testimony"* SL: *"record of the examination"* TL: *"protocol from this interrogation"*]. However, it needs to be stressed that the interpreter rarely omitted unknown words and always made an effort to ask the witness either to repeat her statement or explain the meaning of an unknown word. Consequently, this resulted in the interpretation being repeatedly interrupted by the interpreter's questions and the witness's replies (she requested the witness to explain the meaning of such words as *"dreich", "ditch", "gouge" "offside" "nearside", "chappy", "jammy sandwich", "wee lad", "bonnet"*, etc.]. One of the critical errors in the interpreter's output, namely an incorrectly interpreted sentence [SL: *"The front nearside door was opened"* TL: *"And the front part, front of the car was opened"*] led to a major misunderstanding of the witness's testimony by the prosecutor.

The interpreter's pronunciation and intonation in English were good, with a slight Polish accent. Her rate of articulation was slow, with a large number of pauses.

3.3.3   VCI B setting [court interpreter 2]

Comprehension of source text

The interpreter had some problems with understanding the source-language text, especially colloquial words used by the witness, and had to ask the witness to explain the meaning of unknown words.

Production of target text

Occasionally the interpreter departed from the source text and provided inaccurate interpretations [SL: *"The witness has been summoned to…"* TL: *"The witness is at the…"* SL: *"When he was approaching the end of the exit there was another sign"*, TL: *"The driver .... got to the end of the exit"*, SL: *"... then I saw from the left side a passenger's car coming ...."*: TL: *"... and from the left side passengers appeared"* SL: *"I am a doctor, so I know how to do the first aid."* TL: *"... just because I am a doctor I decided to do first aid* SL: *"It was really bad day"* TL: *"It was a day"*]. Also, in her TL delivery the interpreter omitted certain words and phrases [SL: *"I'd like the IT specialist to show it on the document camera screen"* TL: *"I would like to ask our IT specialist to show it to us"* SL: *"It was really dreich", "I was quite drookit after that", "Thank you", "I left my mates' hoose about 3ish"* – all phases omitted], or added phrases that were not said by the witness or the prosecutor [TL: *"in the light of Polish regulations"*]. However, in this case inaccurate interpretations, additions and omissions did not distort general meaning of the witness' words.

The interpreter made very few grammatical or syntactical mistakes in English or Polish, making her interpretation pleasant to listen to. With regard to the lexical aspect, however, the interpreter had certain problems with colloquial and Scottish terms [like *"nearside door" "offside door" "dub", "jammy sandwich"*] but, whenever the witness said an unknown word, the interpreter asked for an explanation and, apparently, put it down in her notepad. The interpreter performed very well in terms of legal terminology and phraseology, providing correct, specialist TL terms throughout her interpretation.

The interpreter's English in terms of pronunciation and intonation was impressive, and so was her pace of speech.

The seating order was not equally comfortable for all the interpreters. It could be assumed that it would be easier for the interpreter to comprehend the witness if the witness appears on the screen (as in the VCI A setting), since such an arrangement allows the interpreter to see the witness's face and lip movement. However, if the screen is situated at an angle, as it was in the Prosecutor's Office, it is not a comfortable working position for an interpreter. Additionally, being at a distance from the foreign-language speaking witness deprives the interpreter of direct contact with the witness. This direct contact may be helpful, as was observed when the witness sitting next to the interpreter made a drawing for the interpreter to explain the terms "offside" and "nearside" in detail, which the interpreter did not initially understand.

One of the experts observed that during a hearing in the VCI B setting (when the interpreter was next to the foreign language speaking witness and the prosecutor was at a remote location) *"the interpreter asked the prosecutor a few times to repeat e.g. the name of the recording clerk or the number of the article he had referred to. When she was determining the correct spelling of [the witness's] address [...] the prosecutor got slightly impatient and asked if there was any problem."* Further, the *"interpreter omitted what the prosecutor said to the IT specialist about switching the camera back to the witness. On one occasion, the interpreter allowed the witness to speak for quite a long time and the prosecutor intervened asking her to interpret. From that time, the interpreter showed the witness when to stop and told her when she could continue."* Again, this suggests that a set of guidelines is required for the management of the communicative situation.

3.4   Interpreting quality assessment – day 3

On the third day of tests, the scenario was that of a credit card fraud case. The witness did not use any specialist terminology or colloquialisms, but spoke every-day language. The only major problems all interpreters had during their work concerned names and addresses. On that day the hearing was conducted with a real recording clerk, who wrote down the testimony for the record (in other words, not someone acting as a recording clerk, as on the first and second day) and this slowed down the entire process.

Throughout the questioning, the interpreters had to dictate the witness' testimony to the recording clerk. They quickly learned how to do it efficiently and come up with neat, correct sentences with the same information the witness provided, but making them as concise as possible.

3.4.1 Face-to-face setting [court interpreter 2]

Comprehension of source text

The interpreter's comprehension of the SL text was very good. She made a few requests for clarification or repetitions, like in the case of witness' address, in which she finally made a mistake (SL: "*It's 1120 22nd Milnguve Avenue*", TL: "*... 22nd Milnguve Avenue, number 1122*"), or when the witness spoke quite fast and her testimony was incoherent.

Production of target text

The interpreter's output was sometimes inaccurate (SL: "It was like half six in the morning" TL: "... about half past five"; SL: "My husband wanted to surprise me,", TL: "My husband decided to surprise me"; SL: "... we didn't have the direct connection to Cracow from Paris on that day", TL: "there is no direct connection from Paris to Cracow"; SL: "... merchants, that they used to sell all the things and buy the things there as well", TL: "where merchants sell many various things"). The interpreter made a number of omissions, resulting most probably from the fact that the witness' utterances were quite lengthy and the interpreter paraphrased them instead of providing a word-for-word interpretation. However, departures of the interpretation from the original were of minor significance.

The interpreter made no grammatical mistakes in the English language, providing correct delivery in terms of grammar, syntax and phraseology. The same applies to her output in Polish. As regards terminology she made very few mistakes, [SL: "*forging (...) of payment cards*" TL: "*credit card fraud*"]. She also proved highly competent as regards legal terminology.

The interpreter spoke fluently in both Polish and English. Her English pronunciation was excellent, and she did not pause as frequently as she had done on previous occasions. Her rate of articulation was fast at the beginning but when she realized that the recording clerk was not able to keep up with her, she substantially reduced her space of speech and began dictating.

The interpreter remained calm throughout the interpreting process, but often gesticulated vigorously with her hands.

3.4.2 VCI A setting [court interpreter 3]

Comprehension of source text

The interpreter had no major problems with understanding the source-language text, except for names and addresses, but in quite a number of cases was not sure whether he understood the witness and asked her for a confirmation of his understanding.

Production of target text

The interpreter did take notes when interpreting. His TL output contained a large number of inaccurate interpretations and omissions, though none of critical significance [SL: *"in relation to your use of cards (...) and losses which you sustained as the consequence of the actions of detained perpetrators"* TL: *"in the matter of using payment card and the retention of persons who were detained"*.

Many of the interpreter's utterances, particularly in the final part of the examination when he delivered the sight translation, contain grammatical mistakes [TL: *"should need be to"*, TL: *"I would like to explained"*]. Also, the interpreter did not seem to know certain legal terms, and made similar mistakes to ones he made during the first and second examinations.

The interpreter understood nearly everything the witness said but repeatedly asked the witness to confirm whether he was right.

The interpreter's pronunciation and intonation in English were good, and his delivery was not interrupted by long pauses. As regards the interpreter's pace of speech, when he was sight translating examination record, he spoke so fast that even the witness asked him to slow down. It was in this part of his TL output that he made the largest number of grammatical mistakes.

3.4.3 VCI B setting [court interpreter 1]

Comprehension of source text

The interpreter did not have major problems with text comprehension, except for names or addresses (she had problems with spelling).

Production of target text

The quality of the interpreter's performance did not differ much from that of the first day of her interpreting. During this examination the witness' sentences were rather short so as to enable the recording clerk to put everything down and the interpreter dictated the witness' answers. Nevertheless, in some cases her interpretation was inaccurate [SL: *"... about half six"* TL: *"... about six in the morning"*] and incomplete.

She made quite a few grammatical mistakes and her biggest deficiency concerned a lack of knowledge of everyday vocabulary [*"date and place of your birthday;* SL: *"merchants"* TL *"shops"*], lack of knowledge of legal terminology and phraseology [she did not know such terms as *"forensic psychiatrist;* SL: *"remote witness examination"* TL: *"distance interrogation"*], SL: *"convicted for giving false testimony"* TL: *"punished for giving false testimony"*]". However, she seldom omitted unknown words but asked the witness for clarification.

The interpreter's pronunciation and intonation in English were good, with a slight Polish accent. Her rate of articulation was slow, with a large number of pauses.

One of the experts pointed out an interesting outcome of the witness's remoteness during the VCI settings and the interpreter's (in)ability to cope with a novel situation: "*It turned out that the recording clerk did not write down the first question (let alone the answer), because he had not been instructed to do so. The recording clerk could not type very fast, so the interpreter was often asked to repeat or wait.... At the beginning the witness could have been confused as she did not know what was going on.*"

In the VCI A setting (the interpreter was next to the prosecutor and the foreign language speaking witness was at a remote location), the witness clearly did not know what was going on when the record was being corrected, because the interpreter was too busy making corrections to tell her.

In VCI B setting (the interpreter was next to the foreign language speaking witness and the prosecutor was at a remote location), the interpreter made an effort to keep the witness informed about what was going on in the other location, and kept the prosecutor informed when she had to ask the witness for clarifications.

While referring to the communicative behaviour of the interpreters on that day, one of the experts stated that the participants' behaviour did not change much compared with the preceding days. One of the interpreters (in the face-to-face setting) tried to maintain eye contact with the witness.

Commenting on possible difficulties ensuing from the video link our expert noted that the quality of the video link was very good during interpretation. For a short time, although the quality of the image remained very good, there were problems with the sound. However, the participants did not complain about it or ask for repetitions. None of the requests for clarification/repetition made by the interpreters seemed to result from poor quality of the sound or image.

4   POST-TEST FEEDBACK

Immediately after the tests, all participants were requested to provide some feedback on their experiences of the test.

4.1   Interpreters' feedback

Interpreter 1 stated that headphones might have been helpful, as would the possibility for the interpreter to control the equipment. She further commented:

- "the screen should be placed directly in front of the interpreter",
- "in a real life situation, it would be possible to draw pictures (by the witness, interpreter) showing the location of victims. In VCI

interpreting it took more time to explain (and interpret) everything carefully",

- "VCI/RI is a bigger challenge for the interpreter..."

The Interpreter added that more effort was needed to understand fully a person at a distance and to establish a rapport with them.

In the opinion of Interpreter 2:

- "it is always more effective to interpret for a person sitting next to me or at the same table",
- "if the technology works properly, there is virtually no difference between 'real' [meaning face-to-face] interpreting and VC interpreting",
- "the fact that there is distance may cause a higher level of stress",
- "during the VCI the participants are more focused, which has a positive effect on the quality of interpretation",
- "it is also important to feel comfortable in the presence of the camera".

Interpreter 3 observed:

- "the greatest problem was to overcome the stress resulting from the camera staring at me and the witness",
- "the stress caused a reduction in performance. I noticed that quite simple things got complicated".

Interpreter 3 was clearly disconcerted by the presence of the camera in the initial phase of the tests.

In their self-assessment sheets, the interpreters commented that videoconference interpreting when the interpreter was with the prosecutor and the witness was at a remote location appeared to be the most difficult of the three settings. In general, interpreters preferred to interpret in the face-to-face and the VCI B settings (when they sat next to the foreign-language speaking witness and the prosecutor was at a remote location) rather than in the VCI A settings (when they sat next to the prosecutor and the foreign-language speaking witness was at a remote location).

Notably, the interpreters saw little or no difference at all between face-to-face and videoconference interpreting in the two VCI settings in terms of their overall interpreting quality and witness comprehension. General satisfaction with their performance was equally good in all these settings. However, all three interpreters regarded videoconference interpreting either slightly or considerably more fatiguing, stressful, isolating and motivating (motivating was understood as requiring a greater effort to remain focused).

The level of working comfort was perceived by all three to be higher in the case of face-to-face interpreting and lower in VCI. Likewise, though the perception of the stress level in these three settings differed amongst the

three interpreters, interpreting during a videoconference hearing was
perceived as more stressful than face-to-face interpreting by all three;
however, as one of the interpreters stated, the *"VCI setting may cause some
stress or uneasiness"*, but *"the stress level gradually decreases when the
interpreter gets used to the fact of being recorded."*

It must be noted that the interpreters indeed got used to the camera and
the new communication context very quickly. Starting from a high level of
stress and uncertainty, they quickly developed techniques to cope with this
new situation and figured out how to tackle the difficulties in the most
efficient way. By the second day, two of the three interpreters had learnt to
manage the VCI communicative environment reasonably well. On day three,
i.e., the last day of tests, two of the three seemed almost relaxed.

Eye contact was also covered in the feedback. In particular, it was
suggested that it is *"important to have an eye contact with the witness or
prosecutor, as it helps a lot in the communication effort."*

Two interpreters mentioned that special training in VCI is needed, also
including training with regard to voice projection in the VC situation.

4.2   Prosecutors' feedback

Regardless of the interpreters' opinions about their quality of interpreting or
satisfaction with their performance in each of the settings, (or the level of
their stress or fatigue in VCI settings), the Prosecutor was equally satisfied
with the result of each hearing. The interviewed Prosecutor said he had
achieved his goal by learning the facts he required. In general, the client (i.e.
the Prosecutor) was more satisfied with the interpreting quality and
interpreters' performance than the service providers (the interpreters)
themselves.

Interestingly, the Prosecutor (who was very experienced in conducting
VCI hearings having questioned approximately 350 witnesses via VC)
noticed that the interpreters who interpreted during the face-to-face hearing
and the hearing of a witness at a remote location (when the interpreter sat
next to the Prosecutor) were nervous and tried to overcome stress during
their work. However, the Prosecutor did not notice the third interpreter's
nervousness. He thought the third interpreter (whom he saw on the video
screen only) was quite composed. The Prosecutor was surprised when told
that the interpreter's hands were shaking and that this interpreter too showed
signs of stress and nervousness that were evident to those sitting next to him.
It demonstrates that despite considerable experience with VCI, some body
language cannot be deciphered successfully via the screen.

4.3   Witness's feedback

Noteworthy are the observations and remarks of the individual playing the role of the witness, who works as a court interpreter in Scotland and has some experience of VCI/RI.

With regard to the general quality of interpreting, the 'witness' (fluent both in Polish and English) noted that the quality of interpreting did not differ much depending on the setting. Her observations were as follows:

	Face to face interpreting	**VCI A (Interpreter next to prosecutor)**	**VCI B (Interpreter next to witness)**
Interpreter 1	good quality, intended result achieved	some mishaps, generally good	good but many interruptions
Interpreter 2	good quality, coped with obstacles	good quality, great stress control	good pace and quality
Interpreter 3	good quality	good quality despite some obstacles (omissions and additions)	too many omissions and additions

In her opinion, face-to-face interpreting "is *best for quality, understanding and pace"* whereas "VCI A (when the Interpreter sat next to the Prosecutor, while the foreign language speaking Witness was at a remote location) *creates a lot of barriers and may slow down the procedure due to distance"* and accompanying difficulties. VCI B (the Interpreter with the Witness) in turn *"improves time management, understanding and has a positive result on the proceedings. Witness is in control of situation in this setting."*

She also stressed the importance of direct contact saying that the VCI B setting (when the interpreter sat next to the foreign language speaking witness, while the prosecutor was at a remote location) *"was better because it assured better confidence and quality;* [which] *is preferable for the interpreter."* For her, *"VC interviews are a big step forward in interpreting, but there are many aspects that need to be understood before anyone starts work in such a setting. It can improve work within the justice system, but interpreters need training and people using interpreters' services need to understand the role of interpreters in the justice system. They should be an asset, not a prop in these proceedings."*

5   CONCLUSIONS

The three scenarios were interpreted by three different interpreters with different linguistic proficiency, interpreting competence and experience. As was pointed out earlier, all the interpreters worked once in one of the three different interpreting settings: the classic "face-to-face" setting and two VCI-assisted settings. The crucial question of this study was whether, and if so, to what extent, the VC-based setting affected the interpreter's delivery. In order to answer this question the experts compared and assessed the quality of the interpretations; they reached slightly different conclusions.

According to one of the experts, the performance level was approximately the same during all the three interpretations. One of the interpreters did even better in VCI A than in the "face-to-face" and VCI B setting, while another performed poorly in VCI A but substantially improved her output in VCI B. In the expert's opinion, it is predominantly the interpreter's competence and the text difficulty (i.e., vocabulary, accent, manner of speaking, topic) that impacts the interpreter's performance. In other words, the higher the linguistic and interpreting competence of the interpreter, the less his/her output is likely to be affected by the interpreting setting.

According to the other expert, interpreters generally performed better in the "face-to-face" scenario than in the VC-based environment. Despite the fact that according to the statistics of interpreting errors compiled by this expert, there was no major difference between the VCI A and VCI B scenarios, in the opinion of the expert, which is also shared by project partners from TEPIS, the scenario where the interpreter is in direct contact with the witness (VCI B) proves more comfortable for the interpreters. In the final conclusion the second expert wrote:

> It is my impression that any differences in the quality of interpreters' performance in various modes [setting] of interpreting were much more attributable to their [the interpreters'] particular professional skills (knowledge of the vocabulary relating to the topic of interrogation, general command of English) than the mode in which the questioning was conducted. The only clear advantage of sitting together with the witness being the ease with which they could determine the spelling of proper names. Even getting explanations or asking the witness to repeat something was not very difficult with this quality of link.

This difference in opinion could have been expected, despite pre-set assessment criteria. It is hardly possible to assess interpreting performance in an unbiased manner. In this case, the overall picture was further shaded by:

- varying degree of interpreters' competence despite efforts to select experienced and well trained interpreters,
- the process of interpreters' increasing familiarity with the videoconference settings and equipment and the process of natural adjustment to working via video-link,
- too small a sample of interpreters to draw global conclusions; thus further study would be necessary.

The interpreters' performance was affected by the difficulty of the source language utterance, especially when the witness' speech was loaded with many colloquial or local expressions, and a strong Scottish accent, but this is far from surprising regardless of the setting (be it face-to-face or VCI).

However, the best-performing interpreter maintained the best quality in each the setting, and there were no major differences in the quality of the other two interpreters across the various settings.

The quality of interpretation was also affected by factors not directly related to the interpreters' skills. What may have caused additional stress was the fact that speakers in one location did not always realize what was going on in the other location. They sometimes interrupted the interpreter, and in one case asked the interpreter to interpret while he was performing a procedural act (signing the record).

The role of prosecutors cannot be underestimated either, because their willingness or unwillingness to cooperate can make the interpreter's job considerably easier or more difficult, with the important factors being e.g. whether the interpreter can have the record for sight translation, whether the prosecutor is willing to dictate to the recording clerk or wants the interpreter to do so, and whether the interpreter is interrupted or not. Therefore, more generally, "good conversational manners" of all participants in the examination are important for successful interpretation.

As the recording clerk was present only on the last day, no patterns can be observed in this respect, but the prosecutor dictated when the interpreter was with the witness and asked the interpreter to dictate when the witness was alone and the interpreter, the prosecutor, and the clerk were in the same location. It should be recommended that, whenever possible, the interpreters should receive written materials for sight translation (especially the record when it is checked) to reduce the risk of omissions or misinterpretations.

To recapitulate, the tests carried out by the Polish partner (TEPIS) suggest that the competence of the trained and practising interpreters' was at least good in all the investigated settings. It seems that the interpreter's language competence has a predominant impact on their performance regardless of the setting. The most preferable setting from the interpreter's and the witness' point of view, other than face-to face, seems to be VCI B, where the interpreter has direct contact with the witness. The tests conducted by the Polish Partner confirm that there is a need for guidelines regarding the management of the communication process and training in VCI and familiarization with the VC equipment.

6   ACKNOWLEDGEMENTS

The authors wish to thank all the persons involved in the tests: the participating Prosecutors and the Office of the Prosecutor General in Warsaw, the Witness, the Interpreters and the IT staff. Special acknowledgments go to the external interpreting quality assessors Agata Fürstenberg-Kukielak and Anna Setkowicz-Ryszka.

THE POLICE INTERVIEW USING VIDEOCONFERENCING WITH A LEGAL INTERPRETER: A CRITICAL VIEW FROM THE PERSPECTIVE OF INTERVIEW TECHNIQUES

Dirk Rombouts

Local Police Antwerp

1 THE POLICE INTERVIEW AS THE BACKBONE OF A JUDICIAL INVESTIGATION

During many years of conducting police interviews at the Local Police of Antwerp, we sometimes asked fellow police officers what it means for them to carry out a police interview. We received a wide range of answers, some more meaningful and profound than others. Answers included:

- 'A police interview is a goal-oriented interrogation (although there is a difference between a general interview and an in-depth interrogation).'
- 'I start with the "weakest" person in the group and then use the statements I obtained against the other suspects.'
- 'A police interview starts with a casual chat, so that it becomes easier to assess the person you are about to interview.'
- 'Conducting a police interview means in fact having a confidential conversation through direct contact.'
- 'A police interview has to be constructed differently, depending on whether you are interviewing a victim/witness or interrogating a suspect.'
- 'A police interview is a question and answer game, and requires the necessary preparation.'
- 'A police interview is a constant and laborious search for "the truth".'
- 'A police interview has only one objective: to obtain a confession.'
- 'A police interview can only be considered successful if the written version directly corresponds to what was said during the interview.'
- 'A police interview starts with bringing about a good mutual understanding.'
- 'Sometimes the interview consists of people talking across each other, and it turns into an argument between clashing egos.'

We can say that all these answers are meaningful, that all these replies and descriptions shed light on some essential aspects of a police interview and that they all contain elements of the cover term "police interview". They are all answers that refer to the police officers' on-the-spot assessment and understanding of the following questions: what is a police interview, what is its objective and how is it perceived by police officers? It is virtually impossible to draw up a sound, comprehensive definition of the "police interview". In the international specialist literature the following description of a (good) police interview is given:

> The police interview is the fair, objective, authorized and goal-oriented interviewing or questioning of a victim, witness, informer or suspect to gather the qualification, evidence and relevant details of the criminal offence, where the initiative is taken by the interviewer. The interview is a dynamic interaction process with intrinsic and relational aspects. (Bockstaele 2007)

Conducting a police interview on a high-quality level (which is what the justice department expects of its police forces) with respect for the interviewee and convinced of the fact that this interview will be used to give the legal professionals an objective and clear idea of the circumstances requires thorough and continuous training and coaching of police officers.

In the past few decades police forces have encountered a multitude of science-based interview (or conversation) techniques and strategies.[1] Fortunately part of police academies' philosophy is to explore and teach some of these interview techniques either in basic training for police officers or in more specialised courses for the criminal investigation department of the police.

In many interview techniques it is explicitly mentioned that before starting the actual interview (concerning the content, the facts, the modus operandi, the confrontation with collected evidence and forensic investigation, and checking compatibility with witness/victim statements), the police interviewer should invest in "making contact" and "creating a personal bond" with the interviewee and "gain his or her trust" based on mutual respect. This is the so-called "intake conversation". Many authors (including e.g. Gudjonsson 2002 and Zuring 2009) even state that an interviewer who omits, disregards or minimizes these steps at the beginning of the interview and who consequently almost instantly starts the interview itself and only focuses on "the facts" does not have a solid basis to start a well-structured, gradual, objective, accurate and complete interview.

---

[1] These include interview techniques such as: investigative interviewing, cognitive interviewing (and enhanced cognitive interviewing), lie detection through non-verbal and verbal signals, the credibility of witness testimony, questioning of suspects, interviewing vulnerable people, the confession, interviewing minors, questioning psychopaths, interviewing victims and interrogating perpetrators of sexual offences, the video interview, the police interview and personality profiling.

The attitude required from the police officer at the beginning of the interview is stated clearly (in inter alia Rabon 1992, Simons 2007, Vanderhallen 2007 and Beune 2009) as follows: during the first interview the interviewer should invest in establishing personal contact with the interviewee (without becoming over-familiar) and provide an environment where the interviewee will be prepared to talk without any pressure or suggestion by the interviewer. The interviewee should feel, so to speak, "comfortable". By being empathic the interviewer will facilitate the rest of the interview.

It all amounts to the fact that when starting the interview the interviewer should try to make the interviewee feel at ease and bring the interviewee to his or her normal behaviour in a non-threatening situation. The interviewer should be alert and critical during this phase and should assess and capture certain behavioural patterns, sayings, phrasings and non-verbal signals.

None of this is easy given that the police interviewer is often thwarted by people's general assumption that "it is not pleasant to be interviewed by the police". A police interview is not about everyday, trivial things. The search for truth, the strategy and methodology used by the police interviewer to get to the core of the matter will not result in a cosy, social chat.

An important element in this phase of the interview is the unique personal contact that the interviewer establishes with the interviewee. In this phase the attitude of the police interviewer and the approach of the interviewee is often as follows: "We don't know each other. You are going to tell me things you have possibly never told anyone else. I was not present at the events, yet I wish to receive a story as complete as possible. I have all the time in the world to listen to your story."

The start of this unique contact between interviewer and interviewee is initiated and carried out on different levels and in different phases, so that the transition from introduction phase to fact phase is made almost naturally (indemonstrably). Crucial aspects of this essential introduction phase are:

- Is the police officer conducting the interview alone, or with somebody else? What arrangements have possibly been made between both interviewers?
- Welcoming the interviewee.
- Determining the language usage of the interviewee (as/needs? to be able to anticipate).
- What is the level of development and intelligence of the interviewee?
- What is the interviewee's background (profession)?
- Does the interviewee sit in the 'willing chair' or in the 'non-willing chair' (i.e. is s/he cooperative or not)?
- Will the interviewer try to convince the interviewee to talk (without putting the interviewee under any pressure)?
- Physical distance between the interviewer and interviewee, and positions at the table (and possible modifications of this setting).

When this introductory phase comes to an end and the police interviewer arrives at the facts, the details and the circumstances surrounding a crime, the police interviewer will continue to benefit from the personal contact he or she has established with the interviewee, namely by demonstrating an attitude such as "willingness to listen" and "listening actively". In this way, the interviewer will continuously invest in an appropriate approach to the interviewee.

Not only will the interviewer listen quietly and actively to the story of the interviewee without interrupting, he or she will also show empathy and adopt an overall attitude that indicates that he or she is prepared to listen. The interviewer can give small encouragements and hints to keep the interviewee talking; for instance, his or her facial expression can be kind and encouraging. Additionally, the interviewer's attitude and posture (and playing with the physical distance between interviewer and interviewee) can play a certain role in obtaining an accurate statement.

Lastly, during the entire interview the interviewer (if the interviewer is conducting the interview alone) will adhere to a certain rhythm and timing: asking a question – encouraging the interviewee to answer – listening and, most importantly, recording in writing exactly what was said by the interviewee including all possible nuances and twists, since the written statement should be an accurate record of the interview. A good interviewer will feel when the time has come to do this, for example when the interviewee is winding up a certain item. However, typing out the statement at the time remains in any case an interruptive element in the normal course of the interview.

2   CHALLENGES FOR THE INTERVIEWER IN VIDEOCONFERENCES INVOLVING A LEGAL INTERPRETER

2.1   Interviews with legal interpreters

2.1.1   Challenges for the police interviewer

Conducting a police interview with the help of a legal interpreter requires from the police officer extra preparation, insight, attitude and procedure. This is quite a task for the interviewer given the fact that all that is said will be phrased by a third, external channel. Just as in a face-to-face interview where he or she speaks the same language as the interviewee, the interviewer will have to invest in the introductory phase. The interviewer has to create a level of confidence with the interviewee, even if this has to happen through a legal interpreter. The fact that an interpreter is used renders the necessary direct interaction between interviewer and interviewee for the most part impossible.

As far as the verbal channel is concerned, the interviewer is completely dependent on the legal interpreter. An interviewee's non-verbal channel can be detected and analyzed by an experienced police interviewer, although the interviewer will only later (after the translation) hear what part of the verbal output the possible non-verbal channel corresponds to.

It is as if the two signals (verbal and non-verbal) are not sent out at the same time and the interval between both is too long to discover and understand the correct meaning of the non-verbal signal.

Before the interview the interviewer should give the interpreter a short briefing (putting the facts in context, as far as the facts are known by the interviewer) without entering into details. The interviewer should be trained in following the rhythm of an interview with a legal interpreter, which means s/he needs to respect the following order: question – translation – answer – translation.

Finally the police should have at their disposal specially-qualified legal interpreters, who can produce an appropriate and accurate translation that will contribute to a well-structured police interview.

2.1.2   Challenges for the legal interpreter

The legal interpreter should demonstrate the following competences to successfully participate in a police interview:

- The interpreter should have knowledge of the subject (the police interviewer should give the interpreter a short briefing before the interview, without going into much detail).
- The interpreter should have a clear understanding of certain interview (conversation) techniques, in particular respecting silences and pauses that can occur during the interview.
- The interpreter must not take control of the interview; this should be the interviewer's task at all times.
- During the entire interview the interpreter should remain impartial, and should in no way reply to personal questions from the interviewee.
- The interpreter should translate accurately and should pay particular attention to emphases used by the two parties. The interpreter should never decide for her/himself what to stress.
- The interpreter should have a good memory and should be able to order what is said for the transfer of information to be accurate.
- The interpreter needs to have an understanding of certain cultural differences between the interviewee's background and the place (country) where he/she is being interviewed.
- The interpreter should strictly adhere to the code of conduct and should be able to deal with a certain amount of stress that could manifest itself during an interview.

2.2   Interviews using videoconferencing with an interpreter

The need for a videoconference may arise when the interviewer is located at place A and the interviewee at place B. The interpreter may be located at place A or B (i.e. with either the interviewer or the interviewee), or the interpreter may be alone at place C (remote interpreting).

After testing different videoconference-based interview settings in the framework of the AVIDICUS project, the interpreters held different views as to which location they preferred (see Balogh & Hertog and Rybińska & Miler-Cassino in this volume). Some interpreters indicated that it did not matter much to them who they were with, while one interpreter preferred to do the translation while isolated at place C.

However, for the two parties participating in the interview (interviewer and interviewee) the location of the interpreter during the interview did make a difference. Both interviewer and interviewee indicated that it felt more "familiar" if the interpreter was with them and that this caused the communication to be more direct.

The police interviewers commented on the technical aspects such as the camera setup of the videoconference, in particular the necessity of presenting a clear image of the interviewee on the interviewer's monitor. They suggested that three cameras should be provided at the location of the interviewee, so that the interviewer will see on his/her monitor a mosaic of four images at most:

1. a bird's-eye view of the interview room with the interviewee, with or without the legal interpreter
2. an overall, clear view of the interviewee (full-length and not obstructed by, for example, a table)
3. a close-up of the interviewee's face
4. possibly the image of the legal interpreter (showing the head and chest), who in certain cases may find themselves at a third location

On his/her own monitor the interviewee should be presented with a complete image of the interviewer and, if applicable, the interpreter. The same goes for the interpreter: if s/he is located at a third location s/he should see a mosaic of images of interviewer and interviewee.

The reason this set-up is suggested is because it counters the lack of direct contact amongst the three parties and gives the interviewer the opportunity to pick up and analyze the interviewee's non-verbal signals. The interview via videoconference link with a legal interpreter will carry the interviewer and interviewee to a new dimension: watching, listening to and answering an individual through a "television screen" is completely different from the standard, face-to-face interview. Therefore, it is vital that at the beginning of a videoconference-based interview the interviewer invests in the important introduction phase and explains thoroughly the procedure to be followed.

After the video-based interviews (simulations) conducted in the AVIDICUS Project both the interviewer and the interviewee reported that after a few minutes they had forgotten that cameras were recording the interview.

During a videoconference it can be more difficult for the interviewer than in a face-to-face situation to express empathy or to adjust communication channels. It can be harder to convey a message to the interviewee, and to receive and interpret what was said by the interviewee. The interview may quickly degenerate into sterile communication, without colour or relief. The distance created by videoconference seems very large and almost impossible to overcome. The direct contact necessary to conduct an interview successfully is non-existent and this may lead to superficial and not particularly accurate interviews.

Therefore we can conclude that videoconferencing with a legal interpreter is a tool that can be used in certain judicial inquiries, but with the following restrictions:

To be avoided when (non-exhaustive list):

- conducting the first thorough questioning of suspects in certain judicial investigations (e.g. drug smuggling, indecency offences, violent crimes, frontier-running).
- interviewing vulnerable witnesses and victims.
- interviewing minors.
- interviewing psychopaths.

Can be used when (non-exhaustive list):

- Re-interviewing suspects in certain judicial investigations to confront the suspect with for instance new evidence that surfaced during the investigation, detailed questioning about a certain topic that was not sufficiently dealt with during the first, face-to-face interview, and verifying certain topics that came up during the first interview.
- Interviewing as part of procedural issues, for instance in immigration law, and extradition procedures.
- Re-interviewing victims or witnesses to explore certain topics in depth, and if necessary, showing a picture line-up.

3   CONCLUSION

The judiciary and the police should evolve and invest in the technical progress and means of communication of the 21st century. This, however, should not be at the expense of many years' expertise and definitely not at the expense of the professional experience the police services gain within the framework of objective, thorough, structural police interviews respecting the democratic judicial process. It is therefore important to remain alert and to adopt a critical attitude when looking to combine new technologies with years of experience in the field. During their training police officers and legal interpreters should be made aware of both perspectives so as to enable an optimal approach.

REFERENCES

Beune, K. (2009), *Talking Heads: Interviewing Suspects from a Cultural Perspective.* Unpublished PhD thesis, University of Twente.

Bockstaele, M. (2007). *Interviewing techniques. Training course for police inspectors and police officers.* Belgian Police Academies.

Bockstaele, M. (ed.) (2002), *Politieverhoor en personality-profiling.* Brussels: Politeia.

Gudjonsson, G.H. (2002), 'Who makes a good interviewer? Police interviewing and confessions'. In: Bockstaele, M. (ed.), *Politieverhoor en personality-profiling.* Brussels: Politeia, 93-102.

Rabon, D. (1992), *Interviewing and Interrogation.* Durham, NC: Carolina Academic Press.

Simons, A.B. and Boetig, B.P. (2007), 'The structured investigative interview', *FBI Law Enforcement Bulletin,* 76 (6), 9-20.

Vanderhallen, M. (2007), *Werkalliantie in het politieverhoor.* Unpublished PhD thesis, KU Leuven.

Zuring, R. (2009), 'Help! Een getuige', *Blauw* 5 (2), 26-29.

HERE OR THERE? AN ASSESSMENT OF VIDEO REMOTE SIGNED LANGUAGE INTERPRETER-MEDIATED INTERACTION IN COURT

Jemina Napier

Macquarie University

1   INTRODUCTION

In Australia there are approximately 6,500 deaf people who use Australian Sign Language (Auslan) as their first or preferred language (Johnston, 2003). It is estimated that there have been 22 hearing impaired inmates in the New South Wales (NSW)[1] criminal justice system since 2002; ten of whom were identified as Auslan users, and one was a user of a foreign signed language.[2] Any deaf person needing to access courtroom proceedings is entitled to the provision of an Auslan/English interpreter. This service is provided to deaf inmates, as well as to deaf defendants out on bail, deaf complainants or deaf witnesses.

The NSW Community Relations Commission (CRC) provides interpreters in criminal courts in over 85 languages, including Auslan. The interpreting service provided by the Deaf Society of NSW—Sign Language Communication (SLC) (NSW)—provides Auslan/English interpreters in family and children's courts. The policy of both the CRC and SLC (NSW) is to employ only interpreters that are accredited at NAATI Professional level[3]. However, the majority of Auslan/English interpreters are accredited at Paraprofessional level (Bontempo & Napier, 2007), thus it can be difficult to find appropriately accredited interpreters who are available. Additionally, the majority of Auslan/English interpreters are located in the major metropolitan areas; therefore deaf people in regional and rural areas can be disadvantaged in accessing courtroom proceedings when interpreters cannot be found. In these instances, the CRC or SLC (NSW) will often fly an interpreter from the city to a regional courthouse to provide sign language interpreting services.

---

[1]   Australia is divided into 6 states and 2 territories, with federal and state governments and legal systems. Sydney is the capital of the state of New South Wales.

[2]   J. Doherty, personal communication, 20 September 2010.

[3]   National Accreditation Authority of Translators & Interpreters. See Bontempo & Levitzke-Gray (2009) for more information on Auslan interpreter training and accreditation. Go to www.naati.com.au for more information about accreditation levels.

Typically, an interpreter is requested to attend the relevant courthouse, and stay in attendance for the duration or the booking, which can be anything from a 10-minute mention to a 2-week trial. This can become a very expensive provision if the interpreter is flown to a regional area for a very short matter. It is not only in regional or rural areas, however, that it can be difficult to locate suitably qualified Auslan/English interpreters. Due to major supply-demand discrepancies (Orima, 2004), Auslan/English interpreters are in great demand, which means that the CRC can even face difficulties in securing the services of an interpreter for a court hearing in Sydney. In these instances, the CRC will sometimes outsource the booking of an Auslan/English interpreter to the specialist interpreting service offered by SLC (NSW), which caters expressly for the needs of deaf Auslan users. Nonetheless, SLC (NSW) may also encounter problems in filling such a booking request if all the interpreters on their books are unavailable.

To date, statistics from the CRC show[4] that there were a total of 252 court requests to the CRC for Auslan interpreters from 1 July 2009 to 30 June 2010. Of those requests, interpreters were provided on 219 occasions for courts in NSW (211 criminal matters and 8 civil matters)—202 interpreters at NAATI Professional interpreter level (93%) and 17 interpreters at NAATI Paraprofessional level (7%). On 33 occasions (33/252 or 13%), requests were unfilled for the following reasons:

- 23 occasions (9%) for 'no available resource' for requested date/time;
- 9 requests were specifically for deaf relay interpreters;
- 1 request was for a Mongolian sign language.

Furthermore, it is known that SLC (NSW)[5] received 2 referrals from CRC between July 2009 and June 2010, and they have also had requests for 207 Auslan and/or deaf relay interpreters directly from the courts during the same period. Of these requests, 155 were for Auslan interpreters and 52 requests were for deaf relay interpreters. From the total 207 requests, SLC (NSW) were unable to service 7 requests, and 57 were cancelled (either due to not enough interpreters available or cancelled trials as matters were settled within the first couple of days). SLC (NSW) is also aware of one trial in particular that was postponed in the local court as they were unable to provide 8 interpreters per day (5 days), so the trial was re-scheduled by the court.

---

[4] CRC statistics provided through personal communication with Don Alava, the Online Interpreting Booking System Administrator at CRC, 1 September 2010.

[5] SLC (NSW) statistics provided through personal communication with Jasmine Rosza, Manager of the Auslan Interpreting Service at the Deaf Society of NSW, 31 August 2010.

At present, the use of audiovisual link in NSW courts is informed by the *Evidence, Audio and Audiovisual Link Act* (1990). At present, an average of 3 out of 5 matters in NSW courts which involve inmates in Correctional Facilities are heard via audiovisual link (50% in Local courts, 43% in the Supreme or District courts), and the goal of the Department of Corrective Services is to increase this figure to 75%.[6]

This paper reports on an interdisciplinary research project conducted to investigate the effectiveness of remote sign language interpreting services provided through video remote facilities in the New South Wales legal system. The project was commissioned by the NSW Department of Justice and Attorney General, with a view to informing policy about the provision of sign language interpreters in court remotely via video. Remote access to sign language interpreting was tested across five key venues and six scenarios involving deaf people and signed language interpreters. The aim of the project was to assess the impact of using video remote facilities on the quality of the interpretations when interpreters or deaf people are in different locations, and the stakeholder perceptions of interpreted interactions experienced remotely. The challenge in designing the study was to ensure that the variety of possible combinations was tested, and that issues of familiarity and authenticity were addressed. Qualitative findings from the study will be reported to assess the effectiveness of video remote facilities to enable signed language interpreter-mediated legal proceedings; as well as an overview of the challenges involved in the design and data collection aspects of the study. This research informs spoken and signed language interpreter practitioners about issues to consider when interpreting remotely via video, and researchers about issues to consider when designing interpreting research studies.

2 SETTING THE SCENE: A REVIEW OF THE LITERATURE

2.1 Court interpreting

The majority of research on court interpreting to date has focused on face-to-face interactions in the courtroom that are mediated via an interpreter, and it has been well documented that courtroom interactions are impacted by the presence of an interpreter, regardless of the language combination (see for example Berk-Seligson, 1990, 1999, 2000, 2002; Colin & Morris, 1996; Dunnigan & Downing, 1995; Hale, 1996, 1997a, 1997b, 1997c, 1999, 2001, 2002, 2004; Hale & Gibbons, 1999; Morris, 1999a, 1999b).

---

[6] Peter Sharp, Manager of Video Conferencing, NSW Corrective Services personal communication, 5 February 2010).

The challenges for deaf people in gaining access to justice via signed language interpreters have been discussed in various studies and reports (see Brennan & Brown, 1997; Mathers, 2006; Napier & Spencer, 2008; Nardi, 2005; Russell, 2002; Russell & Hale, 2008; Stevens, 2005; Turner, 1995; Turner & Brown, 2001), and report on various issues, including the linguistic issues presented by the fact that signed languages are visual in nature.

2.2 Video remote interpreting

Video conferencing is now more commonly used for the provision of spoken language interpreting, and has been used since the early nineties (see Azarmina, 2005; Böcker & Anderson, 1993; Connell, 2006; Fowler, 2007; Jones, Gill, Harrison, Meakin, & Wallace, 2003; Moser-Mercer, 2005; Mouzourakis, 1996; Niska, 1999), but research has shown that it is challenging for all participants; interpreters can feel alienated; their interpreting performance suffers; and empathy with the client is harder to achieve (Braun, 2006, 2007; Moser-Mercer, 2003; Mouzourakis, 2006). The International Association of Conference Interpreters has developed a code for the use of new technologies in conference interpretation (AIIC, 2000), which outlines recommendations for equipment to be used in order to preserve interpreting quality.

2.3 Video remote signed language interpreting

The advent of technology has enabled deaf people to capitalize on the visual nature of videoconferencing and communicate directly using a signed language. Research has shown that deaf American Sign Language (ASL) users adjust their use of ASL in direct deaf-to-deaf communication via video-conference to cope with the interference from video communication (Keating & Mirus, 2003). Thus it was inevitable that the provision of signed language interpreting services remotely through videoconference facilities or video relay services would become more popular, which is evidenced in the UK and USA in particular (Dion, 2005; Lightfoot, 2006; McWhinney, 2009), and more recently in Australia (Napier, McKee, & Goswell, 2010).

With regard to signed language interpreting, the term 'video remote interpreting' or 'video relay interpreting' (VRI) refers to the process of interpreting via video technology, where at least one of the participants is in a different location. In the USA, the term *video relay interpreting* is used where the interpreter is in a different location to all parties but connected via a telecommunications video relay service (VRS). In *video remote interpreting* the interpreter is in the same location as either the deaf or hearing person.

Typically an interpreter is stationed in one location (e.g., at an interpreting agency with a video facility) and interprets between deaf and hearing clients. These clients may be located together (e.g., a doctor and patient together in a surgery) or separately (e.g., a deaf business person contacting a customer in another city). Interpreters employed to work for a VRI service may be booked for block sessions, reducing the need to travel to and between assignments. There have been concerns that this may potentially be more appealing and may attract more interpreters to VRI work at the expense of face-to-face community jobs (Dion, 2005).

At present deaf people are using VRI or VRS in order to organise short meetings at the last minute, and to make phone calls. With further advances in technology, it is likely that more deaf people will use this service regularly for personal communication, and that an increasing proportion of well skilled sign language interpreters will therefore be employed within this type of service, following trends already established in the USA.

VRI has been identified as an effective solution to providing increased access to signed language interpreters, especially for those in regional or rural areas (Spencer, 2000), and has great potential in reducing the need for proximity (Lightfoot, 2006). Competencies for working as a video relay interpreter have been developed in the USA by the National Consortium of Interpreter Education Centres (NCIEC), and a competency model has been suggested for the training of video relay interpreters (Oldfield, 2010).

Anecdotal reports of VRI note that the use of such technology can impact on the signed language interpreting process and interpreters in several ways, including, for example: the need to adapt signing style to account for the two-dimensional medium, limited options for interpreters to assess deaf client's language needs, less opportunity for interpreters to brief with either party, and difficulties of getting a deaf person's attention if the interpreter is in a different location (Napier, McKee & Goswell, 2010).

Taylor (2005) conducted a study to identify the requisite competencies needed by signed language interpreters to perform video relay work effectively, in order to effectively train interpreting students with those competencies for possible employment as video relay interpreters. Taylor observed and/or interviewed 55 interpreters, managers and administrators in two VRS call centers in the United States, and interviewed 25 deaf 'callers' using open-ended questions. Table 1 shows the differences between traditional and VRS interpreting as identified by Taylor (2005, p.9) as a consequence of her research. In sum, Taylor notes that the core competencies required of VRS interpreters can be divided into three categories: skills, knowledge and personal attributes, which are summarised in Table 2 (taken from Taylor, 2005, p.10). Apart from making recommendations as to the needs for preparing interpreters to work in VRS call centres, Taylor also notes that "there is insufficient supply of qualified interpreters to meet the growing demands of the marketplace. This reality was present before the advent of Video Relay Services, but is more apparent as a result" (2005, p.25).

Traditional interpreting	VRS interpreting
Face-to-face communication	No in-person contact
Three-dimensional perspective	Two-dimensional perspective dependent on high speed compression with times when the quality decays
No physical limitation on signing space	Restricted signing space due to technology
Uses contextual and environmental cues for making meaning	Contextual/environment to support cues are lacking
Relationship between parties is commonly known (e.g. doctor/patient, employer/employee)	Relationships between callers are often unknown
Sociolinguistic factors (gender, age, ethnicity) are overt	Sociolinguistic factors are not always known
Assignments are made in advance	"Immediate" assignments
Ability to accept or turn down assignments (e.g., legal or medical interpreting)	Must accept all calls regardless of content or caller (e.g., young children, new immigrant with limited signing abilities, computer techie)
Potential for extensive preparation	Relies on prior experiences rather than preparation
Generally works alone or with one other interpreter	Team environment
Often self-employed	Works for a corporation
Interpretation is the only role	Multiple roles occurring simultaneously (e.g., operator, customer service representative)
One locale with a relatively limited and predictable number of deaf and hard of hearing consumers (e.g., number of "jobs" in a day often range from one to five)	Wide variety of callers and content (e.g., number of calls in a day can be over 100)
Often regional signs are known	Often regional signs are not known
Consumers see each other and are able to monitor reactions visually and auditorily.	Callers are not able to see or hear each other or monitor reactions.
No special need for technology competence	Technology competence is a necessary skill
Dual-tasking at linguistic and physical levels	Multi-tasking at linguistic, physical and mechanical levels
Generally greater demand for English to ASL interpreting	Greater demand for ASL to English interpretation
Most consumers are experienced using interpreters	Many inexperienced callers placing phone calls
Very little use of intimate register	High number of calls requiring the use of intimate register

Table 1: Differences between traditional and VRS interpreting

Skills	Knowledge	Personal Attributes
Experience	World knowledge	Physical
Adaptability	Deaf related world	Psychological-emotional
Linguistic	knowledge	Professional & ethical
Telephone protocol & voice control	VRS knowledge	conduct
Customer service		
Decision making		
Impartiality		
Technology		

Table 2: VRS interpreter competencies summary

In a follow up study, Taylor (2009) interviewed and observed 143 people over a five month period; including interviews with 64 interpreters and/or managers involved in five VRS call centres across the United States; focus groups with 36 deaf and hard of hearing callers' regarding their current and future VRS needs; and observations of 43 VRS interpreters working. She found that interpreters who worked for VRS call centres still worked regularly in the community. Likewise, deaf people who tended to use VRS regularly also repeatedly requested community interpreters for face-to-face interactions. This more in-depth research led to Taylor expanding on the core competencies required of VRS interpreters as follows: *skills* (metacognitive, language fluency, teaming strategies, call management, customer service and telephone protocol); *knowledge* (experience, practical knowledge, ability to learn, and ethics); and *personal attributes* (ability to maintain confidentiality, tolerance of changes in technology, ability to accommodate and adjust, ability to take care of him/herself, and ability to set boundaries).

Although the focus of Taylor's (2005, 2009) studies was on VRS through call centres, the results are also applicable to VRI in terms of the competencies required of interpreters, and the technological impact on the production and comprehension of signed languages.

Alternatively, a study that focuses on VRI has been recently conducted in the United Kingdom. In her analysis of ten case studies of British Sign Language (BSL)/English interpreter-mediated interaction, Wilson (2010) compared face-to-face interpreter-mediated interactions with situations where deaf and hearing people were together but the BSL/English interpreter was in a remote location. She found that interactions that using VRI were slower, predominantly due to the fact that the number of turns taken in video remote interpreted encounters were higher than in face-to-face encounters. Her analyses demonstrated that as long as large screens were used, that the use of technology did not interfere with the interpreting process. However, she found that participants noted the difficulties of reading fingerspelling and facial expressions through the video conference technology, and deaf people in particular felt that the technology was a barrier to the quality of their interpreting experience. In conclusion, she comments that both face-to-face and video remote interpreter-mediated interactions are effective but that the success is heavily dependent on the situation; thus she recommends that only highly skilled interpreters should be employed for VRI assignments.

The use of VRS interpreting has been explored in Australia by the Australian Communication Exchange (Spencer, 2000), and is currently being extensively trialed (Boyd & Harper, 2010). Furthermore, a recent evaluation of VRI services by the Victorian Department of Human Services (BSR Solutions, 2010) identified three key benefits to using VRI:

1. VRI improved access to health and community services by reducing the average lead time for accessing interpreters;
2. VRI improved quality of health and community service delivery by increasing the number of funded interpreting hours, especially in regional and rural areas;
3. VRI increased capacity to service current and future interpreting demand.

After a significant period of testing and technical development, the Victorian project established recommendations for the technical and environmental requirements for the effective provision of VRI. These include:

a. A designated meeting room (multipurpose or dedicated VRI room) for instalment of VRI infrastructure with blue wall back drop; sound proofing; use of hands free speaker; a means of signalling to an outsider that the room is in use to avoid interruptions; free from distraction; and client confidentiality considerations including privacy and quiet.
b. If equipment is on a trolley and moved around, the floor of the room should be marked to show where the trolley and chairs are to be placed when in use. Although VRI cameras can zoom in and out, the need for the client to see the interpreter clearly and vice versa to enable two-way Auslan conversation should be borne in mind at all times.
c. Display minimum resolution 1400x1050; pan and zoom; split screen to enable all parties to view each other; 25-30 frames per second for 95% of transmission; 115 frames per second for 5% of transmission.
d. Enable link to 3 or more locations.

Evaluations of the Victorian project by deaf consumers and interpreters revealed that all were comfortable with the use of VRI, especially due to the large screens that were used, although the interpreters noted some technological issues (e.g., time delay, problems with set-up, clients not knowing where to look). Overall, however, all the participants commented that they would be happy to use the equipment again. The results of the Victorian project (BSR Solutions, 2010) are promising in terms of using VRI to improve the availability of Auslan/English interpreting services.

2.4   VRI in court

The use of videoconferences in criminal proceedings, especially for witnesses or experts participating in hearings, has been allowed under EU legislation since 2000 (Convention on Mutual Assistance in Criminal Matters between EU countries, Article 10). As Braun & Taylor report in this volume, a 2008 survey by the European working group on E-Justice shows that videoconferences are now widely used in criminal proceedings to speed up cross-border cooperation, reduce costs and increase security (Braun &Taylor's review of current practice in this volume).

The AVIDICUS project has highlighted that the emerging settings include videoconferences with witnesses, experts or suspects in different countries but also between courts or police stations and prisons. These settings are often multilingual, necessitating the use of interpreters to mediate the videoconference proceedings. Videoconference technology has offered a potential solution for current problems with the provision of qualified legal interpreters, especially for minority languages. Thus, "remote interpreting" via a video link using interpreters at distant locations (possibly in different countries), is gaining momentum in European criminal proceedings.[7]

Apart from the findings of the AVIDICUS project and related projects (see elsewhere in this volume), little is known about the viability and quality of video remote interpreting in courts, and training for legal practitioners and interpreters on interpreting in court via videoconference or audiovisual link is almost non-existent. Until the project described in this paper, no research has been conducted about the effectiveness of signed language interpreting services provided through video remote facilities for legal purposes. Given the high stakes involved in legal proceedings mediated through interpreters, it is imperative to analyse the effectiveness of VRI to conduct legal proceedings. Thus, the commissioning of this research project in NSW is timely.

2.5   A study of VRI in NSW courts

The researchable questions addressed in this project were as follows:

a) Communication

1. How easy is it for deaf people to understand interpreters through video remote technology?

---

[7]   http://www.videoconference-interpreting.net/Avidicus.html.

2. How easy is it for interpreters to understand deaf people through video remote technology?

3. What are the challenges for all parties in communicating via video technology?

4. Are there any barriers to having deaf clients or interpreters in remote locations?

5. Is the integrity of the interpreting process affected by the provision of services through video remote technology?

6. What are the optimum settings for sign language interpreters to provide quality services remotely through video facilities?

b) Perceptions

1. What are deaf clients' perceptions of the effectiveness of video remote sign language interpreting services?

2. What are legal professionals' perceptions of the effectiveness of video remote sign language interpreting services?

3. What are interpreters' perceptions of the effectiveness of video remote sign language interpreting services?

The conceptual framework for this project involved ethnographic observation and thematic analysis (Silverman, 2006). It was a qualitative study that involved a quasi-experimental design in that five simulated trial scenarios were tested under similar conditions, but each scenario was treated as a case study as it involved different scripts and/or participants, and involved ethnographic observation and follow-up interviews.

In consultation with representatives from the NSW Department of Justice and Attorney General (DJAG), five sites were identified that have video-conference facilities that can be used to provide signed language interpreting services to courts in NSW. These included:

1. Deaf Society of NSW (Deaf Soc)
2. NSW Community Relations Commission (CRC)
3. Witness Protection (in courthouses) (WP)
4. Corrective Services Cells (CSC)
5. Courtrooms (court)

As the remit of the DJAG Diversity Services is to give consideration to diversity issues in NSW courts, it was decided to focus only on those scenarios that directly involved either the deaf person or the interpreter being in court, and to represent the combination of possibilities with the deaf person remote, the interpreter remote, or the deaf person and interpreter together. Through these discussions it was noted that if the deaf person cannot be present in court, this invariably means they are in custody (CSC) or in witness protection (WP). It was also noted that if the interpreter was in a remote venue, this could be at either the Deaf Society (Deaf Soc) or Community Relations Commission (CRC) videoconference venues, but the impact would be the same. Finally, it was agreed that a control ('ideal scenario') should also be tested for comparison, that is both the deaf person and interpreter together in the courtroom. This gave rise to the recognition of possible scenarios where a deaf person or interpreter might interact with the court via videoconference, also known as audiovisual link (AVL).

It was agreed that testing the possible configurations of the deaf person and/or interpreter being in a remote location was most important, rather than testing every single combination. For example, it would not matter whether the deaf person was in custody or witness protection, the fact that they would be accessing the courtroom from a remote location via AVL was the most important factor. Similarly, it would not matter whether the interpreter was situated at the Deaf Society or the CRC, the fact they are remote was the most crucial aspect. However, as the Deaf Society of NSW has a videoconference system that is not part of the Department of Justice Agency Conference System (JACS), it was decided to test both the Deaf Society and the CRC AVL facilities to ensure that they were equivalent. One additional scenario was also identified: that the deaf person and interpreter may be together in a witness protection room or at a Corrective Services facility. The final five scenarios agreed on for the purposes of testing are outlined in Table 3.

Scenario no.	Location 1	Location 2	Location 3
1	Deaf Soc or CRC (I)	Court	WP or CSC (D)
2	Deaf Soc or CRC (I)	Court (D)	
3	WP or CSC (D & I)	Court	
4	Court (D & I)		
5	Court (I)	WP or CSC (D)	

Table 3: Final five scenarios

2.5.1   Participants

Participants were recruited by the research team, DJAG representatives and with assistance from SLC (NSW). Deaf people with experience of professsional acting were approached directly by the research team to take on the characters in each of the five scenarios. Three actors were confirmed, whose demographics can be seen in Table 4. The deaf actors were asked to simulate deaf people who were more likely to be in the court system, that is, people who are less likely to be well educated, and not particularly bilingual in Auslan and English—people often referred to as having 'minimal language skills' or 'limited Auslan fluency' (Napier, McKee & Goswell, 2010), and were allocated the scenarios as seen in Table 5.

Actor	Gender	Age range	First language
A	Male	35-45	Auslan
B	Female	35-45	English
C	Female	45+	Auslan

Table 4: Deaf actor demographics

Actor	Scenario
A	1 - remote
	2 – in court
B	3 – remote with interpreter
	4 – in court with interpreter
C	5 - remote

Table 5: Deaf actor scenarios

Unfortunately on the day of filming, the Actor C was not able to attend at the last minute. So Actor B stepped in and also participated in scenario number 5.

SLC (NSW) provided sponsorship to the project by providing their in-house interpreters to participate in the data collection at a reduced cost. In the end three interpreters were provided (as seen in Table 6), all of who had NAATI Professional Interpreter accreditation, but only one had experience of working in court. After consultation with DJAG representatives it was agreed that the interpreters were a representative sample of the working population of Auslan/English interpreters, as the majority are female (Bontempo & Napier, 2007; Napier & Barker, 2003), and there is no guarantee that an interpreter would have experience working in court as typically any available interpreter would be booked. The interpreters were randomly allocated to scenarios based on their availability.

Interpreter	Gender	Age range	First language
A	Female	40+	English
B	Female	20-25	Auslan
C	Female	25-35	Auslan

Table 6: Interpreter demographics

Finally, hearing participants were recruited from DJAG employees with the assistance of the DJAG Diversity Services Manager and Senior Development Officer. Participants gave their time voluntarily and acted in the roles of judge, prosecution counsel and defense counsel.

2.5.2   Scenario Data

Five scenarios of a simulated courtroom interaction were developed using scripts from mock-trial scenarios from DJAG and based on real courtroom trial excerpts. The scripts were adapted in consultation with the Diversity Services Senior Development Officer, and a briefing was developed for the deaf actors and hearing participants, giving an overview of the 'character' of the deaf person in each scenario, plus any linguistic issues for consideration. It was decided to use the same two scripts for the scenarios, so Script 1 (Breach of an Apprehended Violence Order), was used for scenarios 1, 2 and 4; and Script 2 (Driving whilst Disqualified) for scenarios 3 and 5 (as seen in Table 7).

Remote witness room	CRC	Deaf Society	Court	Script no.
Deaf person A	Interpreter A		Court personnel	1
		Interpreter B	Deaf person A Court personnel	1
Deaf person B Interpreter B			Court personnel	2
			Deaf person B Interpreter C Court personnel	1
Deaf person B			Interpreter C Court personnel	2

Table 7: Script and scenario allocation

In order to make the simulations as authentic as possible, the interpreters only received brief information about the assignment as would normally be given on a CRC or SLC (NSW) booking sheet, which included: the venue and address, the name of the contact person, date and time of the assignment, the name of the deaf person and the type of court matter.

2.5.3   Process

The data collection process involved complex organisation of multi-location data collection of five scenarios across four sites, using two scripts. The filming took place in four different locations: three in Parramatta (Children's Court, South West Trial Court Remote Witness Room, Deaf Society) and one in the Sydney Central Business District (CRC); which required four researchers to be present to set up each location, film the scenario and interview participants.

Prior to the day of data collection, DVD recorders were installed in the Children's Court, CRC and Deaf Society sites in order to record the video image sent between the courtroom and the remote locations via AVL[8].

Before filming could commence, time was needed to set-up each scenario to ensure that all participants could be seen and heard. Figure 1 illustrates the usual seating positions in court when neither a deaf person nor interpreter is present. It was found that in setting up each scenario, due to the fixed nature of the JACS camera equipment (which could not be moved to focus on different parts of the courtroom or zoom in on people), people had to be moved around so that the deaf person and interpreter in particular could clearly see one another. This often meant that the usual seating positions as seen in Figure 1 could not be adhered to; and the 'views' on the screens either in the courtroom or the remote location room also needed to be adjusted. More detail on these adjustments is given with the description of the results of each scenario.

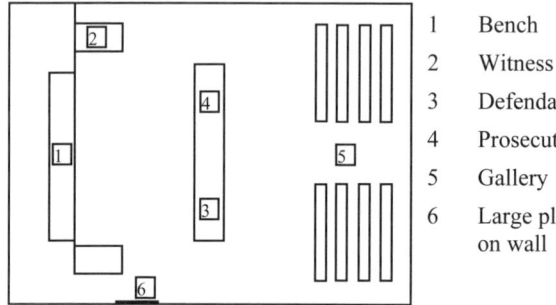

1	Bench
2	Witness Box
3	Defendant and Defence solicitor
4	Prosecutor
5	Gallery
6	Large plasma TV screen mounted on wall

Figure 1: Usual seating positions in court (without interpreter)

Each scenario ran for approximately 10-15 minutes with simultaneous interpretation between English and Auslan. In order to make the simulation as realistic as possible, the deaf actors and hearing participants were requested to respond to the interpretation as appropriate, even though they were following a script. For example, if the script said: "Tell us your full name and date of birth", but the interpreter only signed: "Tell us your full name", then they were asked to follow what the interpreter signed. Or, another example, if the interpreter signed/said something that was unclear, then they were asked to respond as they thought would be appropriate. They were also told that if they deviated from the script (e.g., to clarify something, to interrupt, etc.), then they should return to the script as quickly as possible; and if they had to deviate from the script they should only make one

---

[8]   Typically this recording device is only available in NSW District Courts.

variation before returning to the script and try to make no more than three variations throughout the entire script.

In order to triangulate the data and ensure that all perspectives were captured, each scenario was video-recorded through three points: (1) a static video-camera on a tripod focused on the deaf participant; (2) a static video-camera on a tripod focused on the interpreter (or both the interpreter and deaf person if they were together); and (3) an in-house recording of the footage appearing on the screen through the JACS system[9].

Post-scenario interviews were conducted with all the deaf and interpreter participants using prompt questions that asked their opinions about the use of the technology, their perceived accuracy of the interpretation and whether it was impacted by use of video remote facilities, and their perceptions of the effectiveness of the service. In particular the interpreters were asked about any challenges they experienced, and the deaf people about any barriers they felt they faced. A few of the hearing participants were also interviewed, but due to time constraints many of them had to return to work on completion of the data collection for their scenario. In these instances, the hearing participants were given a hard copy of the prompt questions and asked to email the research assistant with their responses. On completion of the data collection, a follow-up meeting was organised with the JACS Team Leader to clarify the technical specifications used in each scenario. Analysis of the data involved thematic analyses of the various data collected.

2.5.4 Results & Discussion

As already discussed, the project attempted to simulate the range of contexts in which an Auslan/English interpreter may be required to interpret via AVL for a court matter. Throughout the process of collecting the data, it was obvious that employing the services of a sign language interpreter through AVL was effective. In all four scenarios that used AVL it appeared that communication was able to occur. However, to ensure effective communication was possible, some adaptations were needed in some of the scenarios. Without these adaptations the differences between each scenario may have been more noticeable.

To explain the adaptations used during the data collection, for convenience, an overview of each of the scenarios will be presented and discussed separately. Themes from the participant interviews will then be presented with a summary of responses to the research questions.

---

[9]   The first scenario was recorded through the CRC as JACS initially had technical problems, but the remaining 4 were all recorded through JACS.

Overview of scenarios

Scenario 1

In this scenario, the deaf defendant was in custody, the interpreter was in a separate location (at the CRC), and both of these individuals were appearing in court via an AVL. Some possible real-life situations represented by this scenario are:

- weekend bail hearing in regional centre, where no local sign language interpreter is available;
- the inability to transport a defendant to court and no local sign language interpreter is available;
- deaf witness permitted to appear via video link, and no local sign language interpreter is available.

Image 1 is a still-photo taken from the video recording of this scenario. The top picture is divided into two separate images, with the Magistrate on the left side and the Bar Table on the right. The deaf defendant is in the lower, left-hand corner of the image, and the interpreter is in the lower, right-hand corner. This layout was seen on the television screens in all three locations: in the Court, the Remote Witness Room and the CRC. The court and the CRC had large, wide-screen plasma televisions; the Remote Witness Room had a small television screen. Regardless of the television size, in the debriefing after the scenario, both the interpreter and the deaf participant commented that they would have preferred a larger screen, and to not have seen themselves on the screen. The layout of the courtroom for Scenario 1 is illustrated in Figure 2. In this scenario, it was not necessary to move anyone in the courtroom.

Image 1: Scenario 1 – Deaf defendant 'in custody', interpreter (at CRC); both appear via AVL.

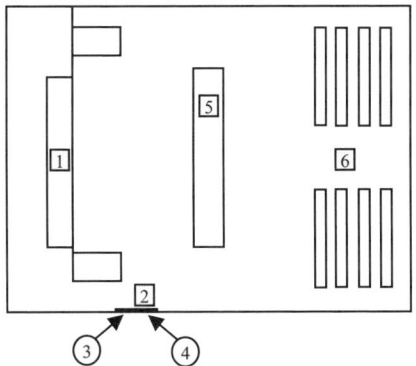

1 Bench
2 Large plasma TV screen mounted on wall
3 Deaf defendant in custody – appearing via AVL connection 1
4 Interpreter at CRC – appearing via AVL connection 2
5 Prosecutor
6 Gallery

Figure 2:Scenario 1 - Deaf defendant 'in custody'; Interpreter at CRC – both appear via AVL

Other technical specifications about the AVL connection for scenario 1 are listed in Table 8.

Connection type	Videoconference mode
Bandwidth used	512kbps
Layout description	3-way split
Other information	JACS established 512kbps connection; Court Officer would only be able to connect at 256kbps

Table 8: Technical specifications for Scenario 1

As noted in Table 8, the connection was established at double the speed of a normal connection than what would be possible if established by a Court Officer. To check whether communication could still be achieved at a lower speed, the researchers re-tested this scenario at 256kbps and found no difference. In addition to the potential real applications of Scenario 1 as mentioned above, another real-life context which would realistically be represented by Scenario 1 is the solicitor-deaf defendant consultation during a court case. In this situation, the court would need to be cleared.

Scenario 2

This scenario is similar to Scenario 1, in that the interpreter is appearing in court via AVL; the difference in this scenario is that the deaf defendant is in the courtroom. Some possible real-life situations represented by this scenario are:

- deaf defendant/witness in a rural/remote setting, with no local interpreter available;
- weekend bail hearing, with no local interpreter available.

Image 2 is a still-photo image taken from the JACS video recording of Scenario 2. The image on the left is a split-screen shot of the Magistrate and the Bar Table. In the picture of the Bar Table, the deaf defendant is seated on the right, the Prosecutor is seated at the left end of the table. The interpreter is pictured separately on the right side of the screen. In the courtroom, the deaf defendant saw the full image of the interpreter on a large plasma screen.

From Image 2 it should be clearly evident that the position of the deaf defendant at the Bar Table would not be ideal, as this is the view that the interpreter had on her screen in the Deaf Society remote location. In a real-life court matter this is precisely where he would need to be seated. In that position the defendant would need to turn to the left to see the interpreter on the television screen hung on the wall of that particular courtroom. However, something more problematic for communication is the fact that the deaf defendant appears to be very small on the screen. Given that Auslan is a visual language, it is imperative that the interpreter and the deaf defendant are able to see each other clearly. To remedy this situation so that the scenario could proceed, we needed to find another location for the deaf defendant. The cameras in the courtroom are in fixed positions, so we needed to work around these limitations. The best solution was for the deaf defendant to sit in the Witness Box, as seen in Image 3.

The resulting position of the participants in the courtroom can be seen in Figure 3. The location of the deaf defendant in the Witness Box should clearly highlight some of the limitations within the current system. Naturally, having a deaf defendant seated in the Witness Box would impact on court proceedings, especially if there were other witnesses. As such, we recognise that this solution does not reflect optimal court practice, but there may be occasions when a deaf witness would be seated in the Witness Box, so this placement is not beyond the realms of possibility. The other technical specifications for scenario 2 are detailed in Table 9.

Image 2: Scenario 2 – deaf defendant in court, interpreter appearing via AVL

Image 3: Scenario 2 – deaf defendant seated in Witness Box

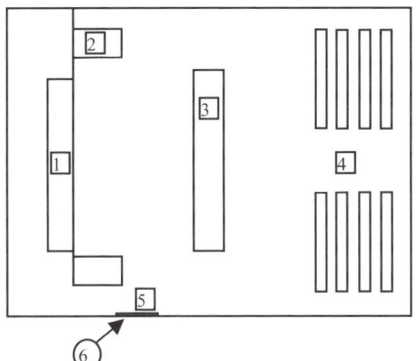

1	Bench
2	Deaf defendant seated in the Witness Box
3	Prosecutor
4	Gallery
5	Large plasma TV screen mounted on wall
6	Interpreter at Deaf Society of NSW – appearing via AVL

Figure 3: Scenario 2 - Deaf defendant in courtroom; Interpreter at Deaf Society of NSW, appearing via AVL

Connection type	Bail video mode
Bandwidth used	512kbps direct connection
Layout description	Bail video mode

Table 9: Technical specifications for Scenario 2

Scenario 3

In this scenario, the interpreter was with the deaf defendant in a remote location, and both appeared in court via the one AVL link. Some possible real-life situations reflected by this scenario are:

- deaf defendant in custody, but unable to be transported to courthouse;
- deaf witness appearing from a remote location and granted permission to appear via AVL;
- deaf witness being protected, thus permitted to give evidence from remote witness room in the same courthouse.

Image 4 is a still-photo taken from the video recording of this scenario. As can be seen in the image, the interpreter and the deaf defendant are seated facing each other, seated a comfortable distance from each other to allow for signing space. Both participants are positioned with their bodies slightly at an angle so that they can be seen as clearly as possible in the courtroom. The television in the Remote Witness

Image 4: Scenario 3 – deaf defendant and interpreter in custody

Room showed a split-screen image of the courtroom, with the Magistrate on the left of the screen and the Bar Table on the right. The technical specifications for scenario 3 can be seen in Table 10.

Connection type	Videoconference Mode
Bandwidth used	512k direct connection
Layout description	Videoconference Layout
Unique technical specs	Court Officer will be able to connect in this mode
Display in RW room?	Split screen of Bench and Bar similar to top image in screenshot from scenario 1.

Table 10: Technical specifications for Scenario 3

Scenario 4

This scenario was the 'control' scenario. This scenario reflects the current practice of having the interpreter and the deaf person in the courtroom. No AVL was used for this scenario to allow for comparison of current practice and the use of AVL. Image 5 shows the position of the deaf defendant and the interpreter in relation to each other. The deaf defendant was seated at the Bar Table as would be expected in a typical courtroom set-up. Image 6 is a screenshot of what was recorded through the court AVL (JACS) system, which shows the Bench on the left and the Prosecutor and the deaf defendant, seated at the Bar Table, on the right. The significance of these two images will be discussed in the analysis of the scenarios below.

Image 5: Scenario 4 – Deaf defendant (left) and interpreter (right) in court

Image 6: Screenshot of scenario 4, recorded through AVL system

The location of all participants in the courtroom is illustrated in Figure 4. The position of the interpreter is the typical one used in the courtroom if there is a deaf defendant present, but the interpreter may be required to sit or stand in other positions depending on the preference of the Bench, or the role (and thus location) of the deaf participant in the court matter. So while this scenario reflects the current practice of having an interpreter in the courtroom, the positioning of the interpreter may vary.

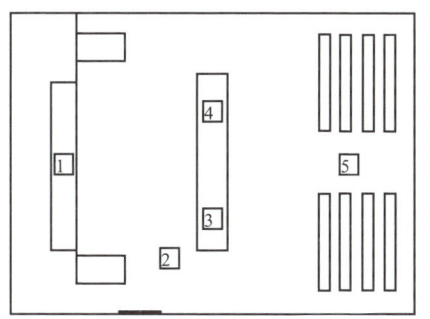

1   Bench
2   Interpreter
3   Deaf defendant
4   Prosecutor
5   Gallery

Figure 4: Scenario 4 - Location of all participants

Scenario 5

This scenario was the last permutation of the combination of participants engaging in a court matter via AVL. In this situation, the deaf defendant was in a remote location, but the interpreter was in court. Some possible real-life situations reflected by this scenario are:

- deaf witness in a remote location some distance from the court where the matter is being heard, but an interpreter is available at the court;
- deaf defendant in custody and unable to be transported to court, but an interpreter is available at the court;
- weekend bail hearing in a location where an interpreter is not locally available, but one is available at another court.

Image 7 is a screenshot from the video recording of this scenario. In this picture the screen is divided into four sections. Moving clockwise from top-left, the images are: the Bench; the interpreter (seated in the Witness Box); the deaf defendant (appearing via AVL from the Remote Witness Room); and, the gallery within the courtroom. It should be noted that once again, as in scenario 2, we had to position one of the participants (this time the interpreter) in the Witness Box. Unlike scenario 2, where there may be real-life circumstances when a deaf person would be seated in the Witness Box, there is no real-life circumstance where an interpreter who is working in a court would be seated within the Witness Box. However, to circumvent the limitations of the current system and the fixed positioning of the cameras within the courtroom, this was the only viable option to be able to proceed with the scenario. As such, this solution highlights one of the major problems and limitations of the current system.

Image 8 is a screenshot of what was seen on the large plasma television screen in the courtroom. Only the deaf defendant was shown on the screen within the courtroom, while Image 7 is what the deaf defendant saw on the screen in the Remote Witness Room.

Image 7: Scenario 5 – Interpreter in court; deaf defendant in custody, via AVL

Image 8: Deaf defendant (in custody) appearing in court via AVL

As mentioned above, the JACS cameras are in fixed positions, so this was the only screen-split that could be obtained to get all participants on screen. The lack of clarity of Image 7, due to the visual distraction of the other participants appearing on the screen at the same time is a significant issue that will also be discussed below.

The location of all participants for scenario 5 is represented in Figure 5, and the technical specifications for scenario 5 are revealed in Table 11.

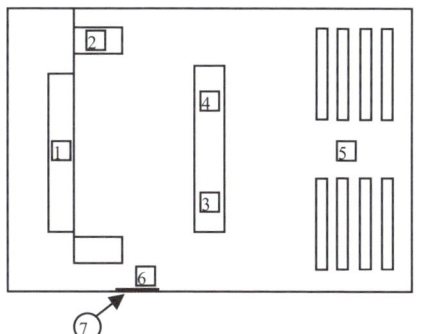

1   Bench
2   Interpreter seated in the Witness Box
3   Defense solicitor
4   Prosecutor
5   Gallery
6   Large plasma TV screen mounted
    on wall
7   Deaf defendant in custody – appearing
    via AVL

Figure 5: Scenario 5 - Location of all participants

Type of connection	Bail Video
Bandwidth used	512k direct connection
Layout description	Bail Video Mode
Unique technical specs	Court Officer will be able to connect in this mode

Table 11: Technical specifications for scenario 5

In sum, overall access was achieved in all five scenarios; there were no significant communication breakdowns, and the interpretations of the trial dialogues were all accurate. Thus it seems that it is possible to provide Auslan/English interpretation in court via AVL, with either the deaf person, or interpreter (or both) being in remote locations. However, it is important to note that adaptations had to be made to make the provision viable.

Now that an overview of each scenario has been provided, detailing the logistics and the screen 'views' that the deaf and interpreter participants had access to, it is worth considering the themes that emerged from the participant interviews. More detail of the ethnographic observations, and linguistic analyses of each scenario can be found in a separate publication (Naiper in press).

2.5.5   Participant interviews

All deaf and interpreter participants were interviewed in Auslan and English respectively after the completion of each simulated trial scenario. The interviews were recorded on videotape for further transcription and analysis. Given there were multiple hearing participants performing the roles of other personnel in the courtroom, it was not feasible to interview each of them separately after completion of the scenarios, so they were asked to provide written feedback in response to a series of questions. Disappointingly not all the hearing participants returned written responses; and for the majority, the comments were quite limited. However, one hearing participant who played one of the court personnel was interviewed after a their involvement in two of the scenarios.

The transcripts and written translations of the interviews were analysed for key themes that emerged across comments from all participants. The issues identified have been organised into six themes: Clarity of AVL; Communication; Roles & Participation; Improving the AVL system; Environmental & Technological Issues; and, other Miscellaneous Issues.

Clarity of AVL

As mentioned earlier, it is clear that communication and being able to effectively conduct a court matter with a sign language interpreter via AVL was possible, regardless of how the technology was used. The interpreters and deaf participants generally commented that the image was clear. However, the size of the participants on the screen and the division of the screen into multiple sections were issues for the deaf participants and interpreters. In addition to these issues, other comments from the participants regarding the clarity of the AVL were:

- (Scenario 1: Deaf defendant) In real-life situations, when I am with an interpreter – face-to-face – if there is some uncertainty or something unclear, then I can easily interrupt and they can go back and clarify the information, or vice-versa if they don't understand me. But, through the AVL system, it's difficult for me to interrupt because the court is in session and things need to keep moving.

- (Scenario 1: Magistrate) I certainly had no problems. It just appeared from the AVL that perhaps the interpreter had big problems. But I don't know what could be done to improve that.
- (Scenario 2: Deaf defendant) You'd have to consider any deaf supporters there might be in the courtroom who might want to express their support for the deaf defendant. In this scenario, with the interpreter only visible on the TV screen on the wall, the other deaf people in the courtroom would not be able to view the screen, so would not have access to what is happening in the courtroom.
- (Scenario 5: Deaf participant) Wasn't clear at all. I felt incredibly disconnected from the proceedings. … If it wasn't for the script, I don't think I would've been able to follow the proceedings very well.

The above comments from the participants confirm many of the observations of the research team regarding technical issues.

Communication

In all scenarios, participants felt that communication was possible, though not always without problems. The 'clarity' factors discussed above certainly impacted on the success of communication. However, in the debriefing interviews the participants made several comments in relation to communication; they included:

- (Scenario 1: Deaf defendant) …you need to explain the AVL process to the deaf client before it begins: "You'll be in this room here. You're the 'witness'. You will communicate via a video camera." It's important to make sure they're aware of the process and understand what's involved before they start.
- (Scenario 1: Deaf defendant) The blue outline around the quadrant of the screen indicates who's speaking and I think that looks good and worked well.
- (Scenario 1: Interpreter) I don't like being away from the deaf person so much. … As an interpreter, it's about that control and being able to go, "Sorry, it's not working." And wondering whether they can hear me. And it just slows everything down.
- (Scenario 1: Prosecutor) The interpreter and the client were not able to see me properly from position (sic).
- (Scenario 1: Prosecutor) I felt like speaking slower so that the interpreter could understand what I was saying.
- (Scenario 1: Magistrate) I was mindful of the interpreter, but also, I know from my experience in court that people don't speak a mile a minute. And certainly from the Bench, they don't. So I was mindful of that.

- (Scenario 2: Deaf defendant) Often when deaf people are working with interpreters, you'll see that they sign everything directly to the interpreter. I think I'm a little bit different; I forget about the interpreter and sign towards the person I want to address. But after this scenario I realise that it's important for the deaf person to watch the interpreter. I found that quite difficult because if I'm only watching the interpreter on the TV screen, then I may not be sure who is speaking and to whom I should respond. But if I'm not watching the interpreter, then she isn't able to interrupt me to ask me for clarification, or to repeat something she might not have understood when I signed it. I admit that I ignored the interpreter in favour of focusing my attention on the participants who were in court with me. … For me, I'm very competent at working with interpreters, but it is hard to maintain focus on the interpreter on the TV screen, and the other participants in the court.

- (Scenario 2: Deaf defendant) Generally speaking, both in the Remote Witness Room, and here in the courtroom, it was difficult to manage the communication. I'm not meaning in relation to working with an interpreter, I guess it's more to do with the nature of the situation. That I'm not communicating with someone immediately present and because I was aware that what I was saying was being recorded. As such, I needed to put more thought into what it was that I had to say. So it actually made me more tense.

- (Scenario 2: Prosecutor) [Everyone was able to communicate] very easily.

- (Scenario 3: Deaf defendant) The way the interpreter and I were seated, facing each other, was fine. … There may have been some small degree of discomfort with being seated so close to each other – I don't know. But that is a possibility.

- (Scenario 3: Interpreter) I had to turn so that the Judge could see me; I was really close to the deaf person.

- (Scenario 4: Deaf defendant) It would be more difficult for an interpreter to interject if they were in a different location.

- (Scenario 4: Prosecutor) I read the script slowly in order to cover my nerve (sic).

- (Scenario 5: Deaf defendant) I found it very hard to feel like I had a connection with the interpreter – for example, if I needed something clarified.

- (Scenario 5: Deaf defendant) In terms of "communication" and "access", it was there, but in terms of it being "equal" and feeling "empowered", I felt at a disadvantage.

- (Scenario 5: Interpreter) I think there was definitely communication there, but it didn't feel as smooth as compared to if she were in the room.

- (Scenario 5: Interpreter) When I was fingerspelling…I was very conscious of having my [indicates holding palm forward, towards the camera].
- (Scenario 5: Interpreter) There was definitely a preference for when I was with her in the room, I felt like I could get more feedback from her, I knew if she was understanding.

Again, data from the interviews corresponds with observations from the research team concerning communication generally, and whether the deaf and interpreter participants could adequately communicate with one another to ensure that the trial process was effective.

Roles & participation

For most of the scenarios, the participants felt they were able to engage in the exchange quite naturally; however, they did notice some issues relating to individuals' roles and participation. This extended to the interaction between the interpreter and the deaf defendant, their initial meeting, and the extent to which they felt 'connected' to the proceedings. Some of the comments surrounding these issues include:

- (Scenario 1: Deaf defendant) I think the communication in this scenario was actually quicker than in a real life court setting. For example, if a deaf person was really going to court, they'd have to wait for the interpreter to arrive, walk into court with them, of course there'd be a level of anxiety, the need to introduce the interpreter to other people, meanwhile the deaf person would be keen for things to get underway. But in this scenario, the interpreter came in, sat down and everything began straight away. It all ran very smoothly.
- (Scenario 1: Interpreter) I slowed down [my signing speed] because I couldn't get the feedback [from the deaf client]. … you always get that feedback as to whether they understand your signing and then you become more natural. But I didn't feel there was that feedback – there was a lack of closeness.
- (Scenario 2: Deaf defendant) Sitting in this [Remote Witness] room, I felt like I had more control around how I said things. In the court I wouldn't necessarily have that same level of control. I feel that in court I'd be more anxious about what I say because I know there'd be other people watching me, so I'd have to be more mindful about what I said and how I said it. … The technology was fine – it was easy to communicate, but I felt quite disconnected.
- (Scenario 2: Deaf defendant) I'm trying to predict how another deaf person might feel if they were in this situation. And I imagine they'd be a bit anxious and wouldn't know what to do and might feel intimidated with the cameras and other people watching them.

193

- (Scenario 2: Prosecutor) … because the interpreter took up the whole screen – so it was just like having another person in the room.
- (Scenario 4: Interpreter) The only bit I felt like it was missing out of the normal situation is just the whole introducing myself to the client and getting to know a little bit more about it right prior to it and just being introduced to the court as well. That all felt like it was missing but I can understand that we just go straight into it.
- (Scenario 5: Deaf defendant) I felt weak and intimidated being in [the Remote Witness Room] on my own. I felt that normally a deaf person would be able to ask an interpreter for clarification, that the interpreter would get the message and stop straight away, but in this situation it wasn't possible. It would require me to draw attention to myself, and while some deaf people might not mind that and would be able to assert themselves and ask for clarification, there would be other deaf people who would be too intimidated by having everyone's eyes on them. The less-assertive deaf person might not say anything, or ask for clarification until after the court proceedings.
- (Scenario 5: Deaf defendant) It's more difficult when we're in different rooms. Also, I'm wondering in the kind of scenario we depicted, would there be time or opportunity for the deaf person and the interpreter to meet for a "warm up"? So the deaf person has to deal with the challenge of possibly having an unfamiliar interpreter that they may not have worked with, or do not work well with, plus having to conduct their business in the court.

One issue that was not considered by the research team was whether the deaf person and interpreter could meet to 'warm-up' before a trial. This was an oversight. It often happens (but not always) in real court cases that the interpreter will be introduced to the deaf client, and they will have a brief interaction so that the interpreter can assess the deaf client's signing style, use of dialect, and establish their role as an interpreter before going into the courtroom. When technology is being introduced into the mix, then this introduction would be even more vital to ensure that all participants feel 'connected'.

Improving the AVL System

During the debriefing interviews all participants were asked for any suggestions they could offer to improve the AVL system. While some were practical solutions to issues they had identified earlier (such as increasing the size of the TV screens), others were more unexpected as follows:

- (Scenario 1: Deaf defendant) Maybe they could have a button for the deaf person to press, which would light up a switch in front of the interpreter to make them aware of the problem, and then they'd know they might have to provide some clarification. They need something to make it easier for the deaf person to intervene if needed.

- (Scenario 1: Deaf defendant) [They] could have three coloured lights to help indicate who is speaking. For example, if the Judge is speaking, then one light lights up to indicate this. I'm only suggesting this because when looking at the small screen it can be quite difficult to know who is speaking, which can be confusing.
- (Scenario 1: Interpreter) I think it's important to have the hearing people on screen, just to get in your own head where they are, who they are, rather than just hearing voices. Because sometimes you can't discriminate the voices.
- (Scenario 2: Interpreter) I don't need to see me, but it was helpful being able to see the Judge. It would have been helpful to see the Prosecutor. … I was not sure if she was asking a question of [the deaf defendant] and then it made me think I'd interpreted incorrectly. But then she started talking and I was like, "Oh! There's someone else here."

Environmental & technological issues

In addition to the issues identified so far, there were others that were directly related to the environment, either in the courtroom, or the other locations connected via AVL. The comments relate to the physical surroundings, but also to some aspects of the technology. Some comments noted during the debriefing interviews include:

- (Scenario 1 & 2: Deaf defendant) The background was too bright.
- (Scenario 1: Deaf defendant) The picture quality was slightly blurry.
- (Scenario 1: Interpreter) There was a bit of a delay. … So it's a bit off-putting.
- (Scenario 2: Deaf defendant) Having the large TV screen on the far wall, opposite the Witness Box was good, but it wasn't always clear who was speaking – if it was the Judge or one of the solicitors. Working through the AVL, I don't think the interpreter was fully aware of the positioning of people within the courtroom so wasn't able to convey it clearly. For it to work effectively, you'd have to clearly inform the interpreter about who is in the courtroom and where they were positioned. Because the interpreter is conveying the speech from all the other participants, and without clearly establishing who is speaking, it is remarkably confusing.
- (Scenario 5: Interpreter) I wasn't sure whether there was any delay or [the deaf defendant's] feedback wasn't immediate, so it was hard to know whether things were going okay.
- (Scenario 5: Interpreter) The only one thing I will say about [the position of the TV screen on the wall] though, is I had to kind of lean

up and that was a bit uncomfortable. If it was for a long period of time, I think that would get pretty uncomfortable. You'd want to be higher up – or just have the TV lower.

- (Scenario 5: Interpreter) I'd say at first, like [signs: POINT POLICE], or [signs: POINT LAWYER] is saying, or [signs: POINT JUDGE] is saying now, but I wasn't sure if that was clear [in the Remote Witness Room]. I think you'd always have to make sure that you say who is talking before you interpret it for them. But if [the deaf defendant]'s seeing this [signs: TV screen divided into four sections], if I'm pointing there, that might actually be nothing and that they're actually over there.

Miscellaneous Issues

In addition to the comments revealed above, one deaf participant commented on the practical application of AVL and when it might be appropriate:

- (Scenario 2: Deaf defendant) There's such diversity in court matters, that I think it would be good to have both options: in court and via AVL. There needs to be a degree of flexibility, based on the nature of the case. If it was a big case, then it would be better for all participants to be in court. If it was only a minor matter, then it could happen via AVL.

2.5.6 Summary of results

To summarise the results from the data, it is clear that AVL can be an effective option for employing a signed language interpreter to work in court. The project explored all possible combinations of an interpreter working through an AVL connection, from within and outside a courtroom. The participants in the project commented on the extent to which they felt fully included or excluded in court proceedings in each of the different scenarios. Noticeably, all the hearing participants' comments for each of the scenarios reflected that they felt the AVL was effective, with the exception of minor technical problems. By contrast, the deaf participants and the interpreters identified some significant areas of concern and limitations of the current AVL system. Their insights are reflected in the comments from debriefing interviews, noted above. In addition to these comments, the researchers analysed the footage for any evidence of other possible concerns. These additional concerns will be discussed below in a summary of the issues noted during the study. As such, fairly well rounded feedback about the process of having an Auslan/English interpreter via AVL in a court matter was gained. To further summarise the results arising from this data, we present responses to the initial research questions for the study.

The first series of questions relates to the effectiveness of the communication via AVL technology.

1. How easy is it for deaf people and interpreters to understand each other through video remote technology?

Four of the scenarios required the use of AVL technology (scenarios 1, 2, 3 and 5), while one scenario (4) was a control and had all participants within the courtroom. According to the participants, they were able to understand each other, with the exception of scenario 5. As will be discussed with regards to the limitations of the study, the fact that the scenarios were scripted may have impacted on the extent to which the deaf participants relied on the interpreter. However, the interpreters (who were not provided with a script) were able to understand the deaf participants in all scenarios.

In addition to being scripted, the effectiveness of the communication may be somewhat deceptive because some adaptations were made during some scenarios, which were beyond standard practice. In particular, in scenarios 2 and 5, participants were seated in the Witness Box. Other challenges, addressed in the next question, would also impact on the ability for the participants to understand each other.

2. What are the challenges for all parties in communicating via video technology?

The participants commented on several challenges and distractions throughout the process, such as: multiple images on the television screen; the slight delay between signing production and seeing it on camera; seeing oneself on the screen; environmental factors such as lighting and distracting backgrounds; fixed camera angles and the position of the TV screens; location of the microphone; the difficulty in watching the television screen and observing what is happening within the courtroom; limited feedback and ability to interact with each other; and the small TV screens which made it difficult to see each other clearly.

In spite of these concerns, the participants felt that communication was possible, but problematic. Less assertive deaf defendants and less-skilled interpreters may be less able to cope with these challenges, which would impact on their ability to understand each other.

3. Are there any barriers to having deaf clients or interpreters in remote locations?

The barriers for using an AVL connection in remote locations depend on the available technology. According to JACS, the technical specifications for the AVL system are uniform across the state. As such, there should not be limitations for using this system in remote locations. The only limitations are the challenges mentioned above, which would be similar to those faced in metropolitan centres as well.

4. Is the accuracy of interpretations affected by the provision of services through video remote technology?

The accuracy of the interpretations is limited by the ability of the parties to communicate effectively through the technology. The data from this project has shown that the interpretation will only be limited if the ability for the interpreter to clearly see the deaf person is reduced, or vice-versa. The factors that impact on the clarity of the interpretation are outlined in the discussion above and in the response to question 2. The accuracy of the interpretation when working through AVL will depend on the interpreter's level of competency, as with any interpreting setting.

5. What are the optimum settings for sign language interpreters to provide accurate, quality services remotely through video facilities?

The optimal settings for effective communication via AVL rely on addressing the challenges outlined above. In addition, the current technical standards for bandwidth should be maintained, or increased where possible. If possible, the interpreter and deaf person should be briefed on the layout of the courtroom and who is present. The technology should be flexible enough to accommodate the option for the interpreter and deaf person to see only each other on the screen, or at least as the main image on the screen. Other participants in the courtroom could be visible on the screen, although priority should be for the deaf person and interpreter to see each other. To ensure correct camera position, the use of portable cameras and television systems should be investigated.

6. What are deaf clients' perceptions of the effectiveness of video remote sign language interpreting services?

Generally the deaf clients felt the AVL system was effective and enabled access to the court. However, they felt more empowered and included, and that they had greater access, in some scenarios more than in others. They also recommended that interpreters and deaf people should be prepared for working through AVL, including knowing who all the participants are, seeing the layout of the courtroom, and seeing how the process will work. The deaf participants also recommended that it would not be appropriate to use AVL for all legal cases. Finally, they questioned whether some deaf individuals could be disadvantaged by using AVL: they may feel dis-connected from the interpreter (in some settings), not assertive enough to state their needs, and potentially feel intimidated by the video equipment.

7. What are legal professionals' perceptions of the effectiveness of video remote sign language interpreting services?

In the scenarios we employed the services of volunteers to play the roles of legal personnel in the courtroom. As such, the feedback received was not necessarily from legal professionals. However, all these participants commented that they felt the communication was effective and smooth. One concern, and possible limitation of the study, was that these participants were relying on a script, which may have given a false impression about the effectiveness of the communication; if there had been no script, we might have seen a more definitive indication of the effectiveness of the communication. The justification for using scripts was to reduce variation between the different scenarios, to allow for easier comparison and analysis. A suggestion for further research is to explore AVL in a longer mock trial that is unscripted to assess more accurately the effectiveness of the communication.

8. What are interpreters' perceptions of the accuracy and effectiveness of video remote sign language interpreting services?

As discussed above, all the interpreters felt that communication through the AVL was effective and accurate. However, to ensure accuracy there were times when the interpreter needed to interrupt and seek clarification and they commented that this was much more difficult through AVL than face-to-face. Furthermore, the inflexibility of the current system, with fixed camera angles and screen layouts, meant that communication was challenging at times.

2.5.7   Limitations of the study

Before concluding the description of this study, there are some limitations that are worth noting. Given that the study did not use authentic courtroom data, various issues were identified that influenced the outcome of the research, as follows:

- The first limitation to note is the fact that deaf actors and DJAG employees were used as participants rather than actual deaf defendants/witness and legal personnel. It was acknowledged in the planning stage that this would have been the ideal, but it was difficult for two reasons: (i) the ethical tension in asking a deaf person who is in a potentially vulnerable position to participate in a research project; and (ii) the difficulty in finding suitable legal personnel to be involved, as the project did not have the budget to match their usual fees, and they would be busy with real cases.
- Secondly, in using simulated trial scenarios and employing professsional actors, the study may not have adequately reflected the real experience for deaf people in the court system who are not well-educated or literate, nor familiar with working with interpreters, or confident at being in a formal setting such as a courtroom. Although the actors were 'in character' and the interpreters were briefed on the 'type' of deaf person they were interpreting for, the interpreters still

seemed to interpret to the actual 'person' present rather than his/her 'character' (e.g., use of fingerspelling for a bilingual deaf person, rather than targeting the monolingual non-English literate character).

- This situation could have been exacerbated by the fact that the interpreters often had to interpret for the deaf person during the set-up of technical logistics before the scenario began, so that the deaf person could understand what was going on. This means it may have been harder for the interpreter to regard the deaf person as a 'character'. Although interpreters were not asked to interpret the set-up, they often took it upon themselves to do so because of delays with the start, and the fact that the lead Research Assistant in the courtroom was talking to the JACS technician via an audio communication link to iron out any technical problems.

- Aside from any potential technical difficulties, well-educated deaf bilinguals who are used to interacting with interpreters and technology may have more facility to adjust to using interpreters via technology; that is, they may be more adaptable to new environments. Thus the deaf actors' perceptions of their experience may not adequately reflect the wider deaf population.

- As the study focused on the technological aspects of interpreting in court via AVL, none of the typical legal procedures were followed: there was no introduction to the case, no reading of the oath/affirmation for the interpreter; and there was no opportunity for the interpreter to 'meet' the deaf client beforehand and prepare. The lack of adherence to these protocols may have affected the interpreter and deaf participants' sense of involvement.

- Scenario 5 should have had a different deaf person, but she unfortunately pulled out at the last minute. This means that scenarios 4 and 5 involved the same deaf person and interpreter for two scenarios, but different scripts were used[10].

- The use of scripted scenarios may have been problematic. The research team tried to account for the potential lack of authenticity by using scripts in advising participants to allow for deviations (e.g., incorrect interpretation, clarify, repair) then return to script. It would have more closely replicated an authentic court case to have no scripts and simply provide participants with briefings and allow them to improvise. Scripts were chosen in order to try to standardise the language used in each scenario (e.g., to prevent more use of fingerspelling in one scenario than another). But it was noted that the

---

[10] We tried to avoid the same deaf person and interpreter being together for more than one scenario to avoid development of familiarity.

use of scripts did impact on the authenticity of the data, especially in relation to potential communication breakdowns. For example:

- Scenario 3 – there was an audio problem in court (when the interpreter was too far away from the microphone in the remote location), but the judge stuck to the script until the Research Assistant in the court intervened. In an authentic setting, if the judge could not hear, he or she would have stopped proceedings to determine the nature of the problem.

- Scenario 5 – the deaf witness lost track of who was talking, and when there was a long pause, she realised she had been asked a question so she referred to script and continued. If there had been no script, there would have been more confusion and need for clarification.

- The final (and major) limitation is that the results have effectively been manipulated as the data collection involved moving deaf people and interpreters to be seated where they could be adequately captured on the fixed cameras. If they were seated where they would normally be expected to sit/ stand in a courtroom, the scenarios would not have been as effective, or in fact possible. So in fact, some scenarios were not realistic at all.

3 CONCLUSIONS

This paper has presented the findings of a study commissioned by the NSW Department of Justice and Attorney General (DJAG), and sponsored by the Deaf Society of NSW, to investigate the effectiveness of sign language interpreting services provided through AVL in NSW courts. The provision of services was tested in key venues with JACS facilities across a range of scenarios involving deaf people, Auslan/English interpreters and non-deaf legal personnel. The aim of the project was to assess the integrity of the interpreting process when interpreters or deaf people were in different locations, and the stakeholder perceptions of interpreted interactions experienced remotely. Qualitative analyses were used to assess the effectiveness of AVL to enable sign language interpreter-mediated legal proceedings. This paper has outlined the various stages of the research and the findings. To conclude, we provide a summary of the issues identified, and the recommendations presented to DJAG. One of the most promising and satisfying aspects of this study is that the results will be directly applied in the provision of sign language interpreting in courts via audiovisual link in NSW courts.

3.1 Summary of issues

This section summarises the issues observed throughout the data collection, in feedback from the participants after the scenarios, and also from analysis of the data. The issues have been grouped into four categories: technological, linguistic, environment, and training and preparation.

3.1.1 Technological issues

(a) Set-up time

Each of the scenarios required an unexpectedly protracted set-up time. This was due to the unique circumstances for each scenario, but also because the limitations of the current system, such as having to seat participants in the Witness Box (scenarios 2 & 5), had to be worked around. Given that the set-up took longer than expected for all of the scenarios using the AVL (1, 2, 3 & 5), it would seem that potential technical challenges would need to be factored into the court schedule to accommodate setting-up the AVL connection. This may result in the use of AVL being problematic for a busy court.

(b) Speed of bandwidth

The speed of the bandwidth needs to be maintained and guaranteed at current minimum standards. For scenario 1, the speed was optimised, but this would be beyond the capabilities of the Court Officers; JACS would need to be involved if this optimisation was required on a regular basis.

(c) Size of television screens

The size of the screens in the Remote Witness Rooms was very small, especially when the screen is divided into smaller sections displaying · different images. The television screens in the other remote locations (i.e., the Deaf Society of NSW and the CRC), were quite large, and even when divided into smaller images, the interpreters felt the picture quality was still acceptable.

(d) Number of images on screen

When the television screen was divided to show simultaneously different images, the deaf consumers and interpreters both found this challenging and distracting – particularly with smaller televisions. Both the interpreters and deaf consumers commented that it was distracting to see themselves signing, especially because there is a slight delay.

(e) Position of microphone

In scenario 3 the position of the microphone in the Remote Witness Room was problematic, resulting in the audio feed to the courtroom appearing to drop out. A research assistant needed to hold the microphone closer to the interpreter as she was speaking so that she could be heard in the courtroom. Given that the interpreter needed to use her hands to sign, and needed to sit far enough away from the video camera so that she and the deaf person could be seen clearly on screen, having the microphone at some distance away and being required to hold it to speak would be impractical.

(f) Use of fixed cameras

The use of fixed cameras within the courtroom and in the Remote Witness Rooms meant that in some of the scenarios (2 & 5) the participants were: a) seated in positions which made it difficult for them to be seen clearly on screen; or, b) were required to sit in positions that were not standard practice (e.g., in the Witness Box). In scenario 3, the interpreter and deaf client were restricted in where they could sit so they could be seen on camera, but still sit comfortably to see each other. Also, the fixed cameras did not always show all the participants in the courtroom, meaning the interpreter or deaf client was not sure who was speaking. At times the camera was pointed at the gallery, which was a redundant image on the screen that was not necessary for the deaf consumer or interpreter.

(g) No recording of interpreter/deaf person when seated in certain locations

Another problem with the fixed cameras is that even when participants were sitting in their usual locations in the courtroom, they were sometimes not seen on camera, so their contribution to the proceedings could not be recorded. This issue is significant for any court matter involving a deaf person who uses a signed language, because without the deaf person or interpreter's signing being captured on video, there is no record of what they have said, or the signed interpretation. Having an accurate record of the original signed messages and the signed interpretations are as equally as important as having an audio recording of any spoken utterances/ interpretations. This recording may be necessary for any subsequent legal matters, such as appeals.

3.1.2   Linguistic issues

(a) Size of signer – difficult to 'read' signing

In relation to the size of the television screen and dividing the screen into multiple images, this impacts on the size of the signer (either the deaf person, or the interpreter). The smaller the image, the less clear it becomes; a smaller image also makes it harder to perceive the subtleties and details of Auslan, such as: fingerspelling, facial expression, eye-gaze, directional verbs, use of space, role shift, numbers, etc.

(b) 3D language rendered in 2D form

Auslan is a visual-spatial language, which uses space grammatically. Signs are produced within the 'signing space' for different purposes, such as: showing direction or location, showing relationships between objects, indicating timelines, and to indicate separate topics – to name a few (Johnston & Schembri, 2007). As such, the language exists within, and exploits, three dimensions. One of the challenges with using a 3D language via a video link is that the option to use 3D space is removed, and the language is portrayed in two dimensions. This may create challenges and result in possible miscommunications. Although the findings of this study did not report any particular problems with the 2D aspect of using video, it has been noted elsewhere (BSR Solutions, 2010) that use of a large screen is ideal to ensure that a person using a signed language can be seen clearly enough. Deaf participants in this study and the Victorian project (BSR Solutions, 2010) noted that when a large screen was used they felt comfortable in watching the Auslan, and were not concerned about any miscommunication. All the participants in this study expressed concerns if they were confronted with a small screen, as some of the nuances of Auslan may be lost. Thus if AVL is to be used, these concerns should be noted and the system used with caution.

(c) Fingerspelling production/readback

In scenario 5 the deaf participant commented that she adjusted the production of her fingerspelling (i.e., spelling an English word using a signed alphabet) so that it would be more clearly visible to the interpreter, who was in the courtroom. She slowed down the pace of her spelling, but also oriented her hand in such as way that it would be more clearly visible. However, this deaf participant is a professional actress and co-host of a television program, so is very comfortable at working via a video camera. The vast majority of deaf individuals would not have this level of metalinguistic awareness, so may not be able to automatically adjust their signing style. This could impact on the overall effectiveness of the communication. The interpreter in scenario 1 also commented that she felt the deaf participant appeared to have slowed down his signing, indicating that he too had sufficient metalinguistic awareness to make this adjustment. This deaf participant was also a professional actor, so possessed a level of awareness that may not be inherent in all deaf consumers.

(d) Attention-gaining strategies/ turn-taking

In all interpreted interactions, regardless of language, there may be occasions when one of the participants or the interpreter may need to seek clarification or interject. For this to occur in sign language, the one who is trying to interject needs to be seen by the other person. In all settings where AVL was used (scenarios 1, 2, 3 & 5), in the debriefing interviews the interpreters and/or deaf participants commented on the challenge in relation to getting the other person's attention, if needed. In the scenarios where the deaf participant and the interpreter were not together (1, 2 & 5) it was difficult for them to get the other's attention if they were not watching the television screen. This may result in inaccurate translations that might go uncorrected or in lost information from a testimony if the person has continued to speak/sign before the misunderstanding is revealed and their clarification is different from their initial utterance. Furthermore, if communication is unclear – either through the inability to seek clarification, or failure to do so – then this could influence the jury's or Bench's impression of the deaf individual, or the interpreter.

3.1.3   Environmental issues

(a) Background

Ideally the background behind the signer should be devoid of as much visual distraction as possible, and should ideally be a solid colour—preferably blue (BSR Solutions, 2010). In scenarios 2 and 5, the deaf defendant and the interpreter were seated in the Witness Box. The wall behind had sections cut out of it, which looked like stripes when viewed on a television screen. In addition, in scenario 5, strips of bright sunlight were shining on the wall behind the interpreter, which produced glare. This, compounded with the high camera angle, the small television screen and the multiple images on the screen, made it very uncomfortable for the deaf person to watch the television in the Remote Witness Room. The deaf participant in scenario 1 also commented that the background behind the interpreter at the CRC was also too bright. The brightness of it impacted on the clarity of the interpreter's hands if they moved within that section of the image on the television screen.

(b) Lighting

As mentioned, above, lighting was problematic if it was too bright or there was too much glare, as on the wall behind the interpreter in scenario 5. If the lighting is too bright or dim, then this will impact on the clarity of the image. Also, strong shadows should be avoided.

(c) Audio

Generally the audio facilities were adequate. However, in scenario 3, when the deaf defendant and interpreter were together in the Remote Witness Room, the audio feed to the courtroom appeared to drop out. After reviewing the data it became apparent that the audio was still working, but was not loud enough to be heard clearly in the courtroom. If the interpreter had spoken louder, then it may not have been an issue, but this would require an interpreter to speak at an uncomfortably loud volume, which would be problematic for any extended period. Basically the problem with the audio feed at this point in scenario 3 was the location of the microphone being some distance from where the interpreter and deaf person were required to sit so they could both be seen on camera.

3.1.4 Logistical issues

(a) For interpreters working via AVL

The three interpreters who were involved in the data collection all had previous experience of interpreting through AVL, though not necessarily within a courtroom. Only one of the interpreters had never been inside a courtroom previously. If interpreters have not had previous experience working via AVL, or within a courtroom, then interpreters should receive training. This would be necessary to prevent problems from arising, and also to enable them to consider the linguistic and environmental issues and how to address them.

(b) For legal personnel on using AVL specifically with Auslan interpreters and deaf people

Training is necessary for court personnel on how to adjust the AVL settings to suit the context, such as: which cameras to use; which video mode (i.e., Bail Video, or Videoconference); adjusting the bandwidth; and involving JACS if necessary. If additional equipment is introduced to address issues listed above, such as portable video cameras, television screens or microphones, then training for this equipment would also be necessary.

(c) Time for briefing regarding technical and linguistic aspects (e.g., establishing who is where)

The deaf participants and interpreters commented that they felt the preparation period was missing from the scenarios. They felt they did not have the chance to meet each other, become familiar with each other's signing style, familiarise themselves with the courtroom, or the other participants. This would be essential so that both the interpreter and the deaf person have a clear understanding of who is involved and is able to draw on linguistic features of Auslan (e.g., the use of space) to indicate who is speaking. A briefing period would also allow for any technical issues to be addressed prior to commencing the court matter.

(d) Establish cues for attention-getting

As noted above, the ability for the deaf person or the interpreter to gain the other person's attention is essential to ensure an accurate interpretation. However, the constraints of working via AVL make this problematic. As such, a briefing period would provide an opportunity for the interpreter, deaf person and court personnel to negotiate cues and protocols for gaining attention. The participants in the data collection noted that being able to seek clarification or interject were essential, but it was made difficult when working via AVL.

3.2   Recommendations

As a consequence of the findings of this research study, six recommendations were presented to DJAG in relation to the provision of Auslan/English interpretation via AVL in NSW courts. It should be noted that the following recommendations were based on the current JACS AVL system. If the system were to be changed and/ or updated, the recommendations would also change. The recommendations focus on the observations of the functioning of the current JACS AVL system in line with the provision of Auslan/English interpretation in five different scenarios. The recommendations were considered by the DJAG Working Party with final recommendations made to the NSW Attorney General for implementation in policy and practice.

Recommendation 1

Based on the current JACS AVL system it is recommended that this system is not used to provide Auslan/English interpreting services in NSW courts, as there are too many issues with guaranteeing effective, equitable access.

At present, the research team feels that the current system is not flexible enough to address the unique requirements of signed language interpreting. Under the current JACS AVL system, the time and trouble involved in establishing the right conditions to ensure that deaf/interpreting access is adequate, means that the AVL system is not the desired panacea. Given the variety of courtroom layouts and available technology (i.e., number of video cameras, size and number of television screens, etc.) and the varying experiences of court clerks in using AVL, the challenge of setting up an AVL interpreting connection would not be worth it, and there would be risks of communication breakdowns.

This recommendation was rejected by DJAG as they felt it important to pursue the use of the JACS AVL system, given there were no major hurdles discovered in this study. However, this position is dependant on Recommendations 2 and 3 and DJAG noted that AVL should only be used in specific circumstances to ensure that the deaf client is not disadvantaged through the lack of availability of a face-to-face interpreter. Where possible a face-to-face interpreter is the preferred option.

Recommendation 2

If the current JACS AVL system has to be used, then it should only be used in certain scenarios.

The results of this project have shown that employing an Auslan/English interpreter to work in a court via AVL is potentially successful, but only effective under certain conditions. In light of evidence from this project and based on the current limitations of the system, we feel that all the scenarios could potentially allow for successful interaction, with provisos.

The recommended preferences for using AVL under the current system are:

- Scenario 3: deaf individual and interpreter together in a remote location, appearing in court via AVL.
- Scenario 1: deaf individual and interpreter are in different locations outside of the courtroom (e.g., interpreter at SLC (NSW) or CRC and the deaf person in remote witness room), both appearing in court via separate AVL connections.
- Scenario 2: deaf individual in court and interpreter in other location. (Note: under the current limitations of the system, this only worked with the deaf individual seated in the Witness Box and because of the large television screen in the remote location).

Scenario 5 (deaf individual in remote location and interpreter in court) is not recommended at all under the current system. In this situation the deaf person in the remote location became too confused by too many divisions and images on the television screen: the interpreter was too small, the camera angle was too high, the lighting on interpreter created too much glare, and the background behind the interpreter was distracting. If these factors can be addressed, then it may be possible to use AVL in this scenario.

This recommendation was accepted by DJAG, with modifications to the ranked order of the scenarios. The revised order is as follows:

- Scenario 1: The system worked well for the deaf client and interpreter. This scenario is a realistic example of where a client may be in custody and the interpreter is in another remote location. The advantage was both the client and interpreter faced the monitor and camera and had limited distractions. The only downside to this scenario was the loss of the face-to-face dynamic and the ability of the interpreter to meet the client before the case to confirm language fluency.
- Scenario 3: Both the client and the interpreter were both in the same remote location. The possibilities for this scenario occurring are

limited. There were physical difficulties with how close the interpreter and client had to sit to be captured on the camera. Their positioning was side on to the camera and made it difficult for court participants to view facial or body language.

- Scenario 2: In order for the interpreter to see the deaf client, the deaf client had to be positioned in the witness box due to the constraints of fixed cameras. To make this scenario work under the current system, guidelines (with magisterial approval) would need to be developed that would indicate the repositioning of parties within the courtroom. A preferable solution would be to recreate Scenario 1 by using the remote witness room and thereby both the interpreter and client are remote.

Recommendation 3

If the current JACS AVL system has to be used, then it should only used for short matters of no longer than 30 minutes in duration.

Even if all the identified challenges with the AVL system could be addressed, utilising the services of an Auslan/English language interpreter via AVL for any lengthy court matter would **not** be appropriate. We recommend that it would only be appropriate for brief matters. Using the AVL system for short matters is where the greatest efficiencies could be found in avoiding the transportation of deaf inmates, and reduced costs for booking interpreters for shorter periods of time and with less notice. Thus the JACS AVL system should not be used to provide signed language interpreters for hearings or sentencing, and should only be used for short matters such as adjournments and brief mentions.

This recommendation was accepted by DJAG, who agreed that the use of AVL should be restricted to short matters of 30 minutes or less or where the face-to-face option was not available. The working party also specified the types of matters where AVL may be used. They include: matters for adjournment and bail matters only when the face-to-face option is not available. The working party agreed to ensure minimal disadvantage by advising that AVL **should not** be used in hearings and expert matters; sentencing; witness testimony; changes to bail; or the finalisation of matters.

Recommendation 4

If the current JACS AVL system has to be used, then technological guidelines must be developed to ensure that technological constraints are addressed.

DJAG accepted this recommendation and noted that technical guidelines must be developed to ensure the JACS team are aware of how to configure the system for each scenario as it arises.

Recommendation 5

If the current JACS AVL system is going to be improved or upgraded the findings of the research should be considered in determining the best course of action.

If investment is made to address the technological and environmental short-comings in the JACS AVL system, in the long run it could prove to be more cost-effective to utilise the services of signed language interpreters in courts via AVL. Services could be provided more effectively and efficiently than requiring the interpreter or deaf client be physically present in the courtroom.

The current system uses fixed cameras, which proved to be problematic throughout this project. It was recommended that the use of portable AVL equipment should be explored.[11] In addition, the size of television screens and the layout of images on the screens would need to be modified to reduce the amount of on-screen visual information. If possible, the interpreter and deaf person should be able to see each other in the majority of the screen. It may be possible to have smaller images of other participants in the court, but it is not necessary for the interpreter or deaf person to see him/herself on the screen. Depending on the mode of AVL being used, the Bench may require a split screen view, with both the interpreter and deaf individual on the screen. Furthermore, the location of the microphones should also be considered to ensure they are able to accommodate the needs of interpreters without impacting on their ability to do their work (i.e., use their hands).

DJAG accepted this recommendation, and noted that when upgrading AVL equipment JACS should consider sign language users and interpreters as potential users of the system and refer to findings of the research study and the JACS response to the Report. The working party is supportive of the proposed monitor software upgrade as per the *JACS Response to the Macquarie University Report* "that the system be reprogrammed so that the interface could be used to maximise the image size on the monitor." This low cost response would make the system more effective and user friendly for deaf clients and other clients with different disabilities. DJAG also emphasised that JACS should note the Victorian research on VRI and their technical solutions in undertaking any upgrade of the system. A portable system might be a consideration for courts that are not being upgraded, and where possible the data from this study should be used to prioritise locations for staged upgrades.

---

[11] See for example the portable equipment provided by Paras Associates Video Interpreter Network in hospitals in the United States and the portable equipment provided by the Department of Human Services Victoria in some of their VRI locations).

Recommendation 6

If the current JACS AVL system has to be used, then guidelines must be developed for personnel who will encounter the system.

Guidelines should include: (a) information for judges and legal personnel on the sign language interpreting process via AVL; (b) guidelines for interpreters on working with AVL in court; (c) mandatory training for sign language interpreters on working with AVL; and (d) training for court personnel on operating the AVL system.

DJAG accepted this recommendation and noted that guidelines must be developed for all potential users; including Magistrates, court staff, legal representatives, interpreters and deaf clients; and could include:

- courtroom setup for each type of scenario;
- instructions for court staff responsible for arranging the system – "Call JACS";
- instructions for Magistrates on when to use the system. An example of this might be:
    - the closing of a court to allow a client to brief their counsel via the AVL
    - never use with deaf (relay) interpreters as it becomes too complex;
- guidelines for clients could be developed in conjunction with the Deaf Society of NSW. The guidelines could be videoed in Auslan and made available on the Deaf Society's website and on DVD for use by Corrective Services NSW.

The recommendations have since been approved by the NSW Attorney General, and implementation is due to begin. DJAG have agreed that use of the AVL system with Auslan/English interpreters will be piloted over a period of three to six months in order to tweak guidelines; and that use of the system will be reviewed after one year to evaluate its effectiveness.

4   ACKNOWLEDGMENTS

Acknowledgements go to Marcel Leneham for his major contribution as the principal research assistant on this project, and his insight when analysing the data; and George Major and Lindsay Ferrara for their assistance with the data collection. I would also like to thank all the participants and also Anne Mangan and Julia Haraksin from Diversity Services at the NSW Department of Justice and Attorney General for their support in organising the data collection, and Patrick Donoghue, Manager of the Justice Agency Conference System, for his technical assistance with the data collection.

REFERENCES

AIIC. (2000). Guidelines for the use of new technologies in conference interpreting. . *Communicate!, March-April.*

Azarmina, P. W., P. (2005). Remote interpretation in medical encounters: a systematic review. *Journal of Telemedicine and Telecare, 11*, 140-145.

Berk-Seligson, S. (1990). *The Bilingual Courtroom: Court Interpreters in the Judicial Process.* Chicago: University of Chicago Press.

Berk-Seligson, S. (1999). The impact of court interpreting on the coerciveness of leading questions. *The International Journal of Speech, Language and the Law, 6*(1).

Berk-Seligson, S. (2000). Interpreting for the police: issues in pre-trial phases of the judicial process. *The International Journal of Speech, Language and the Law, 7*(2).

Berk-Seligson, S. (2002). The impact of politeness in witness testimony: The influence of the court interpreter. In F. Pöchhacker & M. Shlesinger (Eds.), *The interpreting studies reader.* London: Routledge, 278-292.

Böcker, M., & Anderson, B. (1993). Remote conference interpreting using ISDN videotelephony: a requirements analysis and feasibility study *Proceedings of the Human Factors and Ergonomics Society, 37th annual meeting*, 235-239.

Bontempo, K., & Levitzke-Gray, P. (2009). Interpreting Down Under: Sign Language Interpreter Education and Training in Australia. In J. Napier (Ed.), *International Perspectives on Sign Language Interpreter Education.* Washington, DC.

Bontempo, K., & Napier, J. (2007). Mind the gap! A skills analysis of sign language interpreters. *The Sign Language Translator & Interpreter, 1*(2), 275-299.

Boyd, Z., & Harper, P. (2010). *Interpreting for the Australian video relay service.* Paper presented at the Australian Sign Language Interpreters Association National Conference.

Braun, S. (2006). Multimedia communication technologies and their impact on interpreting. In M. Carroll, H. Gerzymisch-Arbogast & S. Nauert (Eds.), *Audiovisual Translation Scenarios: Proceedings of the Marie Curie Euroconferences, 1-5 May 2006.* Copenhagen: MuTra: Audiovisual Translation Scenarios.

Braun, S. (2007). Interpreting in small-group bilingual videoconferences: Challenges and adaptation processes. *Interpreting, 9*(1), 21-46.

Brennan, M., & Brown, R. (1997). *Equality before the law: Deaf people's access to justice.* Durham: Deaf Studies Research Unit, University of Durham.

BSR Solutions. (2010). *Evaluation of Video Relay Interpreting services.* Melbourne: Department of Human Services Victoria.

Colin, J., & Morris, R. (1996). *Interpreters and the Legal Process.* Winchester: Waterside Press.

Connell, T. (2006). The application of new technologies to remote interpreting. *Linguistica Antverpiensia*, 311-324.

Dion, J. (2005). *The changing dynamics of the interpreting industry as influenced by Video Relay Service (VRS), and its impact on the deaf community.* Paper presented at the Supporting Deaf People Online Conference.

Dunnigan, T., & Downing, B. (1995). Legal Interpreting on Trial: A Case Study. In M. Morris (Ed.), *Translation and the law.* Philadelphia: John Benjamins, 93-113.

Fowler, Y. (2007). *Interpreting into the ether: interpreting for prison/court video link hearings.* Paper presented at the Critical Link 5: Interpreters in the community. Retrieved from http://www.criticallink.org/files/CL5Fowler.pdf.

Hale, S. (1996). Pragmatic considerations in court interpreting. *Australian Review of Applied Linguistics, 19*(1), 61-72.

Hale, S. (1997a). Clash of World Perspectives: the discursive practices of the law, the witness and the interpreter. *The International Journal of Speech Language & the Law, 4*(2), 197-209.

Hale, S. (1997b). The Interpreter on Trial. Pragmatics in court interpreting. In S. E. Carr, R. Roberts, A. Dufour & D. Steyn (Eds.), *The Critical Link: Interpreters in the Community* (pp. 201-211). Phildadelphia: John Benjamins.

Hale, S. (1997c). The treatment of register variation in court interpreting. *The Translator, 3*(1), 39-54.

Hale, S. (1999). The interpreter's treatment of discourse markers in courtroom questions. *The International Journal of Speech, Language and the Law, 6*(1), 57-82.

Hale, S. (2001). How are Courtroom Questions Interpreted? An Analysis of Spanish Interpreters' Practices. In I.Mason (Ed.), *Triadic Exchanges: Studies in Dialogue Interpreting* (pp. 21-50). Manchester: St. Jerome.

Hale, S. (2002). How faithfully do court Interpreters render the style of non-English speaking witnesses's testimonies? A data based study of Spanish-English bilingual proceedings. *Discourse Studies, 4*(1), 25-48.

Hale, S. (2004). *The discourse of court Interpreting: Discourse practices of the law, the witness and the interpreter*. Philadelphia: John Benjamins.

Hale, S., & Gibbons, J. (1999). Varying realities: Patterned changes in the interpreter's representation of courtroom and external realities. *Applied Linguistics, 20*(1), 203-220.

Johnston, T. (2003). W(h)ither the Deaf community? Population, genetics and the future of Auslan (Australian Sign Language). *American Annals of the Deaf, 148*(5), 358-375.

Johnston, T., & Schembri, A. (2007). *Australian Sign Language (Auslan): An introduction to sign linguistics*. Cambridge: Cambridge University Press.

Jones, D., Gill, P., Harrison, R., Meakin, R., & Wallace, P. (2003). An exploratory study of language interpretation services provided by videoconferencing. *Journal of Telemedicine and Telecare, 9*, 51-56.

Keating, E., & Mirus, G. (2003). American Sign Language in virtual space: Interactions between deaf users of computer-mediated video communication and the impact of technology on language practices. *Language in Society, 32*, 693-714.

Lightfoot, M. (2006). *Video Remote Interpreting: Parallel Worlds Inform Practice.* Paper presented at the Supporting Deaf People Online Conference.

Mathers, C. (2006). *Sign language interpreters in court: Understanding best practices.* Bloomington, IN: AuthorHouse.

McWhinney, J. (2009). *Video interpreting services in the UK.* Paper presented at the International Association of Translation & Intercultural Studies.

Morris, R. (1999a). The face of justice: Historical aspects of court interpreting. *Interpreting, 4*(1), 97-124.

Morris, R. (1999b). The gum syndrome: predicaments in court interpreting. *The International Journal of Speech, Language and the Law, 6*(1).

Moser-Mercer, B. (2003). Remote interpreting: assessment of human factors and performance parameters. *Communicate! , Summer.*

Moser-Mercer, B. (2005). Remote interpreting: issues of multi-sensory integration in a multilingual task. *Meta, 50*(2), 727-738.

Mouzourakis, P. (1996). Videoconferencing: techniques and challenges. *Interpreting, 1*(1), 21-38.

Mouzourakis, P. (2006). Remote interpreting: a technical perspective on recent experiments. *Interpreting, 8*(1), 45-66.

Napier, J. (in press). "You get that vibe": A pragmatic analysis of clarification and communicative accommodation in legal video remote interpreting. In

Meurant, L., Sinte, A., Van Herreweghe, M. & M. Vermeerbergen (eds.), *Sign language research uses and practices: Crossing views on theoretical and applied signlanguage linguistics*. De Gruyter Mouton and Ishara Press.

Napier, J. (2012). Exploring themes in stakeholder perspectives of video remote interpreting in court. In C. J. Kellett (Ed.), *Interpreting across genres: Multiple research perspectives*. Trieste: EUT Edizioni Universtà di Trieste, 219-254.

Napier, J., & Barker, R. (2003). A demographic survey of Australian Sign Language interpreters. *Australian Journal of Education of the Deaf, 9*, 19-32.

Napier, J., McKee, R., & Goswell, D. (2010). *Sign language interpreting: Theory & practice in Australia and New Zealand* (2nd ed.). Sydney: Federation Press.

Napier, J., & Spencer, D. (2008). Guilty or not guilty? An investigation of deaf jurors' access to court proceedings via sign language interpreting. In D. Russell & S. Hale (Eds.), *Interpreting in legal settings*. Washington, DC: Gallaudet University Press.

Nardi, M. (2005). Vulnerable groups - deaf people at official hearings: A perspective of the European Forum of Sign Language Interpreters. In H. Keijzer-Lambooy & W. J. Gasille (Eds.), *Aequilibrium: Instruments for lifting language barriers in intercultural legal proceedings*. Utrecht: ITV Hogeschool voor Tolken en Vertalen, 69-76.

Niska, H. (1999). Quality Issues in Remote Interpreting. In A. A. Lugris & A. F. Ocampo (Eds.), *Anovar / Anosar estudios de traduccion e interpretaccion*. Vigo: Universidade de Vogo, 109-121.

Oldfield, N. L. (2010). A competency model for video relay service interpreters. *International Journal of Interpreter Education 2*, 41-57.

Orima. (2004). *Supply and demand for Auslan interpreters across Australia*. Canberra, ACT: Australian Government Department of Family and Community Services,.

Russell, D. (2002). *Interpreting in legal contexts: Consecutive and simultaneous interpretation*. Burtonsville, MD: Sign Media.

Russell, D., & Hale, S. (Eds.). (2008). *Interpreting in Legal Settings*. Washington, DC: Gallaudet University Press.

Silverman, D. (2006). *Interpreting Qualitative Data: Methods for Analysing Talk, Text and Interaction* (3rd ed.). London: Sage Publications.

Spencer, R. (2000). *Video Relay Interpreting trial final report*. Brisbane, Australia: Australian Communication Exchange.

Stevens, H. (2005). Justice must be seen to be done. In H. Keijzer-Lambooy & W. J. Gasille (Eds.), *Aequilibrium: Instruments for lifting language barriers in intercultural legal proceedings*. Utrecht: ITV Hogeschool voor Tolken en Vertalen, 77-86.

Taylor, M. (2005). *Video Relay Service Task Analysis Report* (No. Unpublished research report): Distance Opportunities for Interpreting Training Center, University of Northern Colorado, USA.

Taylor, M. (2009). *Video Relay Services Industry Research: New demands on interpreters* (No. Unpublished research report).

Turner, G. H. (1995). The bilingual, bimodal courtroom: A first glance. *Journal of Interpretation, 7*(1), 3-34.

Turner, G. H., & Brown, R. (2001). Interaction and the role of the interpreter in court. In F. J. Harrington & G. H. Turner (Eds.), *Interpreting interpreting: Studies and reflections on sign language interpreting*. Coleford: Douglas McLean, 152-167.

Wilson, C. W. (2010). *Working through, with or despite technology? A study of interpreter-mediated encounters when interpreting is provided by video conferencing link* Paper presented at the Critical Link 6: Interpreters in the community.

TRUE-TO-LIFE REQUIREMENTS FOR USING VIDEOCONFERENCING IN LEGAL PROCEEDINGS

Peter van Rotterdam and Ronald van den Hoogen

Ministry of Security and Justice, The Hague

1   INTRODUCTION

This article provides some true-to-life and other requirements for video-conferencing in courtrooms or studios that are relevant to cross-border judicial proceedings. These requirements have been developed by several European Union member states in two projects, financed by the European Commission. The overview given in this article is not yet complete and is not focused on interpreting via video link. However, it is nonetheless provided here in order for other countries to benefit from it immediately. The final version of this document will contain an agreed set of requirements; that is to say, requirements that have been agreed by the participants in the action 'Implementing Transnational Use of Videoconferencing' to be both neces-sary and sufficient to reach a good level of quality for the use of videocon-ferencing in cross-border judicial procedures. These requirements, which are based on best practice, will not be binding and should be regarded as recom-mendations. The final version will be used in actions regarding the further implementation of 'transnational videoconferencing'.

A courtroom is an area where interaction between different parties in proceedings is of primary importance and where certain legal, traditional and ceremonial aspects also play an important role. Like courtrooms, examining magistrates' chambers, witness rooms and interview rooms in penitentiary institutions are no ordinary workplaces. The special feature of the inter-actions in such rooms is that each of the participants has a fixed role, and, often, a specific position in the room. The fixed nature of their roles dictates who they may be located beside or opposite. Considerable importance is moreover attached to ensuring that each participant can see and hear all other participants clearly and observe both verbal and non-verbal reactions. The use of videoconferencing in both criminal and non-criminal (civil) proceed-ings as a means of hearing witnesses, experts, suspects and immigrants at a distance therefore imposes such stringent requirements on equipment components and the composition, positioning and adjustment thereof that the audiovisual solution may generally be regarded as a tailor-made solution.

2 ASSUMPTIONS

The following basic assumptions have been made: the use of videoconferencing should not disrupt the normal judicial process. Both proceedings and data should continue to be at least as reliable as at present. The audiovisual solution will be implemented in locations such as court rooms, police custody suites and prisons that have been selected by the authorities operating in the chain of organisations in criminal and non-criminal (civil) justice; any adaptation to rooms which may be necessary for such implementation in terms of the requisite lighting and acoustics, etc., can be carried out by third parties in consultation with the appropriate authorities. With the exception of areas controlled by third parties outside the judicial domain, audiovisual data can be transferred via the Wide Area Networks in the judicial domain. The supply of the videoconferencing service to users within the judicial system should be organised centrally.

3 REGULATORY REQUIREMENTS

The Legislation and General Administrative Order in The Netherlands lays down five requirements for the use of videoconferencing. Those five requirements – including the accompanying explanations – are reproduced in full below. The videoconferencing system should be set up in such a way that:

i. The persons concerned are provided with a true-to-life picture of what is happening in the other room

Explanation: The videoconferencing system should be set up in such a way that the person being heard, his lawyer, the judge and other participants are provided with a realistic and clear picture of what is happening at the other end of the connection. This first requirement relates to the quality of the visual and audio connection. The fundamental principle is that sufficient account should be taken of the interests of the persons concerned. Consequently, the videoconferencing system must be of high quality. Only then will a hearing conducted via videoconference link provide a reasonable alternative to a face-to-face hearing. It is not acceptable, for example, for distorted images to be produced by zooming in or out in order to focus on a specific feature of a person. More particularly, the requirement means that sounds and images must be aligned accurately and reproduced without any perceptible delay. Furthermore, the external appearance, facial expressions, lip movements, direction of gaze, gestures and postures of the persons concerned must be clearly perceptible. Other persons present in the other room must also be visible. In addition, it should be possible for the persons concerned to interact with one another, and for the viewer to see how they comport themselves and react to one another through looks and speech. The sound must also be reproduced realistically. Speech must be comprehensible (insofar as this is also possible in the case of face-to-face listening), and it must be possible to speak simultaneously. When the person concerned is looking at a file, for instance, he should be able to communicate merely on the basis of the sound he is making.

ii. The persons concerned can consult with one another without third parties overhearing

Explanation: There may be cases where a suspect, an immigrant, a witness etc. wishes to consult with his or her lawyer (whether or not via an interpreter) without the judge or any other participant in the judicial proceeding overhearing. It is therefore a requirement that mutual consultation should be possible without third parties overhearing.

iii. The persons concerned can exchange documents

Explanation: The third requirement concerns the possibility of exchanging documents. It must be possible for the persons concerned to exchange the necessary documents, e.g. by fax. Even though few documents are exchanged during a judicial proceeding, it may be that one of the parties concerned does not have all the documents in his/her possession. In such a situation, it should be possible to exchange documents, as is the case in face-to-face hearings.

iv. The system is safeguarded against loss or any unlawful form of processing

Explanation: The authenticity of reproduction must be guaranteed. This requirement therefore specifies that the transmission of images and sound must be safeguarded. In other words, reproduction must be inviolable. The system must also be safeguarded in such a way as to prevent recordings from being intercepted unlawfully by third parties.

v. The system can be linked up to other countries' systems

Explanation: In the field of criminal law, videoconferencing will often be used in connection with international judicial assistance. Hence the additional requirement whereby it must be possible for the system to be linked up to other countries' systems, and it must also comply with the international standards applicable to videoconferencing. Those standards have been drawn up by the International Telecommunication Union (ITU), which is part of the United Nations. In the case of videoconferencing which takes place via ISDN, VPN, Internet or SDSL, the applicable standards are currently H320 and H323. In the case of an ordinary telephone line, the applicable standard is currently H324.

4   VIDEOCONFERENCING BEING *NOT* TRUE-TO-LIFE

It is also important to consider what might make one or more of the participants perceive that a videoconferencing facility, its look and feel, is *not* true-to life. The main notion of true-to-life is that each actor can interact with each other actor in a natural way. It therefore follows that a videoconferencing facility is NOT true-to-life if it is difficult to:

- interact with one or more persons in one or other of the rooms,
- make eye contact with one or more persons,
- notice that one is being spoken to, looked at, pointed at or addressed,
- determine the provenance of a sound,
- see how each person comports him/herself,
- see how persons react to one another,
- see what is on each person's desk and what they do with their hands,
- see each person's external appearance, facial expressions, gestures, posture, lip movements and direction of gaze.

The lack of interaction may be caused by insufficient sound and image quality in the video link. Thus, a videoconferencing facility is *not* true-to-life if:

- images are unclear,
- images do not show everyone present in the other room,
- images do not show everything happening in the other room,
- images are not of the same size or quality for all persons,
- images are distorted by camera movements (zooming, tilting or panning),
- images show strange skin colours or shadows or distracting reflections on spectacles, images focus on a specific feature of a person, sounds and images are not real-time (delayed),
- sounds and images are not aligned (no lip-synchronicity),
- sounds are not realistic (volume too high, too low or changes when looking at desk), sounds are indistinguishable when speaking simultaneously and speech is not intelligible.

Interaction may also be hindered by the look and feel of the room if it differs from what is usual in court sessions. So, a videoconferencing facility is *not* true-to-life if the positioning or appearance of the equipment, the floor, walls, ceiling, furniture, lights, acoustics, background noise or environment make a participant feel as if they are not in a court room, or the perceived positioning of or distances to other persons on the screens differ from their actual positioning and distances in a face-to-face hearing.

5   VIDEOCONFERENCING FACILITIES – REQUESTING VERSUS REQUESTED

Transnational videoconferencing is used for any part of criminal, civil and commercial proceedings, in particular for the taking of evidence from remote locations in other states. For the purpose of this document, the focus is on the transnational usage of videoconferencing for criminal law applications, i.e. examining magistrate/rogatory commission. Within the European Union applications in criminal cases are usually governed by national acts and the Convention on Mutual Assistance in Criminal Matters between the Member States of the European Union of May 29, 2000 (further referred to as the "2000 MLA Convention"). Two authorities are involved: the requesting authority (this authority is in one state and wants to hear a person that is in another state and therefore requests assistance from that other state); and the requested authority (this authority is in the other state and receives from the authority in the first state the request for assistance to hear a person).

The seven main participants in a face-to-face rogatory hearing are the requesting judge, public prosecutor, court clerk, requested judge, person to be heard, lawyer and interpreter. Additional actors, like assistant judges or second lawyers, may participate in the hearing. In a face-to-face rogatory hearing the actors are often situated in a 'square', meaning that the person to be heard together with the interpreter are located opposite the (requesting and/or requested) judge and the court clerk, with the public prosecutor on the third side and the lawyer on the fourth side.

In a rogatory hearing via videoconference, the participants are located as follows: The person to be heard, the requested judge and, in many cases, the interpreter and lawyer are located in the VC facility of the requested authority. The requesting judge, court clerk, public prosecutor and, in some cases, a (second) lawyer or the interpreter are located in the VC facility of the requesting authority. Note that the location of some actors is not fixed. The videoconferencing facility should allow all actors to be situated at their normal position. In order to hear a person via a videoconference link, both the requesting and requested authority require a videoconferencing facility, e.g. a court room or examining magistrate's chamber fitted out with video-conferencing equipment. During the videoconferencing session these facilities are connected to each other and are to be regarded as a single (court) room. Each videoconferencing facility should be built in such a way that it can operate in requested as well as in requesting mode and should accommodate the most common variants with regard to how many actors are participating and where they are situated. If the VC equipment is appropriately set out, the court room should remain suitable for face-to-face judicial proceedings. Its VC facility should be able to be used for other types of legal procedures.

6   EQUIPMENT COMPONENTS

All equipment components should as far as possible be standardized on the basis of the same quality of equipment and the same configuration. In so far as the rooms in the judicial premises permit this, an attempt should be made to ensure that the equipment is positioned in the same way in all types of rooms. The following sections cover execution, explanations and compliance with the five aforementioned requirements as regards the aspect of image, sound and audiovisual environment.

6.1   Image

It is recommended that requirements can be satisfied through the use of three types of screens:

- Focusing screen; for transmitting images of the participants in the other room,
- Overview screen; for an overview of the situation in the other room,
- Information screen; for transmitting documents and other information. This includes any screens located in participants' "work stations").

Objectivity: each participant must be portrayed in the same way on a screen. Participants must not be portrayed differently. The lighting intensity, colour balance, resolution and frame rate must be identical for each participant. All the images must be as objective as possible.

Eye contact: as far as is possible, eye contact must be imitated. The smaller the angle in the vertical and horizontal plane between the participant's direction of gaze towards the person shown on the screen and the line of vision of the camera reproducing the image in the other room, the greater the impression of eye contact (eye contact is made where there is 0° of deviation). All participants in room A (e.g. the judge and the lawyer) must have an equally great impression of eye contact with participants in room B (e.g. the person to be heard). The impression of eye contact gained from the position of the judge, for example, must not differ from that gained from the position of the lawyer.

6.2   Positioning

Equipment must be positioned in such a way that only minimal adjustments need to be made to the position participants would normally adopt in a traditional court setting. It must not be necessary, for example, for lawyers and judges to sit at one table or in close proximity to one another. At the same time, the equipment must be positioned in such a way that cases can still be handled without videoconferencing in the relevant courtroom. Furthermore, it must be possible to position cameras, screens, lighting and participants in such a way that the entire set-up is suitable in as many situations as possible in both criminal and non-criminal (civil) proceedings.

Cameras, screens, projectors, lighting, furniture, etc. and participants must be positioned in such a way that they do not block the participants' view of one another or the view of the general public. Cameras (except for overview cameras) must be placed at eye level. Participants should not be filmed from above or below.

The focusing screen must be positioned to reflect the situation in the courtroom as realistically as possible. The perceived distance between the participant being filmed and the observer must be comparable to normal circumstances. In other words, participants, cameras and screens must be positioned to simulate the usual distances between participants. The cameras must be positioned to ensure that: (1) when a participant looks at the person on the screen, the latter is fully aware that he or she is being looked at, and (2) when participants in the other room look at one another, the person watching the screen is fully aware of this. A person observing the other participants on the screen must be able to identify who those participants are looking at.

The overview screen must be positioned in such a way that the public can see everything the judge sees. The overview screen and the focusing screen must be positioned closely enough to each other to ensure that both screens are visible to all participants without them having to move their heads.

6.3   Lighting and contrast

The lighting/colour contrast must be such that facial expressions are always readily discernible; there is no shadowing around the eyes; skin colour is authentically reproduced; users are not dazzled; there are no reflections on screens and no distracting reflections on spectacles; documents are easy to read; and the contrast between the lighting intensity of the participants' facial skin colour and the background must be such that facial expressions are readily discernible.

6.4   Camera-image mapping on screens

The image layout on the focusing screen must be such that the following aspects are clear in respect of each participant: facial expressions, lip move-ments, directions of gaze, gestures, upper body posture, table and objects. The setting in which the videoconference link is used determines how many participants are shown on the focusing screen; the depiction of between 2 and 4 participants per room will usually suffice. The position of the focused images of participants on the focusing screen (e.g. with the interpreter on the left and the lawyer on the right) must correspond to their actual position in the room and hence to the image of the same participants on the overview screen (e.g. with the interpreter on the left and the lawyer on the right).

The image layout on the overview screen must be such that participants are able to judge the actual distances between the persons in the other room on the basis of the images transmitted; observe and recognise persons in the room; determine who is looking at and speaking with whom; and see how the other persons move with respect to one another. The image layout of the information screen must contain the image filmed by the document camera.

6.5   Screens

The number and type of screens required will be determined in consultation with the supplier. The following indications are for guidance only. Viewing angle and viewing distance must be such that all participants can use the same screen in the same way. Size should be large enough to ensure that – in terms of the viewing angle – the persons involved can preferably be shown to the same scale as would be perceived at a normal meeting. Because of the importance of the viewing angle, the screen size must be determined in conjunction with the distance from the screen; a 72 or 120-inch screen may be required. Type should possibly be LCD or similar. Resolution should be high enough to be able to convey a clear indication of facial expressions, lip movements and directions of gaze given the selected screen layout and image contents, possibly at least WXGA or similar. A minimum of 25 frames per second may be required. Facial expressions must be readily discernible and viewing comfort high. There should be no distracting delays or distortions (blur). Contrast should be sufficient for use in areas for reading/writing. Mounting should preferably be fixed, if necessary on wheels (this certainly applies to mobile equipment).

It is recommended to use two screens. One focusing screen, the position of which has yet to be determined; this will show the focused images from the other room, one overview screen, the position of which has yet to be determined; this will show the overall view from the other room. The overview screen must also be usable as an information screen.

6.6   Cameras

The number and type of cameras required will be determined in consultation with the supplier. The following indications are for guidance only:

- *Angle size of overview camera*: must be large enough to ensure that all participants are fully in the picture and make it possible to see people entering the room.
- *Angle size of focusing cameras*: must be large enough to ensure that: (1) the participant's face, shoulders and upper body and hands and objects placed on the table are clearly visible and (2) users do not feel restricted in their movements. All participants must be able to move within an area of 80 x 80 cm without disappearing from view. They must therefore be able to gesture, turn towards other persons present and lean forwards or backwards without disappearing from view.

- *Light sensitivity*: must be such that participants can clearly distinguish one another's facial expressions (this also applies to dark-skinned persons). Cameras should be suitable for colour images.
- *Mounting*: cameras should preferably be fixed and should follow participants as they stand up and sit down. The public prosecutor and lawyer, for example, must be viewed in accordance with the relevant requirements even when they are standing up.
- *Adjustability*: cameras must be fixed to one or more pre-set positions for panning, tilting and zooming; one of the possible positions should be pre-set as a preference.

In the Dutch situation it has been decided that during the implementation phase only fixed cameras should be used; this is in order to avoid the image of some of the actors constantly changing and/or not conforming to other requirements. In practice this necessitates the use of extra cameras and sometimes switching between images on the screen. It is recommended that seven cameras should be used: six cameras, each one directed at a participant (the person to be heard, the examining magistrate, public prosecutor, lawyer, interpreter or clerk) and one camera to provide an overview of the courtroom or examining magistrate's chamber.

6.7   Processor

A digital video-processor should be used to assemble the camera images, possibly on a "picture in picture" basis. The processing speed of the system as a whole must be such that facial expressions are readily discernible and viewing comfort high.

6.8   Sound

Speech must always be readily intelligible. No words must be lost during a videoconference link. The quality of the sound must be continuous, and no extraneous interference or crackling may occur. Speech quality must not deteriorate as a result of speech compression. This means meeting certain requirements as regards lip synchronicity (a delay of less than 0.15 seconds), echo cancellation and background noise and reverberation. Participants must be able to speak at the same time and be understood.

6.9   Microphones

The number and type of microphones required will be determined in consultation with the supplier. Account will also have to be taken of any desire to use a sound system already in place in a room (usually a courtroom) for videoconferencing purposes, provided that it is of adequate quality.

Microphones must be positioned in such a way that all participants are clearly understandable in the other room with no distortions caused by background noise. It is recommended to use microphones that are built-in (into desks or elsewhere), eavesdropping-proof, direction-sensitive, permanently switched on, and not fitted with a mute button. The court clerk has a central mute button, fitted with automatic volume control, and a central volume button, positioned and adjusted to ensure that all participants are clearly understandable in the other room with no distortions caused by background noise. It is recommended that one microphone is used for each participant.

6.10 Speakers

The number and type of loudspeakers required will be determined in consultation with the supplier. The loudspeakers must be positioned and adjusted to ensure that all participants in the other room are clearly under-standable with no distortions caused by background noise. As a general principle, speakers must be positioned on either side of each screen.

6.11 Audio delay unit / amplifier

The audio processor must be suitable for at least sixteen microphones.

6.12 Exchange of documents

Participants must be able to exchange documents securely. This applies to documents in both paper and electronic form. Documents in hard-copy form, e.g. documents submitted at a court session, are shown on the information screens. The documents are filmed using a document camera/visualiser, which will probably be operated by the court clerk. It is recommended that one visualiser should be used. Note that the document camera is also capable of showing objects other than documents. Where a document camera is not available, a printer and/or fax in the room is required.

6.13 Mobile equipment

This section covers execution, explanations and compliance with the five aforementioned requirements regarding the aspect of "mobile equipment" for special situations on a temporary basis, such as in a prisoners' hospital, a secret location of a witness, or in the event of fixed equipment breakdown.

It is recommended that procuring one or more additional sets of mobile equipment (screen + camera + speaker + microphone + accessories) should be considered. Such equipment must be usable either in various combina-tions or in conjunction with a fixed set of equipment. The mobile equipment must be readily transportable (and hence not necessarily on wheels), easy to move between the different locations and flexible in terms of its use. Consequently, more limitations are expected to apply to mobile equipment than to fixed equipment (e.g. as regards the number of participants who can be filmed clearly at the same time). However, every set of mobile equipment must still comply with the five requirements laid down by the legislation.

6.14 Operation

This section covers execution, explanations and compliance with the five requirements outlined above as regards the aspect of "operation". For the operation of the VC equipment it is recommended that one Touch Panel should be used, to be installed at a location in the courtroom yet to be determined. It must be possible to use the audiovisual solution at every connected judicial location. Note that there are limitations on allowing the judge to be fully in control of the proceeding (e.g. there are no operator facilities in a penitentiary institution). Operation must be as user-friendly (i.e. as simple) as possible, and should therefore consist of only a limited number of option, e.g.: switch on (in all the rooms concerned), select type of court session (number and role of participants per room), select other court location (from a pre-programmed list), connect to other location, mute/pause court session, share document, disconnect and switch off. The applications menu should be pre-programmed in order to cover all situations applicable to the room in question including, for example, the hearing of persons by an examining magistrate and other legal proceedings. The menu should also list all rooms to which the videoconferencing facility can connect.

Participants must be clear as to which court session is taking place. In order to verify the establishment of the visual and audio connection between the intended rooms, the name and/or number of the room in which the equipment is located should be fixed to the wall in view of the camera. It must be possible to establish the connection required for the meeting and to make the correct adjustments within one minute. Since the visual and audio connection is between two rooms (point-to-point) only, it must be impossible for a third room to break in into this visual and audio connection.

The system will be operated by a person determined by the court, e.g. a court clerk; such persons will attend a short training in how to operate the system. During use, the audiovisual solution must not require the intervention of an operator (this includes activating the central mute button, e.g. for the purpose of a lawyer-client consultation). The operator and/or security guard must remain on hand in case of any problems. If any problems arise, the local operator must be able to ring a help desk (which should be set up within the judicial system). The help desk should only have to offer assistance in the case of operational failures. In the event of failures of the audiovisual system and/or the network, the help desk should report the fault, which must be repaired before the following working day. It is for the judge to decide whether to abandon a case that has been disrupted in this way. In principle, it should not be necessary to adjust the positioning, focusing or configuration of cameras, screens, lighting or sound. Where this is necessary, however, servicing should be as simple as possible in order to ensure that there is a minimal risk of loss of quality in the videoconferencing system. Equipment will be replaced by the supplier. The supplier should therefore have "hot spares" in place in order to ensure reliability.

6.15 System Management

There should be a simple system of supervision of the audiovisual solution. As stated above, a help desk should be set up to service and support operational use; a supervisor should maintain a list of configurations, a list of usage and a list of faults for each location, and such lists should be reviewed periodically. Furthermore, a strategic board should monitor the use of videoconferencing in judicial proceedings and decide upon alignment between what law requires and technological availability.

6.16 Infrastructure

Network capacity must be sufficient to satisfy user requirements as regards image content. In addition, bandwidth should be the same for all participants in order to ensure that they are all portrayed in the same way and are able to exercise the same degree of influence on one another (resolution, delays). This also applies to use in conjunction with other countries. The location of the network connector must be such that the system can easily be connected.

6.17 Codec

The codec must be suitable for the member state's network. It should be suitable for other temporary connections with encryption (this is in order to make provision for applications such as the hearing of witnesses and experts who are located outside the judicial premises).

6.18 Resistance to vandalism

Equipment, including microphones, should as far as possible be vandalism-resistant. This can be ensured *inter alia* by the type of mounting used.

6.19 Reliability and maintenance

In order to ensure the orderly conduct of meetings using videoconferencing, the audiovisual solution must be highly reliable. The supplier should ensure such reliability by carrying out both preventive and corrective on-site maintenance of equipment components where required for each location; the supplier will be assisted in that task by a facilities manager in each location.

7 CONCLUSION

The requirements outlined in this chapter highlight that 'True-to-life' means more than simply the equipment involved in video-mediated proceedings. True-to-life is a comprehensive concept that covers the room layout, positioning of equipment and participants, lighting and a range of other factors. The discussion in this chapter makes it clear that many of the issues surrounding legal videoconferencing are exacerbated when an interpreter is added to the proceedings.

CONFERENCE INTERPRETING WITH INFORMATION AND COMMUNICATION TECHNOLOGIES – EXPERIENCES FROM THE EUROPEAN COMMISSION DG INTERPRETATION

Jose Esteban Causo

European Commission

1 INTRODUCTION

In the European Commission, the Directorate General for Interpretation, DG SCIC, is in charge of providing interpretation and conference services to most of the European Institutions, including the Commission, the Council, the Committee of the Regions and the Economic and Social Committee. This task has become considerably more challenging with the recent addition of 12 new Member States and a total of 23 different languages that have increased, on the one hand, the geographical distances and, on the other hand, linguistic and cultural diversity.

DG SCIC is the largest interpreting service in the world. In 2010 more than 140,000 interpreter days were provided for nearly 12,000 meetings (about 60 meetings a day; 700 interpreters a day).

SCIC's key mission is to support multilingual communication and consequently to facilitate a transparent, efficient and democratic EU decision-making process by providing:

- quality conference interpretation services;
- support to interpretation training programmes targeted at staff interpreters, universities and students;
- an effective conference organisation for Directorates General and departments of the Commission;
- new technological solutions for multilingual communication (videoconferencing, web streaming, internet chat facilities, etc.) and daily technical support to the Commission's meetings and conference facilities

The European Union has always considered multilingualism to be an important issue and DG SCIC has been a major player supporting the freedom of using different languages. In addition, the Commission has renewed its commitment to communicating with Europe's citizens.

Information and Communication technologies (ICTs) help to improve transparency both in European Institutions and at national government level.

They foster multilingual communication and can play a key role in bringing EU institutions closer to citizens, business and national and local administration.

Conferences, workshops and debates, held in European Institution premises or elsewhere, as well as general information, can be accessible to virtually all interested stakeholders. ICTs can contribute to the Lisbon strategy of boosting overall economic performance by creating new services and new job opportunities. They can also be used to preserve, promote and provide access to European diversity and cultural heritage.

New information and communication tools can create additional and richer communication opportunities. However they require open-mindedness and an ability to change one's approach to communication. The right tool should be carefully selected to match the corresponding communication objective. By either complementing or offering more adequate alternatives to traditional meetings and other communication means, they can increase productivity, reduce governance costs and contribute to environmental protection by diminishing travel emissions.

For all these reasons, DG SCIC is investigating, testing and exploiting ICTs, combining them in different platforms for multilingual communication, which is fully compliant with ISO standards and the good professional practices applicable to conference interpretation.

DG SCIC shares its experience and know-how with other Directorates and institutions to foster e-Governance.

At present, DG SCIC is managing and combining different ICT tools to provide a package of services such as:

A) Multilingual on-line Internet "chats": a real-time written discussion on the web between distant participants choosing to join a discussion on a given issue using their own language.
B) Multilingual Videoconferences: a discussion in which participants at different locations can see and hear each other as though they were together in one place.
C) Multilingual live Web streaming: broadcasting live images and encoded sound on a digital media (intranet or Internet).
D) Interactive Virtual Conferences with interpretation: any combination of two or more of the above.
E) Multilingual Video-on-Demand: delivering recorded images and sound of original and interpreted interventions on a digital medium (intranet or Internet).
F) Dubbing and subtitling in all EU languages with a web based application (both for producing the clip and watching it).
G) Conferences web portal broadcasting both live and recorded events
H) Speech repository: an e-learning web portal with a collection of thousands of selected speeches and a software virtual booth tool to train interpreters

The technological developments in the area of the videoconferences with simultaneous interpretation are of particular interest in tackling multilingual issues in the context of legal proceedings.

2   VIDEOCONFERENCE WITH INTERPRETATION: TECHNICAL BACKGROUND

Videoconferencing equipment commonly on the market is linked via ISDN lines (H.320 standard) or via IP connections (H.323 standard); sound frequency bandwidth is normally limited to 7.5 kHz because of the audio compression algorithm used (usually G.722), but some old installations limit bandwidth to 3.4 kHz (G.711, telephone bandwidth). Video resolution is far below SD television quality, with a low and inconstant frame rate, error frames ("pixelisation") and no "constant" lip synchronization (video-audio frame rate). Regarding audio requirements stated in interpretation standards, the 100 - 12.500 Hz minimal bandwidth is not available in most of the current audio codecs, and compression level and other digital encoding parameters are generally unsatisfactory.

Furthermore videoconferences frequently link standard offices unsuitable for this purpose, or have a poor set-up, which means sound reverberation, ceiling lighting, simple omni-directional microphones integrated in the table, etc.

DG Interpretation receives an increasing number of requests to provide videoconferences with simultaneous interpretation. Since it is also responsible for the management of the technical infrastructure of about 40 meeting rooms, the DG interpretation has for several years been looking for appropriate videoconferencing equipment that would provide adequate sound and image quality for a very specific and demanding task: simultaneous interpretation.

Conference interpreting is not merely a question of repeating words or phrases in another language, or a matter of code switching. It is a highly complex activity that requires the interpreter to simultaneously listen, analyze, comprehend, translate, edit and reproduce a speaker's speech in real time, while looking at the speaker to observe the non-verbal signals of his (her) message, as well as the reactions s/he arouses among the recipients of that message. Not only is the content of the text unrevealed as the interpreter proceeds, but the speaker's underlying intention may also remain obscure, since perceiving it requires larger chunks of text than are available in real-time oral delivery.

When working in remote videoconferencing situations, interpreters must therefore rely on high quality images, synchronised with the sound, which make it possible to distinguish facial expressions and gestures of speakers and participants as well as and variations in the voice clearly.

3   LOOKING FOR SOLUTIONS

DG SCIC has been monitoring videoconferencing equipment available on the market since 1998. As no plug and play system compliant with interpreting requirements was found, suitable components or sub systems from different vendors were combined and tested by the technical units of the Directorate General until a satisfactory result was obtained.

In order to comply with technical standards applicable to remote interpreting, the coding equipment must ensure a high sound and image quality and a perfect audio-video synchronization (lip-sync is essential).

Only broadcast-level codecs (e.g. MPEG-2 or MPEG-4) and isochronous connections or IP connections with maximum level of quality of service can currently provide the minimal requirements in order to make possible the interpretation of interventions from remotely connected participants. However, some improvements are underway thanks to larger bandwidth network connections, more efficient compression algorithms and the fact that telecommunication providers can now offer high quality services.

These high quality requirements are only necessary one way, i.e. to send image and sound to the place where interpreters are. Images from the main event and the interpretation provided can be conveyed to remote places using common codecs and conventional ISDN links (obviously, lip synchronization is not necessary when transmitting interpreted audio).

Tests conducted in 2005, 2006 and 2007 with interpreters were crucial in defining an appropriate technical set-up that has been designed, implemented and used for videoconferences with simultaneous interpretation which are fully compliant with interpretation standards.

The tests showed that it is possible to perform this particular type of remote interpretation without breaching the CODE for the use of new technologies in interpretation, ISO 2603 or other related standards applicable to interpretation.

It is necessary to use an IP network connection that guarantees the delivery of the audio/video stream in real time (in the strict sense of the term).

Using H.264 it is possible to reduce the total bandwidth required to less than 1.5 Mbps for a talking heads in SD quality, thus considerably increasing the possibility of making such connections via public networks.

The set-up permits both a terrestrial transmission, over IP or satellite links and requires quasi-broadcast level cameras, high quality microphones, appropriate lighting, etc. Minimum technical requirements have been established (see Appendix 1).

The system has been successfully implemented on different occasions such as:

- Participation of a European Commissioner in a TV debate organised by the TV channel "France3". The Commissioner participated from a television studio in European Commission premises in Brussels while the other participants and the journalist were in Paris; the Commissioner spoke in English and was interpreted in Paris by France3 interpreters. The videoconferencing link was via satellite and the codec was MPEG-2.

- From a TV studio in Bratislava, a European Commissioner participated in a meeting held in Brussels that gathered 600 participants in a former Brewery, with interpretation provided from Brussels to both ends.

- During the European Union Sustainable Energy Week, an interpreted videoconference in several languages was organised between a conference venue in Grenoble and a meeting room in Brussels, where interpretation was provided for both venues.

- During the "Europe for Citizens" Forum, an interpreted videoconference was organised between the Commission Press Room in Brussels and a conference venue in Rhodes.

- Two European Commission staff forums have been organised with videoconferences between Brussels, Luxemburg and Ispra, allowing a multilingual communication between President Barroso and Commission staff. Interpretation was provided in 3 languages from Brussels to and from all participants.

The system is permanently available between Commission meeting rooms in Brussels, Luxembourg and Grange (Dublin), with fixed installations, allowing simultaneous interpretation from and to every location in four languages (expandable by adding a blade to the encoder per additional four languages).

The set-up used has been validated by senior interpreters designated by the interpreters' representatives.

However, the assessment is based on a specific brand and codec implementation, as well as specific audio and lighting conditions, and a subjective assessment by interpreters. In addition, current standards regarding technical requirements applicable to conference equipment only contain analogue audio bandwidth requirements and do not cover new technologies and devices widely in use nowadays in meetings or conferences. In particular, they do not contain any requirements for digital video and audio sources, nor for real-time video and audio signals transmitted over non-isochronous networks.

The next step has been to look for an objective evaluation method updated to cover digital equipment. To this end, DG Interpretation commissioned from the Fraunhofer Institut in Berlin a study on the "Definition of an objective evaluation method for assessing the minimal quality of digital video and audio sources required to provide simultaneous interpretation". The purpose of the study was to:

a) assess minimum quality levels of audio and video signals and of audio-video synchronization for the provision of simultaneous interpretation. This is needed when interpreters are working from an audiovisual support (i.e. images coming from the meeting room or from any remote location, and projected on a meeting room screen or displayed in a monitor in the interpretation booth)

b) establish objective, measurable parameters to allow simultaneous interpretation of digitally encoded images and sound, irrespective of brand, codec algorithm or codec implementation, etc. coming either from the meeting room itself or from any remote location;

(see Appendix 2)

In addition to videoconference, remote interpretation has been thoroughly investigated since the year 2000. Tests have been done in 2001 and 2003 with different scenarios and configurations, with more than 60 conference interpreters.

In 2005, remote interpretation was provided in 22 languages during a Summit of European Heads of State and Government in Hampton Court (see technical report in Appendix 3).

Technical guidelines have been drafted, based on the acquired experience (see Appendix 4).

APPENDICES

All Appendices are available at the following website:

http://www.videoconference-interpreting.net/BraunTaylor2011.html

Appendix 1:

Interpreted videoconference – minimum audiovisual technical requirements. European Commission, DG Interpreting, updated 10/2010.

Appendix 2:

Definition of an objective evaluation method for assessing the minimal quality of digital video and audio sources required to provide simultaneous interpretation - Final Report. Fraunhofer IDMT, 12/2010.

Appendix 3:

Remote interpretation at Hampton Court. European Commission, DG Interpreting, 11/2005.

Appendix 4:

Technical guidance for remote interpretation. European Commission, DG Interpreting, updated 03/2011.

TRAINING IN VIDEO-MEDIATED INTERPRETING IN LEGAL PROCEEDINGS: MODULES FOR INTERPRETING STUDENTS, LEGAL INTERPRETERS AND LEGAL PRACTITIONERS

Sabine Braun and Judith L. Taylor, *University of Surrey*

Joanna Miler-Cassino and Zofia Rybińska, *TEPIS*

Katalin Balogh, Erik Hertog, Yolanda vanden Bosch, *Lessius Hogeschool*

Dirk Rombouts, *Local Police Antwerp*

1 INTRODUCTION

Because of the scarcity of training opportunities in legal interpreting, and the non-existence of training in video-mediated legal interpreting *per se*, both from the point of view of the legal interpreters themselves, and that of the legal professionals who work with interpreters, the AVIDICUS Project included as one of its core objectives to devise and pilot three training modules on video-mediated interpreting: one for legal practitioners, including the police; one for interpreters working in the legal services; and one for interpreting students.

This chapter presents the three training modules, designed and developed by the AVIDICUS Project. Following a discussion of the background context to the need for training and the technological of such training, the module for student interpreters is presented, followed by the legal interpreters' module, and finally the module aimed at legal practitioners and police officers.

The modules cover two main settings of video-mediated interpreting. *Videoconference interpreting (VCI)* is used when the proceedings take place at two different locations, e.g. a court and a prison, that are linked via VC. The interpreter is situated either in the court or in the prison with the non-native speaker. *Remote interpreting (RI)* is used to provide timely access to qualified legal interpreters. In this case, the proceedings take place at a single location (e.g. a court room), but the interpreter is integrated via VC link from a remote location (e.g. at another court house).

There is currently very little pre-service and in-service training in legal interpreting, let alone in video-mediated forms of interpreting in this area.

Sabine Braun, Judith L. Taylor, Joanna Miler-Cassino, Zofia Rybińska,
Katalin Balogh, Erik Hertog and Dirk Rombouts

Higher education institutions in Europe have only recently begun to offer such training at undergraduate or postgraduate level[1, 2] or short courses on legal interpreting for professional interpreters, as CPD or in-service training.[3] There is also very little provision in terms of certification or accreditation, with one of the few examples being the Diploma of Public Service Interpreting (DPSI), which has been offered by the Chartered Institute of Linguists in the UK since 1994. Even more precarious is the situation with regard to the training of legal practitioners and police officers regarding how to work with an interpreter.[4] A small but growing number of European initiatives, funded by the Criminal Justice Programme of the DG Justice, have begun to address the lack of training and training resources for legal interpreters and legal practitioners/police officers, especially the Building Mutual Trust 1 and 2 projects[5] and the TRAFUT project.[6]

The contribution made by the AVIDICUS project to the training of interpreters and legal practitioners is one further step in this direction, but two questions have emerged:

Firstly, given the scarcity of even the most basic training in legal interpreting, one might raise the question as to whether the integration of training in VCI and RI into such training is ahead of its time. However, as a crucial point, the various forms of video-mediated interpreting are likely to become more frequent, given the following developments:

- New EU legislation, especially the Directive of the European Parliament and of the Council on the rights to interpretation and translation in criminal proceedings (DIRECTIVE 2010/64/UE),

---

[1] e.g. BA Legal Interpreting at the University of Applied Sciences Magdeburg-Stendal/ Germany; Masters in Intercultural Communication, Interpretation and Translation in Public Services at the University of Alcalá/Spain; binational Masters in Legal Translating and Interpreting offered by the Université de Bretagne-Sud in Lorient/France and the University of Applied Sciences Magdeburg-Stendal/Germany (2010/11); Masters in Legal Interpreting and Translation English-Italian at Luspio University Rome/Italy (2011), MA in Public Service Interpreting at the University of Surrey/UK (2009/10); Postgraduate Diploma in Legal Interpreting at London Metropolitan University/UK (2009/10).

[2] See also Lequy and Sander (2009).

[3] e.g. Certificate of Advanced Studies in Legal Interpreting, University of Applied Sciences Winterthur/Switzerland; Short course at the Universities of Applied Sciences Cologne/ Germany.

[4] One initiative has recently been developed by the Norwegian Directorate of Integration and Diversity (IMDi) to provide orientation seminars for judges on how to work with interpreters during court hearings. (Kolstad Zehouo and Fiva 2010 – abstract online); see also Corsellis (2008) on the importance of training legal practitioners.

[5] JLS/2007/JPEN/219, 2008-10 and JUST/2010/JPEN/AG/1566, 2011-13.

[6] JUST/2010/JPEN/AG/1549, 2011-13.

- The European effort to strengthen cooperation and mutual assistance in cross-border criminal proceedings as reflected in the *Green paper on obtaining evidence in criminal matters from one member state to another and securing its admissibility* (COM (2009) 624), and
- The Multi-annual European e-Justice Action Plan 2009-2013 of the Council (OJ No. C 75/01, 31-03-2009).

All of these initiatives provide for and/or encourage the use of videoconferencing in legal proceedings, including as a tool to deliver interpretation. A survey conducted in 2008 by the working party on legal data processing shows that videoconferencing is already widely used in criminal proceedings to speed up cross-border cooperation, reduce costs and increase security (15641/07 JURINFO 75 JUSTCIV 315 COPEN 176). The surveys conducted in the AVIDICUS Project in 2009-10 confirm that the practice of video-mediated *interpreting* in criminal proceedings is also expanding (see Braun & Taylor's report in this volume on the two surveys).

Secondly, the small body of research on video-mediated interpreting,[7] including the research conducted in the AVIDICUS Project (reported elsewhere in this volume) make it clear that video-mediated interpreting is especially challenging. From a purist's point of view, another key question would, therefore, be whether training should be offered for forms of interpreting whose viability is as yet undecided. The AVIDICUS Project has taken the cautious but pragmatic view that videoconference technology can *potentially* offer an effective solution to some of the current problems surrounding the provision of interpreting services, providing that relevant research is conducted to improve understanding of video-mediated interpreting and to enable mitigation of the challenges. As well as highlighting the limitations of video-mediated interpreting where applicable, research outcomes will help to shape the design of the solutions and interpreters' working conditions. The development of training is an integral part of such an approach.

It is against this background that the AVIDICUS Project aimed to develop a series of training modules in video-mediated interpreting, addressing different target groups – legal interpreters, interpreting students, and legal practitioners/police officers. Although in the long run it will be useful to train interpreters and legal practitioners/police officers together, this seemed less practicable at the outset of AVIDICUS, given the current state of the art in training. Also, due to the novelty of the forms of interpreting considered here, it was assumed that initial training would proceed more easily if it were group-specific. Accordingly, three training modules were devised.

---

[7] See http://www.videoconference-interpreting.net/rPublications.html for a bibliography.

The strength of the approach to training adopted in AVIDICUS is the combination of practical aspects with outcomes from the project research. **Research-led guidance** in the training will facilitate reflection upon practice and provide a sound basis for the discussion of appropriate solutions to problems arising.

All three modules are designed so that they can be adapted to local contexts. For example, different pieces of national legislation may be included. The focus may be on those settings of video-mediated interpreting that are most relevant in a particular national context, and different exercises may be included as appropriate.

Furthermore, the delivery of the modules is flexible. They can be delivered within a day or less, but can also be expanded into a small series of lessons to suit different needs. The module for interpreting students, for example, has been designed to become part of a broader module or course on legal interpreting, although feedback from the pilot of this module indicates that it may be desirable to devote a more substantial amount of time to the topic of video-mediated interpreting.

All three modules were **piloted** at least once, using the complementary types of expertise and access to target groups in the AVIDICUS consortium:

The *module for interpreting students* was piloted with two groups of Masters students (31 in total) undertaking the module entitled 'Public Service Interpreting – Trends and Issues' at the University of Surrey (UK), in the spring of 2010 and 2011. Each year, the module was delivered in three 2-hour sessions, and included the opportunity for students to practise VCI and RI in the University's videoconferencing suite. Feedback was collected by means of a questionnaire.

The *module for practising interpreters* was piloted in a two-day training session organised by TEPIS in Poland in January 2011 and in five half-day training sessions held for different groups of accredited interpreters of the London Metropolitan Police Service, in September 2010, and January and March 2011 organised by the Metropolitan Police Service's Language and Cultural Services department. A total of 41 interpreters attended these sessions and were invited to provide feedback in an evaluation questionnaire.

The *module for legal practitioners* is based on the results and observations of three full-day testing days of role plays hosted by the audio-visual centre of the University of Leuven, Leuven, Belgium, on 1st and 25th February 2010 and on 7th May 2010 in the Utrecht Court and Zeist Asylum Centre in The Netherlands. A training session for legal practitioners, in this case some 15 police officers, was piloted in Ghent in November 2010 and it is their recommendations, together with the observations of the police officers taking part in the role plays which form the backbone of the training module for legal practitioners outlined in section 5 below.

One important prerequisite concerns the technological basis required to run the training modules. This is described in section 2 below.

2   TECHNOLOGICAL BASIS

There are three important technological elements to consider for any
practice-based training module in video-mediated interpreting. The first is
the availability of at least two VC 'sites'. For the purposes of simulation and
training, it will be convenient if the two (or more) sites are co-located in the
same building to allow the course participants (and tutors) to change
locations easily within a training session. Alternatively, the training session
could be organised as a collaborative event between two institutions with
compatible VC equipment, e.g. between two universities or between a
university and a public service provider.

The other two crucial elements are the quality of the VC connection and
the quality of the equipment. **Minimum technical specifications** can be
derived from the Videoconferencing manual which was developed by the
European working party on legal data processing and which is available on
the European e-Justice portal (http://e-justice.europa.eu/ → Section on
videoconferencing → Manual → Annex II: Technical specifications). The
following list is a summary of these specifications:

- *VC system:* If possible, a dedicated 'room system' should be used.
  Alternatively, a PC-based system can be used, provided that the PC
  has an acceptable processing speed and that no other 'heavy'
  applications run on this PC while the VC session is in progress.

- *ISDN-based connections*: If an ISDN connection is used, a minimum
  of 6 channels (3 ISDN lines) should be available to achieve a
  bandwidth of 384 kbit/s and a transmission rate of 30 frames per
  second for the video image. If large screens are used, this may not be
  sufficient. In any case, the H.320 or H.310 standards for Video over
  ISDN should be used (H.310 provides a faster connection).

- *Internet-based connections* should use the H.323 standard for Video
  over Internet. A bandwidth of at least 1Mbit/s should be available.

- *Picture*: Systems should use the H.263 and H.264 standards for
  picture quality and a frame rate of 30 frames per second to ensure a
  picture quality that is as close to broadcast quality as possible.

- The most common *audio transmission* standards are G.711 and G.722,
  which provide 7 kHz audio-coding within 128 or 64 kbit/s
  respectively). It should be noted, however, that the International
  Association of Conference Interpreters (AIIC) deems a range of 7 kHz
  insufficient for remote conference interpreting.[8]

---

[8]   See AIIC (2000). The sound problems for interpreters especially in ISDN-based videoconferences have also been highlighted in various studies (e.g. Böcker & Anderson 1993,
Braun 2004, 2007, Mouzourakis 2006).

- *Screens*: good sized LCD screens should be used. They should be large enough for the recognition and identification of facial expressions and exhibits.
- *Microphones*: Echo cancellation microphones with full-duplex audio and audio muting should be used.
- *Cameras and lighting*: If possible, cameras which can be controlled remotely should be used. Light in the VC rooms should be such that a natural atmosphere is created and that especially facial expressions can be seen clearly and without shade.
- *Seating arrangements* should imitate real-life conditions as far as possible and should ensure an ergonomically appropriate seating for the interpreter.

In a training situation, some – but not all – of the above provisions may have to be adapted or foregone. With regard to seating arrangements, for example, it may not be possible or necessary to recreate a courtroom or custody suite in a training environment. Conditions should, however, be such that a useful training experience can be provided.

Regarding the quality of the equipment and the connection, a compromise seems less commendable, however. It could, of course, be argued that those who take the training modules could learn something from VC systems using a low-quality connection such as narrowband ISDN (2 to 6 channels, i.e. 128 to 384 kbps), Skype or similar Internet-based video telephone services for the home market, which may be readily available especially in some institutions. The use of low-quality connections as well as the experience of using low-quality peripheral equipment (screens, microphones and loudspeakers) in a training situation would certainly demonstrate to the course participants the problems and shortcomings of such equipment for the purposes of legal communication and interpreting. However, with high-quality equipment and connections becoming more affordable, the experience of 'bad' technology does not need to take place in a training situation; it could be left to observation of real-life proceedings using lower-quality technology.

Many magistrates courts in England, for example, are equipped with early VC systems for the so-called 'court-prison video links', which are mostly used for remand extension hearings. This equipment barely allows the participants at a remote site (i.e. in prison) to be seen (see Fowler 2007 for a discussion of some of the consequences). The observation of such low-quality video links will be a revealing experience for any interpreting student, practising legal interpreter and legal practitioner. Any training module dedicated to video-mediated interpreting in legal proceedings should, however, be based more appropriate equipment, assuming that outdated technology in real-life courtrooms and other legal settings will be replaced with more appropriate technology in the near future.[9]

Further details of the equipment required will depend on the mode of interpreting (consecutive, simultaneous or whispered interpreting) that is chosen for the training session and relevant to the country in which the training takes place. The AVIDICUS surveys (see Braun & Taylor in this volume) show that at least in Europe the current and emerging VCI and RI settings are mostly based on consecutive interpreting, i.e. the mode in which the interpreter renders short segments of speech after listening first. In this mode of interpreting, no additional equipment is required, although the use of headphones for the interpreters may be considered to reduce noise levels (see Braun in this volume). However, the survey reveals that some countries use simultaneous interpreting, i.e. the mode in which the interpreter relays speech continuously while listening and without the speaker having to pause. Simultaneous interpreting normally requires specific additional equipment, especially a sound-proof booth for the interpreter which in a VC situation needs to be connected to the VC system. By contrast, those situations in which simultaneous interpreting is delivered in the form of 'whispered interpreting', with the interpreter sitting or standing next to the person who needs the interpretation, do not normally require additional equipment. It should, however, be noted that in a VC situation, this mode of interpreting can only be applied for participants who are co-located with the interpreter.

A training situation may have to cover different modes of interpreting so that those participating in the training can form a realistic impression of the specifics of each mode and are enabled to assess the suitability of different modes of interpreting for a particular VC situation in a legal context. The training modules are indifferent to the interpreting mode. Given the current situation in most European countries, the AVIDICUS pilot courses focused on consecutive interpreting.

3   THE MODULE FOR INTERPRETING STUDENTS

This section describes the details of the module for interpreting students, which is aimed in particular at Masters-level students. It is assumed that students undertaking the module have an appropriate level of linguistic aptitude and at least initial experience of face-to-face interpreting to ensure that they will be able to appreciate the challenges of VCI/RI and their implications. It is also advisable (and assumed here) that students who undergo this training have acquired a good understanding of legal

---

[9]   In other settings, there may be good reasons for using lower-quality VC equipment and connections, e.g. to ensure mobility, as discussed by Verrept (2011) in a healthcare setting.

interpreting, including knowledge of the relevant legal systems and the ethical and practical problems and challenges commonly associated with it. It is therefore recommended that the module outlined here should not be offered in semester 1 of any Masters programme, irrespective of whether such programmes have a duration of one or two years.

3.1 Aims and Learning Outcomes

The specific **aims** of this module are:

- to raise awareness of the novel forms of video-mediated interpreting;
- to provide a detailed introduction to the various forms of video-conference and remote interpreting in legal proceedings, an overview of current practice and future trends;
- to enable students to explore the specific challenges of video-mediated interpreting in comparison with face-to-face interpreting (such as the perception of interlocutors via technical channels, absence of visual clues, problems with control over technical equipment and communication management);
- to instil in students a thorough understanding of the reasons for the implementation of video-based communication and interpreting solutions by the judicial services;
- to provide opportunities for hands-on practice of different forms of video-based interpreting;
- to encourage discussion and reflection upon practical experience;
- to provide a synopsis of new research questions arising from the introduction of video-mediated interpreting.

In terms of **learning outcomes**, it is expected that students who have completed this module will have a good insight into the communication technologies used in different forms of video-based interpreting, into the motivations of their use and into the specific challenges that these create for interpreting. Students will also have developed initial know-how to enable them to evaluate when videoconference/remote interpreting are appropriate working modes and when they are not. The syllabus described in Section 3.2 has been developed with these aims and learning outcomes in mind.

3.2 Syllabus

The syllabus for the module is divided up into six main **units**, which is reflected in the teaching material (see Section 3.3). The units are designed so that there is a mixture of teacher-led input, student exploration and discovery, and practical exercises for the students to undertake, either in class or in their own time. Additionally, students should be encouraged to engage in the discussion and ask questions at any time, to create an active learning environment.

Unit 1: Introduction
- The current situation
- Current EU legislation relating to VC use in legal proceedings
- Videoconferencing: definitions and key terms

The unit aims to give an overview of current developments leading to the use of VCI and RI in criminal proceedings, to introduce the emerging legal frameworks in Europe and their implications, and to explain the technological basis for videoconferencing.

The unit firstly highlights the motivations on the part of the judicial services for using these forms of interpreting, including the need to speed up legal proceedings, the pressure to save costs and the shortfall of qualified legal interpreters in some regions. It also draws students' attention to the current tensions between stakeholders regarding the use or non-use of VCI and RI, including the concerns voiced by interpreters that the use of VCI and RI may reduce the quality of interpreting and may have adverse effects on their working conditions. Secondly, the unit provides the students with information on current and emerging EU legislation which mentions and promotes the use of videoconferencing in criminal proceedings, especially the '*Procedural Rights Roadmap*' for strengthening procedural rights of suspected or accused persons in criminal proceedings (OJ No. C 295/01, 04-12-2009) and the ensuing Directives. This will help students understand the legislative and political background for using VCI and RI in criminal proceedings. Thirdly, the introductory unit provides definitions of the key terms associated with videoconferencing and makes reference to the diverse technologies that are used for videoconferencing, pointing to the differences in the appropriateness of these technologies.

The intended learning outcome of this unit is to raise students' awareness of the motivations behind using VCI and RI. By discussing the various technologies used for videoconferencing, the unit also makes students aware of the fact that each setting and potential interpreting assignment involving a VC is likely to be different and merits individual assessment.

Unit 2: Videoconferencing and Interpreting
- Emerging settings and their motivations
- Definitions
- Settings in detail: rationale and potential uses

Building on the basic insight gained in Unit 1 of the module, that future interpreters are likely to face a variety of settings, this unit provides an in-depth analysis of the various emerging settings and motivations behind them.

The unit makes a basic distinction between videoconference interpreting and remote interpreting, as defined in the introduction to this chapter. It then explores the potential uses of each of these forms of video-mediated interpreting, comparing and contrasting them, and additionally looks at the utilisation of VCI in tandem with RI. Most importantly, it draws students' attention to the different distributions of participants and interpreter. The unit explains to students that the form of video-mediated interpreting which has been termed here videoconference interpreting (VCI) is employed when an interpreter needs to be integrated into a videoconference, e.g. to hear a remote witness who requires an interpreter, and that in VCI, the interpreter is normally co-located with some of the participants, i.e. either in the court room or with the witness. This setting is contrasted with remote interpreting (RI), which is mainly used to overcome local shortages of interpreters or to save interpreter travel costs and in which the interpreter is the only person who is in a different location.

As an outcome of this unit, students will be able to distinguish between different settings and understand their different motivations. This will help students realise that the different settings are not normally interchangeable and that each of them comes with their own challenges.

Unit 3: Current Practice
- Examples of current uses of VCI and RI in legal proceedings (based on the two surveys among legal practitioners and interpreters conducted in the EU project AVIDICUS)
- First hands-on practice session: VCI and RI

The aim of this unit is twofold. Firstly it intends to give an overview of current uses of VCI and RI in legal proceedings. Secondly, it integrates the first of two hands-on practice sessions in this module.

In the first part, the unit identifies examples of current real uses of VCI and RI in legal proceedings across Europe, based on the responses to the AVIDICUS project's EU surveys of legal practitioners and interpreters. The focus is on criminal proceedings, but some references to other settings, especially immigration, are also made. The unit shows where and how the different forms of video-mediated interpreting are used today, e.g. VCI in first hearings and remand extension hearings, or planned in the near future, e.g. RI in police interviews. Examples from different European countries are provided, highlighting similarities and differences in the emerging practices. This unit in particular can be adapted to local contexts by including additional material drawn from national or regional contexts as appropriate.

The second part of the unit consists of hands-on practice. This requires a group of at least three students, scripts of legal proceedings and access to VC technology (see Section 2). It is recommended that students get practice in both VCI and RI to explore and apply what has been learned in the first part of the unit and in previous units, but the hands-on part can be adapted to local circumstances, relevance and time available. The following are two examples of how to practice:

1. Practice of VCI: One student takes on the role of a prosecutor or judge and is in VC room 1. Another student takes on the role of a remote witness, speaking another language, and is in VC room 2. A third student, who speaks the language of the remote witness, is the interpreter and interprets for approximately 10 to 15 minutes at either side. The other students observe the VC. Then, roles can be swapped and the exercise can be repeated.

2. Practice of RI: One student takes the role of a police officer and another student the role of a suspect or victim, speaking in another language. They are in one room. A third student, who speaks the language of the suspect or victim, is the interpreter and is in another room. Here again, one student can practise interpreting for approximately 10 to 15 minutes, before roles are swapped to give another student a chance to practise. Students without active roles should observe the VC at the different sites.

These suggestions require at least two students who have the same working languages. If this is not possible, the practice can take place in one language only, and the interpretation can be simulated. (Suggestions for overcoming problems with the availability of language pairs are outlined in Section 4). A group discussion of the practical experience and observations should follow. Students should be encouraged to compare the two settings with each other and with face-to-face interpreting, to discuss the problems they encountered or observed and to establish what would be required to resolve them.

As an outcome, students will be able to appreciate the fact that VCI and RI are different settings catering for different needs. Students should also be able to understand that there is currently no commonly accepted or agreed standard for the practice of VCI and RI. The hands-on session should enable students to experience the differences between face-to-face and video-mediated interpreting and to reflect on their own practice.

Unit 4: From Practice to Research
- Current insights: an overview of what has been learned from the current uses of VCI/RI in legal proceedings, with a focus on the evaluation methods used
- Summary of research findings in other areas of VCI and RI

The practical part of Unit 3 is likely to have raised a range of questions. Given the lack of commonly accepted standards for VCI and RI, it is important for students to develop their own criteria for assessing VCI and RI situations, and hence methodological awareness is required. Similarly, graduates from interpreting programmes may in future be tasked with planning or overseeing the introduction of new forms of interpreting in an institution for which they work. In such a situation, evaluative skills are crucial, as well. Accordingly, Unit 4 familiarises students with the findings of studies that have examined different uses of video-mediated interpreting. The focus is on the research and evaluation methods that were employed in such studies.

As an outcome of this unit, students are expected to be able to distinguish different approaches to researching and evaluating VCI and RI. This will, in turn, raise the students' awareness of the links between a particular research/evaluation method and the research outcomes and will enable them to identify shortcomings in evaluation methods applied in some of the past studies. Along with their own initial practice of VCI and RI gained in Unit 3 of the module, the students will also be able to identify open questions for the practice of VCI and RI that would require further research. These will be summarised in Unit 5.

Unit 5: Implications for future research
- Areas and directions of future research on VCI/RI
- Questions arising from current practice for future research

---

The aim of this unit is to identify research questions relating to VCI and RI. By doing so, it will also draw the students' attention to potential problems of VCI and RI in a more systematic way than previous units, in which students collected their own observations.

The unit firstly identifies the main areas of research for VCI and RI such as the impact of technology on an interpreter's performance, the impact of the socio-cultural specifics of legal interpreting on VCI/RI in legal proceedings and the impact of the video mediation on the communication management and rapport between the participants. It then gives an overview of some of the major questions arising in each of these areas.

After completing this unit, students are expected to have an increased awareness of potential problems in VCI and RI and have begun to reflect upon possible strategies that will help resolve such problems. The unit will also prepare the ground for the second hands-on practice, which forms part of unit 6 and in which students are actively encouraged to identify problems which can be resolved more easily and problems which are likely to persist even with training and familiarisation.

Unit 6: Wrap-up
- Final practice session
- Concluding remarks

The aim of this final unit is twofold. One the one hand, it incorporates a second practical session and on the other hand it draws conclusions regarding the current and emerging usage of VCI and RI in criminal proceedings.

The recommendation for the practical session is to repeat the interpreting practice exercise in Unit 3, using different legal settings and/or scripts. Students should be encouraged to think actively about

- the difficulties of VCI/RI that are easy to resolve through practice and familiarisation,
- the difficulties that are likely to remain and/or require specific interpreting/communication strategies,
- elements that further training in VCI/RI should include,
- possible guidelines and recommendations for interpreters and legal practitioners.

Finally, this last unit highlights the main points of the module and suggests some general solutions to begin to address these issues.

As a variant, the practical guidelines for VCI/RI which are part of the module for practising interpreters (see Section 4) could be included in the Wrap-up unit. In line with constructivist approaches to learning and teaching, which are common in higher education settings, tutors may, however, prefer to let students create their own guidelines first before presenting them with suggestions or a ready-made list.

Each unit of this syllabus is based on a set of teaching materials – PowerPoint slides, exercises and handouts. These are described in the next section.

3.3 Teaching Material

The teaching material for this module was developed in several iterations. Preliminary versions were discussed in the consortium and used in the two pilot courses (see Section 3.4). The final version of the teaching material, which is provided in the appendices, was produced after the completion of the second pilot, incorporating student feedback, the results of the discussions in the consortium and the final project results as at March 2011.

The final version aims to strike a balance between information about current practice in VCI and RI, trends and frequency of use on the one hand, and the need for updating of the teaching material to reflect changing practice, changing legal frameworks and new research insights on the other hand.

The material includes:

- A PowerPoint presentation covering each unit of the syllabus (see appendix 1a),
- A set of exercises for each unit; the exercises are included in the PowerPoint presentation at the end of each unit,
- A handout providing a number of texts from the media relating to video-mediated interpreting, for discussion in Unit 1 (see appendix 2),
- A bibliography of VCI/RI, which is also available at the AVIDICUS website (www.videoconference-interpreting.net),
- Scripts for role-play sessions: role-plays should be based on real material where possible and appropriate.

Whilst the PowerPoint presentation provides a summary of the teacher-led input to the module, the teaching material and the module as a whole have been designed to encourage active student participation. The teaching style should be accordingly, allowing for interaction, reflection and discussion. The exercises included in each unit are intended to aid this process.

In the remainder of this Section, the main aspects of the teaching materials for each unit will be highlighted. Readers are, however, referred to the appendices, which provide the full set of the materials created for this module. A range of exercises has also been created for each unit.

Unit 1: Introduction

The PowerPoint slides for this unit provide an overview of the current situation, outline the main motivations behind the use of VCI and RI and give a list of the main legislative frameworks relating to the use of VCI and RI. The slides include links to the legislative texts for later reference.

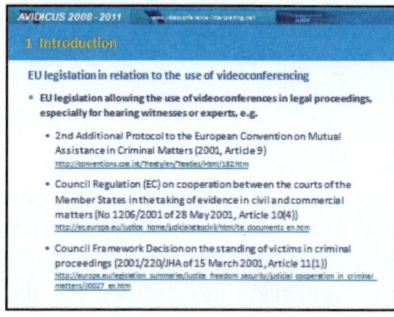 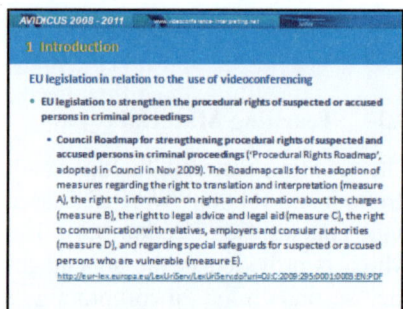

Example of references to EU legislation relating to videoconferencing

The pilot courses have shown that an awareness-raising exercise at the beginning is a good way of achieving student participation from the outset. To this end, several press releases relating to the introduction of video-mediated interpreting in legal proceedings and also other settings were collated into a handout (included in appendices). In the introductory unit, students can be asked to study these texts and to assess the attitude towards video-mediated interpreting they reflect. Students are likely to find that the media often report about the novel forms of interpreting in an enthusiastic but oversimplified way and that bold claims are made with regard to the viability of video-mediated interpreting, the advantages and the potential cost savings. This insight can be contrasted with the points made in Unit 1, especially the concerns raised by professional interpreters' regarding the drawbacks of VCI and RI. Such a discussion alerts students to the mixed reactions towards VCI and RI and creates a focus for the subsequent units. The other exercise in the introductory unit encourages students to research the legislative texts introduced with regard to the references such texts make to videoconferencing.

Unit 2: Videoconferencing and Interpreting

The slides for Unit 2 give graphic representations of the different settings and provides examples of their use.

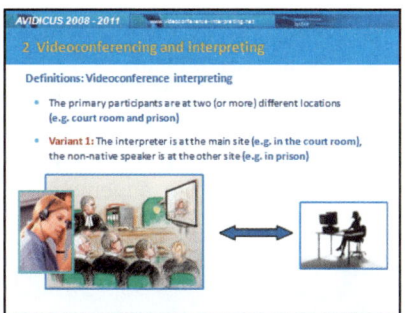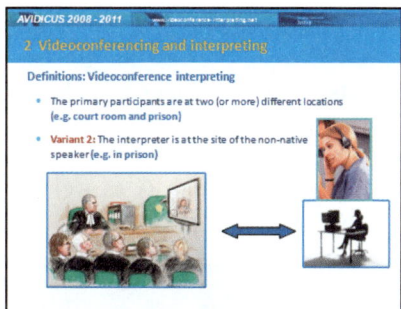

Example of illustration of VCI settings

The exercises ask students to find out which of the settings are used in their respective countries and then encourage them to think about the advantages and drawbacks of the different variants of VCI in court (interpreter co-located in court room vs. interpreter together with remote non-native speaker) from the point of view of the interpreter, the non-native speaker and the judge. This exercise requires students to transfer their knowledge about legal interpreting to the novel situation of VCI. It prepares students for Unit 3, the discussion of current practice of VCI and RI in Europe.

Unit 3: Current Practice

An effort has been made to include examples of current practice from different countries in this unit. For example, some of the slides in Unit 3 contrast the different practices of VCI in first hearings in England/Wales (interpreter normally in court), Belgium (interpreter normally co-located with the judge), the Netherlands (interpreter can choose the location but is normally co-located with the non-native speaker; whispered interpreting is used) and Poland (location of the interpreter not regulated). The exercise in Unit 2 will have primed students to reflect critically on the differences, depending on the conclusion to which they came in Unit 2.

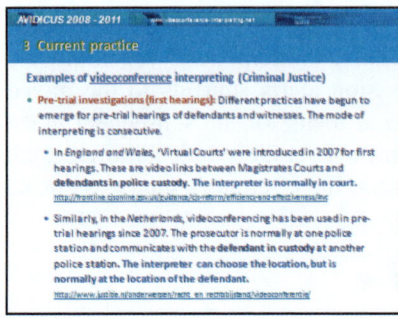
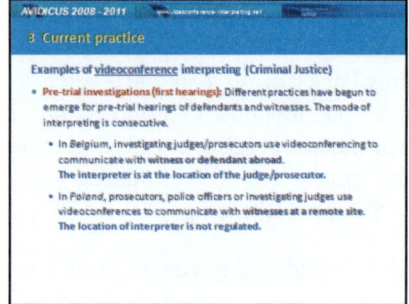

Slides contrasting the practice of first hearings across Europe

The remaining slides in Unit 3 present information gained in the AVIDICUS legal practitioners' survey regarding the frequency of use of VCI and RI across Europe, the reasons for use as stated by the respondents and other aspects. Unit 3 includes a wide range of exercises which mainly challenge students' evaluative skills. Students are, for example, asked to discuss controversial quotes from reports on current practice, interpreters' initial reactions to VCI and RI as well as to reflect upon seating arrangements in VCI/RI situations in court and at police stations.

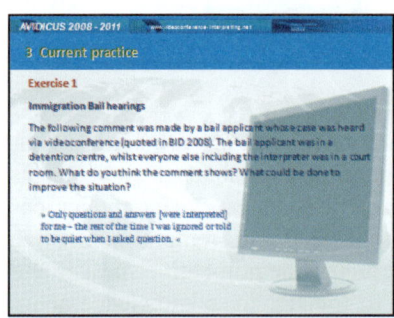
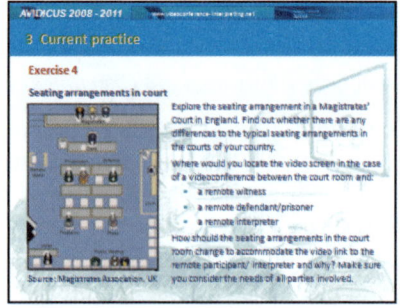

Examples of exercises in Unit 3

The hands-on session should be based on scripts, as stated above. To make it realistic, scripts should reflect the national context. The students can act as role players, with some prior instruction. Alternatively, another tutor, legal practitioner or police officer volunteer could participate in the role play. However, using the students themselves has the advantage of helping them experience and engage with different roles, not just that of the interpreter.

Unit 4: From Practice to Research

The material in this unit provides an overview of the research on VCI/RI conducted to date. It compares the research methods of studies conducted in the EU/UN (with regard to remote conference interpreting), and in healthcare and business settings. It also provides information about the research and evaluation methods that were used in some of the reports on VCI/RI practice. The associated exercises ask students to assess these research and evaluation methods and to design their own methodological approach.

Unit 5: Implications for Future Research

The slides for this unit identify relevant areas for research and present a range of research questions for each area. One of the exercises in this unit invites students to think about how to research a chosen question. The other exercises encourage students to discuss the impact of VCI/RI on various aspects of the interpreting process including the role of the interpreter.

 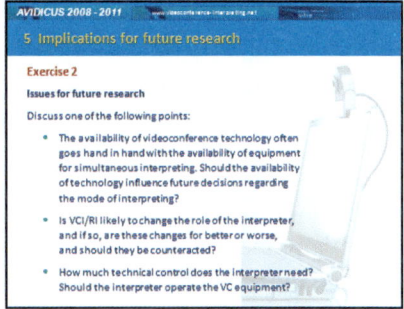

Examples of exercises for Unit 5

Unit 6: Wrap-up

This unit is designed to start with a second hands-on practice session, similar to the first session in Unit 3. The slides for this unit focus on the concluding remarks and provide a list of requirements for VCI and RI and problems that need to be resolved in the future. As indicated in Section 3.2, the final unit could be extended to include slides relating to practical guidelines for VCI/RI, as is included in the module for practising interpreters. Alternatively, students can be asked to come up with their own guidelines first.

3.4   The Pilot at the University of Surrey

The module for interpreting students was piloted with Masters students in the Centre for Translation Studies at the University of Surrey. The pilot course was held twice, in 2010 and 2011. It was integrated into a semester 2 module entitled 'Public Service Interpreting – Trends and Issues'. The module was attended by 9 students in 2010, and by 22 students in 2011. In 2010, an early version of the module and teaching material was piloted. In the 2011 version, more of the information emerging from the research conducted in AVIDICUS, especially information on current practice from the surveys, was integrated. The version of the teaching material used in the second pilot was thus very similar to the final version provided in the appendices. In the module run at the University of Surrey, the six units of the training module described above were covered in the course of three 2-hour sessions.

Session I

Unit 1 (Introduction) was delivered in lecture style, followed by the aware-ness raising exercise using the collection of press releases. Unit 2 (Videocon-ferencing and Interpreting) was presented in seminar-style allowing for discussion of the different configurations of VCI and RI. Most of the associated exercises became part of this discussion. Students were asked to think about the advantages and drawbacks of different VCI variants at home.

Session II

Firstly, the homework was discussed. Then Unit 3 (Current Practice) was presented in seminar style with time for discussion. Once again, the exercises for unit 3 were integrated in the discussion.

In the second part of this session, the students received hands-on experience of videoconference interpreting, with practice in both variations of this form of interpreting, but not in remote interpreting. This had to do with the timeframe and the group size, especially in year 2. Remote interpreting was practiced in Session III.

Before the actual interpreting practice, the students were given a brief introduction to the equipment. The videoconferencing suite used for the sessions is equipped with an Access Grid Node (http://www.accessgrid. org) which supports the standards for Internet-based videoconferencing outlined in section 2. Students were able to see the other room (overview picture and 2 close-ups from different angles) as well as a picture of their own room. The images were projected to a video wall.

In the role-play, a mock trial script involving the hearing of a remote witness was used. All roles involved – interpreter, legal professionals, non-native speaker – were played by the students. Legal practitioners were not involved, because it was felt that the students would gain more from the experience if they carried out the role plays themselves. However, the Surrey students had other opportunities to meet and talk to legal practitioners and legal interpreters in other parts of their MA programme.

All students received a briefing of the mock trial, and then some students were asked to adopt the various roles. They were given a script, except for the student who acted as the interpreter. The students had previously received introductions to the English/Welsh legal system and court interpreting and had worked with similar scripts in prior classes, also in the form of a role-play. In the VCI session, one student took on the role of the magistrate (speaking in English), while a Polish student volunteered to go to the remote site (another room within the same building) to play the part of the witness. Other Polish students took turns at interpreting, both in the main VC room and at the remote site with the witness. Other languages utilised included Chinese, Greek and Italian. The session ended with a discussion of the students' observations.

Session III

Session III covered the remaining units of the module (Units 4, 5 and 6). Students also received further practical experience, this time in remote interpreting. Once more, the students played all the roles. In this session, the script of a police interview was used. Otherwise, the class was run on similar lines to the practical part in Session 2.

The final discussion drew together the students' observations from their own VCI and RI experiences from the 'hands-on' sessions; implications for future research (the direction of future research on VCI and RI and the questions arising); and concluding remarks on generic issues arising and potential solutions.

The students made numerous interesting observations which figured in the discussions after the practical sessions and also enriched the discussion of more 'theoretical' parts of the module. For example, some students who acted in the role of the interpreter noted difficulties with turn-taking ('I didn't know when to talk;' 'When should the interpreting begin?'). Other aspects that were noted included the difficulty of making eye contact with the interlocutors at the remote site and the problems with seating arrangements. One student commented, for example, that 'the interpreter should have visual contact with the witness – the prosecutor was hiding her'. Another student expressed the characteristic uncertainty of interlocutors in VC situations by saying, 'I didn't know where to look to begin with'. A student also raised the issue of the care of the technology and asked what would happen in court if the VC link or technology broke down. In the RI setting, one student admitted to feelings of isolation owning to being in a separate room ('You get the impression you are far away from them'). On the whole, students were, however, positive towards the novel forms of video-mediated interpreting. One student summarised the overall attitude thus: 'Because we're new to interpreting, we take to VCI/RI more easily. Someone who has done it for twenty years or more mightn't take to it so easily'. The attitude taken by the students is in stark contrast to the attitude expressed by some of the professional interpreters (see Section 4).

3.5   Evaluation feedback from the pilot

An evaluation questionnaire was circulated at the conclusion of the final
session in each of the two pilot courses. In total, 26 evaluation questionnaires
were completed by students who participated in the module at Surrey. Not
every respondent completed every question.

Surrey students are of different language backgrounds and different first
degrees. The students' linguistic backgrounds include languages that are
among the most frequently required in legal interpreting in England, e.g.
Chinese, Polish, Russian and Turkish. Some of these students are UK
residents who are likely to attempt to become public service interpreters in
the UK. Others come to the University for the duration of their Masters
degree and expect to return to their home countries after graduation.
Depending on their country of origin, some aspects of legal interpreting may
be more or less relevant to them. However, the innovative nature of the
sessions on video-mediated interpreting in legal proceedings made the
students reach beyond the immediate contexts of individual countries. The
sessions were well attended and feedback was positive.

Students had varying levels of knowledge with regard to VCI and RI
before enrolling on the MA and before commencing the module:

	Totally agree	Slightly agree	Neutral	Slightly disagree	Totally disagree
I knew about new forms of interpreting (VCI/RI) before I joined the MA programme.	3	8	1	9	5
I knew about new forms of interpreting (VCI/RI) before I started the module 'PSI Trends and Issues'.	7	7	3	8	1
I joined the module 'PSI Trends and Issues' because it offered an opportunity to learn about VCI/RI.	8	6	6	4	2

Total responses to each question: 26

Prior knowledge of the two forms of interpreting were reported as coming
from a student's own 'general knowledge' (1 student), word of mouth (1),
other courses (1), news (1), undergraduate degree (1) and the students' own
research on the internet (4).

The majority of respondents felt that VCI and RI require some form of
specialised training and that the VCI and RI sessions sat well within the PSI
module. As to whether the VCI/RI sessions should be made into a stand-
alone module, the response was less clear cut:

	Totally agree	Slightly agree	Neutral	Slightly disagree	Totally disagree
VCI/RI requires specific training.	16	7	2	0	1
The sessions on VCI/RI sit well within the wider context of the module 'PSI Trends and Issues'.	18	5	1	0	0
The VCI/RI sessions should be expanded to become a module in their own right.	8	6	9	2	0

Total responses: 26, 24 and 25 respectively.

Most participants also felt that the time dedicated to VCI and RI was sufficient (16 students), with 7 feeling that the time was not sufficient and 2 holding the opinion that it was too much.

The impression of some students that the time was not sufficient was particularly apparent in 2011, when the module was delivered for the second time. The tutor had included additional information that had been gathered in the AVIDICUS project, especially information about current practice that emerged from the AVIDICUS surveys and this raises a wide range of new practical and theoretical questions. It was felt that more time could have been devoted to the discussion of this.

The students were then asked about the learning content of the VCI and RI sessions:

	Totally agree	Slightly agree	Neutral	Slightly disagree	Totally disagree
The background information about VCI/RI (the forms, motivations for their uses, trends, etc.) provided a useful overview.	15	7	3	0	0
The relationship between the background information and the applications of VCI/RI (e.g. in legal settings) was made clear.	13	10	2	0	0
The examples of current practice and recent studies helped me to understand the advantages and problems of VCI/RI.	20	5	0	0	0
The hands-on practice provided a good opportunity to experience VCI/RI.	18	5	2	0	0
The hands-on practice illustrated a relevant range of settings.	9	15	1	0	0
The discussion/reflection covered my interests and questions.	12	9	4	0	0

Total responses: 25

The participants were generally of the opinion that the course was well-balanced:

	Totally agree	Slightly agree	Neutral	Slightly disagree	Totally disagree
The weighting of background information on VCI/RI, examples of current practice and studies, hands-on practice and discussion/reflection during the sessions was balanced.	11	10	4	0	0
More of the time available should have been spent on exploring background information on VCI/RI.	1	1	14	9	0
More of the time available should have been spent on exploring examples of current practice and recent studies of VCI/RI.	4	8	9	4	0
More of the time available should have been spent on hands-on practice in the videoconference room.	10	6	5	2	0
More time should have been spent on discussion/reflection on the advantages and challenges of VCI/RI.	3	4	13	5	0

Total responses: 25, 25, 25, 23 and 25 respectively.

However, the responses show that a significant number of respondents (16 out of 23) totally or slightly agreed that more time should have been spent gaining practical experience of VCI and RI. This is reflected by the free comments the students gave at the end of the evaluation. It is also consistent with the students' perception that the sessions on VCI and RI could have been expanded.

Materials provided during the sessions, including handouts and scripts, were deemed to be appropriate, both in content and amount:

	Totally agree	Slightly agree	Neutral	Slightly disagree	Totally disagree
The material provided was relevant to the topic.	16	9	0	0	0
The material was sufficient.	9	15	1	0	0
The material deepened my understanding of the topic	16	8	1	0	0

Total responses: 25

The students were then questioned about what they believed they had gained from the VCI and RI sessions, in terms of learning outcomes:

	Totally agree	Slightly agree	Neutral	Slightly disagree	Totally disagree
The sessions gave me the opportunity to learn about new forms of interpreting.	16	7	2	0	0
I feel I am familiar with the major differences between face-to-face, VCI, RI.	19	6	0	0	0
I feel I am familiar with the major advantages and challenges of VCI and RI.	17	7	0	0	0
I feel confident that I can carry out an interpreting assignment involving VCI/RI.	5	12	8	1	0
I feel I could explain the challenges of VCI/RI to a client	10	12	3	0	0
I feel I could advise clients on when VCI/RI can and cannot be used.	6	12	6	1	0

Total responses: 25, 25, 24, 26, 25 and 25 respectively.

The students were generally confident and positive about their learning experiences. They were, however, slightly less confident about using this knowledge in real interpreting situations. This result is consistent with the students' perception that they would like more practice. The overwhelming final response from the course participants was that the practical, hands-on sessions were the most useful part of the course, and that they were not long enough. In Surrey, the module was offered as a generic module with students of different language pairs in the same group, but in the allotted time, it was not possible for every student in the class to participate actively. Some students appreciated the opportunity to observe others carrying out VCI/RI, as it allowed them to see how to conduct themselves in a video link and how problems could be solved. However, as one participant stated, 'all language groups need the opportunity to practise this and experience the challenges.'

On the whole, then, the student feedback suggests that the time spent on the topic of VCI/RI could be expanded to provide more opportunities for a discussion of current trends and uses, and for hands-on practice. This constitutes an important difference to the pilot with practising legal interpreters, who were generally keen on a brief overview, limiting the amount of information that can be conveyed (see Section 4).

The expansion of video-based interpreting suggests that interpreter training programmes should spend more time on the practice of e.g. different configurations of interpreting in a videoconference (with the interpreter being in different locations), additional settings such as combinations of VCI and RI, relay interpreting using a video link and ultimately different modes of interpreting (simultaneous as well as consecutive). In view of likely developments, the tendency among students to welcome more information and practice is a positive outcome of the evaluation.

4   THE MODULE FOR PRACTISING LEGAL INTERPRETERS

This section outlines the module aimed at practising interpreters. It is
targeted at interpreters who have at least some experience in interpreting in
criminal justice contexts. However, if appropriate, it can be adapted to the
local situation (for example, if less experienced interpreters are involved).
That said, it was assumed in the design of the module that participants are be
familiar with the ethical and practical issues arising in legal interpreting.

4.1   Aims and Learning Outcomes

The aims of this module are:

- To increase interpreters' awareness of the motivation and rationale
  behind the use of video-mediated interpreting, including an
  introduction to European legislation;
- To give an overview of current and potential uses of videoconference
  and remote interpreting in various settings and countries;
- To enable discussion of the problems and challenges of videoconference and remote interpreting in legal settings;
- To provide an introduction to the technology and opportunities for
  hands-on practice of forms of video-mediated interpreting (particular
  to local contexts);
- To give guidelines on how to deal with various issues arising during a
  video-mediated interview;
- To provide a basis for further discussion and study.

Upon completion of the module, participants will have a sound
understanding of different forms of video-mediated interpreting and the
reasons behind employing these. They will be aware of potential difficulties
and be equipped with solutions to such problems. Furthermore, they will be
able to give advice on when video-based interpreting forms should and
should not be used. As was the case for the student interpreter module, the
syllabus outlined in the following section has been designed with these aims
and learning outcomes in mind.

4.2   Syllabus

In contrast to the student interpreter module, the module for practising
interpreters was designed to be delivered in one half-day session or, at most,
one whole-day session. This was to allow the module to fit into interpreters'
schedules without impacting significantly upon their livelihoods. It can stand
alone as a course, or, depending on the local context, can be adapted into
existing continuous professional development programmes.

The interpreter module is comprised of five discrete sections. The
teaching format is mixed method: lecture-style sections are combined with

platforms for discussion and practical sessions. Opportunities are also provided for further study and discussion.

Unit 1: Introduction
- The current situation
- Current EU legislation relating to the use of videoconferencing in legal proceedings
- Videoconferencing: definitions and key terms

The module begins by giving background information on the different forms of video-mediated interpreting and their uses. Firstly, the reasons often cited for employing these forms of interpreting are outlined, such as the need to cut delays in legal proceedings, the demand for qualified legal interpreters, and the mounting pressure to save costs in the current economic climate. As in the student interpreter module, participants are encouraged to reflect upon the tensions that can arise between or from these requirements, for instance, the need to save money while ensuring that the ends of justice are met.

The unit then defines key concepts and gives the technological basis for VCI and RI, before introducing European legislation relating to VCI and RI in legal proceedings. This includes older legislation allowing its use (e.g. the European Convention on Mutual Assistance in Criminal Matters) as well as more recent initiatives such as the Procedural Rights Roadmap and the Directive on strengthening the rights of those suspected and accused of crimes to translation and interpreting, the European effort to strengthen cross-border judicial co-operation in criminal matters (e.g. the Green Paper on obtaining evidence in criminal matters) and the European e-Justice initiative to promote the use of electronic tools in criminal justice.

The aim of this section of the module is to increase interpreters' awareness of the practical, economic, political and legal motivations behind using video-mediated forms of interpreting.

The unit should be tailored to the local context in which it is provided, e.g. by adding relevant national legislation, in order to heighten participants' understanding of their own national legislation.

Unit 2: Videoconferencing and Interpreting
- Emerging settings and their motivations
- Definitions
- Rationale and potential uses

This unit looks specifically at emerging legal settings in which video-mediated interpreting is used, as well as giving more in-depth definitions of the different types of video based-interpreting.

Firstly, the unit marks the distinction between *videoconference interpreting* and *remote interpreting*. It provides more detailed definitions for these and draws the participants' attention to the different motivations for using VCI and RI. The module makes it clear that VCI is a solution for integrating an interpreter in a videoconference situation, whilst RI is a solution for integrating interpreters remotely into an otherwise tradition communicative situation. VCI implies that the interpreter is co-located with some of the participants at one of the VC sites (e.g. in a courtroom or a prison), whilst RI entails that the interpreter is the only person who is physically separated from everyone else. The possibility of combining VCI and RI is also highlighted. The unit closes by outlining characteristic areas of application of each form. Discussion of the commonalities and differences of these situations, and the consequences, is encouraged.

By the end of this part of the module, participants will have acquired a solid understanding of the distinctions between the different types of video-mediated interpreting, the different settings in which they are employed, and the reasons for using them in these settings.

Unit 3: Current Practice
- Examples of current uses of videoconference interpreting (VCI) and remote interpreting (RI) in legal proceedings (based on the two surveys among legal practitioners and legal interpreters conducted in AVIDICUS)

This section provides an overview of current practice, describing actual uses of VCI and RI in legal proceedings. It gives a variety of examples of VCI and RI use across different European countries. The examples are based on the responses to the surveys among legal professionals and legal interpreters conducted by the AVIDICUS Project, and cover various stages of the criminal justice process.

The exemplification of current VCI and RI use across Europe serves two purposes. Firstly, the overview puts national developments in the area of video-based interpreting in a European context and thus helps interpreters to gauge potential uses in their respective countries. Secondly it provides further insight into how – and with what kind of variations – the prototypical settings introduced in unit 2 are implemented in practice. This is important given the observation that the interpreters are often focused on a particular setting of VCI or RI that they have encountered (see Section 4.4). The unit encourages interpreters to reflect on the advantages and drawbacks of different practical solutions, compared to face-to-face interpreting and alter-native solutions of video-mediated interpreting. Discussion is invited regard-ing the appropriateness of the current solutions, e.g. with regard to the location of the interpreter in relation to the other participants, the impact of the interpreter's location on such factors as the mode of interpreting, rapport with the other participants, interpreter's working conditions and ultimately the quality of interpreting and the overall the goal of delivering justice.

On completion of this unit, course participants will recognise that different forms of face-to-face and video-mediated interpreting are appropriate for different circumstances, and that this depends on practical concerns and national legislation as well as on the intrinsic challenges of interpreting. This unit in particular will enable practising interpreters to advise judicial services on the appropriateness of video-mediated interpreting solutions in a given setting.

Unit 4: Practical Demonstration
- Live video link
- Role play centred around simulation
- Participation and observation

Here, course participants are offered an opportunity to practise either video-conference or remote interpreting, or both, depending on the specific requirements of the audience. The form of video-mediated practised may also depend on local availability of equipment, rooms and personnel, but an effort should be made to include a live demonstration into the module. In order to make the role plays as realistic as possible, they should, as far as possible, involve real legal practitioners.

In role plays involving VCI, the legal professional (for example, a prosecutor or judge) should be located in one of the VC rooms. One of the course participants should take on the role of the other-language speaker, e.g. performing the role of a witness in a criminal case, and be located in the second VC second room. Other course participants who have the same language combination as the 'witness' should interpret, first alongside the legal professional, then being co-located with the 'witness'.

In role plays to practise RI, the legal professional (for example, a police officer) should be located with someone acting as a suspect in one of the VC rooms. Other participants, who have the same language as the 'suspect', should interpret their conversation from the second VC room.

For those course participants who do not share the working languages of the other-language speaker, the role play should be performed in one language, e.g. both prosecutor and witness speaking in the language of the country. The interpreters participating in the course should render the utterances into their respective working languages. This will give them an opportunity to gain some hands-on experience in video-mediated interpreting. Given the anxieties of some interpreters with regard to VCI or RI (see Section 4.4 and Braun & Taylor's report on the AVIDICUS surveys in this volume), a practical demo should be an important element of any such module, even if a full language match between the role players and the interpreters' working languages cannot be achieved.

In each interpreting scenario, the course participants who are not involved in the role play should observe and reflect on proceedings. In particular, consideration should be given to how video-mediated interpreting differs from face-to-face interpreting, any difficulties arising for the interpreter, and potential problem-solving strategies.

In connection with this, the following unit gives an opportunity to discuss such strategies and further the issues raised by the course participants.

Unit 5: Discussion and guidelines
- Communicating and interpreting in the videoconference situation
- Differences between face-to-face and video-mediated interpreting
- Challenges of video-mediated interpreting
- Initial guidelines for interpreters

The aim of the final unit is to allow the interpreters to reflect upon the role plays and their own experiences of VCI and RI in a systematic fashion, and to provide initial guidelines for interpreters on how to cope with various aspects of video-mediated situations, building on the insights gained in the AVIDICUS project.

The first part of the unit provides a platform for discussion by identifying the specific difficulties often encountered in video-based interpreting situations. Points of discussion include, for example, the difficulties with communication management and the co-ordination of talk, issues with the sound, visibility, gaze and eye contact, and problems with rapport and contextualisation (see also Braun 2006). Although the aim is to provide a systematic overview of such problems, it will be useful to allow some time for brainstorming at the beginning of the unit and let participants report on their own observations from the practical session (unit 4). The systematic overview of potential difficulties described above can then be presented as a summary of the discussion.

The final part of the unit builds on the recommendations for interpreters outlined in Braun (in this volume) and provides practical guidelines and suggestions for problem-solving strategies for the different phases of interpreting assignments that involve a video link. The guidelines refer to the booking phase, the stage immediately before the assignment starts, the assignment itself, especially the beginning and the post-assignment phase.

As an outcome of this section, the participants will be able to appreciate that VCI and RI often magnify or exacerbate existing interpreting problems, but that training and familiarisation may contribute to improving this situation to some extent in that they can help to develop strategies for coping with the specific challenges of video-based situations. On completion of this final part of the module, the participants should also recognise that they have a significant role to play in improving VCI and RI use, by taking the initiative when they discover problems and by working together with the legal services to resolve them.

4.3   Teaching Material

The teaching material for this module has developed over time. At different stages of the piloting phase, it has been refined, based on the course tutor's observation and on the participants' feedback. It is not intended to be static, but should be adapted in the future to capture new developments and to fit local/national contexts. To illustrate the adaptation to a country's context, the PowerPoint slides presented in the module for interpreters make specific reference to the use of video-mediated interpreting in Poland. This can be replaced with other localised information as the need arises.

The materials detailed here are designed to strike a balance between lecture-style information providing definitions and overviews, and the opportunity for discussion, reflection and self study. This format, it is hoped, will maximise the learning experience for participants. The materials include the following:

- A PowerPoint presentation covering each unit of the syllabus (see appendix 1b);
- Questions for further study, included at the ends of units 1 and 2 in the PowerPoint slides;
- Scripts for the live demonstrations – these should be based on real material where possible and appropriate;
- Instructions for the role players.

The teaching material for each unit of the module is outlined below.

Unit 1: Introduction

The PowerPoint slides for this section describe the current problems in the judicial services for which videoconference technologies could be a potential solution. Some basic definitions and key concepts are introduced, in addition to different types of connection and hardware used for videoconferencing. European Union legislation relating to the use of videoconferencing in legal proceedings is then presented. Links to websites detailing the legislation are provided, to allow course participants to explore these further in their own time. Information about national legislation in Poland is included in this unit as an example of adapting the material to local contexts.

The final slide in this unit suggests topics for further study, specifically in relation to the EU legislation: participants are asked to examine the situations in which videoconferencing is allowed or recommended, and then to explore the extent to which the legislation is enacted in their own country.

Sabine Braun, Judith L. Taylor, Joanna Miler-Cassino, Zofia Rybińska,
Katalin Balogh, Erik Hertog and Dirk Rombouts

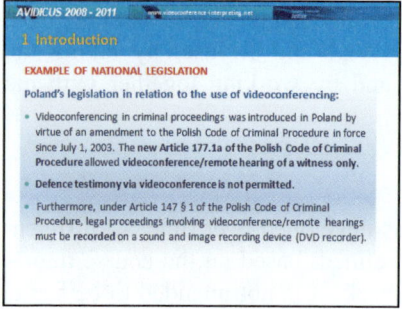
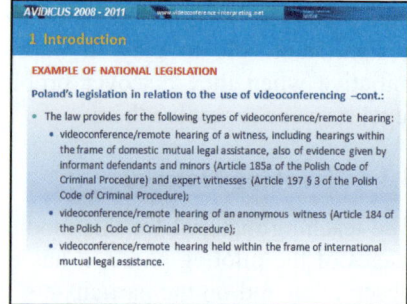

Examples of national legislation

Unit 2: Videoconferencing and Interpreting

As an aid to comprehension, the slides in unit 2 contain graphic representations of the differences between VCI and RI, the different motivations underlying their use and examples of criminal justice settings in which each of these forms of interpreting is characteristically used in Europe.

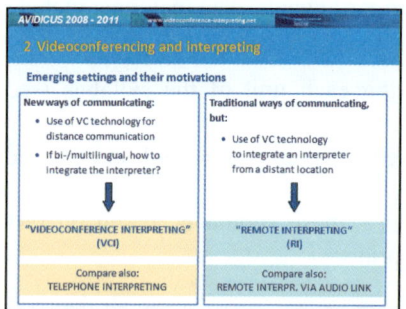

Graphic illustration of motivations and potential uses

On the final two slides, course participants are again encouraged to undertake further study: having ascertained which settings are used in their own countries, they are invited to reflect upon the advantages and disadvantages of the relevant settings from the point of view of the legal services and from the point of view of the interpreter. Furthermore, the interpreters are invited to examine the two variants of VCI for the purpose of hearing a remote witness in court, and to consider the advantages and disadvantages of the interpreter being in court versus being located with the remote witness.

Unit 3: Current Practice

In this section, the slides give examples of current uses of VCI and RI in different legal settings across Europe. The examples deliberately go beyond criminal justice settings so as to have a richer basis for discussion. The slides in this unit also contain photographs and graphics to illustrate and aid comprehension. The illustrations allow those less familiar with the settings to see aspects such as room configuration and location of participants.

Illustration of courtroom layout in Maastricht

This section of the module is particularly amenable to adaptation: instances of VCI and RI use from the local or national context can be illustrated and examined in more depth, as shown in the following slides, using the example of Poland, where legal videoconferencing is a rather recent development.

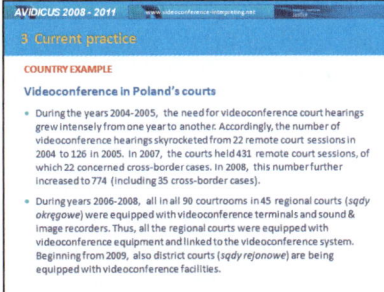
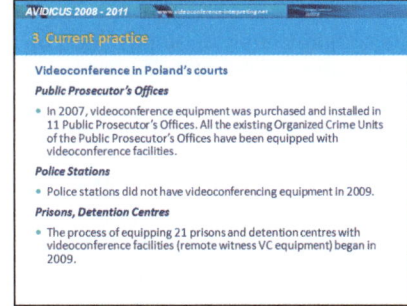

Example of national situation: Poland

Videoconferencing in Polish courts

Sabine Braun, Judith L. Taylor, Joanna Miler-Cassino, Zofia Rybińska,
Katalin Balogh, Erik Hertog and Dirk Rombouts

Unit 4: Live Demonstration

The hands-on practice in unit 4 should use role play scripts based on real material where possible and appropriate. To maintain the realistic aspect of the practical sessions, the scripts should reflect the national context and should involve, as far as possible, real legal practitioners. Any other roles can be taken by other course participants.

The slides relating to this section include questions for participants to keep in mind while observing or participating in the practical session. In particular, the participating interpreters are invited to reflect upon the following aspects:

- What is the most difficult aspect of video-mediated interpreting for the interpreter?
- What is more/less difficult than you would have expected?
- What good solutions do you observe?
- What could you have been handled differently?
- Where do you see potential problems (general problems of video-mediated interpreting or caused by the specific setting(s) practised in the session)?

These questions can be provided on a separate handout for the participants to make notes during the practical demonstration and observation.

Unit 5: Discussion and Guidelines

Here, the slides are intended as a summary of the brainstorming and discussion following the practical demonstration. The first slides summarise the potential problems of video-mediated communication and interpreting. The final slides provide initial guidelines for interpreters for each stage of the communication process. As stated above, this builds on the recommendations developed in the AVIDICUS Project (see Braun in this volume) and covers the time of booking an assignment, the phase immediately before the interpreted session begins, the session itself and the post-assignment phase.

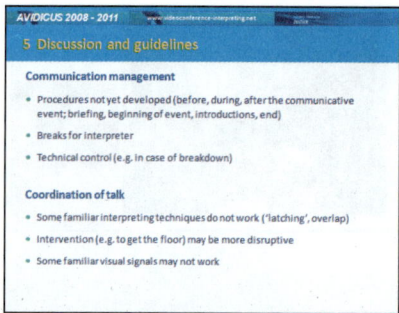
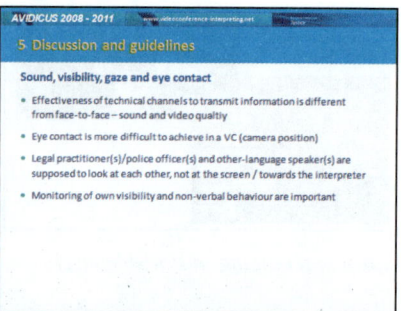

Summary of VCI/RI problems

The presentation concludes with a summary slide to remind participants of the essential points emerging from the current situation and the observations discussed during the session.

The module for practising interpreters was piloted in the UK and in Poland. The following two sections report on each of the pilots.

4.4   Training Sessions with Metropolitan Police certified interpreters (UK)

The sessions in the UK were organised by the London Metropolitan Police Service's Language and Cultural Services department, addressing Metropolitan Police certified interpreters and using the VC equipment that has been implemented in the Metropolitan Police Service in preparation of the force's remote interpreting pilot project.[10] The sessions were delivered by the University of Surrey project team.

The Metropolitan Police Service in London is currently in the process of implementing remote interpreting, whereby interpreters work from a number of central hubs to provide interpreting services for a range of police custody suites in the London area. The Metropolitan Police had decided, partially in consultation with the University of Surrey, that all interpreters on their list should have an opportunity to familiarise themselves with the technology and the concept of video-mediated interpreting before starting to work in via video link. The familiarisation was organised in two phases. Phase 1 provided an induction to the equipment and was carried out within the Metropolitan Police. Phase 2 covered the specifics of video-mediated interpreting, and it was decided that the AVIDICUS training module would be used to cover this phase. There was thus an imminent need for the interpreter training module in the Metropolitan Police Service at that time.

The pilot training sessions included five half-day sessions held at Hendon Police College in September 2010 and January and March 2011. A total of 41 Metropolitan Police certified interpreters participated. As was the case for the student interpreter module, the course and teaching material were refined each time the module was presented.[11]

In contrast to the pilot course for interpreting students described in section 3, the interpreter training sessions with the Metropolitan Police were fitted into a half-day, with the structure below. If local circumstances permit or demand, the module could, however, be expanded into a whole-day session or longer.

---

[10]   http://www.mpa.gov.uk/downloads/partnerships/icv/newsletter/2009-10.pdf, p. 3.

[11]   The training continues to be delivered by the AVIDICUS team after the end of AVIDICUS 1 to cover all Met Police certified interpreters.

1330	Welcome
1345	**Introduction**
	Context
1415	**Practical Demonstration**
	Live link to Charing Cross Police Station
	Role play centred around simulated police interview
	Participate and observe
1545	**Break**
1600	**Discussion**
	Discussion of experiences of practical demonstration
	Provision of Guidelines
	Dos & Don'ts
1700	**Close**

Units 1, 2 and 3 of the training module were mainly delivered in a lecture-style format; however, course participants were invited to ask questions at any time, and discussion of the various uses of VCI and RI was encouraged. Participants were keen to share their experiences with one another. As outlined in Braun & Taylor's report on the two AVIDICUS surveys (in this volume), interpreter attitudes to video-mediated interpreting vary widely, but in the UK, the majority of interpreters are suspicious about these forms of interpreting. Not surprisingly, therefore, some of the interpreters used the discussion to express their concern or discontent with the introduction of remote interpreting.

In unit 4, the practical session, participants were invited to interpret a simulated police interview of a suspect – in other words, a remote interpreting scenario. The role play involved a real police officer. The 'suspect' was played either by a colleague of the interviewing officer with appropriate language skills or by an interpreter. Both the police officer and the 'suspect' were situated in Charing Cross Police Station in Central London.

The participants who wished to practise interpreting took turns to interpret from the interpreting hub at Hendon Police College. Before starting the interpretation, the volunteers were given time to settle into the work space,[12] and were given a briefing by the interviewing officer (via video link).

All of the interpreters whose working language matched the language of the role player had some practice. However, the participants in all five sessions had a range of different working languages. To offer an opportunity to practise to the other interpreters in the group, the police officer and the

---

[12] The interpreters who participated in the sessions had received an induction on operating the equipment so that they were in principle familiar with the VC station in the hub.

role player spoke in English, and the interpreters rendered everything from
English into their working language. Some of course participants were
content simply to observe the role play.

Unit 5 of the module was run as a discussion session, focusing on the
interpreters' own prior experiences of VCI and RI and on the experiences
gained in the practical session of unit 4. These discussions often went beyond
the specifics of video-mediated interpreting and brought up basic issues of
legal interpreting.[13] The final section of the unit returned to a lecture-style
presentation of initial guidelines for interpreters, although discussion was
still encouraged.

At the close of the module, the participants were asked to complete a
feedback questionnaire. A summary of the feedback is given in Section 4.5.

4.5   Evaluation feedback from the MPS training sessions

An evaluation questionnaire was circulated to all participants at the end of
the session. Participants were encouraged to complete this form immediately,
while the module was still at the forefront of their memories. The
questionnaire aimed to gather background information about the interpreters
themselves, their interpreting experience, with particular emphasis on any
video-mediated interpreting practice, as well as their feelings about the
module, its structure and content.

The training workshops run for the Metropolitan Police Service yielded
41 questionnaire responses. Not every respondent answered every question
on the form.

The interpreters on the course were firstly asked in the feedback form to
give their approximate age:

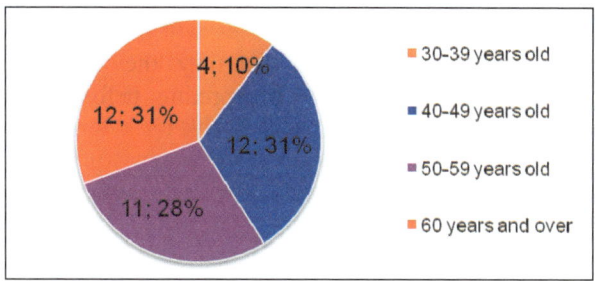

Age range: Total respondents to question: 39

---

13   The most frequent point made by the participating interpreters was that in real life,
interpreters are not always given a briefing regarding the case in question. At the same
time, the discussion revealed that even in traditional interpreting situations, interpreting
practices and the interpreters' approaches to resolving problems differ quite widely.

None of the interpreters who attended the sessions run for the Metropolitan Police Service was under the age of 30, and only 4 were under 40. This may be because a certain amount of experience is necessary for membership of the official list of the Metropolitan Police, and experience is generally (though not exclusively) linked to age. The age figures broadly tally with the amount of interpreting experience the participants are reported as having acquired:

Hours of interpreting carried out	2000 or more	1000-2000	400-1000	Less than 400
Interpreting in general	31	3	1	0
Interpreting in criminal justice	32	3	1	1

Total responses: 35 and 37 respectively

The interpreters were then asked to give an impression of how these hours had been spent – in other words, where in the criminal justice services they had gained experience. Unsurprisingly, given that the training module was being run for the Metropolitan Police, all participants reported having carried out interpreting in a police context. All participants had also carried out some form of court interpreting. 39 respondents had interpreted for the Crown Prosecution Service, and 32 had done interpreting work for prisons. Participants also stated that they had interpreted in appeals tribunals (1), for the probation services (2), and for solicitors (3). Other types of interpreting experiences included 'other legal' (29), medical (16), conference (15), business (14), UKBA/ immigration (5), civil law (1), family law (1), social security (1), social services (1), mental health tribunals (1), Home Office (1), construction industry (1), oil industry (1), presentations (1) and maritime arbitration (1).

Most of the interpreters were of the opinion that they knew at least 'something' about videoconference and remote interpreting before they embarked on the module:

Very much	Much	Something	Very little	Nothing
4	12	22	2	1

Total responses: 41

The sources of this knowledge were varied. Fifteen respondents reported having learnt about video-mediated interpreting in courts and tribunals. Other sources included: conference interpreting (2), induction sessions at the

Metropolitan Police (5),[14] AVIDICUS tests (1),[15] EULITA (1), research (1),
university (1) and the AVIDICUS Symposium (1).[16]

Most participants had carried out some form of video-mediated interpreting prior to undertaking the training workshop:

How many times have you carried out VCI or RI in the following situation:	10 times or more	5 to 9 times	1 to 4 times	Never
VCI in the criminal justice system	20	11	7	1
RI in the criminal justice system	6	6	4	3
VCI in other contexts	4	3	5	2
RI in other contexts	2	1	4	4

Total responses: 39, 19, 14 and 11 respectively

The bias in the figures towards the criminal justice services can be explained by the fact that the module was run for legal interpreters.

Almost two-thirds of respondents 'totally agreed' with the premise that VCI and RI require specialised training (24 out of 39 respondents to the question). 10 said they 'slightly agreed', 4 described themselves as 'neutral', and one interpreter said they 'slightly disagreed' that specific training is necessary.

Having established background details about the interpreters' prior experience, the feedback questionnaire used in the Metropolitan Police sessions went on to elicit information and opinion on the training module *per se*.

Firstly, participants were asked about the length of the module. Almost all interpreters (36 out of 39 who answered the question) found that the length was appropriate for this training. One interpreter felt it was insufficient and two thought that the session was too long.

The majority were also satisfied with the quality of each section of the module. In relation to this question, participants were invited to suggest other aspects that they felt should be covered in the session. Two proposals were offered: 'the decreasing job opportunities for interpreters,' and a 'more practical approach to the deployment of interpreters'.

---

[14] This refers to the induction that all participants received prior to the training module described here.

[15] The interpreter participated in the AVIDICUS comparative study.

[16] The interpreter attended the AVIDICUS Symposium in February 2011 before attending the training session in March 2011.

Please indicate to what extent you agree with the following statements:	Totally agree	Slightly agree	Neutral	Slightly disagree	Totally disagree
The background information (legislation, different forms, their uses, current practice) provided a useful overview.	24	6	6	0	0
The overview of EU legislation helped me to understand the wider context.	23	6	8	0	0
The hands-on practice provided a good opportunity to experience RI.	27	7	4	1	0
The discussion covered my interests and questions.	26	6	3	2	1
The initial guidelines are a useful starting point for RI.	29	6	2	0	1

Total responses: 36, 37, 39, 38 and 38 respectively.

The balance among different components of the course content was also, as a general rule, considered to be satisfactory, although some participants felt that the weighting required alteration:

	Totally agree	Slightly agree	Neutral	Slightly disagree	Totally disagree
The weighting of background information, hands-on practice in the VC room and discussion/guidelines was balanced.	24	6	5	0	0
More of the time available should have been spent on exploring background information (legislation, forms, uses, current practice).	10	8	10	4	2
More of the time available should have been spent on hands-on practice in the videoconference room.	13	8	10	2	2
More time should have been spent on discussion/guidelines.	14	5	10	2	2

Total responses: 35, 34, 35 and 33 respectively.

However, the opinions on how the weight should be altered were divided. Eighteen of the participants (53% of 34 respondents) 'totally' or 'slightly' agreed that more time should have been dedicated to background information on VCI and RI; 21 (60% of 35 respondents) took the view that the practical aspect of the course should have had a bigger share of the available time; and 19 (57.6% of 33 respondents) felt that discussion and guidelines should have been given more prominence in the course timetable. On the whole it seems fair to say that the module catered for different needs and interests.

One point that requires highlighting is that although 60% of the interpreters would have liked more time for the practical session, the majority were content simply to observe their colleagues rather than practise interpreting. This is also in stark contrast to the behaviour of the interpreting students, who were keen to practise (see section 3.5). It can be assumed that the students saw the sessions as an opportunity to gain additional general interpreting practice as well as experience in video-mediated interpreting. Practising interpreters are less likely to feel the need for additional practice. Moreover, the module for students offered a sheltered training environment, which seems to have encouraged students to interpret in front of their classmates. Professional interpreters are in a more competitive situation. They may, therefore, feel less comfortable interpreting in front of their colleagues.

The interpreters were also asked about the materials for the module. A majority considered the materials to be appropriate and sufficient:

	Totally agree	Slightly agree	Neutral	Slightly disagree	Totally disagree
The material was relevant to the topic.	29	4	5	0	0
The material was sufficient.	27	4	6	0	0
The material deepened my understanding of the subject.	25	3	7	1	0

Total responses: 38, 37 and 36 respectively.

The questionnaire then moved to focus on the interpreters' personal learning experiences and outcomes from the training. Interpreters' opinions on general outcomes of the session were sought:

	Totally agree	Slightly agree	Neutral	Slightly disagree	Totally disagree
The session gave me the opportunity to learn about RI.	27	9	2	0	0
I feel I am familiar with the major differences between face-to-face and RI.	30	8	0	0	0
I feel I am familiar with the major difficulties of RI.	25	10	3	0	0
I feel confident that I can carry out an interpreting assignment based on RI.	30	6	0	1	0
I feel I could explain the challenges of RI to a client.	25	8	4	0	0
I feel I could advise clients on when RI can and cannot be used.	21	11	4	0	0

Total responses: 38, 38, 38, 37, 37 and 36 respectively.

The above set of questions provides the most feedback about the training module. Most of the participating interpreters seem to have felt that the course was helpful in preparing for using VCI/RI in real situations.

The evaluation form finished by allowing interpreters to offer free comments, with specific regard to the most and least successful aspects of the module, and to what they feel should be covered in future guidelines. The answers to the question what aspect of the session worked best and why, ranged from 'all of it' (3 respondents) to 'hands on experience and practice' (11), discussion (3), aspects regarding technology (1) and EU legislation (1).

The question what could be improved prompted responses ranging from 'successful and no improvement needed' to the suggestions that more 'individual interpreting problems' should be addressed, that the handouts could be improved and that more time should be spent to gain 'familiarity with adjusting volume and video settings in general'. However, these comments were only made by a small number of participants.

Other comments in relation to this question referred to the time available for practice, requesting 'more practice/hands-on experience' and that the interpreters should be 'given more time to learn the practical work so that [they] know how to use it properly'. These requests are interesting given the point made above that many interpreters preferred observing others to interpreting. However, some interpreters made more specific suggestions with regard to practical aspects, asking for an 'opportunity to practise in all languages', which was not possible in the mixed language groups, and a 'chance to start from the beginning of the process: arrive, place or accept the call, and use the controls'.

When asked about aspects that were not covered in the session and that should be covered in future guidelines, some interpreters responded that the session 'fully covered' everything. One interpreter asked for more coverage of 'potential problems with body language and facial expression'. Another interpreter felt that the chances of him/her focusing on the case during a video link 'could be made easier by a briefing – this is a must'.

Most other comments in relation to this question referred to aspects which were beyond the scope of this session, e.g. a comment that aspects of 'confidentiality in suspect-solicitor consultation' would have to be clarified when the interpretation is delivered via video link. Other interpreters used this comment field to state that interpreters who work in video-mediated situations 'should get a pay rise' and that 'the [interpreting] profession is shrinking at an alarming rate'. One interpreter phrased the same issue slightly differently, asking how video-mediated interpreting can 'keep the good interpreters if income and work volume keep falling'. Although not directly related to the aim of the training session, such comments are indicative of the anxieties in the interpreter community in relation to video-mediated interpreting and mirror some of the attitudes elicited in the AVIDICUS survey among legal interpreters, especially in the UK, where attitudes were

generally more negative than in other European countries (see Braun &
Taylor's report on the two AVIDICUS surveys, in this volume).

The evaluation shows that most participants were happy with the pilot
training courses, in terms of the course content and structure. One interpreter
also commented on RI as such saying that it was 'much easier than expected,
[with a] good picture [and] good voice quality from the remote end'.
However, the responses also show that there are still some deep-seated
concerns and fears on the part of the interpreters with regard to actual use of
VCI and RI in the real world. It remains to be seen whether with increased
training and education, some of these concerns can be put to rest.

4.6 Training Session with interpreters from TEPIS (Poland)

In addition to the training sessions run in conjunction with the Metropolitan
Police Service, the module for practising interpreters was piloted in Poland
by TEPIS, the Polish Society of Economic, Legal and Court Translators.
TEPIS is one of the largest associations of legal translators (and interpreters)
in Europe. The module was run as part of TEPIS' continuous professional
development programme on the 28th and 29th January 2011 in the Videoconference suites of the two regional public prosecutors' offices in Warsaw.

Seven interpreters attended the course. Four were certified court interpreters, referred to as 'sworn translators' in Poland. This means that they
hold the Polish equivalent of a Masters degree (as a minimum), have passed
the State Examination for interpreters, and have thereby gained the right to
practise interpreting and provide services for the police, public prosecutors'
offices, and courts. The experience of these four participants as court
interpreters ranged from two to four years. The remaining three participants
were not certified interpreters at the time of the course; however, they all
planned to attain certification. None of the course participants had any
previous experience in video-mediated interpreting. The interpreters were
split between the two course venues: five (three English interpreters and two
Dutch) in one venue and two (Italian and Russian) in the other.

The Polish pilot of the module was run in two parts, over two days.
Because the videoconference (VC) equipment was only available on the first
day of the course, the practical session (unit 4, above) had to be run first,
before the informative and theoretical sections. However, the pilot course
showed that least some of the theoretical component should ideally be
presented before the practical session, as planned in the module syllabus.

At the beginning of the practical session, time was given for the
participants to familiarise themselves with the VC equipment. IT technicians
from the two prosecutors' offices were on hand to present the equipment,
answer any queries from the participants, and establish the video link.
Prosecutors were present at the beginning of the session to provide
information about current VC practice and the advantages and disadvantages
of using VC technology as a means of obtaining evidence.

The participants then had the opportunity to practise two variants of VCI: in the first case, the interpreter was located with the prosecutor, while the witness was at a second, remote, location; in the second case, the interpreter and the witness were together and the prosecutor was at the remote location. Real legal professionals were not available to participate in the practice interviews; instead, the roles of the prosecutor and witness were played by members of TEPIS for the English, Russian and Italian interpretation, and by the interpreters themselves for the Dutch interpretation. However, the scripts were drafted by prosecutors, and covered the pre-trial interviews of witnesses in drug-trafficking and car accident cases. Before the interviews commenced, the interpreters received a short briefing about the basics of the cases. The course organisers reported that the quality of the VC link was far from perfect; indeed at one point the connection broke completely. Additionally, there was a perceptible time lag at times between image and sound.

The theoretical part of the module was split into two main subsections, and was largely delivered in a lecture-style format. The first of these two subsections focused specifically on the current Polish legislation regarding certified court interpreters in legal proceedings, and included legal concepts, terminology and phraseology. The second part incorporated units 1-3 and 5 of the AVIDICUS training modules, as outlined in Sections 3.2 and 3.3, with specific emphasis on Polish legislation relating to video-mediated interpreting and current practice. The module ended with a discussion reflecting on the problems that had arisen during the hands-on session as well as practical issues relating to video-mediated interpreting in criminal proceedings.

To make the pilot run by TEPIS appeal to a wider audience, a lecture on stress management and workshop on note-taking were also included.

As was the case in the Metropolitan Police sessions, participants were invited to consider further the issues raised in their own time. They were also asked to complete an end-of-course questionnaire. For the most part, the participants commented that they found the training module very interesting (though some remarked that they had found the delay between image and sound in the practical session to be rather disturbing). The need for more hands-on experience, particularly language-specific training, was stressed.

Additionally, the theoretical section of the training module was presented as a *Repetitorium* (revision course), part of the TEPIS Continuous Professional Development programme, in March 2011. Around 80 translators and interpreters attended the course, which discussed the use of VCI in criminal proceedings, the European and Polish legal context of video-mediated forms of interpreting, and current European and global practice. The post-presentation discussion among participants revealed a real desire for specialised training in video-mediated forms of interpreting.

The repetitorium participants were invited to complete a questionnaire on their VCI experience. The questionnaire also sought answers on whether training is required for VCI, whether TEPIS should organise such training, and, if so, whether VCI training should be coupled with any other practical classes or workshops.

In total, 37 participants completed the questionnaire. Of these, 25 are sworn interpreters/translators. Of this figure, only three reported having any previous VCI experience. In response to the question relating to factors potentially influencing the quality of the communication via VCI, one of the three, who had carried out one VCI assignment, cited the quality of the equipment and VC link, as well as human factors such as speech mannerism, accent, pronunciation and pace of speech. Another participant, who had experienced VCI twice, also stressed the importance of using high quality videoconference equipment. The third participant with VCI experience added that the quality of the interpretation could be affected by the interpreter's location and whether or not headphones are required. All 25 questionnaire respondents – including those with no experience of video-mediated interpreting – stressed that some form of training in VCI is necessary, and that any training should include a session on familiarisation with the technology.

5 THE MODULE FOR LEGAL PRACTITIONERS

This section describes the module for Legal Practitioners or Professionals (LPs) such as police officers, investigative judges and lawyers.

Many legal practitioners do have considerable experience in working with interpreters in criminal proceedings. However, as yet very few are familiar with videoconferencing, let alone interpreted videoconferencing or remote interpreting in criminal proceedings. The extent of their experience may be determined by the nature of the legal system in which they work or the availability of these technologies, whereas their (pre-)disposition may well be coloured and shaped by their initial experiences with a technology either poorly mastered or inadequately appreciated. It seems, however, that once the legal provisions are in place in the legal system of the member state, LPs may have to come to terms with this technology and be prepared to use it to maximum efficiency.

5.1 Aims and Learning Outcomes

The aims of this module are:

- To increase legal practitioners' awareness of the motivation and rationale behind the use of video-mediated interpreting;
- To raise awareness of the novel forms of video-mediated interpreting;
- To provide a detailed introduction to the various forms of videoconference and remote interpreting in legal proceedings, an overview of current practice and future trends;
- To give an overview of current and potential uses of videoconference and remote interpreting in various settings and countries;

- To provide an introduction to the technology and opportunities for hands-on practice of forms of video-mediated interpreting (to be adapted to specific local contexts);
- To give guidelines on how to deal with various issues arising during a video-mediated interview;
- To provide opportunities for hands-on practice of different forms of video-based interpreting;
- To provide a basis for further discussion and reflection upon practical experience.

In terms of **learning outcomes**, it is expected that the LPs who have completed this module will have a good insight into the communication technologies and tools used in different forms of video-based interpreting, into the motivations of their use and into the specific challenges that these create for interpreting. Furthermore, the LPs will also have developed initial know-how to enable them to evaluate when videoconference/remote interpreting are appropriate working modes and when they are not. The syllabus described in the following section has been designed with these aims and learning outcomes in mind.

5.2   Syllabus

The syllabus for the training module for LPs is divided up into three **sessions** each consisting of two main **units**, i.e. six parts in all, which is reflected in the teaching material (see Section 5.3). To allow the module to fit into the LPs' schedules, the module is designed to be delivered in, ideally, three half-day sessions or one whole-day session followed by one half-day session. The module can stand alone as a specialised course, or, depending on the local context, can also be adapted into existing continuous professional development programmes. Broadly speaking, the training module is composed of a first theoretical part, followed by a second practical part, and a third part discussing observations, drawing conclusions and suggesting recommendations.

Unit 1: Introduction
- Videoconferencing: definitions and key terms
- Emerging settings: Rationale and potential uses
- Examples of current uses of VCI and RI in legal proceedings

---

The unit aims to give an overview of current developments leading to the use of VCI and RI in criminal proceedings, to introduce the emerging legal frameworks in Europe and their implications, and to explain the definitions and key terms used in videoconferencing.

The unit starts by giving the LPs some background information on the definitions of the key terms associated with videoconferencing and makes reference to the diverse technologies that are used for videoconferencing, pointing to the differences in the appropriateness of these technologies. It also provides information on the different forms of interpreting (consecutive, simultaneous etc.), on the code of conduct and on guidelines for good practice for interpreters.

This unit marks the basic distinction between videoconference interpreting (VCI) and remote interpreting (RI), as defined in the introduction to this chapter. The unit explains that the form of video-mediated interpreting which has been termed VCI is employed when an interpreter needs to be integrated into a videoconference, e.g. to hear a remote witness who requires an interpreter. In VCI, the interpreter is normally co-located with some of the participants, i.e. either in the court room or prison, or with the witness.

This setting is contrasted with remote interpreting (RI), which is mainly used to overcome local shortages of interpreters or to save interpreter travel costs and in which the interpreter is the only person who is in a different location.

It explores the potential uses of each of these forms of video-mediated interpreting, comparing and contrasting them, and additionally looks at the utilisation of videoconference interpreting (VCI) in tandem with remote interpreting (RI).

Finally, the unit also gives a variety of examples of current uses of VCI and RI in different European countries. By the end of this unit, the legal practitioners will have acquired a solid understanding of the distinctions between the different types of video-mediated interpreting, the settings in which they are employed, and the reasons for using them in these settings.

Unit 2: Videoconferencing and Interpreting
- Current issues
- Current EU legislation relating to the use of videoconferencing in legal proceedings
- Surveys among LPs conducted in AVIDICUS

This unit highlights the motivations on the part of the EU and the legal systems of different EU-countries for adopting these forms of interpreting, i.e. the need to speed up national and international legal proceedings, cost efficiency, the lack of qualified legal interpreters in some languages or regions, and security reasons e.g. when transporting prisoners to and from court. This part also draws the attention of the LP to the current tensions between stakeholders regarding the use or non-use of VCI and RI, including for example the concerns of police officers regarding when to use such forms

Sabine Braun, Judith L. Taylor, Joanna Miler-Cassino, Zofia Rybińska,
Katalin Balogh, Erik Hertog and Dirk Rombouts

of interpreting, or the fears of interpreters with regard to safeguarding the quality of interpreting.

The unit refers to the current and emerging EU legislation which mentions and promotes the use of videoconferencing in criminal proceedings, especially the *'Procedural Rights Roadmap'* for strengthening the procedural rights of suspected or accused persons (OJ No. C 295/01, 04-12-2009) and the ensuing Directive on translation and interpreting in criminal proceedings, as well as the envisaged legislation relating to victims' rights, the right to information and so on. The unit should always be tailored to the national legislation in which it is provided.

Based on the responses to the AVIDICUS Project's EU surveys of legal practitioners and interpreters (see Braun 6 Taylor in this volume) the unit shows where and how the different forms of video-mediated interpreting are used today, for instance VCI in first hearings and remand extension hearings, or RI in police interviews. Examples from different European countries are provided, highlighting similarities and differences in emerging practices. The focus is on criminal proceedings, but some references to other settings, especially immigration, are also made. This part of the unit in particular can be adapted to local contexts by including additional material drawn from national or regional contexts as appropriate.

It is to be noted that, in light of the recent Salduz case and others before the ECtHR in Strasbourg, in future at least two legal practitioners will have to be present during VCI or RI, deciding that a lawyer not only has to be present in court but also during the police interview and before the investigating judge (see also the new proposal on this matter by the European Commission of 8th June 2011). Similarly, the guidelines of the Committee of Ministers of the Council of Europe on child friendly justice (17th November 2010) demand interdisciplinary communication training of all professionals working with minors, a development that also has to be taken into account in future VCI/RI training.

Units 3 and 4: Practical Demonstration
- Role plays centred around simulation
- Participation and observation

These units consist of hands-on practice, requiring a sufficiently large group of participants, realistic scenarios of legal proceedings and access to VC technology (see Section 2). It is recommended that the LPs get practice in both VCI and RI to explore and apply what has been learned in the first two units, but the hands-on part can be adapted to local circumstances, relevance and time available. An effort should be made to include some video illustrations and demonstrations into these units (as shown below), by way of comparison and to alternate with the role plays.

What follows is a brief summary of the role plays conducted in the course of this project and which may serve as a model for the training of LPs. The corpus consisted of sixteen role plays of about 25 to 30 minutes each, between Dutch-speaking officials (in this case police officers) and Hungarian-speaking suspects or witnesses. Four role plays were face to face (FF); four were of the videoconference A type (VCI A, i.e. the interpreter sits with the police while the suspect or defendant is in another location); four were videoconference B role plays (VCI B, i.e. the interpreter is in the same location as the other- language speaker while the police officer is in a different location); and four were RI settings (i.e. the interpreter is on his or her own, in a different location from the other participants, both the police officer and the suspect or witness).

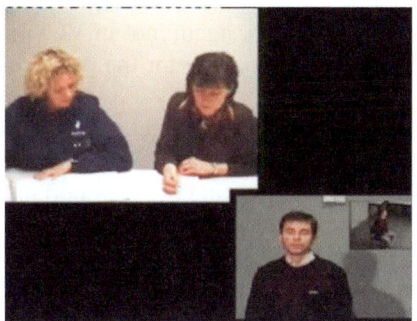

Video illustrations: VCI A Leuven *VCI B Utrecht Courtroom*

RI Antwerp Courtroom

The topics of the role plays were taken from real-life police materials and dealt with four situations: questioning by the police of a suspect of credit-card fraud; questioning of a suspect of human trafficking; interview of a witness to a hold-up in a hotel and, finally, questioning of a suspect of criminal conspiracy. The role plays were not scripted but the participants were briefed on the topic and on the general drift the interrogation or interview should pursue. Occasionally, specific instructions were given to one of the role players as to positioning, behaviour, body language, coherence, register etc. to try and gauge the effect of these parameters on the overall interpreting performance.

The role plays were conducted in Dutch and Hungarian, the latter being a language completely unknown to the police officers which forced them to rely exclusively on the interpreting and prevent them from hazarding any guesses or 'establishing' confirmation of the interpreting on the basis of their proficiency in a more 'common' language. The participants in the role plays were, first of all, four Dutch-Hungarian interpreters, who had between five to fifteen years of interpreting experience, including experience in legal interpreting (though not in VCI or RI). The 'actors' playing the role of suspect or witness were all native speakers of Hungarian, with little or no Dutch at all. The two police officers (one chief inspector and one inspector, one of whom was male and the other female) had long-standing experience in interviewing and the use of legal interpreters though, again, not in VCI or RI. All role plays were video-recorded for later analysis and for the purpose of illustration in the training module.

It is important that in the course of these two units, the LPs get practice in both VCI and RI to explore and reflect on the advantages and drawbacks of different solutions, compared to face-to-face interpreting. An important aspect for later discussion and reflection is the technology as such, for example the quality of sound and image, the lighting and camera-angle, but also the flow and management of communication as it manifests itself in overlaps, hesitations, misunderstandings, eye contact and so on.

This unit in particular will enable LPs and judicial services to understand the appropriateness of video-mediated interpreting solutions in a given setting (inter alia goal of delivering justice, mode of interpreting, location and legislation).

As an outcome, LPs will be able to appreciate the fact that VCI and RI cater for different needs and that, currently, there is no commonly accepted or agreed standard for the practice of VCI and RI. The hands-on session should enable LPs to experience the differences between face-to-face and video-mediated interpreting and to reflect on their own practice.

Units 5 and 6: Discussion, Conclusions and Recommendations

The aim of these two units is to draw the LPs' attention to potential problems of VCI and RI in a more systematic way than previous units, in which LPs collected their own individual observations. Points which will certainly underline these discussions are issues of legislation and national practice in the light of EU Directives and recommendations, the impact of technology on the LPs and the interpreter's performance, the impact of the socio-cultural specifics of legal interpreting on VCI/RI in legal proceedings and the impact of video mediation on the communication management and rapport between the participants. The units will allow the LPs to reflect upon the role plays and their own experiences of VCI and RI in a systematic fashion, and to come up with guidelines and recommendations on how to best cope with various aspects of video-mediated situations.

5.3   Teaching Material

The materials are not intended to be static, but should be adapted further to capture new developments and to fit local/national contexts of legislation and practice. The materials should in any case contain:

- A PowerPoint presentation on VCI and RI, including illustrative links to and examples of VCI and RI, and an overview of national, European and international legislation on VCI and RI (see appendices 1c)
- A handout providing a number of texts relating to VCI and RI (see appendix 2)
- A bibliography of VCI/RI, which is also available at the AVIDICUS website (www.videoconference-interpreting.net)
- Topics and scripts or instructions for role plays
- Instructions for role-play sessions
- Feedback forms and questionnaires.

Units 1 and 2: Introduction, Videoconferencing and Interpreting

The PowerPoint slides for this session provide an overview of the key concepts and basic definitions in addition to different types of connection and hardware in VCI and RI, the current situation, the main motivations behind the use of VCI and RI, and a survey of the main EU legislative frameworks relating to the use of VCI and RI. The slides include links to the legislative texts for reference to allow course participants to explore these further in their own time.

An effort has been made to include examples of current practice from different countries in this unit. For example, some of the slides contrast the different practices of VCI in first hearings in England/Wales (interpreter normally in court), Belgium (interpreter normally co-located with the judge), the Netherlands (interpreter can choose the location but is normally co-located with the non-native speaker and whispered interpreting is used) and Poland (location of the interpreter not regulated). These illustrations allow those less familiar with the settings to see aspects such as room configuration and location of participants.

This section of the module is particularly amenable to adaptation: instances of VCI and RI use from the local or national context can be illustrated and examined in more depth. The remaining slides present information gained in the AVIDICUS legal practitioners' survey regarding the frequency of use of VCI and RI across Europe, the reasons for use as stated by the respondents and other relevant aspects (see appendices).

Units 3 and 4: Role plays

The hands-on practice in these units should use role play scripts or scenarios based on real situations. To maintain the realistic aspect of the practical sessions, the scripts should reflect the national context and should involve active legal practitioners and legal interpreters. Any other roles –suspects, defendants, witnesses etc. – can be taken by other participants. While actively participating in the role plays or as observers, the LPs were invited to reflect upon the following aspects (exemplary selection only; see Units 5 and 6 above for further guidance on the observations):

- What is the most difficult aspect of video-mediated interpreting for the LP?
- What is more/less difficult than you would have expected?
- What good solutions do you observe?
- What could/should have been handled differently?
- Where do you see potential problems (general problems of video-based interpreting or caused by the specific setting(s) of the session)?
- Is a particular setting (FF, VCI A or VCI B, or RI) more conducive to the (legal) requirements of the procedure?
- To what extent is VCI or RI technology an asset or disadvantage? Which technological aspects could be adjusted or improved?
- Does the technology impact on the usual procedure or working arrangements?
- Which interpreting and general communication aspects need to be mastered and managed?

These questions can be provided on a separate handout for the main observers to make notes during the observation of the role plays.

Units 5 and 6: Discussion, Guidelines and Recommendations

Here, the slides are intended, first of all, as a set of general recommendations and, secondly, as a summary of the brainstorming and discussions which followed the role plays practical demonstration. These slides summarise the potential problems and areas of concern for the LPs of video-mediated communication and interpreting (see appendices).

Upon completing the role plays with the LPs, the project team organised three de-briefing sessions, one eliciting written feedback from the police officers, the other a training session for LPs in Ghent in November 2010 and, finally, a general debriefing session of the LPs together with the interpreters and project partners. The following is a summary of the main observations. These may be useful as starting points for discussion.

Role play – screener LP				LAN-GUAGE	DATE	NAME
Conversion native -foreign language	Completeness	5 very good	4 good	3 sufficient	2 insufficient	1 totally inadequate
	Misunderstand-ings	not (absent)				yes (frequent)
Professionalism	Communication	5 very good	4 good	3 sufficient	2 insufficient	1 totally inadequate
	I-form					
	Attitude					
	Inspires confidence?					
Mother tongue	*Language*	5 rich/ very good	4 good	3 correct	2 poor	1 incom-prehens.
	Terminology (specified)					
	Register					
	Macroniveau communication	5 rich/ very good	4 good	3 correct	2 poor	1 incom-prehens.
	Pronunciation / intonation / fluency					
Audiovisual / non-verbal issues		not existing	correct	acceptable	disturbing	unaccept.
	Gaze of interpreter					
	Gaze of legal practitioner					
	Gaze suspect/ witness					
		excellent	correct	acceptable	disturbing	unaccept.
	Posture					
	Gesture					
	Facial expressions					
	Actions					
Technical issues		excellent	correct	acceptable	disturbing	unaccept.
	Being in shot					
	Sound					
	Inaudible					
Visual		excellent	correct	acceptable	disturbing	unaccept.
	Showing objects					
Comments:						

5.4   Training session

This section describes a pilot training session for Legal Practitioners (LPs) -
police, investigating judges, public prosecutors and lawyers. The session
took place at the University of Ghent on 8th November 2010. And included a
number of Legal Practitioners: two investigating judges, a public prosecutor,
police officer, and a chief superintendent and researcher at the University of
Ghent (Criminology – 'police interviews project'). The other participants
were role players (other language witness/suspect – native speakers of
Hungarian) and an interpreter (native speaker Hungarian).

The training session consisted of three parts.

In the first part an introduction to VCI/RI was provided. VCI and RI
were defined and the distinction between the various settings was explained,
as were the aims of the AVIDICUS Project. Some of the Legal Practitioners
already had some experience with interrogation interpreted videoconferencing interviews, others had heard about it and at the outset of the session were
invited to outline their experiences, expectations, ideas and concerns about
VCI/RI. The following are just a few of these initial views. Not surprisingly,
the LPs expressed their preference for FtF settings and the legal instrument
of the rogatory commission. They mentioned the importance of the quality of
the interpreter and the awareness of the cultural context. They were concerned about the possible lack of control over the interpreter and suggested
using two interpreters, one at each side. They also raised the question of
whether VCI/RI could work in difficult and serious criminal cases because of
the nature of these cases, the technical problems and the participants' lack of
experience.

In the second part a number of VCI/RI role plays were offered for
observation and analysis. Each role play took about 20 minutes. The topics
were an interview of a witness and an interrogation of a suspect of credit-
card fraud. The role pays offered the LPs the chance to have hands-on
experience of VCI. After each role play and setting they were invited to
formulate their initial reactions to the exercise. The following are some of the
most relevant observations that were raised during the discussions.

VCI A (INTERPRETER TOGETHER WITH POLICE OFFICER)

The LPs expressed the need to have a close-up image and a full complete
body image of the witness/suspect. The quality of the image was also very
important to them as they wanted to see aspects such as facial expression,
emotions, body language and eye movement. They complained that the
presence of the camera and screen (the remoteness) made it was impossible
for them to have eye contact, which was important for them. Concerning the
interaction and flow of communication, they were more positive and
commended the 'invisibility' of the interpreter. On the whole, the reaction to
this setting seemed positive and appropriate for witness and victim
interviews, but less so for suspects (and certainly not to be recommended in

difficult, sensitive and important cases). If there is not enough or limited control over the interaction and the setting it is difficult to build up confidence.

VCI B (INTERPRETER TOGETHER WITH WITNESS)

Again the need for a close-up and a complete view of the witness/suspect was stressed, and the need for overall quality of sound and image. To be able to see emotions is crucial, and, in particular, the lack of eye contact because of the camera and screen is disturbing.

In this set up a lack of interaction and a feeling of 'distance' were experienced. The LPs had the impression they only had limited control over the interaction and the setting, and hence felt that their interventions were limited because of insufficient non-verbal input from the witness/suspect.

Furthermore, the LPs felt they did not need an image of the interpreter and commented that the close relation (physical togetherness) of the interpreter and the witness/suspect raised issues of trust, reliability, impartiality and independence.

RI (POLICE OFFICER TOGETHER WITH SUSPECT)

Generally speaking, this was the setting preferred by the LPs. To them it was the most natural setting which allowed them more possibilities for direct interaction. Again, they felt the image of the interpreter was not required "because he/she is an instrument". They also discussed whether this setting was more or less difficult or even disturbing for the interpreter.

In part three of the session the experts formulated a number of observations and recommendations that they considered most important.

The interpreter is a neutral instrument as he or she does not belong to the police or court. Indeed, the LPs preferred not to see an image of the interpreter on the screen. This is also why, even though their preference is for FF interpreting, LPs are open to the RI setting with an 'invisible' interpreter.

To guarantee the flow of communication and interaction, the quality of the interpretation is very important. It is crucial that the interpreter does not take a leading role – this is the responsibility of the police or the court – and that they are trained in the specific terminology, strategies and procedures of the different legal settings, e.g. in the use of direct questioning or silences as part of specific interrogation techniques. It would additionally be helpful to have a reference in the register of legal interpreters to those with training in VCI and RI.

The LPs were positive about the usefulness of VCI/RI for the interview of a witness or victim, in 'small' cases involving a suspect (or possibly in case of a need for extra information in cases of a certain importance) but would not recommend the use of VCI/RI in serious, complex cases.

The LPs mentioned their concerns about the technical quality of VCI/RI. They stressed the need for excellent quality equipment, including sound and image, which is tailored to their needs, e.g. the possibility of provision of a close-up or a whole body image.

It was generally felt that interpreters as well LPs (police, judges, prosecutors, court officials and lawyers) need training before using VCI/RI in addition to support and guidelines.

Following on from the Strasbourg ECtHR *Salduz*-case, the specific issue of the rights of the defence during VCI/RI-mediated police interviews (including the confidential contact between defendant/suspect and lawyer) was also raised and the extent to which this might complicate the use of VCI/RI and the role of the interpreter was discussed.

6   CONCLUSION

The main conclusion of the AVIDICUS partners upon completing and assessing the results and comments of the role plays in the project and the pilot training sessions is that there is an urgent need to understand better the mutual responsibilities and roles of the actors involved in criminal proceedings, i.e. both the concerns of the LPs as well as the role of the legal interpreter, in order to arrive at a fair and efficient criminal procedure. The lack of accurate understanding and appreciation of the role of the different parties involved in the procedure, bears a risk of leading to wrong assumptions and unrealistic expectations. This is the reason why Directive 2010/64/EU of the European Parliament and of the Council of 20 October 2010 on the right to interpretation and translation in criminal proceedings, in Article 6 on 'Training', states that:

> [W]ithout prejudice to judicial independence and differences in the organisation of the judiciary across the Union, Member States shall request those responsible for the training of judges, prosecutors and judicial staff involved in criminal proceedings to pay special attention to the particularities of communicating with the assistance of an interpreter so as to ensure efficient and effective communication.

This fundamental but general requirement will become all the more urgent as VCI and RI will become more prevalent in criminal proceedings throughout the EU, adding another layer of complexity to criminal proceedings that involve more than one language.

The training modules on video-mediated interpreting in criminal proceedings designed in AVIDICUS were a first step in offering training for the integration of these novel forms of interpreting for different target groups.

One important point is that the training material needs to be adaptable, allowing for different local and national contexts to be taken into account and allowing for updates, for instance on the legal situation, the technology, and

the further development of the guidelines. In AVIDICUS, this has been
achieved by designing the training modules as a series of workshops, flexible
in length, with PowerPoint and other teaching material as the core on which
others can build.

Another crucial insight is that co-operation between legal practitioners
and interpreters in terms of training should be increased and that both groups
would benefit from joint training. The design of training joint training
modules for legal practitioners and legal interpreters on video-mediated
interpreting will be an important task in AVIDICUS 2.

REFERENCES

AIIC (2000), 'Guidelines for the use of new technologies in conference interpreting',
    Communicate! March-April 2000. http://www.aiic.net/ViewPage.cfm?page_id
    =120.
Böcker, M. and Anderson, B. (1993), 'Remote conference interpreting using ISDN
    videotelephony: a requirements analysis and feasibility study'. In: *Proceedings
    of the Human Factors and Ergonomics Society, 37th annual meeting*, 235-239.
Braun, S. (2004), *Kommunikation unter widrigen Umständen? Fallstudien zu
    einsprachigen und gedolmetschten Videokonferenzen.* Tübingen: Narr.
    Available at http://bit.ly/c1J0xb.
Braun, S. (2006), 'Multimedia communication technologies and their impact on
    interpreting'. In: Carroll, M., Gerzymisch-Arbogast, H. and Nauert S. (eds.),
    *Audiovisual Translation Scenarios. Proceedings of the Marie Curie
    Euroconferences MuTra: Audiovisual Translation Scenarios Copenhagen, 1-5
    May 2006.* Available at http://www.euroconferences.info/proceedings/2006_
    Proceedings/2006_Braun_Sabine.pdf.
Braun, S. (2007), 'Interpreting in small-group bilingual videoconferences: challenges and
    adaptation processes', *Interpreting*, 9 (1), 21-46.
Braun, S. and Taylor, J. L. (eds.) (2011), *Videoconference and Remote Interpreting in
    Legal Proceedings.* Guildford: University of Surrey. Available at www.
    videoconference-interpreting.net/BraunTaylor2011.html.
Corsellis, A. (2008). *Public Service Interpreting. The first steps.* Basingstoke: Palgrave
    MacMillan.
Fowler, Y. (2007), 'Interpreting into the ether: interpreting for prison/court video link
    hearings', *Proceedings of the Critical Link 5 conference, Sydney, 11-
    15/04/2007.* Available at http://www.criticallink.org/files/CL5Fowler.pdf.
Kolstad Zehouo, L. and Fiva, H. (2010), 'He is talking about why you should go to
    prison' – Training judges in the Norwegian courts in facilitating interpreted
    court hearings. *Critical Link 6 26th-30th July 2010.* Abstract available at
    http://www1.aston.ac.uk/lss/news-events/conferences-seminars/2010-archive
    /july-2010/critical-link/.
Lequy, A. and Sander, N. (2009), Neuer binationaler Master-Studiengang "Juristisches
    Übersetzen und Dolmetschen". *Redit* 3, 52-62.
Mouzourakis, P. (2006), 'Remote interpreting: a technical perspective on recent
    experiments', *Interpreting*, 8 (1), 45-66.
Verrept, H., (2011), 'Intercultural Mediation Through the Internet in Belgian Hospitals',
    4th International Conference on Public Service Interpreting and Translation,
    13th-15th April 2011. Abstract available at http://tisp2011.tucongreso.es/ti2011/
    files/book-abstracts.pdf.

APPENDICES

All Appendices are available at the following website:

http://www.videoconference-interpreting.net/BraunTaylor2011.html

Appendix 1

PowerPoint presentations (including exercises):

1a. Student interpreter presentation

1b. Practising interpreter presentation

1c. Legal Practitioner presentation

Appendix 2

Student Handout

AVIDICUS: CONCLUSIONS AND IMPLICATIONS

Ann Corsellis, OBE

1 CONTEXT OF THE PROJECT

EU and domestic legal principle and legislation require equality before the law, irrespective of language.[1]

The scale of movement of people between countries is already significant and increasing, as individuals move between countries for work, education and tourism or to escape war or economic hardship. The Demography Report 2010 provides the following figures:

> In recent years, immigration has been the main driver behind population growth in most Member States: between 2004 and 2008, 3 to 4 million immigrants settled in the **EU27** each year. In 2010, a breakdown of the population by citizenship showed that there were 32.4 million foreigners living in an **EU27** Member State (6.5% of the total population), of those, 12.3 million were EU27 nationals living in another Member State and 20.1 million were citizens from a non-EU27 country.
>
> In 2010, the largest numbers of foreign citizens were recorded in **Germany** (7.1 million persons), **Spain** (5.7 million), the **United Kingdom** (4.4 million), **Italy** (4.2 million) and **France** (3.8 million). Almost 80% of the foreign citizens in the **EU27** lived in these five Member States.
>
> Among the **EU27** Member States, the highest percentage of foreign citizens in the population was observed in **Luxembourg** (43% of the total population), followed by **Latvia** (17%), **Estonia** and **Cyprus** (both 16%), **Spain** (12%) and **Austria** (11%).[2]

Criminal activity is also increasingly taking place at a transnational level, giving rise to the need for prevention strategies, bringing the guilty to justice and protecting the vulnerable in a multi-lingual situation.

The principle of equality before the law applies where there is insufficient shared knowledge of language for reliable communication in criminal justice systems, such as:

---

[1]   See, for example, the European Convention on Human Rights, article 6, paragraph 3, available at http://www.echr.coe.int/NR/rdonlyres/D5CC24A7-DC13-4318-B4575C9014 916D7A/0/ENG_CONV.pdf.

[2]   Demography Report 2010. Latest figures on the demographic challenges in the EU. Eurostat News Release 5/2011,available at http://epp.eurostat.ec.europa.eu/cache/ITY_ PUBLIC/3-01042011BP/ EN/ 3-01042011-BP-EN.PDF.

- cases within member states, involving defendants, witnesses and victims who do not speak the language of the country in question;
- individual cases that cross national borders;
- implementation of mutual recognition of legislation;
- judicial co-operation between EU member states e.g. the prevention of terrorism or trafficking of drugs or people.

This situation is likely to escalate and, unless dealt with properly, risks damage to the fabric of the criminal justice system in every member state and to a corresponding lack of trust in those justice systems.

The cost of meeting the legal requirement for equality is correspondingly increasing. For example the costs of legal interpreting and translation in the London Metropolitan Police are as follows:

> The Metropolitan Police expenditure on interpreters and translators for 2009/10 was £9,598,849, covering approximately 40,000 assignments. During 2010/11, 38,000 assignments were covered at a cost of £8,829,552. These figures represent the full cost of claims for interpreting and translation processed during the period of the report (fees and expenses). Further costs may have been incurred which were processed locally, or outside of requested reporting parameters.
>
> Furthermore, the figures represent fees incurred in respect of interpreting assignments, where interpreters are deployed to facilitate face-to-face communication between officers and speakers of languages other than English, and written translation assignments, which will include official letters requesting the co-operation of judicial authorities in other countries, when officers are required to travel abroad to pursue investigations.[3]

The skills and structures to meet the demand are lacking, to varying degrees, in all member states (Hertog & van Gucht 2008) and have not kept pace with contemporary life, despite repeated requests over the last twenty years. For example, the level and type of language skills needed, in the languages required as opposed to those traditionally taught, are generally unregulated and sparse. The costs of developing and putting the hitherto neglected but necessary skills and structures in place must therefore be added to operational budgets.

Many member states are pursuing unsatisfactory short-term compromises, which would be disastrous if they became long-term solutions.

Member states are in a position whereby they are obliged to observe EU and domestic legislation in this regard or face censure, while being ill-equipped to do so and reluctant to incur the cost. Meanwhile, the demand continues to rise.

---

[3] The figures do not include the operating costs of Language & Cultural Services, the MPS department which manages interpreting and translation provision across the MPS.

2   PURPOSE OF THE PROJECT

The advent of new technology, such as videoconference technology for interpreting, is seen as providing a potential cost-effective easy solution. The purpose of the AVIDICUS project has to some extent been to start to find out whether this is really true, why and where.

The short answer is that it can be true in intelligently selected situations but only with the appropriate level of skills, technology and structures. The use of video-mediated interpreting would not be appropriate in circumstances such as very sensitive police investigations, breaking bad news to families or complex court hearings. In many other circumstances it has the potential to provide accurate communication across languages and accommodate relevant legal processes.

The project recommendations (see following chapter) describe under which conditions video-mediated interpreting can be used effectively and how it should (and should not) be used. The recommendations are based upon the project findings that emerge from a range of careful, inter-disciplinary assessments in different circumstances, locations, languages and approaches (see the other contributions in this volume). They focus on training, in-service training, familiarisation and co-operation between the stakeholders to expand upon these points, such as:

- the criteria for using video-mediated interpreting;
- the skills needed by legal services, legal interpreters and translators (LITs), administrators and policy makers;
- monitoring and evaluation of processes.

3   PARTICIPANTS IN THE PROJECT

The core project participants were carefully chosen to reflect:

- the main groups of professionals involved: interpreters and translators, applied linguists, police officers, jurists, lawyers, IT specialists and administrators/policy makers;
- the regional spread of member states;
- different types of European legal system – inquisitorial and adversarial.

Consultations took place within the wider groups of interested parties, such as interpreters and legal professionals (see Braun & Taylor's report on the two AVIDICUS surveys in this volume).

4 METHODOLOGY

The project methodology was designed in view of the fact that it had to:

- retain its clarity of logic and approach in a multi-faceted and complex subject area;
- observe the interests and processes of justice on an informed basis;
- accommodate the varying needs and perceptions of the different professions involved;
- be sufficiently rigorous to withstand challenges;
- be understandable to a range of interested parties not necessarily acquainted with academic research of this nature, on the basis of common sense;
- be as complete and rounded as possible within the time-frame;
- provide a solid foundation for further research, investigation and evaluation;
- produce feasible recommendations, which:
    - are directed towards the long term aims;
    - recognise the inevitable short-term incremental objectives;
    - manage expectations e.g. IT as the panacea;
    - manage time-frames e.g. it may take at least five years to produce a sound EU wide system;
    - balance cost and quality.

5 IMPLICATIONS

The AVIDICUS investigation and the increasing use of video-mediated interpreting reveal the strengths and weaknesses of existing arrangements. The use of technology in criminal justice contexts can only be of best value if the elements involved can be consistently relied upon. The chain of communication is only as strong as its weakest link. The chain includes the legal service interlocutors, the interpreters or translators and the technology. Failure by any one of them risks the integrity of the whole. If, for example, the interpreting is inaccurate, the IT equipment is inadequate or the legal services do not perform correctly, justice is jeopardised.

By way of a small example, if the right procedures are not in place, employing seemingly useful technology can produce errors like the one overleaf, even when intentions are positive and legislation is in place.

Welsh is an official language in the UK. It follows therefore that road signs in Wales have to be in Welsh and English. In this instance, the authorities e-mailed the translation agency and diligently placed the reply they received on the road sign. Unfortunately, the Welsh text says, "I am not in the office at the moment. Send any work to be translated".

The need for overall competence is self-evident. But let us look at what is needed to achieve reliability across the board and, just as importantly, who is going to make this happen.

6   WHAT IS NEEDED

There can be variables relating to context or content, which cannot always be controlled. Therefore every element or link in the chain that it is possible to influence needs to be underpinned and to dove-tail with one another to achieve the integrity of the whole and provide a safety net for the variables. There is a need for a reliable consistency for the following main players:

- interpreters
- translators
- IT specialists and the equipment they produce and maintain
- interlocutors in varying degrees, i.e. the legal staff can be fully trained, whereas the witnesses, defendants and victims can probably be no more than familiarised with how to communicate through video-mediated interpreting
- administrators and policy makers.

Consistency is required in terms of the level and type of:

- standards of skills
- procedures and processes
- codes of ethics and good practice e.g. confidentiality
- administrative frameworks – "back office" and budgets
- accountability – to the justice system, to the public and colleagues
- professional frameworks.

This reliability and consistency, for the five main groups of players, can only be achieved through the usual routes of nationally consistent professional systems and structures (such as for lawyers) for:

- selection of suitable individuals
- training, in-service training and education to enable the exercise of informed judgements e.g. when to use video-mediated interpreting and, where there is a choice, which form should be used
- objective assessment
- independent accreditation
- deployment
- employment
- support and supervision
- continuing professional development to keep them up-to-date.

It follows that such systems and structures should be:

- of equivalent type and standard, which does not necessarily mean exactly the same but of sufficient similarity to promote a recognisable and acceptable consistency
- negotiated, compatible and agreed
  - between disciplines, so that, for example, the level and type of language skills are set against a proper analysis of what is truly needed in the work-place; the training given to the legal service interlocutors enables them to accommodate the interpreting and translation processes and the bi-cultural nature of the situation; the IT specialist provides and maintains equipment that is entirely appropriate to the situation; and the administrators enable them all to succeed in their tasks
  - nationally, so that there is a coherent and solid body of skills and systems which can promote and maintain the agreed standards; liaise internally and externally; and remain agile in response to change
  - internationally, to accommodate the need to function reliably across national borders.
- accountable and transparent to each profession involved, to colleagues in other professions involved in the same task, to the particular task overall (justice), to the "client" and to the public.

It is worth considering briefly what might happen if what is required is not in place, if there were gaps or an unforeseen matter of significance should suddenly occur without the necessary safety net to deal with it.

These are a few fictitious examples. What would be the situation if:

- the method of collecting evidence in country A were not admissible in a trial in country B?
- a judge did not insist upon lawyers correctly accommodating the interpreting process?

- an interpreter from country A was alleged to have breached confidentiality in country B, which country's professional body would be responsible for instigating disciplinary codes?
- the IT equipment was not compatible?

7 WHO IS RESPONSIBLE FOR WHAT?

Who is to do all that and how are they to do it? A good deal of what is necessary is already in place.

For example, in the public service arena, lawyers, police officers and so forth are already subject to the codes and principles of the statutory professions to which they must belong. These have long-established systems for selection, training, assessment, accreditation and accountability, with growing international recognition. Members of those established professions already have the mechanisms which enable them routinely to up-date their expertise. They need only sufficient additional in-service training, supervision and support systems to enable them to work with interpreters and translators, through technology when required, and across cultures. Recommendations for the work with interpreters through technology are set out in the following chapter.

IT specialists and their equipment are subject to the demands of an increasingly competitive commercial market. They need to be given very clear specifications for the task and be monitored through the usual mechanisms for public spending.

Both regulated formal professions and commercial IT companies should be able to negotiate and monitor the necessary inter-disciplinary and international arrangements in ways which are transparent and accountable – although it might take longer than they anticipate to iron out the details.

Who is responsible for implementing the remaining requirements is less clear. Administrators and policy makers, in some member states, may lag behind the demands of the work place and changing social patterns. They do not always put in place the frameworks and budgets necessary to move forward. Reasons given for this are not always logical. Political will plays a part, for that is where the decision making starts. Lack of funding, time and energy are cited when often all these might be used more effectively by adopting better practices. EULITA (European Legal Interpreters' and Translators' Association) has been given funding for an EU project to try to offer regional work-shops to remedy this – and in the hopes that such skills may transfer from the legal to other contexts such as healthcare.

This leaves us with interpreters and translators, where a good start has been made through six other EU projects in addition to AVIDICUS. They began in 1998, are more or less sequential, and are:

- Aequitas – which recommended the equal and adequate standards required[4]
- Aequalitas – which sought to disseminate those standards throughout the EU[4]
- Aequilibrium – which looked at the necessary liaison working arrangements between the language and legal professions[4]
- Status Quaestionis – a survey of developments in legal interpreting and translating in all member states, which showed an uneven patchwork of provision[4]
- EULITA – the establishment of the European Legal Interpreters' and Translators' Association, designed to promote EU-wide standards and act as a focus of information exchange[5]
- Building Mutual Trust, which offers a selection of sample teaching and other materials for legal interpreters, translators and legal services and their trainers. They are designed to guide and enable competent and interested university language tutors, or trainers of legal service professions, to offer their own courses. These core materials can be adapted to national systems and particular student needs, while retaining consistency in the level and content.[6]

The basic tools have therefore been developed and made available, although much still needs to be done, in liaison with the other groups. While national and international equivalencies of standards are not as yet always applied, academics have already begun to make a significant and valuable contribution in aspects which concern them, including:

- systems for selection of students
- training and in-service training
- assessment at various levels
- evaluating professional practice
- researching new developments

However, it is not the role of academia but for practising interpreters and translators themselves (some of whom may also be academics) to establish

---

[4] See http://www.agisproject.com.
[5] See http:// www.EULITA.eu.
[6] See http://www.lr.mdx.ac.uk/mutual-trust/.

the essential national and international professional structures and systems for:

- accreditation and registration
- accompanying codes of conduct and disciplinary procedures
- deployment – one should have sufficient people with the right skills, in the right languages, in the right places
- employment – 24/7 rapid contact systems, working arrangements, fees & expenses, health & safety and so forth
- supervision, support, monitoring and mentoring

It is here that matters become tricky. The levers for change are various and lacking. On the one hand, progress may be spurred on by the EU Directive (October 2010),[7] requiring implementation of quality standards and registers of legal interpreters and translators in each member state within 36 months of its approval.

On the other hand, inconsistencies abound over working arrangements. Some authorities will request levels of language skills far below what is recognised for reliable transfer, in order to pay less to the holders of such inadequate skills. It does not appear to occur to them that interpreters, with the post-graduate levels of skills and experience needed for the task, are in demand elsewhere.

This is where the differences become apparent between conference interpreters, such as those working for the EU, and public service interpreters, such as those working in the legal system. The difference is not in standards of accuracy because that should be the same, but in attitudes towards the interpreters. The skills of conference interpreters and translators are respected. Few, if any, members of the European Parliament (MEPs) would accept a lower standard of interpreting (or translation); or would wish to pay lower fees less than that standard warranted. They may have a proper concern over the significant budget that goes towards interpreting and translation, while also recognising the right of their country's citizens to be able to read, in their own language, what is being done in Brussels on their behalf. Many MEPs acquire fluency in a second, or even third, language to reduce the amount of I&T needed for less crucial interchanges. However, perhaps because of their awareness of the multi-lingual nature of the contemporary world, they do not resent or marginalise either the interpreters or the situation they find themselves in but seek solutions.

---

[7] Directive 2010/64/EU of the European Parliament and of the Council on the right to interpretation and translation in criminal proceedings. Available at http://www.europarl.europa.eu/oeil/file.jsp?id=5840482.

This does not yet apply to the public service sector. As their conference interpreter colleagues did before them, public service interpreters are going to have to put in place what is needed to form regulated professions before someone else imposes it upon them, to their detriment. A formally regulated profession is an entity in its own right and independent of others, including government. The professional elements required are the same as those required for other regulated professions such as law. They have been described elsewhere, including in the reports to the Commission of the EU projects on legal interpreting and translation listed above (Corsellis 2005, 2008, and Hertog 2001, 2003).

The elements required include national and independent examinations with related training and education through accredited courses, and assessment standards, based upon a sound collaborative analysis of what is required in the work place. They also include national and independent professional registers based on criteria which include language combinations, qualifications, experience, security vetting and the interpreter's agreement to observe the code of conduct and understanding of the published disciplinary procedure where breaches are alleged. National and independent Membership bodies for those who meet the entrance criteria and Trades Unions, where appropriate, are further requirements.

In order to achieve the four elements above, the following are needed:

- time
- organisational skills - plan incremental stages
- less money than one might think
- team work
- commitment
- focus
- conflict resolution skills
- communication
- support from colleagues in the other professions they work with.

8   EMPLOYMENT AND DEPLOYMENT OF LEGAL INTERPRETERS AND TRANSLATORS (LITs)

LITs are normally professionals who work on a freelance basis, which helps to accommodate the logistics of an unpredictable demand and, just as importantly, to signify their independent and impartial status.

In practical terms the legal services need to be able to contact LITs when they need them, on a 24/7 basis, and know that LITs have had a prior objective assessment of their skills and good practice and are subject to agreed codes of conduct. They need standard forms of engagement to hand. Most of all, legal services need access to a sufficient number of qualified legal interpreters in the languages required and based in the right places. The time-scales must accommodate the needs of the situation, such as the legal limitations on the number of hours individuals may be detained by police before being charged.

Contact and employment systems are still developing and vary in both competence and effectiveness. They include:

- direct contact with individual LITs
- not-for-profit units which could deal with:
  - contacting the appropriate LIT
  - associated administration
  - record keeping
  - promoting local training and in-service training
  - supporting, mentoring and supervision of LITs
  - liaising with associated professions, local communities and so forth
- commercial, profit making companies which may or may not provide the list of services above according to the tender involved, and may or may not take a top-slice that diminishes the LITs fees below what they find reasonable.
- cooperatives, which are beginning to emerge among LITs.

Given the many exigencies outlined in this paper, it may be argued that video-mediated interpreting has its proper place as an alternative to face-to-face interpreting. However, there are nice balances to be considered, which is why training of, and guidelines for, the legal services to make such judgements is necessary. The AVIDICUS recommendations outlined in the final chapter of this volume respond to this need.

In face-to-face interpreting, the interpreter can see the whole room, and – as the AVIDICUS findings reported in this volume show – physical proximity is likely to allow a finer comprehension of communication and interactions than through video-mediated interpreting. On the other hand video-mediated interpreting can, once the investment in the equipment is covered, reduce the costs of travel, travel time and subsistence expenses and also speed up the process of accessing interpreting. This is particularly relevant when the parties are separated by some distance, are located in different countries, or are subject to weather conditions such as those experienced during a Nordic winter.

Therefore those involved, from legal and language disciplines, should be in a sufficiently informed position to decide which method of interpreting is to be preferred, on each occasion the matter arises, without compromising the legal process. They should be able to understand and weigh up the various factors and subsequently justify their decision if necessary.

9 CONCLUSION

There are times when we choose to buy or use a process which is simple because there is "less to go wrong". This is not an option in this context. Communication alone is complex. Communication through an interpreter is more complex and communication through technology and interpreting more complex than that. Simple it isn't. In addition there are a range of variables, which may or may not be possible to foresee or control. Therefore, every element that can be foreseen has to be carefully considered, prepared, organised and quality controlled for video-mediated interpreting to be effective and adequate.

REFERENCES

Corsellis, A. (2005). Interpreters at the hub of disciplines. *SKASE Journal of Translation and Interpretation* 1(1), 37-46. Available at: http://www.skase.sk/Volumes/JTI01/index.html.

Corsellis, A. (2008). *Public Service Interpreting. The first steps.* Basingstoke: Palgrave MacMillan.

Hertog, E., (ed.) (2001), *Aequitas Access to Justice across Language and Culture in the EU.* Antwerp: Lessius University College. Available at http://www.agisproject.com.

Hertog, E., (ed.) (2003), *Aequalitas Equal Access to Justice across Language and Culture in the EU.* Antwerp: Lessius University College. Available at http://www.agisproject.com.

Hertog, E. and van Gucht, J. (eds.) (2008). *Statis Quaestionis. Questionnaire on the Provision of Legal Interpreting and Translation in the EU.* AGIS Project JLS/2006/AGIS/052. Antwerp/Oxford/Portland: Intersentia. Available at: http://www.agisproject.com/ Documents/ Status%20Quaestionis_Druk.pdf.

RECOMMENDATIONS FOR THE USE
OF VIDEO-MEDIATED INTERPRETING
IN CRIMINAL PROCEEDINGS

Sabine Braun

University of Surrey

1 INTRODUCTION

The recommendations presented in this chapter constitute one of the major outcomes of the AVIDICUS Project, which set out to assess the viability of video-mediated interpreting in the criminal justice system. The project has provided an initial assessment of interpreting in two relevant video-conference settings: a) in criminal proceedings which involve a VC, e.g. the hearing of a remote witness, with an interpreter being located at either side of the VC ('videoconference interpreting' – VCI), and b) in proceedings which use a video link to access an interpreter who is not physically present ('remote interpreting' – RI). The review of current practice undertaken in AVIDICUS (see Braun & Taylor in this volume) suggests that there is a growing demand for both forms of video-mediated interpreting throughout Europe in all areas of criminal justice. At the same time, the review reveals a considerable fragmentation of knowledge and a high level of uncertainty among legal practitioners (e.g. judges, prosecutors, solicitors), police officers and interpreters about these forms of interpreting.

Equally importantly, the findings from the AVIDICUS Project and related project initiatives, reported in several chapters of this volume, suggest that whilst basic practical problems with video-mediated interpreting may be resolved quickly through initial training and a process of familiarization, the combined complexities of technological mediation (through videoconference) and linguistic-cultural mediation (through an interpreter) also create deeper-rooted behavioural and communication problems which require further research to be fully understood. In particular, further research is required to investigate how the double mediation through videoconferencing and interpreting affects the specific goals of legal communication and to elicit adaptive strategies to mitigate such effects.

Prior research on legal videoconferencing has sounded a note of caution over the increasing use of videoconference technology in legal proceedings. Haas (2006: 61) emphasises that there is "a growing body of scientific evidence that shows video-mediated personal interactions are perceived as significantly different by the participants and observers than in-person interactions". Federman (2006: 450) claims furthermore that a multiplication of the complexity of legal communication "by the mediation effects created through videoconferencing introduces the significant possibility of inconsistency, inaccuracy, and altered judgment". Federman's claim is based on the assessment of the findings of videoconference use in immigration hearings, which also involved an interpreter, although the focus of the analysis was not on the interpretation.[1] Research dealing specifically with video-mediated interpreting has generated mixed findings, making it difficult to infer the potential risks and challenges. As Roziner & Shlesinger (2010) highlight, most of the studies conducted to date show almost no difference in the actual interpreting performance between traditional and video-based interpreting, but they reveal that the majority of interpreters have negative perceptions of video-mediated interpreting and are less satisfied with their own performance in video-based interpreting. This latter finding is corroborated by the AVIDICUS survey among legal interpreters regarding their attitudes to video-based interpreting (Braun & Taylor in this volume). With regard to the actual interpreting performance, the AVIDICUS comparative studies in relation to spoken-language interpreting as well as Napier's study in relation to video-mediated sign-language interpreting (all reported in this volume) suggest that video-based interpreting in criminal proceedings is more challenging than traditional interpreting in comparable settings, although given the small sample sizes it is currently difficult to draw final conclusions with regard to the significance of these differences.

At the same time, the growing number of migrants in Europe,[2] who for the purposes of specialised communicative situations such as legal proceedings need to rely on the services of an interpreter, implies an increased demand for public service interpreting, including legal interpreting, with the effect that the 'appeal' of video-mediated interpreting as a potentially cost-effective and sustainable solution is likely to rise in criminal justice institutions. There is a consensus, reinforced by the new European Directive on the rights to interpretation and translation in criminal proceedings,[3] that the criminal justice services need to provide language and interpreting support in criminal proceedings (and are responsible for appointing sufficiently qualified interpreters, see van der Vlis in this volume), coupled with an increasing perception that certain measures can be

---

[1] The outcomes of this study are reported in detail by Ellis (2004). See Braun & Taylor's contribution on current practice in this volume for a summary of this study.

[2] See e.g. Demography Report 2010. Latest figures on the demographic challenges in the EU. Eurostat News Release 5/2011. Available at http://epp.eurostat.ec.europa.eu/cache/ITY_PUBLIC/3-01042011-BP/EN/3-01042011-BP-EN.PDF.

[3] Directive 2010/64/EU of the European Parliament and of the Council on the right to interpretation and translation in criminal proceedings. Available at http://www.europarl.europa.eu/oeil/file.jsp?id=5840482. See also Morgan (in this volume).

adopted to make the use of videoconferencing effective. The Harvard Law
Review, for example, concedes that "improving the technology used, limiting
use to preliminary hearings, and requiring the respondent's consent could
help balance the efficiency videoconferencing purportedly provides with the
substantive requirements" of the judicial system (2009: 1192).

The new European Directive and also the European E-Justice Action
Plan[4] specify that the demand for qualified legal interpreters can be met with
the help of videoconference technology. Time will tell to what extent this
will be possible and to what extent training, familiarization and increasing
knowledge, improved technology and improved system designs will facilitate
video-mediated interpreting in criminal proceedings. An important task in
bridging the gap between current experience and (future) demand will be the
development of (European) standards for video-mediated interpreting in
criminal proceedings (and other types of legal proceedings). As a first step in
this process, the formulation of recommendations and guidelines is an
important instrument to avoid known problems and to disseminate the
findings of the growing body of research to all stakeholders. The
introduction of such recommendations is the aim of this final chapter of the
present volume.

Section 2 will firstly summarise the main risks and challenges associated
with video-mediated interpreting, based on the findings of the research
conducted in the AVIDICUS Project and the findings emerging from similar
research. Section 3 will then present three sets of initial recommendations on
the use of video-mediated interpreting in criminal proceedings, addressing
the three major target groups in this process:

- Judicial authorities planning to implement video-mediated interpreting
  services,
- Legal practitioners and police officers,
- Legal interpreters.

In line with the global aim of the AVIDICUS project and this volume, the
emphasis in these recommendations is on how to implement and use video-
mediated interpreting in criminal proceedings without jeopardizing the fair
access to justice of all (European) citizens, regardless of their knowledge of
the language used in the proceedings. Section 4 will conclude this chapter,
highlighting the key aspects for allowing *appropriate* use of video-mediated
interpreting in criminal proceedings.

---

[4] European E-Justice Action Plan of the European Council (OJ No. C 75/01, 31-03-2009).
Available at http://eur-lex.europa.eu/LexUriServ/LexUriServ.do?uri=OJ:C:2009:075:
0001:0012:EN:PDF. See also van der Vlis (in this volume).

2   VIDEO-MEDIATED INTERPRETING IN CRIMINAL PROCEEDINGS: RISKS AND CHALLENGES

The AVIDICUS project undertook different studies in order to gain a better understanding of the difficulties arising in video-mediated interpreting in a legal context, including a review of current practice, two surveys among judicial institutions/legal practitioners and legal interpreters, and a series of empirical studies comparing traditional legal interpreting with the different forms of video-mediated interpreting. Additional information comes from the feedback received during training sessions delivered to practising interpreters, trainee interpreters and legal practitioners (see individual chapters in this volume). Drawn together, the findings of AVIDICUS paint a comprehensive picture regarding the challenges of video-mediated interpreting in criminal proceedings. The suspension of the physical co-presence of the interpreter and/or some of the primary interlocutors has been found to have potentially wide-ranging implications, which researchers have only begun to investigate. This section will give an overview of the main problem areas and risks upon which any recommendations, guidelines and standards should build. It is intended as rationale for the three sets of recommendations (for judicial authorities, legal practitioners and legal interpreters) that will be presented in Section 3.

The overview will begin with a brief review of the specifics and general challenges of legal communication and legal interpreting (2.1) and then discuss various issues related to videoconferencing and interpreting, especially the implications arising from the distribution and number of participants involved in the communication (2.2), the view and image of the remote site that the participants receive (2.3), the role of the participants' own image (2.4) and the sound quality and its implications (2.5). Furthermore, a number of communication-related problems will be discussed, especially the difficulties in creating a 'rapport' with the remote interlocutors (2.6) and videoconference-specific difficulties with the management and coordination of the communication (2.7), and related to this, the interpreter's working environment (2.8). Further problems will be outlined by way of overview in section 2.9.

2.1   Legal communication and legal interpreting

Legal communication comprises specific genres and has specific purposes ranging, for example, from collecting evidence to assessing, presenting and disputing evidence, making and pronouncing decisions and reviewing and appealing these decisions.

The primary interlocutors – i.e. police officers, prosecutors, judges and other legal practitioners, and suspects, defendants, victims or witnesses – may have shared or conflicting goals of communication, depending on who

talks to whom, the stage the proceedings have reached, and which of the
above purposes is at play.

When the primary interlocutors do not share a sufficient amount of
linguistic knowledge, an interpreter is required to mediate the communication. As Hertog (2002: 145) points out, today there is a need for legal
interpreters both at transnational level, i.e. in cross-border cases, and at
national level because of "an ever-increasing number of individuals who do
not understand or speak the language of the country but end up involved in
its legal system". Given the specialised nature of legal communication, the
need for an interpreter at national level arises even when the other-language
speaker has some basic knowledge of the language of the host country but
would be unable to understand the specialised discourse of legal
communication.

What is characteristic of cross-cultural, interpreter-mediated legal communication is an asymmetry of power. This arises because the communicative situation involves, on the one hand, institutional representatives of the
legal institutions of the host country, who are normally legal professionals
with a sound knowledge of the law and legal language and, on the other
hand, other-language speakers who may be unfamiliar with the legal system
of the host country, under stress, vulnerable, emotional, uneducated, not used
to public speaking, using non-standard language or illiterate.

Legal interpreters have to be able to take all of this in their stride. This
requires training and an appropriate qualification. The specifics of legal
interpreting and the skills and knowledge required of a qualified legal
interpreter have been outlined by Berk-Seligson (1990, 2009), Corsellis
(2008), Hale (2007), Hertog (2002), Kadric (2001), Mikkelson (2000) and
many others. Legal interpreting requires at least:

- a profound knowledge of the relevant working languages, including
  knowledge of all registers from specialised legal terminology and
  formal language to dialect, colloquial language, slang and swearing,
- culture-specific knowledge of the host country and the country,
  territory or culture of the other-language speaker,
- a sound knowledge of the legal systems of the host country and the
  country of the other-language speaker and a clear understanding of the
  differences between them,
- appropriate interpreting skills and strategies for all relevant modes of
  interpreting (two-way consecutive interpreting, whispered simultaneous interpreting and sight translation), i.e. the ability to relay the
  message accurately, completely and stylistically appropriately –
  which, it should be noted, is more than 'just' speaking two languages,
- knowledge about how to deal with cultural and ethical challenges
  often arising in cross-cultural communication, including knowledge
  about how to prevent or resolve potential misunderstandings,

- the ability to cope with emotionally loaded, inconsistent and/or conflicting communication goals, and any other consequences that cross-cultural legal communication, as described above, involves,
- the ability to coordinate the interaction between the primary interlocutors and the interpreter, including the ability to intervene appropriately to deliver the interpretation and ensure that nothing is lost.

In any situation of legal interpreting, whether in a traditional setting or a video link, a legal interpreter will encounter linguistic and socio-cultural problems such as specialised terminology, regional and social variations of language, and culture-bound references or culture-specific behaviour. Interpreting is cognitively demanding, and problems associated with an overload of cognitive processing capacity can be observed in almost any interpreting situation. On the surface, such problems often show up as hesitations, drawing out words, self-corrections or language mixing (see also Mead 2002, Gile 2009[2]) but cognitive overload also leads to problems with accuracy, completeness and appropriateness of the rendition.

In the AVIDICUS comparative studies, the occurrence of such problems was by no means confined to the forms of video-mediated interpreting, but – as the reports by Braun & Taylor, Balogh & Hertog and Miler-Cassino & Rybińska in this volume show – the studies revealed a tendency for such problems to be more frequent and magnified in video-mediated interpreting.

As stated above, given the many challenges of legal communication, legal interpreting requires training and a qualification. Furthermore, legal interpreters need to abide by a code of conduct which makes reference to such crucial notions as impartiality, awareness of conflicts of interests, and awareness of limitations. However, in video-mediated interpreting the interpreters also face a range of new or additional challenges which are not ordinarily part of their training as yet and for which recommendations and guidelines – and arguably an amended code of conduct – are required. These challenges are described in the subsequent sections.

2.2   Distribution and number of participants

One of the most important questions in video-mediated interpreting is how the primary interlocutors and the interpreter are distributed, i.e. who shares and does not share the same location. The concept of 'remoteness', i.e. the lack of co-presence, and the impact of this, has also been one of the main concerns in research on videoconferencing and distance communication as such. In the context of legal interpreting, a basic distinction has to be made between the remoteness of the interpreter, which leads to 'remote interpreting' (RI), and the remoteness of the other-language speaker or both the other language speaker and the interpreter, which leads to 'videoconference interpreting' (see Section 1 for definitions). Figures 1 to 3 summarise the different constellations currently in use in criminal proceedings.

Figure 1: Remoteness of the other-language speaker (interpreter in the main location): Videoconference Interpreting A

Figure 2: Remoteness of the other-language speaker and the interpreter: Videoconference Interpreting B

Figure 3: Remoteness of the interpreter: Remote Interpreting

One consideration in all of these settings is the question of how the separation of the primary interlocutors from each other and/or from the interpreter affects the interpreting performance. However, since, as Hale (2007: 145) points out, "[t]he behaviours of all participants influence the interaction and effectiveness of the interpreting activity", a related considera-tion is how the physical separation affects the communicative behaviour of the primary interlocutors themselves and what the possible knock-on effects on the interpreter's task and performance and the possible impact on the proceedings are. Such questions can be said to be particularly relevant in the context of legal communication because most forms of legal communication (police interview, statement taking, court proceedings etc) are highly interac-tive, and the legal interpreter is traditionally a member of the group of communicators and is therefore highly 'visible' for the primary interlocutors.

With regard to the impact on the interpreter, the consensus is that remote interpreting, i.e. the form of interpreting in which the interpreter is separated from all other interlocutors, is the most difficult form of video-mediated interpreting, although the AVIDICUS survey shows that the difference in perception between remote interpreting and videoconference interpreting is not large. All such forms were seen by a majority of interpreters as being considerably or slightly more difficult than traditional interpreting. The reasons for this will be described below (see section 2.6).

As far as the effect on the primary interlocutors is concerned, Braun (2004, 2007) has found a number of changes in their communicative behaviour, including a tendency to over-elaborate and a lower degree of coherence in their utterances. As was pointed out in Section 1, Haas (2006) comes to similar conclusions.

It also needs to be noted that the different forms of video-mediated interpreting are not necessarily interchangeable. The reasons for the use of remote interpreting (RI) are quite different from the reasons for using either form of videoconference interpreting (VCI). With regard to VCI, the AVIDICUS comparative studies have made it clear that there is no 'best' place for the interpreter but that different participants have different views. Many interpreters feel that they would like to be co-located with the non-native speaker. This is also confirmed by other studies (see BiD 2008, Ellis 2004).

Another consideration is whether the equipment is needed for only one or multiple settings, i.e. whether it is, for example, likely that the same equipment is used in court for different purposes and stages of the proceedings, with interpreters in different places.

The setting and number of participants and the purpose of the communication will determine the specification of the equipment required, i.e. the number and size of screens, the number of cameras, any ancillary equipment such as document readers, or additional functions such as document or application sharing, the room layout and the place for the VC equipment. The subsequent sections will return to the importance of identifying an appropriate place for video screens and cameras in relation to the participating interlocutors and the interpreter.

2.3   View and image of the remote site

Interpreting is known to rely heavily on non-verbal clues such as mimic, gesture, posture (cf. Bühler 1985, Poyatos 1997) and on the interpreter's general visual perception of the communicative situation. Some of the major problems of videoconference communication are that it imposes constraints on the perception of non-verbal clues and general visual perception, and also that it makes direct eye contact virtually impossible. Research into visual perception in monolingual video-mediated communication suggests that the video channel, even when providing high quality video images, supports the perception of visual clues less efficiently than face-to-face communication (see Braun & Taylor's overview of current practice in this volume). Reflecting upon the role of visual perception in remote interpreting, Moser-Mercer (2005) concludes that a better understanding of the functions of visual information and of the interpreters' perception of these is required.

For the time being, an important point is that the view in videoconferences never provides a complete view of the remote site; only an 'extract' of the remote site is visible, and due to the two-dimensional nature of a video screen, there is no peripheral vision.

Within these constraints, the view of the remote site that the interpreter requires depends to a certain extent on the number of primary interlocutors, but as a basic principle, every participant in a VC **including the interpreter** should be able to

- see the participants at the other location(s),
- be seen by the other side,
- see his/her own image (see section 2.4).

This is necessary for two reasons. Firstly, the interpreter (as well as all other participants) needs to be able to re-construct the situation at the remote site (e.g. who is sitting where in relation to each other, who is speaking to whom) from what s/he can see and hear via the video link. In complex situations, this will require more than one screen and camera and possibly a high amount of cognitive processing on the part of the interpreter. Secondly, the interpreter needs to see the remote participants in order to gauge their reactions. If this is not possible, the interpreter will feel that s/he interprets 'into the void', and this has been identified as one of the main reasons for the distance and isolation felt by interpreters, especially in remote interpreting (see Mouzourakis 2006).

However, there is another layer of complexity. Given that visual and non-verbal communication plays a crucial role in making sense of what is said and resolving potential ambiguities, the interpreter should not simply be able to see the remote participants, but s/he will require a view of their faces, facial expressions and possibly lip movements to aid comprehension of what is being said. This has important consequences for the position of the primary interlocutors in relation to the cameras that deliver the video image for the interpreter:

- The interpreter should have a frontal view of the remote participants.
- At the same time, it is important that the interpreter does not become the centre of attention simply by appearing on a video screen. In other words the setup should not create a situation in which the primary

interlocutors have to turn away from each other in order to see the interpreter.[5]

- In videoconference interpreting A (interpreter in main room), the interpreter should therefore be seated next to the main speakers so that s/he can be seen at the remote site together with the main speakers.
- In videoconference interpreting B (interpreter at the remote site together with the other-language speaker), the interpreter should be seated next to the other-language speaker so that both are in direct view at the main site (e.g. the court room).
- In remote interpreting (interpreter separated from all primary interlocutors), more than one screen may have to be implemented in different positions at the main site to enable the primary interlocutors to look at each other and at the interpreter (on screen) at the same time, rather than turning away from each other and directing their gaze at one central screen towards the interpreter.

With regard to VCI B, one of the AVIDICUS comparative studies experimented with positioning the interpreter slightly behind the other-language speaker but this led to a number of problems for the other-language speaker, e.g. having to turn his/her head towards the interpreter and away from the screen, which was found to be undesirable by all parties involved (see Balogh & Hertog in this volume).

In remote interpreting, the ideal situation would be that the interlocutors, e.g. a police officer and a suspect, are able to keep sight of the interpreter on the video screen while looking at each other (as expected). In the AVIDICUS study, some of the instances of remote interpreting used a set-up in which the screen was perpendicular to the interlocutors (in police interviews). This turned out to be problematic in the sense that the police officers and suspects looked towards the interpreter on the screen rather than at each other (see Braun & Taylor's report of the AVIDICUS comparative study in this volume). Only a longitudinal study will be able to show whether this can be resolved by adapting the position of the interlocutors.

The considerations regarding the view of the remote site are closely linked to the quality of the video image. Given that it is essential for the interpreter to recognise gestures, facial expressions and also the speaker's lip movement, the image quality needs to be of highest standard. Low-quality images would mean that the interpreter has to do additional cognitive processing to infer any visual information that is lost. The image quality also needs to be stable, i.e. the interpreter's visual input should not be disrupted

---

[5] See also van Rotterdam and van den Hoogen (in this volume), who make similar points with regard to the room layout for legal videoconferencing in general.

by a sudden drop in the image quality or split-second pixilation of parts of
the image as a result of bandwidth problems or error frames in the image
transmission. Initial technical standards for the image quality in remote
interpreting have been outlined by Esteban Causo (in this volume) with
regard to conference interpreting and by van Rotterdam & van den Hoogen
(in this volume) with reference to legal videoconferencing. What has to be
tested further is whether the standards suggested for legal videoconferencing
in general will be also robust enough for legal *interpreting* via video link.

2.4   Own image

Apart from seeing the remote interlocutors, the interpreter should also have
access to his/her own image (also known as the "picture-in-picture" or "near-
end image"). Seeing his/her own image is an important control mechanism
for the interpreter.

In the simplest case, having sight of his/her own image enables the
interpreter to confirm whether s/he is in shot and facilitates the control of the
interpreter's visual signs. This is particularly important in the consecutive
mode, which is currently the most used mode in video-based interpreting in
criminal proceedings in Europe (see Braun & Taylor's overview of current
practice in this volume), as the interpreter needs to be able to intervene and
interpret at suitable points. Many interpreters use visual signs, e.g. raise their
hand, to signal that they would like the speaker to stop. In video links, this is
crucial because verbal intervention is more disruptive than in face-to-face
communication (see Braun & Taylor's report on the AVIDICUS comparative
studies in this volume). The own image provides a useful means of
controlling whether the visual signals are visible and effective.

Access to the own image also helps the interpreter to assess how s/he is
perceived at the remote site, as the interpreter's 'image' arguably contributes
to building confidence and trust. Since the perception of someone on a screen
tends to be more intense than the natural perception in face-to-face
communication, the control of one's non-verbal behaviour is likely to
become more important than in face-to-face interaction. Finally, although
real eye contact is impossible to achieve in a videoconference, access to the
own image will enable the interpreter to create the illusion of eye contact,
which is another important element of creating trust.

2.5   Sound

If there is any shared outcome in the small body of research on video-
mediated interpreting, it is that the sound quality of the equipment used is
crucial for an interpreter in any situation. Some interpreters argue that sound
even takes priority over the image (see Braun & Taylor's report on the
AVIDICUS surveys in this volume). In a comprehensive model of legal
interpreting and its challenges, such a weighting may be unsustainable, but

clearly sound is one of the most important elements of communication for the interpreter to rely on. Sound quality has a strictly technical dimension, i.e. the audio transmission capacity of the equipment used, but it is also influenced by number of environmental factors. Both will be outlined in this section.

With regard to the technical dimension, Esteban Causo (in this volume) highlights the problem that the sound transmission in common videoconference equipment is normally limited to a frequency of 7500 Hz – and in some older equipment even to 3400 Hz – because of the audio compression algorithms used (usually G.722 and G.711 respectively), whilst the audible human frequency ranges from approx. 20 to 20000 Hz. Although Esteban Causo refers to the difficulties of *simultaneous* interpreting (especially the simultaneity of processing the speaker's utterances and producing an equivalent message in the target language), sound problems affect interpreters in all modes of interpreting. In the AVIDICUS studies, which were conducted using market-ready equipment and in which the consecutive mode of interpreting was used, listening comprehension problems and ensuing mishearings were among the most serious problems (see Braun & Taylor in this volume for example).

Based on the studies conducted in supra-national institutions in relation to remote conference interpreting, the International Association of Conference Interpreters (AIIC) states in their interpretation standards that the minimum frequency bandwidth available for remote (simultaneous) conference interpreting should be at least 100 - 12.500 Hz.[6]

Esteban Causo also highlights further conditions that may have an adverse effect on the sound quality, emphasising that "videoconferences are frequently linking standard offices unsuitable for this purpose, or have a poor set up, which means sound reverberation [...], simple omni directional microphones integrated in the table, etc." (Estaban Causo in this volume). This point is particularly relevant in legal interpreting, where video equipment is often fitted into existing environments (court rooms, police custody suites etc). Moreover, interpreters frequently complain about the noise in court rooms, generated, for example, by rattling papers, poor room acoustics or people moving in and out of the court room while a session is in progress. In a video link, this is likely to magnify the technologically induced sound problems.

As related issue, interlocutors may – in the course of the communication – also change their position in relation to the installed microphones, raise or

---

[6] See AIIC (2000). The sound problems for interpreters especially in ISDN-based videoconferences have also been highlighted in various studies (e.g. Böcker & Anderson 1993; Braun 2004, 2007; Mouzourakis 2006).

lower their voices, or change their voice modulation. This has further implications for the design of the VC system as a whole, the peripheral equipment such as microphones and loud speakers, control options (especially volume control) and possibly other parameters. All of these need to be taken into account in the design of technical solutions to minimize the risk of miscomprehension and distortion of the communicative message. They are part of the initial technological recommendations outlined by van Rotterdam & van den Hoogen (in this volume) with specific reference to legal interpreting. Miler-Cassino & Rybińska (in this volume) also highlight that video-mediated interpreting may require training for the interpreters in voice modulation and voice projection.

The impact of any sound quality problems are likely to be compounded in situations where the interpreter does not have a frontal view of the remote speaker(s) to see their lip movements and facial expressions (see Section 2.3) or when speakers mumble, speak a dialect or with a strong accent, or have difficulty speaking, all of which is particularly relevant in the context of legal interpreting (see Section 2.1).

As pointed out in Section 2.3, non-verbal and visual clues are crucial for interpreting, and this is especially true when the interpreter faces listening comprehension problems. This is where sound quality, video quality and view of the remote site come together. Hence, an appropriate view and a high-quality image, as well as high-quality sound, are vital.

Equally importantly, image and sound need to be synchronised. Any discrepancy between sound and image will require additional processing effort on the part of the interpreter to 'piece' sound and image together. Given the point made in Section 2.1 that interpreting is cognitively demanding and that interpreters often work at the limit of their cognitive processing capacity even in traditional interpreting situations, it is clear that any additional distraction from less than perfect technical parameters is likely to turn this into a processing overload. This is exacerbated by the fact that because of the novelty of many videoconferencing situations, interpreters are less likely to develop coping strategies when a processing overload occurs (e.g. when a speaker speaks too fast) than in traditional situations. Thus, the risk that less than perfect technological conditions may adversely affect the interpreting performance is very high.

Another point that was explained in Section 2.1 is that legal interpreting often involves a high degree of interaction, i.e. two-way communication or, when an interpreter is involved, three-way communication. This requires turn-taking and sometimes entails overlapping speech. Another technological parameter that is therefore vital is that the equipment used for video-mediated legal interpreting should be full-duplex systems, allowing sound from both locations to be transmitted at the same time without the sound 'cutting out'. Having said that, the AVIDICUS tests, which used full-duplex systems, revealed that even such systems create a certain degree of interference and sound 'loss' when two speakers in different locations speak at the same time, especially when they speak with a raised voice (which, in turn, is a characteristic feature of videoconference communication, mainly to compensate for a lack of 'rapport' with the remote site – see Section 2.6). In the AVIDICUS tests, overlapping speech was one of the main reasons for omissions and the loss of information (see Braun & Taylor in this volume).

In remote interpreting in criminal proceedings, another problem may arise. In this setting, interpreters are likely to work in centralized hubs. Whilst conference interpreters normally work in soundproof booths, this is not common in legal interpreting, but soundproofing will have to be considered in interpreter hubs to control the level of noise created when many interpreters work in the same space.

2.6   Rapport with the remote interlocutors

In videoconferences, the interlocutors are in different environments at their respective sites and may be exposed to different influences (e.g. background noise or disruptions). The physical separation of the interlocutors creates a latent uncertainty about what 'the other side' does, i.e. the atmosphere or communicative situation at the remote site is generally more difficult to gauge. In a seminal work in the field, Short *et al.* (1976) have postulated that the rapport between the interlocutors in a VC is usually weaker than in traditional face-to-face communication, leading to a feeling of reduced 'social presence'. In her study of video-mediated interpreting in business settings, Braun (2004, 2007) found that the reduced social presence manifests itself, for instance, in unnatural ways of speaking, especially a tendency to speak louder and, in some cases, also a tendency to over-elaborate and to be less coherent. The interlocutors also seem less focussed on what they want to say.

The majority of the interpreters who responded to the AVIDICUS survey (see Braun & Taylor in this volume) confirmed the problems with rapport. They felt that the use of a video-link in interpreting makes it more difficult to build a rapport with the (remote) interlocutors. Many of the interpreters who participated in the survey among legal interpreters, the comparative studies and/or the training sessions (all reported in the various chapters in this volume) saw this as one of the main problems of delivering interpreting via video link. The AVIDICUS comparative studies furthermore replicated some of the problems identified in Braun (2004, 2007), especially the tendency to speak louder and to be less focussed on the communication.

Legal interpreters are used to working in close physical proximity to the primary interlocutors. Some of the interpreters who participated in the AVIDICUS comparative studies reported that the closeness helps grasp all the subtleties of the communication and to resolve communication problems. As one of the comparative studies shows, the decreased rapport may also mean that problems at the other side are misjudged or go unnoticed (see e.g.

Miler-Casino & Rybińska in this volume for an example in which the prosecutor did not notice at all how nervous the remotely situated interpreter was).

Furthermore, the interpreters felt that video-mediated interpreting takes
longer and is more tedious. One of the AVIDICUS comparative studies,
which compared the duration of face-to-face and remote interpreting as well
as the effort required to resolve communication problems confirmed the
interpreters' impressions (Braun & Taylor in this volume). For example, the
videoconference sessions were on average 19% longer than the face-to-face
sessions, and many interpreting problems required a lengthier exchange
between the interlocutors to be resolved.

The comparative studies also reveal that videoconference participants
seem to try and compensate for the weaker rapport by putting more effort
into the communication, resulting in, for example, the tendency to speak
louder. The interpreters who took part in the test reported that they had to
concentrate more and that they tired more quickly. These points will be
discussed further in Section 2.8.

In the training sessions delivered to practising interpreters as part of the
AVIDICUS project (see Braun *et al.* in this volume), some interpreters
furthermore highlighted the importance of the 'human factor'. They pointed
out that their presence often has a positive or reassuring effect on the other-
language speaker, as they are the only person to share his/her language. All
in all, the difficulty in establishing a rapport in video-mediated
communication seems to be partially responsible for negative reactions of
interpreters to video-mediated interpreting.

Yet another problem of video-mediated communication concerns the
contextualisation of the situation. A remote witness in another country or a
remote suspect in another borough of a big city may refer to a location with
which an interpreter who is used to working in a particular area may be less
familiar. In other words, the interpreter may not be aware of the specifics of
the remote location.

Remoteness and its effects are issues that will require a substantial
amount of further research. A crucial task in minimising the risks of video-
mediated interpreting would be the investigation of the possible long-term
effects of video mediation and interpreting on the participants in videoconferences and the dynamics of the proceedings. Until this is possible, the
introduction of video-mediated interpreting should be slow and incremental,
allowing for adjustment as more research outcomes become available.

2.7 Communication management

As explained in the previous section, remoteness is an overarching condition
of videoconferences that seems to affect all aspects of communication,
including communication management. The management of the
communication in legal settings has several dimensions. On the one hand, it
concerns procedures at all stages (and before and after) a communicative

event. Questions arise with regard to the briefing for the interpreter when s/he is not physically present, but also over the opening procedure in the VC, the introduction and other aspects. What is required here is a set of guidelines for each communicative event to ensure an appropriate standard of communication. In the meantime, time should be set aside at the beginning of the communicative event to make sure procedures are established for the event in question to minimize the risk of miscommunication.

Another aspect of communication management is technical control, e.g. in the case of breakdown. As Ellis (2004) points out, it should not be left to the interpreter to solve technical problems. It is in fact the fear of an increasing dependency on the technology that also contributes to creating negative attitudes among interpreters towards video-mediated interpreting. Appropriate technical support and clear procedures are likely to be reassuring for the interpreters.

It is also essential that the interpreter has a certain amount of control over the technology. Among the interpreters who took part in the AVIDICUS comparative studies and the training, the opinion regarding technical interventions was divided. Whilst some wanted to have everything set up beforehand and did not want to operate any equipment during the interpretation, others would have welcomed the opportunity to have some control over the technology even while interpreting, especially panning the camera around and zooming in. Whether this is practicable will depend on the setting and the number of participants, but should be considered in the planning stage.

A third and equally important dimension of communication management in dyadic communication is the actual co-ordination (or synchronisation) of the talk. In the various settings of legal interpreting, the interpreter is traditionally part of the group of interlocutors, and the delivery mode is mainly consecutive. In the interest of a smooth conversation flow, the interpreter usually keeps pauses between the end of a speaker's turn and the delivery of the target text to a minimum and sometimes even starts his/her rendition while the speaker is still completing his/her turn. Ideally the interpreter should be visible for all interlocutors and should be able to maintain eye contact with the interlocutors to handle turn-taking in this tripartite communication situation.

One of the factors that influences the co-ordination of the talk in videoconferencing are transmission delays, however slight, present even in high-quality broadband connections. Such delays let pauses between turns appear longer, which in turn creates uncertainty and produces the wrong signals (such hesitations usually being interpreted as inability to produce an appropriate reply or as disagreement). On the other hand, attempts to resolve 'deadlock' situations created by long pauses frequently result in overlapping speech, e.g. when an interlocutor starts to restate his/her utterance just as a response from the remote site arrives (see also Braun 2007).

Furthermore, it seems that the artificial sound source in a videoconference does not accommodate overlapping speech in the same way as natural speech does (see also Section 2.5). This is compounded by the fact that turn-taking problems have been observed in the AVIDICUS studies to be much more frequent in video-mediated interpreting than in face-to-face interpreting for several reasons. One reason is the slight transmission delay, which makes it more difficult for an interpreter to intervene without too much disruption. Another, with similar effect, is the generally decreased rapport between interlocutors in a VC (see Section 2.6), which slows down the interlocutors' verbal and nonverbal reactions and makes the assessment of the remote interlocutors' behaviour (e.g. whether or not they are about to stop speaking) more difficult.

Moreover, interlocutors who are agitated and speak fast or interlocutors who are not very experienced in working with an interpreter may find it difficult to adapt to speaking in short 'chunks' and to pause for the interpreter. They may continue speaking when the interpreter begins the interpretation and thus create extended overlap with the interpreter, which for the reasons outlined above is difficult to resolve when the interpreter is in a different location (see also Braun & Taylor in this volume).

The conclusions to be drawn from the communication management problems in video-mediated interpreting are multiple. One concerns the selection of equipment. As was pointed out in Section 2.5, full duplex sound is required to minimise problems arising from overlapping speech. However, as mentioned in Section 2.6, practice shows that full-duplex audio does not guarantee the elimination of problems with overlapping speech. Therefore, adjustment, i.e. a change of strategies, on the part of the interpreter will be required. This, in turn, may take some time, even though prior research (Braun 2004, 2007) and one of the AVIDICUS studies (Miler-Casino & Rybińska in this volume) suggest that the adjustment may not take long. It will, however, be useful for interpreters to have a chance for a 'dry run' especially as part of a training or familiarization session.

The wider implication is that the way the interpreters work, including the way to gain the floor, may partially change. If the interpreter is less successful with his/her attempt to intervene and stop the speakers at appropriate points, a detainee, for example, may speak in longer turns and information may be lost. Given that many legal interpreters are used to interpreting in very short chunks and some are not well trained in memorization and note-taking techniques, this is an important point for interpreter training.[7]

Even wider is the implication that the changes in turn-taking may change the dynamics of the communication, giving a police officer, for example, less of a chance to intervene and ask a quick follow-up question. The consequences are as yet unclear but will be one of the research questions that will be followed up in AVIDICUS II.[8]

Other conclusions to be drawn from the problems with the co-ordination of talk in videoconferences concern situations with more than two primary interlocutors, where overlapping speech between the primary interlocutors is likely to occur. Such overlaps are likely to cause additional communication problems, especially when primary interlocutors do not share the location of the interpreter (i.e. all primary interlocutors in remote interpreting or those at the other site in videoconference interpreting).

2.8   Working environment

The introduction of video-mediated interpreting raises important issues for the working environment of the interpreters, both in the sense of the actual physical environment and in the sense of the atmosphere or ergonomics. This has also been one of the major considerations in the various studies conducted in supra-national institutions in relation to remote conference interpreting (see Roziner & Shlesinger 2010 for an overview).

With regard to ergonomics and atmosphere, the AVIDICUS survey and the feedback from the interpreters participating in the comparative study indicate that interpreting in front of a video screen is more tiring than interpreting in the traditional way, confirming prior research on remote conference interpreting (e.g. Moser-Mercer 2003). The reasons have to be further researched but it can be assumed that the following aspects of seeing, speaking and listening in a videoconference play a part.

Focussing on a two-dimensional screen which only allows 'extracts' of the remote location to be seen, without any peripheral vision (see also Section 2.3) is likely to require more cognitive resources to construct and understand the situation at the remote site. In short, video-mediated interpreting is likely to require more concentration.

As was pointed out in Section 2.6, videoconference participants have a tendency to speak louder in order to compensate for their uncertainty of whether everything that is said actually arrives at the remote site. Both

---

[7]   This is one of the reasons why the AVIDICUS training module for practising interpreters piloted in Warsaw by TEPIS was embedded in a more comprehensive CPD measure which also included note-taking training (see Braun *et al.* in this volume).

[8]   EU DG Justice grant, JUST/2010/ JPEN/AG/1558, 2011-2013.

speaking with a raised voice and listening to speakers who raise their voices is likely to add a strain on the interpreter's cognitive resources. In combination with the problems of listening comprehension due to difficulties with currently available sound quality (see Section 2.5), the effort required for listening to and analysing the speaker's utterances could be considerably higher than in traditional interpreting situations.

Fatigue can be assumed to be directly linked to the interpreting performance. One of the AVIDICUS comparative studies analysed the distribution of interpreting problems on the timeline of the face-to-face and video-based sessions (Braun & Taylor in this volume). This analysis revealed a greater increase in the number of interpreting problems during the video-based sessions, which became more noticeable in the second half of the sessions. The video-based sessions show, for example, a steep increase in the number of paralinguistic problems, which are often indicative of a cognitive overload. Moser-Mercer (2003) reported similar findings from her study on remote conference interpreting.

In connection with this, the duration of an interpreter's turn in a video link will require attention. The conference interpreting profession has adopted 30-minute turns as the standard duration of a working turn for a conference interpreter. Our data and Moser-Mercer's study show a decline in the interpreting quality (increase in the number of errors) after approximately 15 to 20 minutes, suggesting that interpreters may not be able to work for an extended period of time in a video link. What is noteworthy is that the guidelines for remote interpreting issued by the Wisconsin Circuit courts, which recommended 30 minute turns in 2006, were revised in 2010 and now recommend 15 minutes as the maximum length.[9]

The physical working environment of the interpreter is another concern, but given the varied nature of video-mediated interpreting in terms of the distribution and number of participants, type of communication etc., it is difficult to make generalizations with regard to potential challenges. One crucial issue is noise level, as pointed out in Section 2.5. Another concern is the work space including e.g. screen size, desk, view of the other (onsite and remote) participants, lighting and temperature. Such detailed technical recommendations were beyond the scope of AVIDICUS, which focused on the quality of interpreting and aimed at initial general recommendations for video-mediated interpreting. However, the technical recommendations formulated by van Rotterdam and van den Hoogen (in this volume) for legal videoconferencing as such cover important issues relating to the audiovisual environment of videoconferences and can serve as an important starting point for more detailed technical recommendations on video-mediated interpreting.

---

[9] http://www.wicourts.gov/services/interpreter/docs/telephoneinterpet.pdf.

2.9 Further problems and conclusions

Although the focus of the AVIDICUS Project was on the *quality* of interpreting in video-mediated communication, the work also brought up a range of other points that will require consideration. These are, inter alia:

- possible differences in acceptance of videoconference communication in different cultures,
- possible correlations between the viability of video-mediated interpreting and language pair, type of crime/offence, age group, gender and cultural specifics of the other-language speaker,
- possible consequences of the fact that people who are suspected of, accused of or involved in a crime may be under stress, vulnerable, aggressive or violent in the videoconference situation.

The AVIDICUS comparative studies, which used simulations of real-life situations, have pointed to a number of generic problems that can be addressed immediately. However, not everything can be anticipated and researched: each setting and solution has its own specifics. The following key points are, therefore, of utmost importance to mitigate risk:

- The introduction of video-mediated interpreting into criminal proceedings should be incremental, with in-built pilot phases at each stage and a real commitment to adjustment as the need arises before moving on to the next stage.
- At present, until further research has been conducted, video-mediated interpreting should only be used for low-impact crime and short procedures,
- A crucial prerequisite for all forms of video-mediated interpreting is the use of trained, qualified and experienced legal interpreters as well as the use of legal practitioners and police officers who are experienced in working with an interpreter.

The recommendations made in the next section of this chapter will take up these key points and elaborate a range of further points for the three relevant target groups (judicial authorities, legal practitioners and police officers, and legal interpreters).

Two further important points that are incorporated into the recommendations are the provision of training for legal interpreters and legal practitioners/police officers and close co-operation between all stakeholders. Judicial institutions, legal practitioners, police officers and interpreters need to co-operate to create the best possible working conditions and to make sure that the fairness of justice is not jeopardized. This requires listening to each other and interacting with each other, from the planning stage onwards. Co-operation is also required when it comes to assessing the suitability of a video link. Experienced interpreters will have developed good insight into the communicative challenges of legal communication and will be able to advise on the appropriateness of a video link. Interpreters who have experience in both interpreting and videoconferencing will, of course, be of most value with regard to providing advice, and their voices should be heard.

3 RECOMMENDATIONS FOR THE USE OF VIDEO-MEDIATED INTERPRETING IN CRIMINAL PROCEEDINGS

3.1 Recommendations for public/judicial services

1. Identify your needs

Map out your setting. Identify, for example, who talks to whom, who needs to see/hear whom, where the main parties and the interpreter are located, whether the distribution and especially the location of the interpreter is flexible and how long the interaction is likely to take.

2. Involve expertise at the planning stage

Involve interpreting/linguistic, legal and technological expertise to work out the specifics of your setting and to approve your solution.

3. Use the best available technology

Provide high-quality sound and video for all parties involved and additional equipment for the interpreter as required (e.g. head-phones); use a separate document camera (for the presentation of documents, images and other material that can facilitate interpreting)

4. Provide an appropriate work environment for the interpreter

Provide an ergonomic and quiet work environment for the interpreter; allow the interpreter to control the equipment (e.g. volume control).

5. Allow a 'trial and error' phase

Run a pilot before any large-scale purchase, implementation and roll-out of equipment. Identify critical instances in communication process and make necessary adjustments.

6. Allow for a stage-by-stage introduction of new technology

Start with low-impact crime, evaluate the effect of technology at each stage and assess the implications for the next stage.

7. Use qualified participants and interpreters

Use trained and experienced legal interpreters. Use legal staff members who are experienced in working with interpreters.

8. Offer training to the interpreters and legal staff

Offer an early-stage induction before rolling out the technology. Provide continuous professional training (including awareness of wider context, mastery of technology, communicative situation and supportive techniques such as stress management).

9. Agree risk-assessment procedures

Agree procedures for deciding whether or not a video link in combination with interpreting is appropriate. Consult experienced interpreters.

10. Develop guidelines/protocols for your procedures

Specify who is responsible e.g. for booking, timing, testing, starting and controlling the connection; describe the procedure before, during and after the session (briefing of interpreter, beginning of session, introductions, rules during session, debriefing) for all participants.

11. Make provisions for breakdown

Develop a protocol for communication breakdown or technological breakdown; do not leave it to the interpreter to resolve breakdowns.

12. Work towards a code of best practice

Judicial services, legal practitioners and interpreter associations should cooperate to develop joint codes of best practice for videoconference and remote interpreting.

3.2 Initial recommendations for interpreters

1. When you are booked

- Ask about the specifics of the video link, e.g. where the main are parties located, whether your location is flexible or not (i.e. whether you have to be in one particular location, e.g. a court or a prison, or whether you can choose the location), how long the videoconference is likely to take etc.
- If there is time, ask to visit/inspect the site before.
- Ask for the connection to be tested in your presence.

2. Before the session

- Check whether you can see/hear and can be seen/heard; make sure you are not too close to the camera and your seating position is comfortable.
- Ask for a briefing to be given to you and e.g. exhibits to be shown via the video link before the actual session starts.
- Agree procedures for the beginning of the session (e.g. how and by whom the introductions – including, where required, a language or dialect check of the other-language speaker – will be done and whether/when a brief explanation of the 'rules' of videoconferencing is required).
- Agree procedures for the entire session including signals for meta-communication (e.g. visual signals to stop a speaker or to ask a speaker to slow down).
- Bear in mind that the situation is new for everyone, including the other participants.

3. At the beginning of the session

- Follow agreed procedures; don't feel you have to take on responsibility for explaining the videoconference setting.
- Check whether you can see/hear and can be seen/be heard by all participants at the other end.
- Check whether the agreed signals are effective; ask for adjustment if necessary.
- Don't rush, allow yourself time to get used to the situation and the remote participants.

4. During the session

- Monitor your source text comprehension closely to avoid mishearings.
- Monitor your output: be clear and explicit but avoid repetitiveness and over-elaboration.
- Control your voice: don't speak louder than you normally do.
- Use the agreed signals to gain the floor; if you use your hands, make sure they are visible for the other side.
- Always ask if you are unsure (e.g. in the case of a possible mis-hearing, a local reference at the remote site or lapse of attention).
- Don't be afraid of intervening, even if you feel this may be more disruptive than in a face-to-face situation.
- Keep a comfortable seating position: avoid leaning into the screen/camera.

- Control your non-verbal behaviour: create the illusion of eye contact and control your facial expression, using your own image (if available).
- Increase the rapport: try not to move out of shot; if you have to, explain what you are doing.
- Point out disturbances at your end (e.g. noise, changes in visibility of participants).
- Ask for a break if necessary (including a break to resolve a problem at your end).

5. After the session

- Immediately: ask for a (short) debriefing with legal practitioners/ police officer if deemed necessary.
- Back home: note your observations after your first sessions and reflect upon the situation.
- If you encountered problems, identify their source, especially if there are recurrent problems.
- If necessary, discuss the problems with the judicial services.

3.3   Initial recommendations for legal practitioners and police officers

1. When you book an interpreter for a video link

- If you deploy an interpreter to work in a video link, make sure that the interpreter knows that a video link is involved.
- Inform the interpreter about the specifics of the video link, e.g. where the main parties and the interpreter will be located, whether the location of the interpreter is fixed or whether the interpreter can choose (e.g. whether s/he is in court or in prison), how long the video interaction will take etc.
- If there is time before the session, invite the interpreter to visit the site.
- In the schedule for the session, allow time for:
  - briefing the interpreter on-site or via video link, as required by the setting,
  - the connection to be tested in the presence of the interpreter,
  - breaks for the interpreter at appropriate points, when the session is long.

2. Before the session

- Allow enough time for set up at the beginning of the session.
- Briefing: give the interpreter a briefing (concise, factual) and, where relevant, show exhibits to the interpreter.

- Agree/state procedures for the beginning of the session (including the introductions and a brief explanation of the 'rules' of videoconferencing if deemed necessary) and the entire session.
- Check whether everyone can see/hear and can be seen/heard as appropriate.
- Allow the interpreter to agree signals for meta-communication.
- Bear in mind that the situation is new for all participants.

3. At the beginning of the session

- Follow the agreed procedures; as a legal practitioner/police officer, you are responsible for the session and the video link (it is not the interpreter's responsibility).
- Check again whether everyone can see and hear as appropriate.
- Check whether the agreed signals are effective.
- Stop the session if adjustments need to be made (e.g. if somebody is out of shot).
- Do not rush; allow everyone time to get used to the situation and the remote participants.

4. During the session

- Communicate clearly: phrase your points in clear and plain language to avoid misunderstandings.
- Control your non-verbal behaviour: eye contact, facial expression.
- Increase the rapport: indicate clearly what you are doing (e.g. if you move out of shot).
- Monitor your output: speak slowly and clearly but avoid repetitiveness and over-elaboration.
- Control your voice: don't speak unnaturally loudly.
- Always give the interpreter enough time to interpret.
- Respect and reply to the interpreter's request for clarification or for resolving a videoconference-induced problem.
- Respect an interpreter's request for a break (at appropriate points).

5. After the session

- Immediately: try to have a short debriefing with interpreter if required.
- Back home: note observations after your first sessions and reflect upon the situation.
- If you encounter problems, identify their source, especially if there are recurrent problems.
- If necessary, discuss problems with your institution.

4 CONCLUSIONS

The main sources of input for the three sets of recommendations outlined in this chapter were the outcomes of the AVIDICUS comparative studies, the review of current practice, the AVIDICUS surveys and the feedback from the AVIDICUS training sessions (all reported in the various chapters in this volume). One of the most important outcomes was the range of potential risks and challenges arising from the combined use of videoconferencing and interpreting in criminal proceedings. These were summarised in Section 2 of this final chapter of the present volume.

Generally speaking, in spite of using partially different methodologies and assessment methods, the three comparative studies conducted in the AVIDICUS Project came to very similar results with regard to the viability and quality of video-mediated interpreting in criminal proceedings. All forms of video-mediated interpreting were found to magnify known problems of (legal) interpreting to a certain extent. As a consequence, the number of serious interpreting problems was generally higher in the forms of video-mediated interpreting compared to face-to-face interpreting. Furthermore, a range of additional problems for the interpreter were observed including, for example, problems with the view of the remote participants, gaze and eye contact, sound and listening comprehension, communication management and the co-ordination of the talk, and rapport with the remote interlocutors.

The interpreters also faced challenges from the changing communicative behaviour of the primary interlocutors (who, for example, raised their voice unnecessarily, were unsure about where to look or whom to look at or did not react to the interpreter's signs to stop speaking). Furthermore, the video-mediated sessions took longer than the face-to-face sessions. The absence of procedures for video-mediated interpreting (e.g. what to do at the beginning of the session) led to uncertainty and further problems with the coordination of the talk.

The work carried out in AVIDICUS points to an urgent need for training as well as to the need for an incremental approach to the introduction of video-mediated interpreting with in-built pilot phases and a real commitment to adjustment as the need arises.

Given what is at stake in legal proceedings, the problems uncovered in the original AVIDICUS project should not be taken lightly. The major conclusion underlying the recommendations is that a sufficient quality of interpreting performance is the *conditio sine qua non* for the use of video-mediated interpreting in criminal proceedings. At the same time, the potential advantages of videoconferencing, when appropriately used, the influence of training, technological improvement, system design and clear guidelines must be investigated further, especially at a time when traditional ways of conducting criminal proceedings and gaining access to qualified interpreters seem to be increasingly difficult to maintain. The recommendations presented in Section 3 are intended to facilitate *appropriate* use of the technology.

REFERENCES

AIIC (2000), 'Guidelines for the use of new technologies in conference interpreting', *Communicate!* March-April 2000. Available at http://www.aiic.net/ViewPage. cfm?page_id=120.

Berk-Seligson, S. (1990), *The bilingual courtroom: Court interpreters in the judicial process.* Chicago: University of Chicago Press.

Berk-Seligson, S. (2009), *Coerced Confessions: the discourse of bilingual police interrogations.* New York: Mouton de Gruyter.

BiD (2008), *Immigration bail hearings by video link: a monitoring exercise by Bail for Immigration Detainees and the Refugee Council.* London: BID.

Böcker, M. and Anderson, B. (1993), 'Remote conference interpreting using ISDN videotelephony: a requirements analysis and feasibility study'. In: *Proceedings of the Human Factors and Ergonomics Society, 37th annual meeting*, 235-239.

Braun, S. (2004), *Kommunikation unter widrigen Umständen? Fallstudien zu einsprachigen und gedolmetschten Videokonferenzen.* Tübingen: Narr.

Braun, S. (2007), 'Interpreting in small-group bilingual videoconferences: challenges and adaptation processes', *Interpreting*, 9 (1), 21-46.

Bühler, H., (1985), 'Conference Interpreting: A Multichannel Communication Phenomenon', *Meta*, 30 (1), 49-54.

Corsellis, A. (2008), *Public Service Interpreting. The first steps.* Basingstoke: Palgrave MacMillan.

Ellis, S.R. (2004), *Videoconferencing in Refugee Hearings. Ellis Report to the Immigration and Refugee Board.* Ottawa: Immigration and Refugee Board of Canada Audit and Evaluation Committee. Available at http://www.irb-cisr.gc.ca/eng/disdiv/proeva/revs/video/ Pages/index.aspx.

Federman, M. (2006), 'On the Media Effects of Immigration and Refugee Board Hearings via Videoconference', *Journal of Refugee Studies*, 19 (4), 433-452.

Gile, D. (2009), *Basic Concepts and Models for Interpreter and Translator Training.* 2nd edition. Amsterdam/Philadelphia: John Benjamins.

Haas, A. (2006), 'Videoconferencing in Immigration Proceedings', *Pierce Law Review*, 5 (1), 59-90.

Hale, S. (2007), *Community Interpreting.* Basingstoke and New York: Palgrave Macmillan.

Harvard Law School (2009), 'Access to Courts and Videoconferencing in Immigration Court Proceedings', *Harvard Law Review*, 122 (1151), 1181-1193.

Hertog, E. (2002), Language as a human right. In C. Garzone & M. Viezzi,(eds), Interpreting in the 21st century. Amsterdam: Benjmins, 145-158.

Kadric, M. (2001), *Dolmetschen bei Gericht: Erwartungen, Anforderungen, Kompetenzen.* Vienna: WUV, Universitätsverlag.

Mead, P. (2002), Exploring hesitation in consecutive interpreting – an empirical study. In Gazone / Viezzi (Eds), *Interpreting in the 21st century.* Amsteram: Benjamins, 73-82.

Mikkelson, H. (2000), *Introduction to court interpreting.* Manchester: St. Jerome.

Moser-Mercer, B. (2003), 'Remote interpreting: assessment of human factors and performance parameters'. *Communicate!* Summer 2003. Available at http:// www.aiic.net/ ViewPage.cfm/article879.htm.

Moser-Mercer, B. (2005), 'Remote interpreting: issues of multi-sensory integration in a multilingual task', *Meta*, 50 (2), 727-738.

Mouzourakis, P. (2006), 'Remote interpreting: a technical perspective on recent experiments', *Interpreting*, 8 (1), 45-66.

Poyatos, F., (ed.) (1997), *Nonverbal Communication and Translation: New perspectives and challenges in literature, interpretation and the media*. Amsterdam: John Benjamins.

Roziner, I. and Shlesinger, M. (2010), 'Much ado about something remote: Stress and performance in remote interpreting', *Interpreting*, 12 (2), 214–247.

Short, J., Williams, E. & Christie, B. (1976), *The social psychology of telecommunications*. Chichester: Wiley & Sons.